RETIRED

THE PARENTING SURVIVAL KIT

How to Make It Through the
Parenting Years with Your
Family, Sanity, and Wallet Intact

ALETA KOMAN, M.ED.,
with EDWARD MYERS

A PERIGEE BOOK

A Perigee Book
Published by The Berkley Publishing Group
A division of Penguin Putnam Inc.
375 Hudson Street
New York, New York 10014

Copyright © 2000 by Aleta Koman, M.Ed., and Edward Myers
Book design by Tiffany Kukec
Cover design by Jill Boltin
Cover photograph of father and son copyright © by Roy Gumpel/Tony Stone Images
Cover photograph of mother and daughter copyright © by The Picture Book/Photonica

Grateful acknowledgment for permission to reprint excerpts from other works can be found on page 452.

First edition: March 2000

Published simultaneously in Canada.

The Penguin Putnam Inc. World Wide Web site address is
http://www.penguinputnam.com

Library of Congress Cataloging-in-Publication Data

Koman, Aleta.
   The parenting survival kit : how to make it through the parenting years with your family, sanity, and wallet intact / by Aleta Koman with Edward Myers.
      p.   cm.
   Includes bibliographical references and index.
   ISBN: 0-399-52580-7
   1. Parenting.   I. Myers, Edward, 1950–   II. Title.

HQ755.8.K66 2000
649'.1—dc21
                                                                    99-051915
                                                                    CIP

Printed in the United States of America

10 9 8 7 6 5 4 3 2 1

Disclaimer: All case histories and examples mentioned in this book are composites of two or more persons. All personal names (except for those of the psychologists and other theorists I quote) have been changed. All potentially identifying details—professions, ages, places of residence, family backgrounds, etc.—have also been changed. All quotations (again, excepting those of psychologists and other theorists) are paraphrases with some details changed to protect identities. Any similarity between these examples and any actual persons, either living or deceased, is purely coincidental. This book is not intended as a substitute for psychotherapy with a qualified professional.

To the loving memory of my grandmothers, Sarah and Sylvia; to my beloved son Jason, who has taught me so much about the dance of parenthood; to Woody, my beloved soul mate; to my parents, Morty and Rhoda; and to my three exceptional siblings—Stuart, Ivy, and Abby—with gratitude and love.

—A. K.

To my wife, Edith, and to my children, Robin and Cory, with delight, thanks, and love.

—E. M.

CONTENTS

ACKNOWLEDGMENTS

SO MANY PEOPLE have made this book possible. I wish I could thank each and everyone individually, but this acknowledgement section allows only a start in expressing my gratitude to the wonderfully supportive people in my life.

First and foremost, I'd like to thank and acknowledge the skill and wizardry of my co-author and friend Ed Myers. I feel so lucky and honored to have worked with such an exceptional writer and editor. Ed's dedication, creativity, insights, and editing brilliance are surpassed only by his enormous strength of character and his parenting wisdom. This book would not have been possible without his guidance, thoughtfulness, and literary gifts. Thanks for always understanding my thoughts and perspectives on parenting. Working with you has been a dream come true.

My deepest respect, admiration, and gratitude go to Faith Hamlin, my literary agent and friend. Without Faith's visionary guidance and belief in my expertise, this project would never have been possible. Faith was able to bring Ed and me together to form a wonderful writing team. Her exceptional foresight, professional skills, and intuition have surpassed my expectations. I will be forever grateful for her friendship, support, and mentorship.

I would also like to gratefully acknowledge Sheila Curry, senior editor at Perigee Books, for her literary expertise and support of *The Parenting Survival Kit*. I am fortunate to have had the opportunity to work with a person of such skill and professionalism.

To Woody, my soul mate and partner: You are a peaceful harbor of love and support. Your character is only second to your parenting skills and wisdom. You have been my inspiration and have served as a role model for what parents can be when they truly believe in their children and love them unconditionally.

Your kindness, patience, authenticity, love, and friendship are gifts I deeply treasure.

To my son Jason: The teen years have been challenging for both of us, but I feel we've done a good job of weathering the storms. I thank you for being you and for having the strength of character and the wonderful wit and sense of humor to be true to yourself even when I may have disagreed with you. I love you unconditionally. I am truly lucky to be your mom.

Words can't express the gratitude and love I feel in my heart for family and friends who have stood by me through all the years, and whose love and loyalty have gone the distance. Your contributions have been numerous both personally and regarding this project. Under the circumstances, I must limit myself by listing just a few for your special efforts:

To my parents, Morton and Rhoda: I thank you for your belief and support of all my talents and abilities, but particularly in your unending and continuous love and confidence in my personal journey. Thanks for always being there.

To my special grandmothers, Sarah Miller-Goldstein and Sylvia Greenburg-Levine, who loved me unconditionally, and with whom I had an adoring, cherished bond of deep love and affection that has always sustained me and given me the courage to be the best that I can be.

To my brother and sisters, Stuart, Ivy, and Abby: Thanks for all your pride and belief in me, and in this book. Our love for each other sustains us and will always support us through the good times and bad.

For all the members of my family, past and present, and for those that will come in the future: I cherish and love all of you. You are all a part of my personal history, my heart, and my soul. I am eternally grateful for the roles you have played in my life.

Heartfelt thanks as well to all of my colleagues, mentors, and friends, who have shared so much with me over the years. It has been a privilege to know you, to work with you, and to love you.

Last but certainly not least, I want to acknowledge all of the children and families whose lives have touched mine over the years. It has been a privilege and an honor to work with you, and to know each and every one of you.

—A. K.

KIDS DON'T COME WITH AN INSTRUCTION MANUAL

PARENTHOOD IS WONDERFUL.
   Parenthood is difficult.

Like many parents, you may feel confused by the tension between these two statements. You feel great delight in your child, and the process of raising her from birth to adulthood brings untold satisfactions. At the same time, the tasks of parenthood are so numerous, so intricate, so unrelenting, so protracted, so ambiguous, and often so thankless that, when caught up in the rush of day-to-day activities, you feel frustrated, exhausted, and resentful. The situation is all the more difficult in a culture that gives frequent lip service to "family values" while being less child-friendly in many respects than other western nations.

My work both as a therapist and as a teacher—not to mention my personal experience as a mother—has convinced me that nothing truly prepares parents for the task of raising children. Even people who have prior hands-on experience with kids aren't altogether ready for the endless demands of parenthood; first-time parents end up especially hard-hit when the new baby arrives. To complicate matters, kids don't come with an instruction manual. Most mothers and fathers learn the tasks of parenthood chiefly through on-the-job training. This situation is probably how it's always been; even so, I sense that American parents feel more and more adrift as they raise their children in an era of shifting values, frantic schedules, widespread job insecurity, and growing financial stress.

In writing *The Parenting Survival Kit*, I don't claim or intend to answer all nuts-and-bolts questions about raising children. Rather, I am offering a large and useful array of ideas on a wide range of parenting issues. I strongly believe that the best approach to these issues is to address practical and psychological concerns simultaneously. This approach has worked well both in my clinical practice and in my teaching. Drawn from those two realms of professional experience, *The Parenting Survival Kit* provides information that addresses many of the big questions that parents often struggle to answer:

- What do children truly need?

- How can parents meet their kids' needs yet simultaneously attain some degree of personal fulfillment?

- What can ease the stress, worry, and fatigue of parenthood?

- How much involvement in one's children's lives is sufficient, and how much is excessive?

- How can parents deal with the lingering side effects of their own upbringings?

- Where is the balance between solitude and intimacy with others during the high-stress years of parenthood?

At the same time, I hope to provide specific suggestions for specific parenting problems and crisis points. I'm not trying to supply a detailed response to a comprehensive listing of topics; rather, my intention is to offer initial overviews and useful information on a range of common difficulties, conflicts, and core issues that most parents encounter at some point during the child-rearing years. I also want to suggest resources that can add to your knowledge and understanding of parenthood. The goal: helping you "survive" your crisis and move on. That's why I call this book a survival kit.

The Parenting Survival Kit is organized for easy use.

Part 1 offers an overview of why the parenting years are so stressful and a compendium of ideas for making life easier for both parents and children.

Part 2 consists of an alphabetical guide to specific issues and crises, each with more detail than in part 1.

Part 3 is a resource guide for parents—a listing that includes everything from traditional sources of help (such as books, hot lines, agencies, and support groups) to relatively new forms of assistance (such as issue-focused Web sites and chat rooms).

Throughout this book, the overall principle I'm working from is this: If you can understand the issues involved at a particular stage of parenthood, you can attend to both your child's and your own needs better than if you're relatively unaware of what's happening. My purpose in writing *The Parenting Survival Kit* is to help foster that understanding.

Please note: this book has several unifying themes, but in some respects I've structured it as a compendium of articles. For this reason, feel free to pick and choose among the topics, finding those that are most relevant to your own situation.

My best wishes as you experience the adventure of parenthood!

A NOTE REGARDING USAGE

I AM WELL aware that the English language is predisposed toward several kinds of linguistic gender bias, including use of the generic "he": "Listen to your child without interrupting what he's saying." However, many efforts to remedy this situation have been stylistically awkward or ridiculous (e.g., "Listen to your child without interrupting what he or she is saying"). As a result, I have opted simply to refer to "the child" as male in some chapters and as female in others.

PART ONE

SEVEN STRATEGIES FOR SURVIVING THE STRESS OF PARENTHOOD

"**I** WAS A sane person until I had kids."

The speaker of these words is a bright, caring, highly accomplished woman—a dedicated mother and the head nurse of a busy hospital oncology ward. If *she* isn't sane, we're all in big trouble. Yet despite her abilities and accomplishments, she often questions her ability to cope with the cumulative demands of home and workplace. She's not alone in feeling that way. Questioning your ability to cope often comes with the parental turf. Still, it's sobering to me as a family counselor, teacher, and mother how many people express similar self-doubts. Here are just a few of the complaints and laments I've heard from parents about the tangled tasks they face:

- "I never realized how nerve-racking parenthood would be, or how frazzled I'd feel day after day."

- "I've been in the army, I've worked for big corporations, and I've run my own business, but being a dad is hands down the hardest job I've ever done."

- "My kids are constantly fussing and bickering with each other. Sometimes they drive me bonkers with their fighting. I thought parenthood would be like *Sesame Street*, but sometimes it's more like *Mortal Kombat*."

- "The hassles never end. I'd do anything for my kids, but they really wear me down. Going to work is a treat by comparison. Even going to the bathroom and having five minutes to myself is a luxury. Sometimes I go in there and sit on the toilet just to be alone."

- "I'd had a bad week at work, but it was Friday. Then I picked up my kids from their after-school program and headed for the supermarket, which was packed with shoppers. As if that wasn't bad enough, we were in a crowded checkout line and my son, who's six, suddenly asks in this loud voice: 'Wait a minute! So when those sperms meet up with the egg, how'd they get there inside the mommy, anyway?' "

The truth is, parenthood and stress go hand in hand. Children have almost infinite needs, but parents have finite energy, resources, time, and patience. It's not an easy combination. And the situation is all the more complex in the contemporary world, where parents have to juggle the demands of the workplace *and* the home front, often with less support (from grandparents, aunts and uncles, or an extended community) than used to be available.

So what's to be done? There's no easy answer, but simply expecting to "muddle through" isn't an adequate response to the problem. Instead, you should try to overcome the pressures more systematically. Throughout this book, I'll suggest specific ways to deal with specific dilemmas you face as a parent. But if you start with yourself, you'll be better prepared to meet crises as they occur.

Seven Strategies for Preserving Your Sanity

1. Have Realistic Expectations

2. Make a Commitment

3. Adjust Your Attitude

4. Nurture Yourself

5. Work Together

6. Go at Your Child's Pace

7. Make Your Home a Haven

STRATEGY #1

HAVE REALISTIC EXPECTATIONS

One of the bedrock problems facing parents today is distorted expectations about parenthood. As a teacher and psychotherapist, I'm constantly amazed by the sunny views of parenting that many people hold before they actually bring their first baby home. "I didn't think this would be so difficult," is a typical lament. Or, "There's so much work to do, I never get a moment's peace from dawn to dusk." Or else a plaintive, "Doesn't this *ever* get any easier?"

Welcome to reality. The secret is out: parenthood is hard work. Unfortunately, many people tend to view the task through rose-colored glasses. Why? One reason may be biological—nature's way of keeping you committed to reproducing the species before you come to your senses and decide on a round-the-world cruise instead. Another reason is that there's almost no limit to the variety and intensity of forces that affect how you perceive parenthood. In short, you're being brainwashed. Here are some of the most common and powerful influences:

- *Images of parenthood in the media.* How many movies, TV programs, magazines, and ads have you seen that portray parenthood as endless bliss, fun, and play? In these settings, how often does parenting seem as complex, difficult, confusing, or ambiguous as in real life?

- *What your parents told you (or didn't tell you) about parenthood.* The "party line" within your family may have been a home-grown equivalent of the media version. For instance, one mother told her daughter, "Motherhood means you never let your children down." If you take such words to heart, how realistic will your expectations be toward yourself as you raise your own children?

- *In-laws.* Even if your parents are open-minded and supportive about your efforts to raise a family, your in-laws may have opinions, suggestions, and comments that can intensify your anxieties and frustrations.

- *The intrusion of the past.* Unresolved feelings about your own childhood will almost certainly affect your decisions, attitudes, and feelings about raising your children. If you feel angry about having been raised by a dismissive or abusive parent, for instance, that anger may spill over into your own actions toward your kids. It's difficult to avoid this kind of influence unless you identify these lingering emotions about the past.

- *Changing parental roles.* For at least twenty-five years, Americans have been redefining parenthood, including the definition of what makes a good mother or a good father. The demands of the work world have also influenced parental roles. It's hard to know what to expect of yourself as a parent as American society keeps changing; to some degree, the changing roles change *us.*

All of these situations can influence your expectations about parenthood. Worse yet, they can intensify the stresses that are an inevitable part of raising children—stresses that will complicate your life and, in turn, intensify the stresses that your kids experience.

How can you respond to this situation? To the degree possible, prepare yourself in advance for what parenting will really be like. Try to get the media images—parenthood as a state of endless, glorious fun and games—out of your mind. Parenting *is* fun, but it's also a lot of hard work. Be realistic. Don't expect either constant delight or constant drudgery. Parenting is both wonderful *and* difficult.

So go ahead and talk to your parents; ask their opinions and insights; find out what parenthood was like in their time. Take what you can from their experience, knowledge, and wisdom. Leave the rest. But don't assume that your parents' choices in raising you were inherently right (or, in the eyes of some people, inherently wrong). Some aspects of parenthood may be timeless, but many specific issues have changed dramatically over the past few decades. You face different tasks from what your parents did. Approach them for insights, but base your decisions on a wider range of opinions. Read books. Talk to your friends who have children. The more informed you are, the better off you'll be.

If you already have at least one child, you face a different situation from when you were a first-time parent. You know the ropes. You've shed your starry-eyed assumptions. You've developed abilities to manage the complex demands of parenthood. For these reasons, you probably feel you know what you're getting into as you contemplate another child. You're probably right.

However, it's important to consider a few additional aspects to the situation.

- *The changes you'll experience in having another child may seem almost as great as the change from no children to one.* The reason is partly logistical. You'll be dealing with kids at different developmental stages. You'll be juggling two or more sets of needs. The time issue may be especially pronounced—as Geoff, the father of three boys, put it, "The main difference [with having more than one kid] is that I now have absolutely *no* time that's my own."

- *Financial issues may become more complex.* In some respects your second child is less expensive, since you will have already purchased most of the basic equipment (crib, car seats, high chair, etc.) for Kid #1. You may even be able to reuse clothes you bought the first time around. On the other hand, a new baby's arrival may complicate your work schedule and increase child care expenses. Your income may drop as your expenses rise.

- *The potential for disruptive surprises will increase.* Family life is nothing if not unpredictable. With only one child, however, parents at least have their kid outnumbered, so it's easier to deal with crises. Two or more children in the house can mean far more curveballs heading your way. "I got home one night and found the household in an uproar," one woman told me. "Our five-year-old had picked up a stomach virus, so my husband was putting her to bed. Meantime, our three-year-old twins were up to mischief. One was feeding doughnuts to the dog while the other had filled the kitchen sink almost to overflowing." You think life is chaotic with *one* kid?

Reading these summaries, you may regard my portrait of parenting as too negative. The truth is, I adore kids. I regard parenthood as one of the most fulfilling, delightful, and wonderful experiences of my life. I know hundreds of people who feel the same way. I wouldn't trade parenthood for anything. In sounding cautious and in emphasizing the stressful, demanding, often difficult side of the task, I'm just trying to be realistic. Many parents who adore their children and do everything possible for them openly admit that parenthood isn't a bed of roses. It's hard, messy, confusing, repetitive, often frustrating work. As Susan, the mother of a son and a daughter, says, "Parenthood is the hardest thing I've ever done, but it's also the most fulfilling."

MAKE A COMMITMENT

It may seem unnecessary to focus on parenthood as a commitment. However, many people become parents with an impulsiveness unlike anything they'd allow in other realms of their lives; otherwise clear-thinking men and women often don't see the full implications of committing themselves to parenthood.

In fact, becoming a parent usually marks the dividing line between young adulthood and adulthood. You may be mature, responsible, and accomplished, but life before you have children is flexible in ways that end once you're a parent. Before you become a parent, you're freer to do whatever you want, and you have fewer responsibilities. You can act spontaneously. You have financial leeway far exceeding what you'll ever have as a parent. You can experiment with life more or less on whim. The independence allowed by this phase of adulthood is often wonderful, and for many people it's the gateway to creativity and satisfaction. There's nothing wrong with pursuing life in this manner. Once you're a parent, however, you step into a substantially different mode of adulthood.

Part of the commitment to parenthood is, therefore, to acknowledge the magnitude of the changes involved. Parenting requires enormous work, time, and energy. It also demands a degree of maturity and selflessness that is a "stretch" for many people. To be a good parent, you must have—or develop—an ability to love your child unconditionally. You must be capable of taking action without always thinking, "What's in it for me?" You must do what's necessary without looking toward the payback.

I happen to believe that most people are fundamentally good, and that selfless behavior is a capacity residing deep within the human personality, yet our culture—and especially the consumerist culture that's now predominant—often stresses personal gratification. The me-first aspects of American culture don't square with what parenthood requires. Being a parent means that your gratification focuses on others. Many of the satisfactions of parenting are subtle. Some occur after long periods of waiting. Most of them are internal. What makes parenthood delightful is the joy of loving, the joy of giving, the joy of nurturing a helpless, dependent creature into a capable human being. The thrills of seeing a person mature from birth all the way to adulthood is a magical experience. But easy? Forget it. Challenging? Almost constantly. And part of the commitment you should make as a parent is to the long-range agenda of your child's well-being, regardless of the rough times, demands, and frustrations that inevitably crop up along the way.

STRATEGY #3

ADJUST YOUR ATTITUDE

One of the best means for making and keeping your commitment is to adjust your attitude. Even if you start with reasonable expectations, many events throughout the parenting years will challenge your patience, stamina, and imagination. Nothing ever happens quite as you'd expect. The result for many parents is frustration, disappointment, and fatigue. If you can adjust your attitude as circumstances change, however, you'll ease the pressure on both yourself and your child.

A major part of adjusting your attitude is a willingness to focus on *process* rather than *product*. Don't be obsessed with end results; instead, try to be in tune with the experience of doing whatever you've set out to do. This willingness to go with the flow (rather than to become preoccupied with goals) is one of the greatest gifts you can give your children.

TOLERATE DISORDER

Raising children is a messy business. Even once you're past the stages when kids throw food on the floor, dump the books off the shelves, and scatter toys everywhere, you'll be dealing with all sorts of clutter and upheaval. Obviously you have to insist on a certain level of hygiene and safety, and every parent has his or her own comfort level in accepting messiness. But it's easy to go too far. If you can't tolerate a degree of benign disorder, parenthood will drive you nuts. You'll probably drive your kids nuts, too. My suggestion: Don't be rigid. Let your housekeeping standards slide a bit. Clean up when the clutter or messes risk your family's safety, health, or aesthetic sanity; otherwise go with the flow. Dress your kids for comfort, not fashion. Encourage them to tackle art and cooking projects even if they make a mess (though it's fine to insist that they help clean up afterward!). Allow them to get dirty in appropriate situations, such as playing outside. A certain amount of untidiness goes along with childhood creativity.

DEAL OPENLY WITH GUILT

For parents, guilt goes with the turf. Children have more or less infinite needs; you have finite energy and time; it's inevitable that you'll feel you're shortchanging your child at least some of the time. How can you not feel guilty? Yet guilt serves no purpose and often complicates any situation. To deal creatively with guilt:

- *Weigh the pros and cons.* Let's say you're worried about a job-related issue, such as whether you're spending too much time at work and too little with your family. Rather than wallow in guilt, size up the situation. List the pros and cons. If you decrease your hours at work, what will happen? If you increase your time at home, what are the consequences? Base your decisions on assessments of cause-effect relationships, not free-floating guilt.

- *Change your state of mind.* If you can't change your situation, can you change your *response* to it? Sometimes our emotional reactions to problems exhaust and debilitate us more than the problems themselves do. Is it possible that the guilt you feel is out of proportion with what is inspiring it? Children are amazingly resilient. Although your child may be clamoring for your time and attention, she may be quite capable of tolerating your absence (or action in response to some other circumstance) without suffering any harm. Eliminating your guilt may do your child far more good than stewing over your problems.

- *Stop complaining.* Many people jeopardize their own or their family's happiness with constant complaining. Negative attitudes exhaust both the person holding them and those around them. Everyone gets tired of hearing endlessly negative words. If you find yourself obsessing about the same old issues, take stock of the situation. Are you really so powerless? Is the situation so awful? Are there no options to choose from? It's possible that you face genuine problems; it's likely, though, that incessant complaints will compound them, not solve them.

PRIORITIZE

Many otherwise creative parents bog down because they allow family life to become too complicated. Everything seems an ordeal; nothing goes according to plan. Most of this situation is avoidable. The key is to change your attitude about what needs to be done.

- *Reduce the number of activities in your child's (and your own) day.* Kids today are often severely over scheduled; the same holds true for parents. If you cut the sheer number of obligations that you and your child have to meet, you'll both be much happier.

- *Simplify your schedule.* This isn't just a matter of *limiting* the number of commitments, but of *reorganizing* how you deal with them. Cluster errands. Use downtime to your advantage, such as shopping when your child is at a music lesson.

- *Pad in extra time.* Give yourself more time for the transitions from one activity to another. Avoid pressuring your child to rush-rush-rush. Allow a little extra time for decompression after stressful activities.

Delegate

Many parents I know cause themselves untold problems by believing that they alone can accomplish everything that needs to be done. Whether through perfectionism, a controlling personality, or a habitual belief that they must tackle every task, contemporary parents often hesitate or refuse to delegate responsibility or ask for help. The result: high tension and severe fatigue. It's an unfortunate situation, especially since tired parents often make avoidable mistakes or grow irritable with their children.

A better response is to enlist help from carefully chosen helpers. Such helpers may be your own parents, in-laws, and other relatives, or they may be hired assistants such as child care persons, "mother's helpers," or housekeepers. Many people complain that they can't afford such help. That may be so; on the other hand, some partial solutions (such as hiring a local middle-school student to read to your kids or help put away groceries) aren't expensive, and the benefits far outweigh the costs.

Avoid Burdening Your Child with Your Own Ambitions

You may have assumptions about your children that serve on some level (usually unconscious) to compensate for the past. A classic example is the father who, regretting that he never excelled as an athlete, prods his son to play lots of sports. The father's vicarious ambitions probably won't relieve his own sense of failure, and they may easily become burdensome to his son. Pressures of this kind can prompt parents to ignore the *process* (in this case, his son's learning to enjoy sports and be physically fit) in favor of the *product* (being a successful athlete).

A less extreme example involves children's art. Let's say that you pride yourself on your knowledge of painting. In college, you minored in studio art and have dabbled in several media since then. Now your daughter has started school and is beginning to experiment under the tutelage of a gifted art teacher. You're proud of what she's doing—she shows both talent and interest. You feel tempted, however, to comment on what she's done and, if possible, to nudge her toward more ambitious accomplishments. This is understandable but risky. If, while looking at your daughter's paintings, you have expectations that she should be an artist—after all, it would be a shame if she (like you) never explored her talent properly—you may well end up pressuring your daughter in counterproductive ways. Allow her to explore her talent as she wishes. You may or may not have limited yourself by not pursuing your artistic leanings, but that's your issue to face, not your daughter's.

NURTURE YOURSELF

Parenthood is probably the least selfish aspect of your life. By its very nature, being a parent draws your attention away from yourself and focuses it on the children in your care. Whether you have a primarily domestic role in raising your kids or a more indirect, breadwinning role, parenthood exerts a tremendous gravitational pull on your commitments, activities, thoughts, and emotions. This center of gravity is part of what makes parenthood so satisfying; at the same time, it can also make parenthood difficult, demanding, and wearisome.

Unfortunately, focusing intently on your children may prompt you to lose yourself in the shuffle. Loving your kids, you forget to love yourself. Looking after your children's needs, you neglect your own needs. There are two reasons why this focus may sound acceptable, even virtuous—parenthood as a transcendent, egoless experience—but risky.

First, you can't run on empty. This is as true for emotional energy (including love) as for physical energy. Just as ignoring your physical health can ultimately jeopardize your ability to meet your children's needs, ignoring your emotional health can limit and perhaps eventually damage your kids' well-being. And self-love, being a significant component of emotional health, is crucial. By "self-love" I'm not referring to a self-indulgent, self-centered state of mind—a tendency to attend to yourself at the expense of others, or to see yourself as the center of what's important. Rather, I mean simply a matter-of-fact acknowledgment that you, too, matter; that your needs have their own place in the scheme of things; and that you are fundamentally good and worthy of respect for your contribution to your family's well-being. If you are a stay-at-home parent, you are performing one of the most difficult and important tasks that human beings can undertake. If you are a breadwinning parent, you are doing tasks of crucial importance, too. If you are combining these tasks—whether as a single parent or as a co-parent—you are juggling domestic and professional duties in ways that are also demanding and worthwhile. You deserve your own and others' respect regardless of the parental role you play.

The other main reason self-love is important is that it doesn't contradict or negate your love for your children; on the contrary, self-love makes loving your children possible because your appreciation of yourself is a fundamental part of your delight in life and your ability to give to others. If you don't love yourself, you'll find it difficult to love your kids. If, on the other hand, you love yourself—if you value yourself, know yourself, and have a sense of "center"—then that self-love will emanate to others, including your children. They'll sense your confidence, energy, and strength, and these attributes of your personality will give them confidence, energy, and strength in turn.

But it's important to admit that self-love isn't always easy to attain. Looking after your own needs isn't always possible. The demands of life wear you down, leaving you exhausted and cranky. Dissatisfactions you feel about your past (including your own childhood) nag at you and jeopardize your sense of confidence. Fears of the future complicate your choices, prompting you to question your judgment, abilities, and stamina. The endless responsibilities of parenthood burden you until you wonder if you're doing justice to your children. Given these stresses, it can be difficult to love yourself fully and give yourself the sustenance you require.

LOWER YOUR STANDARDS

One reason you may not nurture yourself is that you may hold unrealistically high standards. You feel that you should always appreciate your kids. You should always be kind, supportive, and cheerful. You should always succeed in protecting your children from pain and disappointment. You should never lose your patience. In short, you should be the perfect mother, the perfect father. This set of expectations is risky—a guaranteed path to disappointment and self-criticism. If you revise your expectations and perceive the tasks of parenthood more realistically, however, you'll ease the pressure you feel to succeed in every way all the time. Easing pressure will boost your self-confidence, which in turn will benefit your children.

RAISE YOUR EXPECTATIONS

This recommendation seems to contradict the previous suggestion, but in fact it addresses another issue. Although many people view parenthood as a monolithic experience, it includes an enormous variety of skills, many of which can be improved with practice. There's no question that most parents can benefit from addressing some of these skills. For instance, Tom habitually derided his limited cooking skills, since his children didn't like the food he served them and their nutrition suffered accordingly. Rather than berate himself as a bad cook, however, Tom bought some cookbooks, asked his wife and several friends for advice, widened his culinary repertoire, and started serving his kids different, better meals. Similar situations can face other parents regarding other issues, among them domestic skills, sports, academic pursuits, and even interpersonal tasks such as learning to hold your temper. In this sense, raising your standards (by developing certain skills) can go hand-in-hand with lowering your standards (by having more realistic general expectations).

SEEK SOLITUDE

Solitude is a necessity for all parents, but obtaining it isn't easy. At many stages of parenthood, even a half hour of quiet time is hard to find. Even the briefest periods of solitude, though, can help mend frayed nerves. One of the most important things you can do is allow yourself some solitude throughout any given day, week, month, or year. Almost anything will do: a brief walk, ten minutes' reading time, a bit of TV, a short nap. Whatever you can do alone that recharges your battery will help you feel better about yourself and thus indirectly help your children.

SEEK COMPANY

Another seeming contradiction: in addition to time alone, you may need more people in your life. Until recent decades, parenthood used to be a community affair. Parents lived in extended families that included grandparents, aunts, uncles, cousins, in-laws, and more distant relatives, many of whom assisted in the tasks of raising children. Contemporary American culture presents us with a far different situation, one in which not only the extended family, but often the nuclear family as well, has deteriorated or disappeared. Twenty-eight percent of all children in the United States live in one-parent households. As a result, the burden on parents (not to mention kids) is often severe. Whether you're raising children alone or with a spouse, however, isolation can damage your self-confidence, stamina, and creativity.

Parents should therefore seek company. Relatives may have much to offer, including a long-term sense of connection. A network of good friends will make a big difference, too. Other options include backup care, a parental support group, or an organized play group—whatever lightens the load, offers solidarity, and reduces a sense of isolation. Sharing child care is only the first of many reasons to do this; the chance to compare notes about parenthood is also important. Figure out who you know who's going through experiences similar to yours—or who has gone through them already. Find someone who will listen to you nonjudgmentally. To survive parenting—particularly in the early years— find places where you can let your kids crawl around and let off some steam. And, ideally, where you can find some fellow-parents to keep you company.

SEE PARENTHOOD AS A SPIRITUAL PATH

Most parents take their responsibilities seriously and do whatever they can for their children. During the past few decades, however, there's been a tendency for some people—especially among the baby boomers—to see parenthood as a sideshow to life's main events, variously defined as professional, recreational, artistic, or spiritual pursuits. This shift in attitude may be in part a backlash against the heavy emphasis on duty in earlier generations. It's also partly a rebellion against the long-time double standard that constrained women with most of the parental responsibilities while leaving men freer to pick and choose among life's options. At times the shift is plain old boomer self-indulgence.

Regardless, it's risky to relegate children to a secondary level of importance. (The risks are especially obvious in families where one parent leaves the scene or shirks parental obligations altogether in order to "find" himself or herself.) One possible way to resolve the tension between other-oriented obligations and self-oriented pursuits is to see parenthood as a spiritual path. This approach exists in many religious traditions; it's perhaps most obvious in Hinduism, which offers the mid-life "householder stage"—the *dharma* (path) of attending to family obligations—as a legitimate alternative to more isolated means of reaching spiritual fulfillment. Buddhism, Judaism, and Christianity all offer variations on this theme.

STRATEGY #5

WORK TOGETHER (BUT ACCEPT THAT MEN AND WOMEN PARENT DIFFERENTLY)

I feel reassured and delighted that more and more American men are getting involved in their children's care on a day-to-day basis. This development appears to be gaining momentum and benefits not only kids and their mothers, but also men themselves. In some respects the trend toward fatherly involvement may be one of the most important social changes in our country over the past several decades. (My hope is that the courts will pay more attention to fathers' increased family involvement as they address custody issues.) However, it's not without some complex side effects.

One is that husbands and wives are still trying to figure out how these changes affect them. Roles are changing; so are duties. What was once a clear-cut division of labor—men as wage-earners, women as caregivers—is now much more complicated. The task of sorting out both abstract issues (such as gender roles) and practical issues (such as who does what) will take many years to come.

Another issue is that men and women appear to have different parenting styles. In fact, men and women appear to have different parenting *content*. I discuss these differences later in this book: see chapter 6, "Communication Between Spouses"; chapter 16, "Fathers"; and chapter 32, "Parenting As Partners." For now, let me say simply that a mother and a father may have different or even conflicting ideas about how to raise their children. This situation often requires considerable effort to find the common ground. At times it leads to arguments and misunderstandings. In any case, I strongly urge couples to sort through the issues openly, fairly, and creatively. Women and men can either cheer each other on, support each other, and do everything possible to work together; or they can criticize, hassle, nitpick, and in many other ways complicate life for each other. The first course of action will lead to improved parenting within the family and intensified closeness within the marriage. The second course will jeopardize the couple's trust and happiness, and perhaps the children's as well.

ACCEPT THE DIFFERENCES AS A NET GAIN

Researchers have found that men and women attend to their children in different ways. The differences are complex and not easily summarized, though the overall patterns suggest that women tend to interact more verbally with kids, while men tend to interact more physically. What matters most is that in many ways, children can benefit from *both* styles of interaction. Neither is necessarily better than the other. Accepting these differences will tend to reinforce each partner's confidence in what he or she is doing. By all means talk over your differences, but be supportive. You probably have a lot to learn from each other. Keeping an open mind will benefit your kids far more than arguing over the "right" way to raise a family.

DON'T UNDERCUT YOUR PARTNER

Sometimes one parent feels so strongly about doing things a certain way that he or she inadvertently undercuts the other parent. I see this fairly frequently among women who outwardly welcome their husbands' participation in domestic matters but inwardly resent the male presence in what has traditionally been a female sphere. "He doesn't cook right," one friend said of her husband. "He makes really big quantities of stuff and uses too many pans. The kitchen ends up looking like a war zone." In fact, this novice cook probably has lots to learn. But by criticizing his cooking when the food itself has done no harm, the wife risks frustrating her husband and even driving him back to a more limited fatherly role. Why not tolerate his well-intentioned and perfectly adequate efforts? Why not give him room to experiment, learn, and grow? Patience will pay off in the long run. Validate and encourage one another. Look to the long view, since the gradual accumulation of skills will benefit everyone in the family.

Every parent needs his or her partner's support. Although each of you will have your own ways of doing things, try to overlook inconsequential differences. If you have different ways of shopping, cooking meals, or doing laundry, and if those differences don't really matter, ignore the issue. Talk over the more substantive differences, but separate what matters from what doesn't. Also, ignore the temptation to nag. It's all too easy to focus on the negative and to take out your frustrations on your mate. Instead, concentrate on what's positive. Try to see the cup as half full instead of half empty. (There's nothing wrong with deciding it's both.)

NEGOTIATE TO REDUCE STRESS AND TENSION

Most spouses work hard to help each other; however, economic pressure and assumptions about roles can create lots of resentment. Here's an example: Marilynne and George's son, Pete, is sick and must skip school for a few days, so the couple is trying to decide who should stay home with the child. Marilynne works as a part-time librarian; George is a full-time middle school teacher. Marilynne feels frustrated because she's the one who, having the part-time job, usually attends to the couple's children when they're sick. She resents being pegged as the stay-at-home parent just because she's the mom. On the other hand, George is the primary breadwinner and has the less flexible schedule, so he feels that the division of labor makes sense. If you find yourself in this sort of situation, sort things out together. Explore the full range of options. Take turns doing sickroom duty. Don't polarize the situation so that one of you carries the whole burden of any one task. Doing so diminishes the importance of the other parent's career, responsibilities, and sense of commitment.

DIVIDE UP CHORES IN ADVANCE

It's nice when spouses can turn on a dime and do whatever domestic tasks need to be done. Even in relatively egalitarian households, however, it's easy to lose track of who's doing what. Mapping out responsibilities can be a way to deal with this situation. Make a list outlining chores, who's performing them, and deadlines. You may not realize how many separate tasks your spouse is accomplishing each day until you see them in black and white. Who's buying groceries? Who's doing the laundry? Who's cleaning the house? Who's shuttling this or that kid to baseball practice, piano lessons, and doctors' appointments? Once you sketch the list of necessary chores, it'll be far easier to divide them as equitably and as realistically as possible, given your unique circumstances. Setting things up requires some work, but the outcome is a more straightforward plan for running the household—and a set of assumptions that makes misunderstandings and resentments less likely.

TAKE TIME TO BE A COUPLE

The couple relationship is the foundation of your family. Everything else grows out of that relationship. Making a living and raising your children may demand most of your energy, but you should set aside at least a little time to nurture one another as partners. Pay attention to each other. Listen closely. Read your spouse's body language. Unfortunately, the little things add up. If your spouse is complaining about small but important issues, consider how they add up into something bigger. Everyone needs to feel important, nurtured, and appreciated.

Try to set some time aside for fun. You may feel that you can't afford a baby-sitter or an evening on the town, but you can't afford to burn out, either. Share some good times as well as the meaningful but exhausting tasks of parenthood. And if you're having trouble spending time together, you need to talk about that issue as well. Why is it hard to spend time with one another? What are the problems you're having, whether individually or as a couple, that prevent you from relaxing and enjoying each other's company? Is the problem external—something economic or career-oriented, perhaps—or is it an internal problem, something of an emotional or spiritual nature? Explore what's causing the problem. Address those issues before the stresses involved do any damage to your relationship.

FIND TIME TO NURTURE YOUR SEXUAL RELATIONSHIP

Many couples complain that once they're parents, romance and passion fade out of their lives. One or both spouses are simply too tired to make love. During the early years of parenthood, especially, when many mothers are nursing, some women just don't feel interested in sex. Such disinterest and fatigue are common, normal, and often temporary.

However, many couples also find that even when parenthood seems less stressful and the demands start to ease, an active love life drops down on the list of priorities. If so, the couple should at least discuss the situation openly. Partners may or may not be able to change anything right away, but most people will feel more comfortable if their thoughts and feelings are out in the open. Discussions can help avoid misunderstandings. Some partners may worry, for instance, that the decline in lovemaking shows that their spouse no longer feels any sexual attraction; it's often reassuring to learn that the situation is solely a matter of physical fatigue. In other situations, unspoken cumulative resentments may have been left unstated, thus undercutting affection. In any event, it's possible that discussions will lead to planning more time to talk together and sort out your feelings. Get organized. Find time away from your children. Plan times together that are relaxing and special. Celebrate your relationship as a couple. Make sure that you communicate to each other what you're feeling about your relationship.

STRATEGY #6

GO AT YOUR CHILD'S PACE

A great source of stress in contemporary American families is the parents' insistence on doing too much too fast. It's true that most parents have high-pressure schedules, including heavy work obligations, long commutes, family duties, and often the additional tasks of helping elderly parents. Even so, many parents insist on going full speed ahead in ways that stress out their kids.

A better strategy: to the degree possible, go at your child's pace. I mean these words in a general sense. If you can follow the overall rhythm of what your child needs rather than scheduling day-to-day activities according to preconceived notions, everyone in your family will benefit. Kids often need a far less programmed existence than many adults assume. You don't have to take on a frenetic role as cruise director or social secretary. Just watch your child closely, follow your hunches about what he needs, experiment a bit, and go with the flow.

LET YOUR KID BE A KID

Many parents love their children but over- or underestimate what they are capable of doing or understanding at particular developmental stages. One example of this situation is the toddler who throws tantrums. The boy's mother tolerates such behavior initially; after a year, though, she feels that her son should outgrow his need to express himself in this manner and "pull himself together." The mother's frustration with chaotic behavior is understandable, but it's naive to assume that a three-year-old will act more maturely than he's capable of acting, given this stage of development. At the same time, Mom shouldn't let the boy run amok. What's needed is to carefully set limits, to avoid rewarding manipulative or fussy behavior, and to reward more organized forms of self-expression. Similarly, the parents of older children should allow their kids the full range of behaviors appropriate to each age under the proper circumstances. Gaining insights into the fundamentals of child development will help mothers and fathers understand the realities of what they face as their kids mature.

SET LIMITS

As suggested above, letting your kid be a kid doesn't mean not setting appropriate limits; on the contrary, limit-setting is crucial. Too many parents tend to shy away from teaching their children to behave in ways that lead both to personal satisfaction and to responsibility toward other people. Kids who grow up without proper limits are often restless and unruly, as even a brief visit to a school or shopping mall will attest. What, though, are proper limits? This book can't address this issue in detail, but various discussions throughout provide an overview (and suggestions for pursuing the subject) that readers will find useful.

MAKE TIME FOR PLAY

Too often, adults see play as frivolous activity—"just" play—whereas play is how children learn, relate to others, discharge stress, and explore. Play is how children express their physical delight in the world. Play is how kids learn to deal with social issues like taking turns, waiting, sharing, exerting self-control, and being patient. Play is also the means by which children learn about roles and relationships, and it's how children release tension. Play is how children exercise their imaginations. Play is also how kids unite all their disparate experiences into a whole. For all these reasons, parents should make sure that their children have enough time for play. Given the fast pace of modern life and the heavy pressures that most adults routinely face, it's easy and tempting to forget how central play is in all children's lives—including play *with their parents*, who may tend to delegate others (kids, teachers, child care personnel, etc.) to be playmates.

On a related issue: don't allow electronic or other high-tech playthings to take the place of less glitzy toys that children need for their development. The media, computers, video games, and all manner of gadgetry are fast supplanting art materials, ordinary toys, and "props" such as blocks, cardboard boxes, pots and pans, and costumes in many kids' lives, resulting in an increased impoverishment in children's imaginations, motor skills, and familiarity with the world.

CELEBRATE THE EVERYDAY WORLD

In centuries past, children spent much of their time side by side with adults. Kids learned a lot from their parents and grandparents about domestic skills, work-related knowledge, family history, cultural lore, and information about the wider world. Parents and children now spend much more time apart than in the past, especially once kids enter preschool or kindergarten. Even after each schoolday, many kids' activities center on play groups, scheduled activities, or clubs. The result is a decline in what children learn from their parents. This decline itself is lamentable, for it limits important kinds of parent-child sharing.

In addition, it limits certain ways in which children can learn to enjoy the ordinary aspects of life. Rather than teaching their kids to cook, for instance, parents may do all the food preparation themselves but simultaneously sign up their children for off-site cooking classes. To counter this tendency, emphasize the importance of everyday activities. Family cooking projects, for example, can serve multiple purposes. Preparing meals attends to the group's nutritional needs, teaches important life skills, emphasizes the importance of focusing on others, and celebrates the goodness of life.

TAKE TIME TO BE ATTENTIVE

Many parents today are in such a rat race that they can't calm down, relax, or tune into their own physical or emotional needs. Is it surprising that in this manic state, they can't focus on their child, either? That they can't observe their child's behavior and find out what's going on inside him? This is a risky situation. Preoccupied with work, today's parents inadvertently tune out their kids. But if you can tune *into* your kids, you can tune *out* the static of the world—work, politics, international crises, everything—and the sound is so clear and so beautiful that it's a big relief. This not only helps your child; it helps you as well.

STRATEGY #7

MAKE YOUR HOME A HAVEN

Family life has grown more complex and stressful during the past several decades. Some of the complexity and stress is a consequence of external factors: economic pressures, cultural changes, and the disintegration of community. Some of the complexity and stress, however, is internal: the result of shifts in attitudes and expectations by family members. Whatever the sources of these changes, their effects are often disruptive. Family members often have less time together than in the past. Parents are more likely to be absent from the home for long periods of time, which leaves children either on their own or looked after by parent surrogates. Tension between parents, between kids, and between parents and their kids has increased. Outside influences—peers, celebrities, the media—often displace parents as the chief influence on their children. As a consequence, children often feel adrift or pressured. The instability of contemporary family life takes a significant toll on the mental well-being of millions of American kids.

Even some "solutions" further complicate the problems they are intended to solve. For instance, many parents worry that their children don't have enough to do. It's no longer possible simply to tell kids, "Go out and play," leaving them to their own devices in an era when even relatively safe neighborhoods seem unpredictable and hazardous. Kids complain of feeling bored or having no place to go. Parents feel stressed by obligations to entertain their children or else guilty that they're depriving their kids of meaningful activities. The response? A tendency to schedule—and often overschedule—a whole array of activities. Of course, many kids benefit from extracurricular activities. It's not that scheduled activities shouldn't occur—simply that the level frequently exceeds what children need or can tolerate. This frenzy of lessons, sports, and classes can intensify rather than relieve kids' anxieties. Sometimes the heavy schedules reflect parents' guilt over their own absence rather than indicating the children's real interests.

So how should parents respond to the uncertainty and riskiness of contemporary life without programming their kids' time into a state of gridlock?

First, try to create a peaceful, relaxed environment at home—a calm place where children can unwind, disengage from their often demanding lives, and enjoy themselves and their family members without a lot of distraction. It isn't necessary (or even desirable) to turn your house into an amusement park, nor must you invest in a lot of equipment—fancy sports gear, a high-tech "home entertainment center," or whatever. Elaborate activities at home can be as stressful to kids as elaborate activities off-site. Rather, the goal is a warm, easy-going atmosphere that allows children to put up their feet, engage in unstructured pastimes, hang out, and goof off.

A particularly tricky issue in this regard is so-called quality time. Most mothers and fathers these days have demanding, even crushing work obligations. One or both parents may be absent most or all of every workday. On returning home, they're probably exhausted and tense. The notion of quality time—limited (sometimes very limited) but satisfying periods of parent-child companionship—was created to help parents cope with time away from kids. The idea is that, given a shortage of parental resources, high quality will make up for low quantity. It's a reassuring concept. Unfortunately, it doesn't necessarily meet children's needs. First, it assumes that quality alone will compensate for quantity. The truth remains that part of what kids (especially young kids) want from their parents is simply a lot of time together. Second, the notion of quality time assumes that kids will be able to obtain what they need at the particular time that parents choose to be available. Third, it assumes that the kids won't feel pressured precisely by the expectations of quality. ("We've got twenty minutes before I have to leave, so let's have some fun together, okay?") The dilemma of quality time is that it's often more reassuring to parents than to kids.

The solution to this problem may, in fact, require significantly more change than simply trying to get home half an hour early. There may be economic trade-offs or other concessions necessary to address your children's needs. Certain career moves may have to wait. The reality of the situation isn't appealing to contemplate, but you may have to sacrifice some degree of personal advancement or financial payoff to satisfy your kids' emotional expectations. This isn't to say that you indulge them—setting up fancy activities such as trips, projects, or whatever. On the contrary, I mean simply *being available on a more routine basis*. Part of what kids need is just time. Plain old time—time to be kids, time to hang out with their parents.

Whether you're able to increase your parent-child time or not, here are some ways in which you can make your home a haven.

DIMINISH THE IMPORTANCE OF STRUCTURES AND SCHEDULES

Let your kids take more substantial control of what they want to do. Given the intensity of school activities, your children may feel a need to "go into neutral" for a while. Playing alone, hanging out with friends, reading, or even staring out the window may be attractive, low-intensity pastimes that soothe frazzled nerves.

EXPECT THE UNEXPECTED

One of the things that having children teaches parents is to be "in the moment." You can never truly predict what they'll need, or when. Go ahead and make plans, but be prepared to shift, reschedule, and turn on a dime. If you have an active project in the works but discover that your kid is tired or feeling overwhelmed, be ready to adjust without blaming the child. Sometimes the activity you find yourself shifting to may end up being more satisfying than what you planned. Perhaps you've planned an outdoor activity because your three-year-old seems so hyper; then, suddenly, he turns out to prefer sitting on your lap while you read to him—a pastime you have found him unlikely to tolerate till now.

TUNE OUT THE STATIC OF LIFE

Contemporary life is often absurdly frantic. Set limits and boundaries. Screen phone calls with an answering machine. Limit intrusions by the media—television, radio, or computer on-line services. Diminish the amount of TV that your children watch, since the sensationalistic and often violent imagery of many shows can intensify kids' anxieties about the world.

ENGAGE IN SPIRITUAL PRACTICES

If your family is part of a religious tradition, take time to participate in its family-oriented or community activities. If you have no ties to organized religion, consider practicing some kind of independent spiritual activity, such as meditating, doing yoga, practicing an art, listening to music, or contemplating nature. Such activities may or may not directly involve your children; even if you engage in a spiritual practice alone, it's likely to benefit your family. Calm yourself first. You can't expect your kid to relax if you yourself feel totally wired. Do whatever suits you that helps you gain perspective on family life and ease your own stresses.

FOCUS ON FAMILY ACTIVITIES

If you feel that your children need more to do, try to organize activities around the family. Let's say that your kids express an interest in painting. Rather than registering them for an art class at the community center, do projects together at home. The results may be disorganized and messy at first, but your kids will gain from the family time together as well as learning the specific skills you teach them. The same holds true for activities such as cooking, music, sports, and science. If you lack skills in these areas, visit your library or bookstore to obtain books or videotapes to provide information.

DISENGAGE FROM COMPULSIVE CONSUMERISM

The constant pursuit of material well-being intensifies rather than alleviates stress within most families. Your family doesn't need more gadgets, goodies, and belongings. Most American children suffer from an excess rather than a lack of possessions. One of the reasons kids complain about boredom is that while swamped in toys and amusements, they haven't been challenged to entertain themselves or to exercise their imaginations. In addition, consumerism leads to spending so much money that parents work harder and harder, and thus end up less able to spend time with their children. Most children I've spoken with in my several professional roles say that they would prefer to have more time with their parents rather than more material goods. Make do with what you have. Enjoy each other without relying on a lot of props and distractions. Focus on *being* rather than *buying*.

The seven strategies we've discussed can significantly ease the stress you experience throughout the parenting years. Even using one or two of these strategies can make a difference. There's no question, however, that many of the issues parents struggle with aren't general issues, but specific ones. Sometimes they are one-shot tasks to accomplish. Sometimes they are recurrent problems you have to solve over and over. Sometimes they are quandaries that crop up only during particular developmental stages. In any case, the work of parenting can require you to focus on these issues with great intensity.

PART TWO

PARENTING ISSUES AND CRISES— AND HOW TO DEAL WITH THEM

ONE

ATTACHMENT AND BONDING

THE POPULAR IMAGE of parent-child attachment is tidy, cute, and hopelessly idyllic. Attired in a spotless white nightgown, the new mother gazes blissfully into her newborn's eyes; the baby, safe in Mama's arms, gazes back in rapturous adoration. This brief moment of eye contact seals the pact of mutual love forever.

If only the reality of this situation were so simple! In fact, attachment isn't an automatic occurrence at the moment an infant comes into the world. The outward image is different, more complex, and messier than what most people envision. Almost all mothers are exhausted after giving birth; many can't sit comfortably, let alone gaze blissfully into a baby's eyes. A new mom may be sweating profusely in response to postpartum hormones. She may be in pain from her milk-engorged breasts. She may be feeling ambivalent about the wrinkled, bruised, noisy child she holds: perhaps delighted but also confused, overwhelmed, even depressed. How, she wonders, will she ever relate to this demanding little creature?

Yet despite the messiness and stressfulness of a newborn's arrival, parents shouldn't worry about parent-child attachment. Somehow it usually takes care of itself. If you are concerned about the issue of good attachment between yourself and your child, rest easy. This process happens over a period of time and generally takes shape without problems.

THE NATURE OF PARENT-CHILD ATTACHMENT

When you watch a parent holding a newborn baby, you know that powerful forces are at work. You can sense the baby's need for the parent and the parent's protectiveness toward the baby—almost as if a magnetic field were pulling parent and child together. When you watch that parent interacting with the same child a year later, you know that similar forces are at work, though they have changed: the child's helplessness is now a more complex dependence; the parent's total protectiveness is now a mixture of protectiveness and encouragement to explore.

What you have watched is partly the interaction between the child's attachment to the parent and the parent's bonding to the child. Both attachment and bonding are instinctual behaviors in higher animals, including humans, though human beings' expressions of the instinct depend on cultural and personal factors such as sex roles, personality, and upbringing.

In a 1985 interview with Edward Myers, British psychologist Colin Murray Parkes explained the importance of attachment: "The attachment of the child to the mother is something that's essential to the survival of that child throughout its childhood. On the whole, a baby won't survive unless someone comes along and feeds it and protects it from dangers. There's reason to suppose that the attachment between child and parents is just as much an inborn biological entity as having a left arm or a left leg. This is something you inherit."

In short, a child's attachment to her parents is a normal, crucial aspect of early development. It is a process, however—something that takes place over a period of time—rather than a brief event. Many factors influence this process, including:

- Whether the pregnancy was planned or unplanned

- The state of the parents' marital relationship

- The family's stress level (for instance, the effect of financial worries)

- The parents' temperament and physical well-being

- The parents' family histories (for instance, the emotional distance from or closeness to each parent's own mother and father)

- The parents' emotional maturity and readiness for child-rearing

This isn't to say that any one of these issues will necessarily disrupt either the parents' ability to bond with the child or the child's ability to form an attachment to the parents; rather, it means simply that disruptive issues—physical illness, emotional problems, severe financial strain, and so forth—can affect how easily and quickly a parent "connects" with a child. A relatively happy, relaxed, untroubled parent will probably have more time and emotional energy available to focus on the practical and emotional demands that a new baby inevitably presents. A relatively unhappy, tense, troubled parent is more likely to feel distracted and depleted by a baby's demands. The more complex and stressful the parents' circumstances or the baby's needs, the more complex the attachment process.

Yet in reality, most parents bond well with their children, and most children form good attachments to their parents. That being said, it's worthwhile for parents to understand the nature of attachment and its formation.

ATTACHMENT IN INFANTS

What an infant needs is primarily a loving, consistent, attentive primary caregiver. Throughout most of human history, this caregiver has generally been the infant's mother, though a nurturing father, grandparent, or other relative may suit the child's purposes as well. In theory, other people (including hired caregivers) may be able to provide both physical and emotional care from the time of a child's birth onward; in practice, such arrangements don't always provide the consistency, intensity, and duration that infants need.

Regardless of the caregiver, how does the attachment process occur on a day-to-day basis? First of all, through feeding. Oral gratification not only satiates the infant's hunger, it also provides her with what psychologists call object constancy—a sense that the "other" (the parent or other caregiver) is reliably available to satisfy the child's appetite. This is why a consistent, stable caregiver is so important. The issue isn't just having needs met (such as for food, warmth, safety, and physical affection); it's a matter of having needs met *by the same person*. Consistency of response from the same caregiver is part of what makes attachment possible. In addition to feeding, other forms of nurturing include keeping the child warm and dry, cuddling, touching, and affectionate interactions such as singing, smiling, and making eye contact in trustful, calm, kind ways. In addition, communication of other sorts is a significant part of the attachment process. Communication in this sense includes speaking, singing, and reading.

The result of these various sorts of nurturing, according to Mary Ainsworth, a prominent authority on attachment, is that "Warm, sensitive care liberates and enables autonomy." To put it another way: when a child feels sure that her parent is available and reliable, she is then able to disengage from the parent and explore her environment. Abundant, nurturing care allows a child to develop confidence. Although this confidence means initially that the child will stay close to the parent, it also leads to the kind of independence necessary for moving out into the world.

Building on research by the English psychiatrist John Bowlby, Ainsworth and other researchers have attempted to define the consequences of attachment. By means of an experiment called the "strange situation"—in which six-month-olds were left alone briefly in an unfamiliar room, then reunited with their mothers—Ainsworth and other researchers have distinguished three patterns of attachment:

- *Secure* infants either sought closeness to or contact with the parent, or else greeted the parent at a distance with a smile or a wave. The securely attached child protested or cried when separated from the mother but greeted her pleasurably when she returned. These were relatively easy babies to control.

- *Avoidant* infants avoided the parent. They gave the impression of independence, explored the environment without using the mother as a home base, and didn't turn around or didn't seem affected when she left. They snubbed the mother on her return.

- *Resistant/ambivalent* infants either passively or actively showed hostility toward the parent. The ambivalent child tended to be clingy from the outset, were afraid to explore alone, and became anxious and agitated upon separation. Once the mother returned, these children often cried profusely and sought contact with mother but simultaneously arched away from her.

This theoretical framework is just that—a framework. It sketches infants' characteristic reactions in accordance to one conceptual scheme. Other factors affect how children react to the world around them. Temperament is one such factor—that is, an in-born tendency toward being relatively outgoing, relatively shy, etc. In addition, physiological factors (such as diet or illness) may affect children's responses to people, things, and events around them. Attachment isn't the sole variable that accounts for how children respond to their environment. However, it's a useful concept and one worth considering as you try to understand your child.

ATTACHMENT IN OLDER CHILDREN

Given the attachment theory, what are the implications for later life? It's hard to summarize, but some theorists have done research suggesting that:

- Secure two-year-olds are generally enthusiastic, persistent in solving tasks, and effective in using maternal assistance when tasks are more difficult.

- Secure preschoolers are significantly more flexible, curious, socially competent, and self-reliant than their counterparts.

- Secure school-age children are more sympathetic, more assertive about what they want, and more likely to be leaders. They are more self-confident, creative, and independent. In addition, they tend to find peers who are equal in self-esteem and who are confident, outgoing kids.

- These findings persist through the full span of school ages.

- Secure adults tend to be relatively comfortable establishing closeness to others, depending on others, and having others depend on them; they also don't worry as much as others about being abandoned or about someone getting too close to them.

In my own clinical practice, I've seen that securely attached kids are more independent, confident, and able to explore their world. Why? Because securely attached children not only feel sure about their acceptance from their parents, they have also internalized feelings of self-love, self-worth, and self-esteem. The combination of internal and external security provides these children with a safe base for venturing forth into the world, taking on leadership roles, and accepting the good things that life has to offer. They are more positive, less fearful, less insecure, and less anxious. They have an easier time relating to friends and peers. They are less likely to hook up with bullies and to follow a leader. In peer group situations, they're much more likely to be the leaders or to set the standards. They seem to be more in touch with their creativity and imagination. They are psychologically at home with themselves and less anxious about being alone. They are very self-contained, but they're also very socially adept. And they are psychologically much more attuned to others and aware of the complexities of relationships and people around them.

ATTACHMENT IN TEENAGERS

Attachment changes—sometimes dramatically, sometimes subtly—as a child grows. The nature of attachment in a toddler is clearly different from and more complex than attachment in an infant. Changes occur during all stages of childhood. None are more dramatic, however, than the changes that take place during a child's teens—changes that often prompt parents to feel confused and resentful.

Unlike humans, most animals require only a brief period of nurturance, after which the young leave the parents and disappear forever. Human attachment behavior is much more complex than in other species. "Humans are characterized by an extraordinarily long period of childhood by comparison to all the other animal species," Dr. Parkes explained to Edward Myers in the interview mentioned earlier. "And certainly as a proportion of their total life span, the human period of dependency on parents is much, much greater. Nonetheless, it does appear that 'round about adolescence, there is a rather rapid dwindling of attachment to parents, which perhaps explains the amount of conflict that begins to arise at the time. At the same time, this is perhaps associated with the development of sexual bonds to members of the opposite sex of about the same age group. Before very long, there's a tendency to form a further attachment to somebody else." That is, attachment starts to shift during the teens.

But Parkes notes that the shift in attitudes and behavior is not a total change. "This doesn't mean, however, that there is no residual attachment to the biological parents. I think that although that wanes rather rapidly, it remains a real thing. And there are very few people who stop caring about what happens to their parents at all." In short, even during the teens—a time when many sons and daughters regard their parents with great ambivalence—one part of the mix will be a strong emotional attachment. The implications: when your child reaches his or her teens, brace yourself to be pushed, pulled, and buffeted in many directions. Your child will simultaneously need you and resent you. The events and emotions resulting from these contrary feelings are notoriously difficult for everyone involved. Generally speaking, you're more likely to weather this stage successfully if you keep in mind that teenage ambivalence about parent-child bonds is normal and, given enough patience and time, will eventually stabilize.

FOSTERING GOOD ATTACHMENT

As you read this discussion, you may feel a huge burden descending onto your shoulders. How can you make sure that your child experiences good attachment? My short answer is: Relax.

The longer answer is: Rest easy—your child's attachment to you, and your own bonding to your child, will probably take care of itself. There's no cause for undue worry. Strong forces—your love for your child and your child's need of you—will take care of what needs to happen.

If you need reassurance, though, keep these points in mind:

- *Secure attachment will likely result from the ordinary ways in which you care for and love your child.* Feeding, diapering, snuggling, playing, and all the other ways in which parents care for babies "in the moment" will accomplish most of what needs to happen.

- *Consistency matters more than any specific, one-time action.* If you're simply a "good enough" parent—not perfect but attentive, concerned, and loving— you and your child will both be fine. Making occasional mistakes (delaying a feeding, forgetting to change a diaper, or not being quite as tender when you're exhausted) won't do any harm.

- *Don't worry about "spoiling" your baby.* According to Mary Ainsworth, "It's a good thing to give a young child physical contact, especially when they want it and seek it. It doesn't spoil them, it doesn't make them clingy or addicted to being held."

- *Older children will provide many of the cues you need to understand the changes in their attachment to you.* The toddler pushing you away, the seven-year-old insisting on walking to school, the ten-year-old refusing to be kissed—these are all ways in which children alert you to the internal changes in their psyches. If you honor them and don't take their behavior personally—if you offer them affection but don't force it on them—you will nurture their attachment to you as they grow.

- *Teenagers will move away from you in ways that many parents find confusing and hurtful.* This process, too, is part of their development. It's important to stay involved with your teen on a day-to-day basis, and to continue to be warm, nurturing, and physically affectionate with both sons and daughters. Give them the leeway they need and they'll come back to you in the long run. (See chapter 50, "The Teen Years," for further discussion of this issue.)

BEHAVIOR AND CHILD DEVELOPMENT

W HAT IS APPROPRIATE development at each stage of childhood? This question has complex answers—so complex that psychologists and pediatricians have written scores of books on the subject—and no brief chapter can cover this issue in detail. For this reason, what follows is an *outline* of predictable milestones. Other chapters in this book directly address related topics, among them chapter 3, "Boys"; chapter 14, "Expectations"; chapter 20, "Girls"; chapter 25, "Letting Go and Holding On"; and chapter 50, "The Teen Years." In any case, keep in mind that I'm presenting a sketch, not a detailed analysis, of developmental issues.

NORMS—NOT TIMETABLES

Developmental milestones are useful but deceptive: useful, because they provide you with an overview of how children change and grow over the years; deceptive, because the overview doesn't predict a specific child's behavior. In short, developmental milestones refer to *norms* within a group of children. They aren't timetables for what your own child will experience. Each child will develop in her own way at her own rate. Her development will vary in relation to other children's; in addition, her development in particular areas (such as verbal or motor skills) will also vary in relation to other areas (such as intellectual growth). The upshot of this situation is that you shouldn't be alarmed if your child appears to be developing at a different rate compared to other children, or if her development seems inconsistent. Child development is often erratic. It may proceed smoothly for a while, then accelerate, then slow down or even regress before proceeding again.

NEWBORN TO AGE THREE MONTHS

The first three months of life are a time of tremendous intensity; the newborn is totally dependent on others yet limited in her ability to express her needs. At the same time, infants are remarkably sophisticated creatures in many ways; and because they are inherently programmed to change and grow, they almost seem like a different species within three months' time. (For a detailed overview of child development theory, see the Further Reading section, especially the books of Swiss psychologist Jean Piaget.)

Sensory/Cognitive Development
- Grows alert to loud sounds, bright colors, striking patterns

- Startles when hearing loud noises

- Responds well to human voices, especially the mother's

- Shows rapid awareness of outside stimuli

- Repeats pleasurable behavior, such as thumb sucking

Emotional Development
- Calms down in response to holding, cuddling, or rocking

- Learns to make eye contact with parents

- Shows recognition of parents' voices

Verbal Development
- Cries frequently in response to hunger, pain, fatigue, etc.

- Coos by end of first month

Motor (Physical Skill) Development
- Shows disorganized activity at first, with many involuntary motions

- Can't sit, stand, or crawl

- May be able to roll partway onto side by about four weeks

INFANCY

The first year of life reveals some of the most dramatic changes that a human being will ever experience. From a state of almost total helplessness, the child develops into a still-dependent but remarkably expressive creature capable of complex motion, perception, and communication.

AGE THREE MONTHS

Sensory/Cognitive Development
- Explores the world through the senses (watching, listening, and touching, but also sucking, tasting, and cuddling)
- Delights in observing contrasting black-and-white or brightly colored objects
- Delights in looking at the mother's face, especially when the infant is nursing
- Shows awareness of other people
- Recognizes parents' voices
- Tracks objects, especially black-and-white ones
- Mirrors or imitates mouth movements and facial expressions
- Exhibits oral behavior—puts everything in mouth

Emotional Development
- Cries to show distress, pain, or fear
- Responds strongly to one primary, consistent caretaker
- Coos to show happiness or excitement
- Turns head in direction of parent's voice
- Senses mother's touch and smell when nursing, and enters a relaxed state

Verbal Development
- Makes preverbal or babbling sounds
- Makes a greater variety of sounds—chuckles, gurgles, squeals, etc.
- Starts to change intonation in utterances

Motor (Physical Skill) Development
- Learns to hold head steady
- Takes "swimming" position—weight on abdomen only, with legs, arms, and head lifted
- Moves arms toward objects, but cannot grasp them
- Kicks forcefully
- Plays with own hands

AGE SIX MONTHS

Sensory/Cognitive Development
- Bites or tastes objects
- Follows moving objects more consistently
- Starts to grasp the relationship between size and distance (i.e., a car will look small when distant but larger when close)

Emotional Development
- Smiles readily
- Loves throwing kisses and being held and kissed
- Shows assertiveness in reaching for objects
- Shows anger when deprived of toys
- Enjoys watching and interacting with parents
- Enjoys peek-a-boo and other disappearance/reappearance games
- Smiles often

Verbal Development
- Loves to vocalize preverbal sounds
- Learns to make new sounds by changing shape of mouth
- Starts to recognize different tones and inflections in others' speech

Motor (Physical Skill) Development
- Lifts legs high while lying on back
- May grasp feet
- Rolls onto stomach

- Sits upright briefly
- Grasps objects with hands
- Bangs objects or transfers them from hand to hand

AGE NINE MONTHS

Sensory/Cognitive Development
- Continues to master depth perception
- Develops a growing ability to read facial expressions
- Strives to coordinate motor activities with sensory input (such as making a mobile move)

Emotional Development
- Manifests stranger anxiety when unknown persons appear
- Starts to learn how to assess others' moods and imitate them
- May show jealousy
- Shows anguish or alarm when parents leave the room

Verbal Development
- Loves to vocalize, both alone and in response to others
- Babbles phraselike sequences of sounds
- Forms first syllables, such as "mama" or "dada"
- May respond to own name
- Responds to "no"
- Imitates coughs

Motor (Physical Skill) Development
- Turns in circles
- Crawls by pulling weight over forearms
- Sits steadily for long periods of time
- Grasps objects skillfully
- Waves or shakes hands purposefully
- Pulls body upright to standing position
- Loves to handle objects

AGE ONE TO TWO

Around age one, the child has started to walk and talk but hasn't yet mastered these skills; by the age of two, she is exploring the world with constantly growing physical and verbal sophistication. She is also beginning to exert her will. Rather than tolerate what her parents demand, she now insists on a greater and greater degree of independence.

Sensory/Cognitive Development
- Begins to experiment with cause-and-effect (such as knocking toys down to see what happens)
- Begins to experiment with trial and error to accomplish goals
- Starts to consider specific problems and find mental solutions
- Develops ability to use symbols (such as words; see Verbal Development below)

Emotional Development
- Manifests separation anxiety if parents leave
- Shows "magical thinking"—believes that perceiving something (such as parents' departure) makes it happen permanently
- Shows initial venturing away from parents for short periods of time
- Delights in transitional love objects—blankets, plush animals, etc.
- Shows initial capacity for independence—experiments with evading parents as a game, etc.
- Says "no" more often; starts to throw tantrums
- May show fear of thunder and lightning, big animals, and the dark
- Struggles to distinguish between fantasy and reality

Verbal Development
- Enjoys vocalizing for its own sake
- Responds verbally to other people
- Responds accurately to many simple commands ("Up," "Come here," etc.)
- Gradually acquires a larger vocabulary
- Gradually uses questions like "What's that?" and "Why?"
- Combines words ("All gone," "Want mama," etc.)

- Uses "no" or "not" in understandable phrases or sentences
- Employs about ten different phrases or sentences regularly

Motor (Physical Skill) Development
- Crawls
- Gets into things—cabinets, bookcases, drawers, etc.
- Stands alone competently
- "Cruises" alongside walls, furniture, etc.
- Starts walking with assistance
- Starts to pile blocks
- Stoops to pick up objects
- Puts small objects into larger ones
- Touches and handles many objects
- Turns knobs on appliances

AGE TWO TO THREE

Between the second and third years, the child consolidates the skills that she has acquired in the year before. Energetic, willful, and demanding, she is a force of nature—at once delightful and exasperating to her parents.

Sensory/Cognitive Development
- Develops greater sophistication in dealing with the world symbolically (such as describing things or actions with words)
- Explores experiences through pretending (such as playing house, hospital, and so forth)
- Perceives events entirely in relation to own experience (i.e., egocentric view)
- Thinks at a very concrete, rather than abstract, level

Emotional Development
- Sees the world almost entirely through the lens of her own needs
- Manifests frequent mood swings
- Expresses sadness or stress

- Throws frequent temper tantrums

- Pouts or sulks when frustrated

- Struggles to distinguish between fantasy and reality

- May show a preference for time with and attention from the parent of the other sex

Verbal Development

- Rapidly increases vocabulary

- Mimics adults' verbal inflections

- Grasps simple commands

- Starts combining nouns with verbs to form sentences

- Begins to use pronouns such as "I" and "me"

- Asks frequent "why" questions

- Starts to understand a few prepositions ("on," "under," "with")

- Forms three- and four-word sentences

- Begins to refer to future events

- Uses regular plurals (those formed by adding -s to a word)

Motor (Physical Skill) Development

- Picks up small objects with thumb and forefinger

- Begins to eat with spoon

- Stacks blocks to make towers

- Scribbles randomly

- Washes own hands to some extent

- Begins to show readiness for using toilet on his or her own

- Unwraps packages

- Removes hat, shoes, and socks independently

- Jumps in place

- Runs well

- Can balance momentarily on one foot

- Can pedal a tricycle by age two and a half

- Folds and creases paper
- Unscrews bottles and jars

AGE THREE TO FOUR

A three-year-old can seem much more settled than a child a few months younger; she may be relaxed, content, and comfortable with herself and with the people around her. By three and a half, however, the situation often changes, with growing restlessness and demanding attitudes toward others.

Sensory/Cognitive Development
- Many issues resemble those during age two to three
- Remains egocentric (such as believing that the moon follows her when she walks)
- Struggles with differences between fantasy and reality

Emotional Development
- Begins to grasp what's acceptable and what's not
- Grows increasingly aware of others' feelings
- May show empathy toward familiar people
- Shows frustration when sharing
- Tends to be egocentric and self-obsessed, viewing the world almost entirely through her viewpoint

Verbal Development
- Uses language with greater fluency
- May ask for help or clarification on tasks
- Asks questions rhetorically
- Expresses refusals in complex ways ("I don't want to" rather than "No")
- Is able to talk on the telephone
- Introduces questions with "where," "what," and "why"
- Understands the gender contrast of pronouns such as "he" and "she" or "him" and "her"
- By age four, tells stories that mix fantasy and reality
- By age four, can carry on elaborate conversations
- By age four, develops a more elaborate sense of humor

Motor (Physical Skill) Development

- Exhibits high level of activity

- Plays in complex, active ways, with many games

- Enjoys building projects with blocks, clay, and other materials

- Has adequate motor skills to create elaborate art projects

- Turns corners and rounds obstacles at a running pace

- Turns wide corners on a tricycle

- Balances on one foot for up to five seconds

- Throws and catches a ball

- Draws crude circles

- Uses scissors to cut a sheet of paper in half

- Stirs liquids with a spoon

- Pours from a pitcher to a cup

AGE FOUR TO FIVE

Though physically capable, the four-year-old can be emotionally unpredictable. Many children are secure at this age, but they have entered a period of willful confidence. Boasting, bragging, and exaggerating are common, and many children test adults' patience with outbursts of wild activity and language.

Sensory/Cognitive Development

- Continues to struggle with differences between reality and fantasy

- Ascribes lifelike qualities to nonliving things (such as stuffed animals)

- Struggles with issues of conservation (such as that a quantity of water stays the same whether it's contained in a tall, narrow glass or a short, wide one)

- Explores issues of classification (such as that dogs of varying shapes and sizes are nonetheless all dogs)

Emotional Development

- Attains greater (if still sporadic) emotional equilibrium

- Acquires an increased ability to compromise

- Gains an increased sense of emotional cause-effect relationships (e.g., "If you hit your sister, she'll be angry and hit you back.")

Verbal Development

- Tells elaborate stories, both realistic and fanciful
- Demands detailed answers to questions
- Exhibits a tendency toward self-praise ("I'm smart," "I have good ideas," etc.)
- Understands the concept of opposites
- Rhymes words
- Uses articles ("a," "an," and "the") consistently
- Can define some words
- Bosses and criticizes others
- Elicits attention of adults
- Hesitates to admit inability

Motor (Physical Skill) Development

- Enjoys art projects that involve cutting, building, and painting
- Is capable of more strenuous walking, running, and hiking
- Walks down stairs alternating feet from step to step
- Carries a cup of water several feet without spilling
- Turns sharp corners on a tricycle
- Climbs ladders at the playground
- Can touch thumb to the tip of each finger in turn
- Cuts a straight line with scissors
- Draws stick-figure people that feature heads, eyes, and legs
- Dresses independently

AGES FIVE TO SEVEN

By age five, the child "settles down" to some degree. She can be conformist in attitude, eager to please her parents and other adults. She is capable of many activities but probably more conservative in attitude and behavior than she was at four years old. Then, by the child's sixth birthday, the situation may grow more complicated: While generally cooperative, enthusiastic, and warm, the six-year-old can be impatient, demanding, and difficult.

Sensory/Cognitive Development
- Starts to understand issues of conservation, as during age four to five
- Refines ability to classify objects
- Refines distinction between animate and nonanimate objects
- Grasps more distinctions between reality and fantasy

Emotional Development
- Starts to identify with the same-sex parent in learning about gender roles and relationships
- Imitates and mirrors others through role modeling and play
- Feels a great need to be cherished for intrinsic worth, not just accomplishments
- Continues to have an egocentric, self-absorbed worldview
- Manifests a worldview that's a mixture of fantasy and reality
- Struggles with the complexity of information and issues
- May continue to struggle to distinguish between fantasy and reality

Verbal Development
- Can tell a long story accurately
- Embroiders stories to make them more fantastic
- Is capable of politeness and tact in speech
- Asks many questions about how things work, what things are for, and what words mean

Motor (Physical Skill) Development
- Hones previously learned skills (throwing, catching, running, etc.)
- Learns sports with increasing sophistication and motor control

AGES SEVEN TO TEN

During the three-year span between ages seven and ten, the child consolidates many skills but also acquires a host of new ones. These years are a time of less dramatic physical change than during preceding stages, but they are revolutionary in another way, since children start to focus less totally on their own perceptions and begin to perceive and learn about the complex world around them.

Sensory/Cognitive Development
- Develops a capacity for abstract rather than concrete thought

- Shows increased capacity for logical reasoning

- Begins to understand hierarchical relationships (such as the relationships of the parts to the whole)

- Understands conservation more fully

- Widens understanding of categories (such as what mammals have in common, and how they differ from reptiles)

Emotional Development
- Manifests increased self-confidence and self-worth

- Starts to focus on the peer group as central to his or her social experience

- Develops more resourcefulness, greater self-reliance, and more self-awareness

- Manifests an increasing ability to think critically about ethical issues such as integrity, character, and individual versus community rights

- Manifests a tendency toward stereotypical gender behavior

Verbal Development
- Acquires a significantly larger vocabulary

- Perfects many aspects of spoken language

- Masters many skills relevant to reading and writing

Motor (Physical Skill) Development
- Shows a growing mastery of new skills and a high level of industry

THE PRETEEN YEARS

The years preceding the onset of puberty have tended to be a period of relative stability in a child's overall development. By age ten, the child has undergone many of the striking changes that take place during middle childhood, yet she hasn't yet experienced the confusion and transformation of adolescence. This period of stability continues to occur for most children. However, physiological and cultural changes are shortening what used to be a predictable calm before the storm. The average onset of puberty is earlier now, and social pressures prompt children to imitate adolescent values, attitudes, and behavior.

Sensory/Cognitive Development
- Significantly refines capacity for abstract thought

- Refines grasp of hierarchical relationships

- Develops greater ability to acquire and store detailed information

- Advances in grasp of cause-effect relationships

Emotional Development
- Shows a heightened sensitivity to any kind of disapproval or rejection from the peer group, teachers, and family members

- Manifests a tendency toward black-and-white ethical thinking

- Tends to be judgmental and stereotypic in ethical issues

Verbal Development
- Grows increasingly sophisticated in use of language

- Acquires slang vocabulary and usage as part of peer-group bonding

- Experiments with linguistic taboos (profanity, insults, etc.)

Motor (Physical Skill) Development
- Shows marked increase in physical strength and stamina

- Shows marked increase in agility and sophistication both in large and small motor skills

- May grow fascinated with sports as a pleasurable end in themselves, and as a means of expressing power and a sense of mastery

THE TEEN YEARS

Precisely because adolescence ushers in the most dramatic stage of child development since toddlerhood, I'm devoting a separate discussion (chapter 50, "The Teen Years") to this transformation.

THE PARADOX OF PARENTHOOD

One of the great paradoxes of parenthood is that much of what mothers and fathers "do" is simply to let the child develop. You can't *make* her move from one developmental stage to the next; all you can do is allow the transition to occur in its own time. Attempting to rush the process is often counterproductive. Most parents see the reality of this situation regarding physical growth—

you can't force your child to grow taller, for instance, or to move from baby-hood to toddlerhood two months earlier. However, some parents try to inter-vene in other ways. Parents who enroll young children in enrichment programs—classes purporting to teach toddlers or even babies prereading skills, math facts, art appreciation, and the like—may be needlessly pressuring their kids. The truth is, children develop largely in their own ways at their own pace. Force-feeding them academic or cultural information isn't likely to speed up the process.

To help your child develop healthily and on schedule, I recommend a low-stress, straightforward attitude. Love your child simply for who she is. Cele-brate her being, not her accomplishments. Give her a good, safe environment to explore. Provide a variety of interesting toys to play with. Read to her and, later, when she indicates her own readiness, support her eagerness to read. Throughout her life, bring her into contact with kind people of diverse back-grounds, abilities, accomplishments, and trades and professions. Encourage her curiosity and interests. Listen to her concerns, worries, delights, and perplexi-ties. Grant her the leeway to understand who she is and where she fits into the world. In its own way, what I'm recommending is a tall order; it does not, how-ever, require you to push or pull your child from one stage of development into another. Mostly it means that you should be available when she needs you but otherwise allow her to invent herself as she goes. By providing what I suggest here, you will give her 90 percent of what any parent can give a child.

What if you feel that she is genuinely at risk of developmental problems? Sometimes concerns *are* appropriate. If you have reason to believe that your child isn't reaching age-appropriate milestones—or if her teacher or pediatri-cian flags a concern—don't panic. Most "problems" of this sort are, in fact, merely individual quirks of timing. Children don't learn to walk, talk, or read at the same age. Early or late achievement of certain goals doesn't necessarily indicate developmental precocity or delay. Before you start to worry, though, check with your child's doctor. Discussing your concerns with a thoughtful pediatrician will often ease any worries. Nine times out of ten, your child's sit-uation will fall within normal developmental guidelines. What if there's still reason for concern? The next step would be to obtain a referral to a psycholo-gist or a developmental specialist for an evaluation. Even then, you may well find that your child is simply developing in accordance with her own individ-ual schedule.

THREE

BOYS

"My daughters were six and three when Sean was born," says Ellen, "and I thought I could handle any issue a kid could throw at me. But with Sean I felt like a first-time mom. Nothing prepared me for raising my son! From day one he was fussier, more demanding, and much, much more active. He's a good boy, but he's a boy. I never know what to expect."

....

Josef felt concerned when the teacher called to say that his son, Evan, was acting out. "I asked what he was doing. They said, 'Running in the halls.' So when he got home I asked Evan, 'Why were you running in the halls?' He said, 'I've got all this energy!' I said, 'Run around at recess.' And you know what he told me? 'The school canceled recess!' No recess! And the teacher's wondering why Evan is running in the halls!"

....

Speaking of her teenage son, Jake, Melissa feels hurt and confused. "We used to be close. He was a great pal till age eight or so. Now he'll scarcely talk to me. He hangs around with some friends—sometimes five or six at once—and yuks it up with them nonstop. But when I ask him what's new, he says, "Nothing," and that's that. I can't pry a word out of him."

DIFFERENT AFTER ALL

INFANCY, TODDLERHOOD, THE preschool years, and other phases of development are often similar for both sexes. In many respects, parents can expect their sons and daughters to behave in ways that follow more or less the same patterns over the years.

Yet it's also important to realize that boys and girls differ in significant ways. Most cultures of the world have acknowledged these differences throughout history, though often to the detriment of girls, who have tended to be perceived within male-oriented societies as inferior, deficient, or pathological. It was long overdue when, in recent decades, feminist psychologists objected to the exaggeration of gender differences as an influence on behavior, interests, and accomplishments. But some claims—that gender differences are *solely* a cultural construct—have gone too far. Some theorists assert that only education, gender roles, and stereotypes make girls seem different from boys. Then, during the past few decades, theorists such as Nancy Chodorow and Carol Gilligan set the stage for a change of perception. In her book *In a Different Voice*, Gilligan, a psychologist at Harvard University, argues that girls undergo significantly different developmental changes. Neurobiologists such as Laurie Allen at UCLA and Rubin Gur at the University of Pennsylvania have made discoveries, meanwhile, suggesting that the male and female brains differ in important aspects of structure, development, and function. Many of these assertions are controversial; each claim inspires a persuasive counterclaim. The overall meaning, however, is important. Boys and girls may be different after all.

We don't yet know the implications of these differences. They may be fairly subtle—minor variations of physiology that cultural influences can exaggerate. On the other hand, the differences may be more substantive—major variations in their own right. What we do know is that many people, including mothers, fathers, teachers, principals, and others, react strongly to the real and perceived differences between boys and girls. And these reactions often shortchange not only girls but boys as well.

WHY CAN'T A BOY BE MORE LIKE A GIRL?

I have a friend who is an intelligent, caring, highly committed mother of four children. By luck, Jackie has ended up with an interesting experiment in gender differences: she has two girls and two boys, born at about eighteen-month intervals in a girl-boy-girl-boy sequence. Jackie has a broad perspective on the similarities and differences between boys and girls. Her reaction doesn't prove anything—kids are amazingly individual—but it's suggestive. And it runs counter to what Jackie herself expected. "I figured, Hey, kids are kids. Who cares what their plumbing is like? It's how you raise them that matters. And I figured on treating them the same. But I wasn't ready for Derek and Ian, who I still can't figure out. I hate to say it, but I just don't understand them at all—they're like little wild animals I can't quite tame, almost a separate species."

Jackie's reaction isn't unusual. In her case, it may not be a problem, since she has enough intellectual, emotional, and financial resources to deal with the challenges of raising a large family. For other parents, the situation is more daunting. Many parents (not just mothers, but fathers as well) consider their sons a major challenge. Boys can seem so demanding, energetic, uncooperative, and chaotic that even well-intentioned parents lose patience in trying to deal with them. Other adults can be still more frustrated by the situation. Teachers, among others, often see boys as inherently difficult or, in popular but risky jargon, dysfunctional. Whereas adults often used to perceive boys as the norm (which often led to overindulging them), many adults now perceive girls as the norm (which often leads to pressuring or suppressing boys as deviant). Both responses are limited and shortsighted. In a sense it takes the old question "Why can't a woman be more like a man?" (as it appears in Rogers and Hammerstein's musical *My Fair Lady*) and twists it into an equally unfortunate lament: Why can't a boy be more like a girl?

The issue doesn't show up only in individual parents' reactions. To some degree, even the institutional response to boys tends to suggest that girls' behavior is normal, while many or most boys' behavior is aberrant. The situation becomes frustrating when boys start school. At that point, "they're thrown into schools where, on average, boys aren't as good at things as girls," according to Michael Thompson, a Boston-area psychologist quoted by Carey Goldberg in a *New York Times* article about researchers who study boys. "Girls read faster and sit more nicely, and boys are more physically restless and impulsive." The result? "[W]e sometimes don't make accommodations for the boys' developmental levels, so we humiliate them and get them mad . . . and they come to resent it and dislike it and dislike authority and react back against it." Further evidence for the predominant view of boys' behavior and activity levels shows up in the rate at which American boys are diagnosed with attention-deficit disorder and other learning disabilities: six times the rate for girls. Throughout society as a whole, there's an increasing tendency to view boys as inherently troubled, even destructive.

NATURE *AND* NURTURE

What seems likely is that child development for boys (as for girls) is a combination of nature and nurture. Recent research in neurobiology suggests that boys differ from girls to some degree in brain structure, neural functioning, and hormonal influences. At the same time, culture responds differently to boys and girls, who then respond back to the culture. The result is a complex dialogue between individual children and the society around them.

The challenge is to find a more creative blend of nature and nurture. Boys deserve better than to be stigmatized by institutions that ignore or rebuff their physical and emotional needs. Society deserves better than to produce sullen, angry boy-men who contribute little to the community. What's the answer?

NEW IDEAS ABOUT RAISING BOYS

Several researchers and theorists have now suggested promising new ideas about raising boys. One of these theorists, Michael Gurian, is a therapist and educator who works with families, schools, churches, and youth organizations to focus attention on boys' issues and problems. Another, William S. Pollack, is a psychologist who teaches at the Harvard Medical School and codirects the Center for Men at McLean Hospital in Cambridge, Massachusetts. Both offer interesting, useful perspectives on what boys need from their parents and from society.

IN PRAISE OF BOYS

In *The Wonder of Boys*, Michael Gurian argues that boys' behavior is both physiologically and culturally determined. Boys, Gurian states, differ significantly from girls both in neuroanatomy and in the effects of male hormones. In addition, boys are "hard-wired" toward vigorous physical activity, greater risk-taking, and aggressive behavior as a consequence of millions of years of human development, during which boys' and men's lives centered on hunting as a skill and a way of life.

The result: boys need multiple outlets for discharging physical energy, but they also need creative environments that emphasize competition, high performance, a preference for participation in group activities, a search for independence, and a need for male role models. Our society lets boys down because we fail to provide the settings and the guidance necessary for boys to thrive, learn, and live in accordance with their needs. In this sense, the difficulties that boys face are the consequence of both physiological nature and modern culture's failure to respond to that nature imaginatively. Only by rising to the occasion both individually as parents and collectively as members of society can we reverse the damaging trends that neglect boys and encourage harmful behaviors.

RESCUING BOYS FROM "BOY CULTURE"

William S. Pollack agrees with Michael Gurian that boys are in crisis. Unlike Gurian, however, Pollack feels that the source of the problem is almost entirely cultural. Pollack's recent book, *Real Boys*, notes that some issues affecting boys do, indeed, have physiological origins, but he discounts these as secondary. The real problem is what Pollack terms the "Boy Code": "the outdated and constricting assumptions, models, and rules about boys that our society has used since the nineteenth century." The Boy Code "express only half of their emotional lives . . . their 'heroic,' tough, action-oriented side, their physical prowess, as well as their anger and rage." It also "dictates . . . that [boys] should suppress all other emotions and cover up the more gentle, caring, vulnerable sides of themselves." The result is gradual but devastating damage to boys' sense of wholeness, emotional creativity, and openness to themselves and other people—"a wellspring of grief and sadness that may last throughout their lives."

Why do boys subscribe to the Boy Code? One reason is that the code is essentially unstated, a set of rules and expectations that no one teaches outright, but that modern society teaches anyway, though often indirectly. A second reason is that parents—even parents who want their sons to lead emotionally rich lives—inadvertently stress the Boy Code by shaming, teasing, or simply misunderstanding boys. A third reason is that boys often learn the Boy Code in unsupervised settings, whether on school buses, at summer camp, or in locker rooms. Adult abdication of responsibility leads to spreading the Boy Code by default.

Pollack finds the current situation predictably bleak. "While it may seem as if we live in a 'man's world' . . . we do not live in a 'boy's world.' Boys on the whole are not faring well in our schools, especially in our public schools. . . . Thrust into competition with their peers, some boys invest so much energy into keeping up their emotional guard and disguising their deepest and most vulnerable feelings, they often have little or no energy to apply themselves to their schoolwork." Yet Pollack isn't resigned to accepting the damage. "My clinical experience and research—as well as research done by others—have shown that most boys, when lovingly nurtured themselves, will in turn nurture and show empathy for others. We have learned that the way parents care for their sons has an even more powerful effect on a boy's behavior than we had realized, an effect at least as strong as biology in determining a boy's nature. How you treat a boy has a powerful impact on who he becomes."

WHAT YOU CAN DO FOR YOUR SON

Given recent research, how can you respond to your son's needs so that he can develop fully and become, in Pollack's words, "a real boy"?

Here are two sets of suggestions—the first derived from *The Wonder of Boys*, the second from *Real Boys*.

MICHAEL GURIAN'S RECOMMENDATIONS FROM *THE WONDER OF BOYS*

- Help boys to express their needs rather than believing that, as parents, we know what they need.

- Support boys in working hard to attain their goals; accomplishments should be earned, not simply granted.

- Teach boys to turn their failures into opportunities, especially opportunities to take stock of themselves and grow.

- Teach boys who they are, especially in light of male biology, and enable them to appreciate and respect their maleness and live wisely.

- Give boys more of the discipline and structure they need in order to know how to live and how to love.

- Give them more elders to model after, learn from, and believe in, thus teaching them more about honor, respect, and integrity.

- Eliminate (to the degree possible) influences in their lives that desensitize and dehumanize them. (In this regard, Gurian is referring to overreliance and overtolerance of the media, including TV and computer games.)

- Give them increased opportunities to develop their skills and talents through increased mentoring and availability of supportive adults.

- Give them more adult time and more consistent but flexible authority.

- Give them more of an incentive to serve others, thus more contentment within themselves.

Gurian's *The Wonder of Boys* is a complex book and contains many other suggestions to parents; in addition, the author has published a sequel (*A Fine Young Man*) that focuses on the teen years. Both books are useful, and they deserve a wide audience.

WILLIAM S. POLLACK'S RECOMMENDATIONS FROM *REAL BOYS*

Real Boys, like Gurian's *A Fine Young Man*, is a detailed, thoughtful book, and summing it up in a brief list of suggestions doesn't do it justice. But given the limits of space, here are some particularly important recommendations.

- *Talk openly about the Boy Code.* One of the chief problems that boys struggle with is our culture's silence about its expectations. Discuss the quandaries that the Boy Code presents, and help him deal with them.

- *Teach others about the problem of the Boy Code.* Spread the word about how society's expectations limit boys' emotional development. Resist stereotypes. Object to assumptions (whether among teachers, coaches, or other parents) that stunt or damage boys.

- *Teach your son about masculinity by talking about the men you value and respect.* By pointing out men who have defined themselves more fully, rather than according to society's precepts, you can show boys good examples of deeper masculine values.

- *Rotate parenting responsibilities.* Spouses in two-parent families can show their sons the breadth of human roles by sharing parental responsibilities.

- *When your son is hurting, don't hesitate to ask him whether he'd like to talk.* Many boys won't respond right away; if you follow their lead, however, they may open up eventually. The key is to wait until your son is ready to talk with you.

- *Avoid shaming your boy if he refuses to talk with you.* Any effort to humiliate a boy into talking will only reinforce the Boy Code.

- *When your boy seeks reconnection, try your best to be there for him.* Let him know that you'd be happy to spend time discussing whatever he wants to talk about.

- *Experiment with connection through action.* Many boys are more likely to open up while doing something else—playing a sport, doing a chore, or going for a walk.

- *Don't hold back.* Even if boys seem emotionally standoffish, they need and value parents' affection.

HELPING BOYS TO BE WHO THEY REALLY ARE

The true crisis for boys nowadays isn't that they have too much freedom, but that they lack the kind of freedom that matters most—emotional freedom. Although many boys are self-indulgent, smug, arrogant, antisocial, and even violent, these unpleasant attitudes and behaviors are *not* signs of strength. Quite the contrary: the noxious attributes that so many boys manifest actually scream of weakness. Many boys feel isolated, debilitated, depressed, and weighted down by the oppressive roles and expectations that burden them. Ironically, boys are trapped. Only when parents and other adults can discard outmoded expectations will boys have a chance to be free.

As a parent, you can't solve the entire problem for your son. You can, however, make a huge difference in helping him understand himself, his needs, his abilities and limitations, and his place in the world.

William S. Pollack sums up the situation most eloquently:

Unless they are conditioned not to be, boys are eminently loving and caring human beings. . . . If we withhold our love and affection, our boy feels ashamed and then hardens himself. If we don't stay active in his emotional life and listen to his feelings well, he comes to believe that his emotions are not welcomed. . . .

Real boys need to be with people who allow them to show all of their emotions, including their most intense feelings of sadness, disappointment, and fear. Real boys need to hear that these feelings are normal, good, and "masculine." They need to know that there really isn't any feeling, activity, or behavior that is forbidden to them as boys (other than those that could end up hurting them or somebody else). They need to be taught connection rather than disconnection. . . . They need to be convinced, above all, that both their strengths and their vulnerabilities are good, that all sides of them will be celebrated, that we'll love them through and through for being just the boys they really are.

FOUR

CHILD CARE

WHEN A RECENT poll questioned American parents about which aspects of family life they found most stressful, the number one response was *child care*. This outcome is hardly surprising. Child care is expensive, unpredictable, and often difficult to find. To make matters worse, child care issues are heavily intertwined with most parents' work lives at a time when employers give lip service to "family-friendly values" but often complicate Americans' efforts to balance family and work commitments.

In fact, locating and choosing appropriate child care can be a stressful, even overwhelming task. Many parents feel insecure and confused about what to look for in child care. There are so many different options. Is a child care center best for your child? Would home care be preferable? Should you hire a live-in nanny or au pair? To complicate matters, even the most satisfactory arrangement will change as your child grows and develops. So if you feel insecure about these issues—or confused, worried, anxious, numb, or panicky—you're certainly not alone.

DEVELOPMENTAL ASPECTS

The answers to the child care quandary will differ depending on your child's developmental stage.

INFANTS

My advice for parents with infants is to stay home with your child as long as possible. Three to six months is a good minimum. Longer is better. The reasons for my stressing parental care for infants are the bonding, consistency, and the one-to-one care that infants need to grow and thrive. It's best to have a family member with the child at this early stage. The mother or father is usually the ideal person for this role, though a grandparent can be equally good. The goal in any case is to have a loving, attentive, warm, nurturing, consistent, kind caregiver for the child. If a parent or other relative isn't available, the next best person is a loving, warm child care provider who can be with your infant long-term at home.

If care isn't possible in your own home, I recommend competent, caring attention from an experienced person in her home. (I'm referring to a trained nanny, not an au pair. Au pairs are a difficult issue to assess. Although some are wonderful young women, they are really exchange students more than trained child care providers.) A nanny is most appropriate when infants have overcome the developmental phase called "stranger anxiety." Home care can offer a good alternative to care by relatives. One reason for my preference for family over a child care center is that there are usually fewer children present, hence a smaller chance of exposure to viruses. (Infants' immune systems aren't well developed yet.) In addition, home care usually provides an environment that's more similar to your own home than a child care center would be. There may also be fewer children demanding the caregiver's attention. (See page 61, for information on acceptable child-caregiver ratios at various developmental stages.)

Some people prefer child care centers over home care. The reason is that if you have a family day care provider but she has no backup arrangement, the parents can run into scheduling problems. This situation is especially difficult for families in which both parents work outside the home. But are child care centers acceptable for infants? The answer may well be yes; however, check out the situation carefully. If you're going to put your infant in a child care center, make sure that the staff-to-child ratio is appropriate. Make sure as well that the center meets the standards for the Office for Children Regulations or Department of Child and Family Services in your community. (Later in this chapter I'll discuss appropriate criteria in detail.)

TODDLERS AND PRESCHOOL-AGE CHILDREN

At two or three years old, the ideal transition is a part-time preschool program. This arrangement isn't always feasible, however; most parents don't have the luxury of staying home part-time or gradually easing back into work. In that case, what are your alternatives? If you can't work out a gradual transition, try to find the best early childhood center available. They are usually affiliated with college early childhood programs. Centers of this sort often have more help available because they have students involved—often students majoring in early childhood studies. The supervisors are usually well trained, too, because they are specialists in the field. Other important options include arrangements that allow parents to have lunch with their children, if possible; good phone access to the director or teacher at any time; and no restrictions for parents to visit, observe, and be available to their preschool children.

Some other issues to consider when you're looking at a particular center:

Parental participation. Some centers are cooperatives; the parents spend time with the kids on a rotating basis. Other centers simply have liberal policies regarding parental visits. Either way, parental involvement is a plus for kids and parents alike. Young children love to have parents visit and see what they're doing in school. It strengthens the link between home and school, and it gives children many more opportunities for transition in a safe, trusting, loving way. By this means, the first school experience is one that the child associates with home, which helps the child to begin his or her school experience in a positive frame of mind.

Your intuitions about the place. When you go to the center, how do you feel? How do you imagine your child feeling about the time she spends in that environment? How does it feel when you talk to the director and the teacher? Do they appear open, warm, loving, kind, patient, nurturing? Or do they seem rigid, tense, easily distracted, uncomfortable, or noncommunicative? Especially in the early years, these people will be powerful role models for your child, so their attitudes and personalities are crucial. If the teacher or director has similar values to yours, that's more comforting for your child and makes for an easier transition. Your gut-level sense of things will be the best barometer regarding how your child will adjust to that environment. Your own comfort level will also help to tell your child that you trust this place—it's safe, fun, and relaxed.

An objective assessment. To be sure that you're content with your choice, ask questions, get references, and talk to parents whose children have been there. Call your local office of Children and Family Services. These agencies often have ratings for centers, including files about possible complaints. Call the Better Business Bureau, too, to see if there has ever been a complaint about the center.

One caveat: just because you like the place doesn't guarantee that it's the best environment for your child. For instance, some children are shier and need smaller groups. You should take your child's age and personality into consideration. Shop around to feel sure that a particular center is the best choice for your child.

THE ENVIRONMENT

In addition to making decisions based on your child's developmental stage, you'll have to size up the child care setting to make sure it's safe and appropriate. This process can be fairly straightforward, but you should proceed thoroughly and carefully.

SIZING UP THE GENERAL ISSUES

Always investigate these issues before you enroll a child in a school:

- *Location.* The closer the center is to your home, the more likely your child will have friends from your neighborhood. Close proximity to home also decreases the stress level from transportation hassles.

- *Cost.* What can you afford? High-quality care is expensive. Do you prefer more hours of child care at a somewhat lower level of quality, or do you prefer less time at a better center? What are the costs, and what payment arrangements are available?

- *Scheduling.* What time periods are available? What is the vacation schedule? Is there backup care for vacation schedules or optional programs in the summer? What is the sick policy for caregivers? Do they have backup teachers?

- *Caregivers' credentials.* Check the teachers' and director's backgrounds. Ask to see their résumés. What are the education and training backgrounds of staff members? Once you've narrowed your list, jot down questions to ask the director when you have your interview. Answers to your questions should be forthright, candid, and relaxed.

- *A visit to the site.* Bring your child to see the center. Most day care directors will be happy to let your child visit. If not, it's a red flag, so take any reluctance into account.

- *Turnover rate.* Since child care pay is often low, it's important for centers to have salaries, training, benefits, and incentives that keep providers there long-term. What arrangements has the center made to encourage consistency of staffing?

- *Management.* Who is the director? Does she seem comfortable, cordial, and open-minded? Do you feel at ease talking with her? Does she answer your questions openly and honestly? Can she admit that she may not have all the answers? Does she come across as rigid or rule-obsessed with little room for flexibility?

- *Diversity.* Do you see children from varied ethnic or cultural backgrounds? Is it an open environment that encourages diversity?

- *Child-staff ratios.* (See the boxed discussion on page 61.)

- *Disciplinary policies.* Ask how caregivers set limits for the children. How do they actually handle specific situations, such as aggressive or disruptive behavior? Pose concrete examples and ask for typical responses.

- *Parental visits.* What is the drop-in policy for parents? What are the expectations for parental participation or volunteerism?

- *Toilet training and hygiene.* At what age are children expected to be toilet-trained? For children who aren't toilet-trained, what are the procedures to minimize unsanitary conditions?

- *Health and safety.* What are the health policies and procedures? How is a sick child treated? Do they have a separate room or facility for sick children who are waiting for their parents to pick them up? Is there a nurse on duty? Is there a physician on call?

- *Play facilities and equipment.* Is there adequate space indoors and outdoors for play, both for large and small motor activities? Are there learning centers for exploratory play? Are there dress-up corners for dramatic play? Is there ample space for building with blocks or other construction toys? Are water and sand tables available? Are they well equipped with hands-on materials for children to learn their cognitive skills? What is available for music, art, and body movement activities? Are there special teachers for any of these activities? Are there gym, dance, or yoga activities for the children?

- *Overall "feel" of the place and the program.* Most important: are the staff members warm and friendly, and do they take a developmental approach? Do they look to educate the whole child—the full range of social, emotional, cognitive, motor, and language skills? Look at the faces of the children who are there when you're observing the classroom. Do they look happy, healthy, cared for? Does the teacher look happy, healthy, relaxed, and calm? Is he or she enjoying the children and their activities together?

IDEAL RATIOS

Provider-child ratios aren't the only criterion for judging a child care facility, but they are significant. For infants, the ratio should be one care provider for every two children. A one-to-one ratio is even better. For toddlers, the ratio should be one provider for three toddlers. Some states say one to five, but I believe that three or four toddlers is enough. For preschoolers, the ratio should be one provider for ten children; one to eight is better for three-year-olds. Four- and five-year-olds need one provider for twelve students in a class. The fewer the children per caretaker, the more attentive the care children will usually get. And there's less stress on the providers, too, which ultimately helps the children.

If all of these issues check out satisfactorily, and if you feel comfortable with the director, you will probably feel trusting and comfortable with the center overall.

CHECKING OUT THE FACILITY IN DETAIL

In addition, you should ask about or observe what you can about specific aspects of the program and the physical setting.

- Is the center warm, cheerful, bright and kid-friendly?

  - Is it well maintained?
  - Are decorations at child's-eye level, and is furniture scaled to fit children?
  - Ideally, tables and chairs should be square or round to encourage social interaction.
  - All the bathrooms should be kid-sized.
  - The center should be a child's world that allows kids to do as much for themselves as possible.
  - Is your child's room stimulating, understimulating, or too stimulating for your child?

- Is the center clean?

  - Toys, furniture, and equipment should be washed and in good condition.
  - Are learning materials well maintained?

- Is the center safe and childproofed?

  - Are child safety precautions observed?
  - Is there a fire extinguisher in each room?
  - Are the heaters covered safely?
  - Are the outlets covered; and are there safety seals on all the electrical outlets?
  - Are there safety locks on cupboards?
  - Are safety inspectors' certificates prominently posted and up-to-date?

- What is the balance of activities?

  - Kids need both routine and variety. Do you see evidence that both needs are provided for?
  - Are books numerous and easily available?
  - Is there a reading corner or some other quiet area, ideally furnished with chairs and pillows?
  - Are there other activity centers—places where children can sit quietly, play pretend, or explore dramatic plays or toys?

- How do caregivers communicate with the parents?

  - Is there a phone in each room?
  - Are there scheduled conferences?
  - Is there a center newsletter?
  - What other means are available for parents to keep track of their children's activities?

- Are staff members careful about hygiene, particularly around diaper changing?

- What are the sleeping arrangements for children when they nap?

  - Does each child have his or her own crib, or are there mats on the floor?
  - Can they bring their own blankets from home?
  - How are the mattresses covered?

- Is there good ventilation, heating, and lighting?

Last but not least, trust your instincts. If something doesn't feel right to you, investigate it before you enroll your child. You can always talk to an educational consultant, to another child care provider, or to another parent who has enrolled a child there. (This is always a good way to get some of your questions or concerns answered.) If something doesn't feel right, check out another place that will make you happier and more comfortable.

SAFETY AND SEPARATION ISSUES IN CHILD CARE

Parents often ask me how to tell if their baby-sitter, family day care provider, nanny, or au pair is safe and adequate. The short answer is: Look at your child. Is she happy? Does she like being with this person? Does she like going to school? Does she look forward to it? Does she talk enthusiastically about the teachers or about the nanny, au pair, or other child care provider? If she's with other kids, does she talk about them happily? Does she seem to be making friends? Does your child explore the physical space with curiosity and excitement about life? Positive responses to these issues are all indications that you've made a good decision.

What should you do if your child cries every morning or seems afraid to go to day care? Be open-minded. The issue may or may not be the child care arrangement itself. It may be reactive—anxiety over separation from the parents. To cope with separation anxiety:

- Early on, have a "transition day" into the new setting.

- Put a picture of your family in the child's cubby at the center.

- Let the child take something from home—a stuffed animal, a blanket, or a toy—as a transitional object.

- Write little love notes to put in your child's lunch box.

- Talk about the difficulties of going off to work and school—the sadness of saying good-bye.

- Ask the director what the center's policy is about talking to the child over the phone. (Sometimes parent-child phone calls aggravate the problem, so step carefully in using this tactic to ease your child's stress.)

Separation anxiety is normal. It means that your child is attached to you, which is good and healthy. However, separation is also a guilt-provoking experience for parents. Try not to feed into it too much. Instead, try to make your child feel secure by reminding her who will pick her up each day. Young children don't have a lot of control, so it's important to give them a sense of control by telling them what to expect. Go through her schedule with her; tell her exactly who will pick her up at the end of the day so she has as much consistency as possible. Reassure her. Remember: At this age there's a lot of magical thinking, and separation anxiety originates in a child's fear that when you leave, you'll be gone forever. Make sure you remind your child that you haven't disappeared; you'll always come back.

FIVE

COMMUNICATION BETWEEN PARENTS AND KIDS

COMMUNICATION IS THE heart of all good, healthy, intimate relationships. Your child's age and developmental stage will influence the level at which he can communicate with you; at any age, however, communication is the means by which children build healthy self-esteem, obtain what they need for physical and emotional growth, and get their ideas and opinions heard in a positive way. Communication is crucial to intellectual, social, emotional, and linguistic development. At the heart of good communication is several key features:

- Being able to speak openly with another person without being reactive
- Speaking without casting blame, condescending, making demands, putting others down, or preaching
- Making clear statements
- Engaging the other person in a dialogue
- Becoming aware of the effect that you have on others

GAINING AWARENESS OF COMMUNICATION

All parents face difficult communication issues. At the start of parenthood, when you're caring for a baby, your child can't even talk with you; you must communicate by nonverbal means. Later, as your child grows into toddlerhood, you must deal with the remarkable but complex stages of your child's efforts to acquire language. Other stages and tasks soon follow. Even the parents of highly verbal children must deal with multiple aspects of parent-child communication over the years. And of course parents have their own communication issues, quirks, and challenges to face as the parenting years go by. How, then, can you foster good communication within your family?

First of all, try to monitor the nature of your parent-child interactions. Are the words you speak and hear truly a dialogue between you and your child, or are they perhaps partly exchanges between yourself and someone else—such as your own parents? When you hear yourself speaking to your child critically, for instance, you may be repeating verbal exchanges that your parents had with you. (One of the most common remarks that parents make to me is, "My gosh, I sound just like my parents!") If you find yourself in this situation, stop yourself before you say anything you might regret. Think about the situation. Stall for time. Take a few minutes just to tell your child, "I need to think a while." Or say, "I'm feeling so tired right now, I can't really think clearly. Let's talk again in a few minutes." Once you're calmer, come back and listen to your child without interruption or judgmental behavior. It's hard to hold back, but doing so will serve you well in the long run.

Second, try not to overgeneralize from specific conversations. It's always important to separate your child's *behavior* from your child's *being*. Labeling a child can be destructive. Even abrasive or frustrating conversations may not justify an across-the-board accusation. Instead of asking, "Why are you always so fussy?" ask, "What's bothering you this afternoon?" or "I've noticed you seem unhappy this afternoon—what's bothering you?"

Third, stay open-minded about your own communication style. It may not be what you think it is. Consider recording some of your conversations as a way of perceiving how you really communicate with your children. The experience of hearing yourself as others hear you may become the first step in relearning how to communicate with your children.

. . . .

STEPS TO GOOD COMMUNICATION

Here are seven steps that can help foster good parent-child communication. You may not be able to follow all seven in sequence all the time (or at all), but being aware of them will help.

Step 1: Listen to your child without interrupting.

Step 2: After listening, paraphrase out loud what your child has just said to you.

Step 3: Empathize with or validate your child's feelings. Say, "It sounds like you were really feeling sad and angry." Or, "I sense that I've hurt your feelings." Or, "I'm sure the situation has been frustrating."

Step 4: Ask for clarifying statements. "So tell me again—what did Suzy say to you?" Or, "Help me to understand this better." Do so without judging and without offering opinions; just be curious and ask questions for clarification.

Step 5: Start the negotiating process. Ask your child what options he sees. What could he do differently if he could do things over again?

Step 6: Offer suggestions and gentle guidance. "What would you think about talking with him again?" Or, "Would such-and-such have been a good solution?"

Step 7: Working together, choose an option that might work next time.

PARENT-CHILD COMMUNICATION

First, when you communicate with your child about some aspect of his behavior that's bothering you, use what I call "I-messages." Instead of making categorical statements—"You're such a spoiled brat," or, "You're so self-centered"—use statements that simply state how you feel.

- "I'm feeling angry."
- "I'm feeling hurt (frazzled, stressed, tired)."
- "I worry when you don't show up on time."
- "I feel very tired, so when your room is a mess I feel even more exhausted and frustrated."

Using I-messages instead of accusations, judgmental statements, or blame-casting can help start a dialogue about solving the problem at hand. Rather than putting your child on the defensive, I-messages identify your frustration and its source, which in turn can lead to productive questions:

- "How can we keep your room in better shape?"
- "What's a better way to make sure you get home at the right time?"
- "What's a good way to help you do your chores?"

Second, when you're empathizing with your child, make sure you really validate your child's feelings. Typical validating comments are:

- "I can see this is very tough for you."

- "I know that must have made you feel very badly."

- "I'm sure that made you feel very sad when Suzy didn't let you play the game."

- "It must have been very disappointing when you didn't get the part in the play."

Third, keep in mind that communication is more than simply words. If you are negotiating about an issue, set realistic goals, then help your child meet them. For younger children doing simple tasks, a timer may be useful. For older children, a checklist or chart may be preferable. Consistent, calm actions will reinforce the verbal statements you've made.

COMMUNICATION BETWEEN KIDS

Like parent-child communication, kid-to-kid communication is complex and often problematic. Some of the complexities are an inevitable result of children learning to get along and sort out issues as they grow and change. Other problems crop up as side effects of American culture, which often emphasizes confrontation over compromise and individualism over collaboration. Contemporary kids often learn to force their preferences on others rather than work together. An abrasive, me-first communication style is a nearly inevitable result of this situation. Here are some suggestions to help foster more creative communication among your kids.

- When kids communicate with other kids, teach them that it's not a win/lose situation.

- In family communication, encourage everyone to listen to everyone else's point of view. Don't prejudge other people.

- Try to be open-minded and flexible.

- Come up with an option that might satisfy as many people as possible.

- Try to foster the idea that situations aren't always right/wrong, good/bad—events and people are complicated. There are many gray areas in people's personalities and circumstances.

In short, help your child see all sides of the situation—or at least as many as possible. This task is easier said than done, and it will be influenced by your own attitudes toward communication. Whether you are an inflexible parent or a flexible parent will make the most difference in how your kids communicate. At any stage of childhood, you are the most important role model for good, open communication. If you're a flexible parent, you'll be open to negotiating with your children; you will include them in the process of compromise, talk with them, allow them to be heard, validate their feelings, empathize with them, and help them to come up with possible options and solutions. Taking this approach—being open to your children's feelings—will go far in helping them learn respect and patience in communicating with others.

SIX

COMMUNICATION BETWEEN SPOUSES

D EVELOPING A HEALTHY, intimate relationship between partners isn't easy; disagreements are part of every close relationship. Sometimes these disagreements are simply part of the normal give-and-take of marriage and parenthood, while at other times they can be masks for other problems. The core question isn't always what it seems. The words you hear may be, "Isn't this your third golf game this month?" when the real question is, "Aren't I important to you anymore?" With a greater than 50 percent divorce rate for first marriages and approximately a 58 percent divorce rate the second time around, it's crucial that spouses learn to communicate effectively.

THE CENTRAL ISSUES OF MARITAL COMMUNICATION

In my work as a therapist and counselor, I sense that most marital problems stem directly or indirectly from difficulties in communication. Why do some marriages succeed while others fail? Since all couples have disagreements, the difference often lies in the partners' ability (or inability) to communicate effectively. This issue is admittedly a big and complex task. Some loving couples struggle to cope with it and, despite their best intentions, fail. Some less-close partners successfully overcome their obstacles by communicating well. The truth is, almost all marriages can benefit from a closer look at marital communication.

Underlying many marital anxieties and tensions is one or both spouses' belief that they aren't getting enough time or attention from each other. They feel as if they're no longer a priority. Sometimes communication breaks down because there's an abundance of stress and a shortage of time, particularly given the demands of raising children. Hectic schedules often leave couples attempting to communicate late at night, early in the morning, or at other times when most people feel depleted. Try to pick a more promising time to sort through issues and problems. It's important for couples to have good private time together—to go out for an evening, to talk without being interrupted, to be husband and wife without the extra stresses and burdens of the household and the kids.

Here are some primary rules for good marital communication:

IDENTIFY YOUR ANGER AND FRUSTRATIONS

You may have good reason to feel frustrated with your spouse, but it's important for you to understand what the specific issues are.

LEARN TO FIGHT FAIRLY

Wild accusations, sneak attacks, public humiliation, sarcasm, and other indirect "tactics" almost always backfire and complicate the situation. Pick a time for discussions when both of you are calm, undistracted by other matters, and relatively well rested. State your concerns directly, without exaggeration or efforts to score points. Allow your partner to respond in full.

CHOOSE YOUR BATTLES CAREFULLY

Every marriage has friction points. If you insist on tackling every unresolved issue, however, you may lose the opportunity to resolve those that matter most. Don't insist on winning every fight.

TACKLE PROBLEMS PROMPTLY

Don't let resentments and animosities build up until they explode, or until your partner goes outside the relationship to find support and understanding.

MODEL HEALTHY RELATIONSHIPS

Demonstrate mutual respect. Serious efforts at communication will pay off in ways that far transcend your marriage; your kids, too, will benefit from your efforts at solving problems and working together.

DIFFERENTIATE SORE POINTS FROM CORE PROBLEMS

Couples often state that the marital "sore points" they fight about are money, sex, chores, vacations, kids, friends, and in-laws. Those are certainly the most common surface issues. But are those really the core problems? Often, the underlying causes are really issues of control, power struggles, and changing roles and expectations. Here again, the flash point can occur when one spouse feels taken for granted. In any intimate relationship, conflict is inevitable, and there's always ambivalence built into intimacy. Getting to the root of the problem, though, means facing the root causes of these arguments or clashing communication styles. That task isn't easy.

What are the underlying problems here? Sometimes they are unresolved wounds from childhood. If your marital clashes are intense—or if you're arguing constantly—the conflict may be a result of tension surfacing from an earlier phase of your life. A classic example of this situation is Marie. After long-standing conflicts with her domineering father, she got married to escape the stress of family life—only to end up resenting her husband, Gerry, whom Marie considers similarly oppressive. Is Gerry the tyrant that Marie sometimes regards him? Maybe, maybe not. But until Marie faces her past conflicts, she'll have difficulty perceiving how many of her current marital difficulties are real and how many are projected from her father-daughter relationship. The truth is, we often shift expectations from one relationship to another. We may place unmet needs from childhood onto our spouse; we may want our spouse to remedy all of our frustrations; we may expect our spouse to anticipate what we want or need. This shift may occur anyway, but the tasks of parenthood, given the strains and stakes involved, may intensify the process for many couples.

Many marital conflicts focus on kids. This is almost inevitable. Spouses often have different parenting styles. The differences may be cultural, individual, or gender-oriented. In any case, you may experience conflicts over how to raise your children. As a result, kids may learn to play one partner against the other. The result may be further conflict. How should you respond? It's very important, if your child comes to you with a request or demand, to clarify the situation before reacting. Ask, "Have you talked to your mother (or father) about this yet?" If the child says yes, ask what the answer was or say, "Wait a minute, we have to discuss this further." That way you're empowering both of you. You're not diminishing your spouse, and the two of you can come up with a unified, comfortable response. Sometimes you have to go along with your spouse—at least for that particular incident—so that you don't diminish your spouse's authority in your child's mind. Later, at a quieter moment, you can reevaluate that decision and come up with a different solution for next time.

DO'S AND DON'TS OF COMMUNICATION
WITH YOUR SPOUSE

Marital communication isn't easily reduced to a handy list of tips. There are some obvious issues, though, that deserve specific attention.

- Do level with your spouse in a calm, cool, collected manner.

- Don't try to communicate when you're tired, anxious, or stressed by outside demands.

- Do find a quiet, peaceful time and place to talk.

- Don't use unfair fighting tactics such as accusing, blaming, name-calling, or yelling.

- Do stick to the core problem rather than expanding it to other issues.

- Don't bring up old incidents that are irrelevant to what's at hand.

- Do confront the problem in an assertive, honest way.

- Don't avoid conflict when something is bothering you; likewise, don't sulk quietly or express your frustrations in passive-aggressive ways.

- Do focus on the issues, not on who's at fault.

- Don't try to accept all the blame; alternatively, don't blame your spouse.

- Do listen to your spouse's response without interrupting, judging, or thwarting his or her own feelings and experiences.

- Don't try to repress your feelings of anger and resentment.

- Do empathize with your partner's feelings whenever possible.

- Do focus your communication on the process, not on winning the argument. Lead your discussion to a win-win outcome in which you both feel heard and validated, and in which you find options for resolving your difficulties.

- Do look at both sides of the issues you're facing.

SEVEN

COMPUTERS AND KIDS

Marc, age sixteen, is obsessed with computers. He takes computer pro-gramming classes at school and plans to major in computer science when he starts college in two years. His parents admire his technical abilities and feel pleased that he has found a pursuit he loves. They are concerned, however, that Marc's passion has grown too consuming. He has no interest in friends, sports, music, or anything else. He spends all his free time at the computer, often far into the night.

Until she entered middle school, Sandra felt comfortable with computers, enjoyed exploring her family's PC, and played computer games with friends. In sixth grade, however, her attitude changed. Sandra complained that boys commandeered the best computers and wouldn't let girls join their projects. Some boys also teased her, calling her a geek or, even worse, a "geekette." When her parents offered to speak with the teacher, Sandra asked them to hold off; she said she "doesn't want to get labeled a nerd." Sandra's parents worry that their daughter may be losing a chance to gain valuable skills.

Lewis's mother, Jane, felt that her son was making good use of computers. The twelve-year-old used his PC to write school assignments; he sent e-mail to various friends; he enjoyed surfing the Net. One afternoon, though, Jane walked into Lewis's room and caught him downloading photos from a pornographic Web site. Furious, she banned him from using his computer for a month.

BRAVE NEW DIGITAL WORLD

WELCOME TO THE digital world, where computers and parenthood collide. It's an exciting situation, one with great potential for helping children explore the world; at the same time, kids' use of computers includes some risks as well as benefits and thus requires careful forethought. If you haven't yet had to sort through the many issues involving computers and children, just wait. You will.

Computers are drastically changing how people communicate, work, play, and perceive the world. Few people doubt that the digital revolution will alter most or all aspects of human experience to some degree. This holds true for children's experience as well as adults'. The speed and the degree of change resulting from the spread of computer technology has given rise not only to jubilation, however, but also to significant concerns. These concerns are probably most intense when they focus on children's use of computers.

The most widely publicized issue prompting parental concerns about computers is undoubtedly the Internet. In recent years, newspapers and magazines have published dozens of stories about Internet chat rooms or Web sites that feature pornography, salacious discussions, or contact with people who may have harmful intentions toward children. The biggest outcry has been aimed at World Wide Web sites that distribute pornographic photos. Other worries focus on chat rooms in which children may inadvertently interact with adult pedophiles posing as children. At least one well-publicized murder in New Jersey resulted from a convicted sex offender's successful effort to locate potential victims through the Internet. Violent and hate-oriented Web sites cause growing concern, too, especially in the aftermath of the Columbine High School massacre in Colorado. Parents understandably wonder if computer use will leave their children vulnerable to predators and sleazemongers.

These concerns are valid. Cyberspace includes some sordid neighborhoods. Among the inhabitants of this world are a troubling variety of weirdos, opportunists, and criminals. It's unquestionably important to monitor your children's access to certain Internet sites and, when necessary, to restrict their access. Ideally, use your concerns about the "sleaze factor" as an opportunity for discussions with your child about the negative influences in cyberspace. The long-term goal is to teach your child to self-monitor the situation and develop the ability to understand the pros and cons of what he or she encounters.

At the same time, it's important to note that sleazy Web sites aren't the only issue—or even the biggest issue—facing parents when they evaluate how computers affect their children. Other aspects of the digital revolution are problematic, too, though usually not as garish or flagrantly repulsive. However, they are issues worth pondering precisely because the risks and benefits involved are often ambiguous.

DIGITAL SNAKE OIL

Although it's true that computers are often dramatic in their influence on modern culture, it's also true that some of that influence is less substantial, less remarkable, and less beneficial than proponents claim. Hardware and software companies tout their wares as revolutionary, but many products are decidedly a mixed bag. Products for children are no exception.

Here's an example. Kids' art programs are full of gimmicks, and the accompanying pamphlets often suggest that children using the software will create splendid works of art. At best, this suggestion is an overstatement. Kids enjoy playing with digital art programs, and they can learn from them about color, design, proportion, and texture. That's fine as far as it goes. But is using art programs better than using traditional artistic media—paint, pencils, crayons, paper, glue? I doubt it. Most of the computer-generated art projects I've seen children produce have an artificial, unimaginative look about them; they're far less interesting and attractive than even the most ordinary kids' art made from standard materials. There's nothing wrong with children using art programs now and then, but it's unfortunate when kids don't experience the delight of using their hands to make projects out of many different materials. It's certainly a wild exaggeration to say that by using computers, children learn more about art—or anything else—than they do from traditional disciplines.

THE ISSUES OF PROPORTION AND DISPLACEMENT

Even if you pick child-friendly computer activities for your kids, there are two additional questions to consider. First, when are such activities appropriate? Second, how much is enough? Some parents believe that harmless computer games or benign Web sites are invariably a positive experience for children. This is the Digital Age. Kids need to acquire computer skills for the twenty-first century. Surely any use they make of this technology is good, right? Unfortunately, the situation isn't so simple. Some of the potentially negative aspects of computer use for children are:

- The sedentary nature of computer activities
- A lack of varied experiences
- Eyestrain
- The cultivation of simplistic attitudes
- The development of impatience
- Social isolation and loneliness
- Increased risks of depression

It's not inevitable that kids will suffer these consequences. If children's contact with computers is part of a wide-ranging exploration of the world, kids will almost certainly benefit from the experience. The key issues, in my mind, are timing and proportion. I see no reason for kids to have much contact with computers before age three. I'm troubled to read that hardware manufacturers are now promoting computers they regard as user-friendly for toddlers and even babies. Children will have plenty of chance to acquire computer skills; they don't need to start when they're barely walking. They have more important developmental tasks to tackle. To make matters worse, many parents allow or even encourage kids to use computers more often, and at greater length, than seems appropriate.

My biggest concern is that even benign computer activities can harm children by displacing other important forms of play. Many kids are already too sedentary; they spend much of their free time watching TV or videos. Computers provide yet another pastime that displaces active play. You may argue that computers are far more creative than television—they can offer kids an opportunity to learn new skills, including art, science, languages, geography, and so forth. To some degree this argument is valid. Computers have much to offer. However, this ideal isn't often fulfilled in reality. Most kids use computers to play games or surf the Net. Although potentially creative, these activities often fall short of the creativity they're touted for. They are, moreover, all sedentary. The truth is, computers often displace other activities that children need and benefit from.

The resulting risks include:

- Limiting kids' opportunities for other kinds of play, including outdoor play

- Diminishing opportunities to practice various motor skills, including large motor skills (running, kicking, climbing, playing sports) and fine motor skills (drawing, writing, painting, etc.)

- Reducing children's chances to practice using many materials and artistic media, including paint, pencils, crayons, paper, clay, etc.

- Limiting certain kinds of human interactions, including kid-to-kid problem solving, compromise, story telling, etc.

- Stunting the development of patience and ability to tolerate frustration, since computer programs always allow the participant to bail out at any time

- Limiting the growth of the imagination (including the ability to create fantasy, and to perceive the differences between fantasy and reality), since computer games, etc., usually present a ready-made world rather than allowing kids to create their own

- Limiting verbal communication and expression of thoughts, feelings, and ideas

CYBERSLEAZE

There's no question that loathsome materials are rife on the Internet. Even subscribers to family-friendly Internet service providers (ISPs) may end up bombarded by digital ads from Web sites with names like hotbabes.com, girlpix.com, and worse. It's easy for children to tap into sites that tout every imaginable sexual obsession. Innocent chat rooms may lead to contact with people who are the cyber equivalent of wolves in sheep's clothing. But how bad, really, is the problem? To what degree are your children at risk if they're free to roam the Internet?

The general consensus among level-headed observers of the digital scene is that the risks to children have been overstated. The Internet contains many objectionable places and people, but so does the physical world. Seeking what's worthwhile and avoiding what's vile requires the same sort of vigilance as under any other circumstances. Most of the mishaps involving children's use of cyberspace have occurred when parents allow kids to roam the Internet entirely unsupervised. Forethought and good parent-child communication can prevent most problems.

Here as in so many other aspects of raising children, the key is calm parental involvement. This phrase means different things at different developmental stages. Generally speaking, you should stay involved with what your kids are doing. Don't overreact, but don't assume that a single quick technological fix will address all issues and ease all concerns.

STAYING CONNECTED (IN MORE WAYS THAN ONE)

Technological solutions are only one response to the problem of cybersleaze, and in many ways technology should be a fallback rather than the primary line of defense. Just as you teach your children to be responsible, thoughtful, and cautious when out in the world, you can teach them the same responses when exploring cyberspace. The most important element in computer safety for children is parental involvement and age-appropriate supervision.

- Teach your child responsible use of computer hardware and software
- Establish reasonable, age-appropriate rules for your child's use of the Internet
- Supervise access to the Internet
- If necessary, use filtering and blocking software
- Guide them into being savvy computer consumers

As in every other aspect of your child's development, you should stay aware of his interests, activities, and abilities. You wouldn't simply drop a six-year-old off at a playground and leave for three hours; neither should you leave your ten-year-old alone at a shopping mall. A child's use of the Internet should begin with shared activities, including explanations of procedures, rules, and etiquette. If you aren't familiar with Net protocol, buy any of the many guidebooks to help you learn. If you're not aware of what the Net has to offer, explore the possibilities together. Modeling proper behavior will set the tone for your child's later attitudes toward use of this technology. Older children won't require (or tolerate!) constant parental observation, but that shouldn't rule out supervision.

In addition, you should establish clear expectations for computer use. Children with Internet access at school have probably already signed an "acceptable use policy," or AUP. Such policies state rules for Internet use and outline privileges and responsibilities. An equivalent policy for computer use at home may seem rigid, but it's important and worthwhile precisely because it's unambiguous. An AUP is especially important for teenagers, who will benefit from the freedom it allows provided that they honor the restrictions it demands. The payoff for responsible Internet use—and the consequences for violations—are literally set down in black and white. For guidance and suggestions about AUPs, see *The Family Internet Companion* listed in the Resource Guide at the back of this book.

FILTERS AND GADGETS

However, since it's ultimately difficult to supervise children's Internet activities, you may need to supplement personal interaction with products called *filters* or blocking software. These are programs that deny access to Internet sites that you consider inappropriate. Using a filter, you can indicate which sites are unacceptable; in addition, some blocking programs include a prepackaged listing of objectionable sites. Some software even includes an on-line service which (for a fee) will update the list as circumstances change. In addition, many Internet service providers (ISPs) provide filtering for subscribers, which allows you to block your children's access to specific sites or categories of sites. Contact your ISP for details. The Resource Guide includes a listing of companies that provide blocking software, as well as listings of Web sites with information about filtering.

RECOMMENDATIONS FOR ON-LINE SAFETY

- Make sure your kids understand that the computer is for the whole family, not just individual use.

- Place the computer in an easily accessible, visible area—the living room or family room—rather than in your child's bedroom.

- Learn about your ISP, including its policies on security, filtering options, etc.

- Caution your children about on-line "pretenders"—people who claim to be someone other than themselves (e.g., a man pretending to be a child).

- Insist that your children never respond to suggestive, obscene, or belligerent messages, and ask them to alert you to any that they receive.

- Insist that your children never provide personal information—names, addresses, phone numbers, etc.—to anyone they encounter on-line.

- Do not allow downloading of photos from unfamiliar sources.

- Do not allow your children to upload their own photos to unfamiliar persons.

- Prohibit your children from meeting with anyone they have met through the Internet unless you approve of and supervise the encounter.

- Monitor overall on-line activities.

- Take action on anything you consider suspicious or disturbing.

- Don't use the computer as a baby-sitter or child care surrogate.

THE DIGITAL GENERATION GAP

One of the trickiest issues in dealing with kids and computers is the digital generation gap. To put it bluntly: children often know far more about computers than their parents do. They have grown up with computers as a given; they have no emotional prejudices against them; they often start using them from an early age; they usually pick up and retain technical information more easily than most grown-ups do. Even parents who consider themselves computer-literate may feel shocked by how much their children know about this technology. Less computer-savvy parents may feel totally in the dark. As a result, it's often difficult for parents to monitor and control their children's use of this technology.

LEARN AS MUCH AS POSSIBLE

Even if you feel threatened by your children's digital expertise, it's important to know what you can about their activities. Read one of the more accessible computer guides. Take a course in home computer use. Review the user guides that come with your kids' games and programs. Ask your children to explain what they're doing.

STAY INTERESTED

Just as you may not understand what your kids like about the music they listen to, you may not understand their tastes in computer activities, either. Even so, it's important for you to remain connected to their world. Don't let your kids drift off into isolation. Ask questions about what they like and why. Transform solitary pastimes into family activities.

INTERVENE WHEN NECESSARY

If you discover that your child is engaged in activities you find troubling, intervene. Your questions may prompt a crisis; however, it's important not to sidestep the issues. The issue may be one of proportion—that is, your child may simply be spending too much time involved with the computer and not enough time with other people and activities. On the other hand, there may be an intrinsic problem (such as access to an offensive Web site or use of a violent computer game) that requires more direct action. Either way, do not renege on your parental responsibilities just because you find the technology daunting. Use the crisis as an opportunity for discussion and sorting through decisions.

GENDER DIFFERENCES

A number of studies indicate that until the age of about nine or ten, boys and girls have equal interest in computer activities. After that age, however, a shift occurs: boys grow more interested in computers while girls' participation declines. It's still uncertain what these patterns mean. One explanation is that in school computer centers as elsewhere, boys often dominate, literally or figuratively elbowing girls off the keyboard. Another explanation is that since software producers generally market more products that appeal to boys—often games with competitive or violent themes—girls simply lose interest. In any case, the pattern is disturbing. Girls as a group tend to remove themselves from settings, including computer classes at school, where they can acquire computer skills.

If you have a daughter, here are some important approaches you can take.

CONSIDER THE BIG PICTURE

What I've described here may not be simply a response to computers as a technology or to computer culture as an aspect of American society. Your daughter's reaction may, in fact, be part of a larger issue. By this I mean the tendency of some girls to withdraw from realms generally considered to be "boys' turf." The big picture may be something more general than computers alone.

This is a complex issue—one best discussed in more detail. (Please see chapter 19, "Gender Bias," and chapter 20, "Girls.")

FIND ALTERNATIVE ACTIVITIES

If your daughter finds computer activities boring or unappealing, it's possible that she simply hasn't found the right activities. Many computer games are, in fact, designed specifically for boys. Girls often find them dull, pointless, or offensive. Look elsewhere. A growing number of software companies now market games that appeal more to girls or to both sexes. In addition, many Internet sites focus on girls' interests. As the spread of digital technology continues, the available offerings may become more and more suited to girls.

CONSIDER THE POLITICAL CONTEXT

Some girls feel uncomfortable with computers because the people in charge of the equipment do nothing to make them comfortable—or even work outright to discourage girls' participation. "Those in charge" may include teachers, brothers, or parents. In sizing up your daughter's discomfort with or disinterest in computer technology, consider the political context. Do teachers at school give girls equal access time to equipment? Do brothers or other family members monopolize the equipment? Are there other aspects of the situation that could be discouraging your daughter from having her fair share of computer use? If others are standing in the way of your daughter's computer use, you may have to intervene and rectify the situation.

CONFLICTS

IN FAMILY LIFE, conflict is inevitable. You will annoy or challenge your child at times; he will annoy or challenge you in turn. There will be disagreements and misunderstandings. The situation isn't altogether pleasant, but anger, frustration, and irritability can be normal, healthy emotions within the context of family life. The important response is to be open about what you're feeling, open to others' feelings, and willing to deal with the give-and-take of solving problems together. Conflicts that result from these feelings are generally manageable and potentially creative. After all, family life is the first (and often ideal) place in which children learn the intricacies of getting along with other people.

At the same time, it's true that conflict requires time, attention, and sensitivity to manage creatively. Dealing with conflict thoughtfully makes the difference between pleasant, relatively low-stress family life and unpleasant, stressful family life.

VALIDATE YOUR CHILD'S FEELINGS

When your child has acquired enough language skills to speak about his feelings, one of your tasks is to mirror his emotions verbally. By "mirror" I mean that you should reflect back to him what he's saying, but in a way that clarifies the situation. He may not even *understand* what he feels; mirroring his emotions will help him learn to perceive his own state of mind.

- "It seems like you're very angry with me today."

- "You must feel annoyed to throw the toy on the floor like that."

- "It must be hard to have a new baby in the house."
- "You seem frustrated with what your teacher said."

When you validate your child's feelings, you allow him to express all sides of himself, including expressions of normal aggression and anger. You are also respecting your child's feelings. This accepting, nonjudgmental attitude helps him identify his feelings and have more control over them in the future.

The process of mirroring emotions shouldn't be limited to "negative" feelings; you should also comment on your child's pride in a job well done, kindness or generosity toward others, delight in pleasant experiences, and so forth. This process is especially constructive among younger children, who respond warmly to parents' acknowledgment of good behavior. Helping your child become aware of his positive states of mind (and feel good about them) will limit his need to act negatively to get your attention.

BE SUPPORTIVE AND NONJUDGMENTAL ABOUT FEELINGS

Similarly, you should help your child understand that feelings aren't right or wrong; they just *are*. Some emotions may feel unpleasant, but they won't hurt your child or anyone else. Although feelings are complex and often intense, they are usually normal. Let him know, too, that he can feel simultaneously happy and sad; he can even feel love, dislike, and anger all at once. These are normal emotions that people have in a close relationship. Reassure your child that his feelings aren't good or bad, since this reassurance can help him accept himself, which in turn can ease feelings of wariness or hostility toward others. This sort of emotional awareness also helps children understand what others are feeling and doing. If another kid acts in negative ways, your child is less likely to take the offense so personally. By being empathic—and by modeling empathic behavior—you are helping your child to develop a capacity for empathy as well.

LOOK FOR ROOT CAUSES

There's usually a root cause beneath every misbehavior or misconduct. Your child may feel jealous of a new baby in the house; he may resent you for working long hours; he may feel stressed by an impending move in the family. It's crucial that you consider not just the immediate situation—a fussy, angry, or uncooperative child—but also whatever is going on within the child or his environment. Go beyond the behavior to consider what may be causing these problems. To the degree that you can figure out the larger picture, you'll make better sense of why your child is acting out or feeling as he does.

ALLOW CHOICE—AND THE ILLUSION OF CHOICE

Many conflicts occur when children can't decide how to respond to a situation. They feel uncertain about what's going to happen, or they want both of two contradictory options, such as going to the movies *and* staying home to play. To some degree, the response to these standards depends on your child's age.

If your child is under six or seven, you should respond by offering only a few different choices. "I'll fix you either a sandwich or some pizza." "You can either play with Matthew or come with me to the park." "Here are three outfits you can wear, so pick which one you prefer." Limited choices provide both a measure of independence and an absence of overwhelming possibilities.

Older children need more flexibility. Even middle school kids will want a variety of options about what they'll do or not do; adolescents should have opportunities for even greater input. This isn't to say that you'll grant free rein, since you, the parent, still have a right to call the shots. But it's appropriate to allow children increased responsibility as they grow and develop. Be prepared to compromise and negotiate. At the same time, it's fine to stress that family life requires compromise all the way around; your child, too, must do his part to accommodate others.

CHOOSE YOUR BATTLES

If you make every disagreement or misbehavior into a battle, both you and your child will end up frustrated and exhausted. You shouldn't react to every provocation, taunt, hassle, or incident that family life presents; there just isn't enough time in the day to struggle with your child every time he disagrees with you. More to the point, it's not healthy—either for your child or for your family—if every issue becomes contentious. But when your child confronts you with frustrating challenges, how do you respond?

EMPHASIZE COOPERATION AND NEGOTIATION

Don't set up a divisive mood in the family or a stress on winning arguments, disagreements, etc.; focus instead on how family members should work together.

LET YOUR CHILD "WIN" SOME OF THE TIME

It's frustrating and anxiety-producing when children feel that adults have all the power (even when it's true!).

MINIMIZE EXTERNAL SOURCES OF CONFLICT

For toddlers and preschoolers, especially, the physical environment can be a source of temptations that lead to conflict; if you don't want your child to touch certain prized belongings, for instance, keep them out of reach. Thorough childproofing can make your life much less stressful.

REASSURE YOUR CHILD ABOUT YOUR PRESENCE

Some conflicts occur because children are simply attempting to get your attention. Rather than let their anxieties lead to attention-getting misbehavior, give them as much comforting, reassuring attention as possible, and do so *before* they feel a need to behave in negative ways to gain your attention.

BE AWARE OF DEVELOPMENTAL LEAPS

Certain developmental stages can lead to conflicts over one issue or another, since your child may be acquiring a need for greater independence, autonomy, or responsibility. The most obvious leaps occur during toddlerhood and adolescence, but many others take place. If you insist on adhering to long-standing assumptions about what's appropriate or inappropriate, you may end up in needless conflict.

EXPRESS EMPATHY

Empathy is one of the keys to resolving conflicts. Try to remember how you felt at your child's age. Read books on what behaviors are developmentally appropriate. Give more praise than criticism. Set age-appropriate limits. Use your sense of humor to defuse tensions and open your child's mind to alternatives. Never attack your child's character; instead, describe and focus on his behavior.

MODEL APPROPRIATE BEHAVIOR

Your child will heavily model his behavior after your own. If you're tense, he will be tense; if you are accusatory, he will be, too; the same holds true if you deal with conflict by shouting, throwing tantrums, or giving others the "silent treatment." He will, in short, tend to act as you do. For this reason, you have to emphasize that you have specific expectations which not only your child, but you yourself, must follow. Demanding that he work through conflicts rationally and peacefully simply won't pay off if your own behavior is irrational or belligerent.

WHEN NECESSARY, EXERT YOUR AUTHORITY

That being said, you may reach a point when your child's behavior is relentless, chaotic, disruptive, or dangerous to himself or others, and when nothing you say or do seems to ease the situation. If so, you may have no alternative but to exert your authority. Your child may not like it; you may feel terrible about it; but it has to be done. You are the parent—and you have both the legal right and the moral responsibility to do what's in your child's best interests.

This situation will vary, of course, depending on your child's stage of development. It's awkward but relatively simple with a toddler or preschooler to take a stand, be decisive, and do what needs to be done. It's much more difficult with an older child. Still, this is part of your role as a parent. Sometimes the shortest and simplest statements are more effective than a drawn-out explanation. Keep things brief and direct. As corny as the words may sound, there will be times during the parenting years when you have to say, "This is how it's going to be" or "This is what I've decided to keep you safe." I recommend that you use these categorical statements only as a last resort; if you rely on them too frequently, you'll damage your parental authority. But you shouldn't hesitate to draw the line when it's necessary.

TRACK THE SOURCES OF YOUR OWN RESPONSE

Sometimes a conflict isn't what it seems. If your reaction to your child's behavior is particularly strong, or if you can't seem to shake a negative response to what's happening, consider what other issues might be entering the picture. It is possible that aspects of your own past—memories of your own upbringing, for instance, or conflicts with your parents—are influencing what you're saying and doing in the present. This isn't farfetched. All of us have learned much of what we know about parent-child interactions from our own families; the past retains a powerful grip even decades later.

Given the complexity of these issues, you probably can't resolve the situation in the middle of a conflict with your child; rather, it's best to step back, cope as well as possible, and face the wider issues later. For most people, this involves working with a counselor or therapist. See chapter 33, "The Past," for an overview of what's involved.

READ YOUR CHILD FOR SIGNS OF STRESS

Like adults, children often show signs that indicate stress reactions. Such reactions aren't necessarily a major problem in themselves; however, they can indicate that your child is under pressure and needs more empathy, affection, guidance, or support than usual. Characteristic signs include biting or chewing of nails, picking at skin, clearing the throat, sucking fingers, verbal tics or stuttering, facial twitching, erratic appetite (over- or undereating) or sleep disturbances. Trying to find the root cause of these behaviors is crucial; scolding or shaming your child won't help and may well aggravate the situation. What if you notice your child exhibiting one or more of these signs? First, ask your child how he or she is doing. Indicate that you've noticed some changes in behavior, and that you're concerned. Try to sort out the issues together. If you can't reach an understanding together, check with your child's teacher, the school guidance counselor, or your pediatrician for further input.

LET YOUR CHILD VENT HIS FRUSTRATION

All children feel aggressive impulses, frustration, anger, and other "negative" emotions. Forcing your child to ignore, deny, or repress these feelings will backfire and cause further difficulties; however, he also needs to learn appropriate ways to express what he's feeling without disturbing other people. Acquiring the verbal skills to put frustrations into perspective is one such way. In addition, it's important for your child to have channels to vent frustration and release tension.

One channel is physical activity: running, jumping, playing at a playground, and taking part in age-appropriate sports. Other channels involve punching pillows, hitting a punching bag, or releasing energy in other harmless ways. Less physically active children can let off steam by drawing pictures, singing, playing with clay, or using puppets or dramatic play to act out aggression and frustration. Respond to these outpourings of emotion without taking them personally. These are all useful ways for children to learn self-control without denying the reality of their emotional experiences.

HAVE REALISTIC EXPECTATIONS

Make sure that the rules in your household are realistic, since setting expectations too high or too low will frustrate your child and lead to conflict. Expecting a three-year-old to sit alone for an hour while assembling a puzzle is a recipe for disaster; in contrast, sitting with your child and helping him assemble the puzzle is far more appropriate. Similarly, expecting a teenager to focus on family get-togethers to the exclusion of peer-group activities will almost inevitably lead to conflict. Half the task of avoiding and resolving conflicts with children has to do with knowing what's truly realistic at a given developmental stage. For more information about child development, see chapter 2, "Behavior and Child Development."

DEAL WITH LOADED ISSUES

Some of the most intense family conflicts stem from loaded issues that warrant special attention. (These issues vary depending on your child's age.)

LYING AND STEALING

Some parents have a particularly strong response when children lie or steal. This is understandable; dishonesty is a social and ethical issue as well as a family issue. In some situations, lying and stealing (especially when recurrent or compulsive) can suggest the presence of psychological problems. Still, it's important not to overreact. Try to view the situation developmentally.

Young Children

Most toddlers don't have a clear sense of personal property; in many ways they're too egocentric to understand others' claims to their own possessions. (Toddlers perceive everything as theirs.) For this reason, it's a normal part of early childhood to take someone else's belongings now and then. If this situation is frequent, however, there may be an underlying feeling that warrants attention—feelings of isolation, bereavement, jealousy, or insecurity. Avoid stigmatizing your child for infractions of this sort; strive to find the underlying cause and address it.

Lying presents similar issues. Children often tell tall tales that are part of their magical thinking and creative fantasy life. If you can accept all your child's feelings and behaviors without being too reactive, you will ease your child's need to protect himself by lying. If you punish your child when he admits to lying, you'll set up a cycle of obsessive self-protection. Many children lie out of a simple desire for wish fulfillment or to protect themselves from the consequences of their behavior. One child I know boasted he'd gotten a dragon for Christmas. From an adult point of view, this statement was a lie. From a child's standpoint, though, his claim was more complex than that: He was wishing for something magical. The boy's fantasy of owning a powerful beast served to reassure the child because he felt weak and helpless; the story gave him a sense of power that he lacked otherwise. Reacting to the tall tale, his parents, rather than scolding him, reassured him, which left the boy in peace to explore his fantasy and let it fade away when he felt more secure. In addition, having imaginary friends is creative, and it often empowers a child and proves a sense of companionship when he feels lonely. At times it's a reaction that can be therapeutic and adaptive to external stress or to internal changes or conflicts.

Older Children

As kids reach the middle school years, the issues of lying and stealing become more complex. Children should have a clear sense of personal property by age six or seven; infractions against the rule not to steal will meet increasingly severe consequences at school. The same holds true for honesty. In general, these rules are appropriate, and it's important to teach children a sense of personal responsibility and integrity. Here again your own behavior will set the standard.

Whatever else you do, don't punish your child for telling the truth. If he makes a mistake or commits an error of judgment but later admits what really happened, respond favorably to his willingness to rectify the situation and always praise his honesty. Emphasize that dishonesty is as unacceptable to you—if not more unacceptable—as the actual misbehavior. If you can react calmly to what has happened, you give the message that you can accept him flaws and all, and you accept his long-term efforts to learn and grow. Anger and disciplinary action for misbehavior that your child has confessed to will only backfire. The exception: when misbehavior is repetitive or occurring on a larger scale. At the same time, make sure that your child understands the need to deal honestly with the consequences of his actions; if he has damaged a store-owner's merchandise, for instance, he should accept the responsibility of explaining to the shopkeeper and making restitution. Don't isolate him in this task; stand by him. But expect him to face what has happened.

DEPENDENCE AND INDEPENDENCE

Embedded within many conflicts are issues of dependence and independence. On the one hand, your child may resent you for allowing him too little freedom, which restricts his ability to grow up; on the other hand, he may feel pressured to grow up too quickly. For a child to separate and individuate successfully, he needs a strong sense of security—security in terms of both trusting himself and trusting the people around him. He also needs enough freedom to explore his abilities and develop new skills. An imbalance between security and freedom may lead to tensions between the parents and the child. To the degree that you can monitor these issues and the balance between them, you'll be more responsive to what your child needs. For further discussion of these issues, see chapter 25, "Letting Go and Holding On."

SELF-RESPECT

If your child feels respected, and if he sees a high degree of self-respect and self-esteem in his parents, then he will respect himself, too, and have higher standards for his own behavior. He will have a strong sense of himself and a clearer sense of security. He'll be less inclined to whine, blame others for his difficulties, or act out. He'll be more capable of taking responsibility and standing up for himself. He will feel more complete as a human being, more accepting of himself.

By contrast, a child who doesn't feel respected will feel incomplete, restless, and insecure. He will feel less sure of what he needs and less confident of getting his needs met, which will incline him toward demanding, fussy behavior. He may be less capable of controlling his impulses and more likely to lash out at others.

Children are, of course, highly individual. Some are independent as a result of their temperament. Some seem tough; nothing much seems to bother them. However, I believe that in general, children feel highly affected by how others treat them—and especially by how their parents treat them. As a result, I strongly urge parents to do whatever they can to reinforce their children's self-respect. Children who feel secure and good about themselves will be disinclined to conflict with others. If your child feels confident of your love, there will be conflicts anyway, of course, since conflicts are inherent in family life. But the conflicts will be manageable and creative—part of the process of learning to get along with others and compromise as you try to fulfill each others' needs.

NINE

DISCIPLINE

IN THE PAST, many parents have tended to view discipline as a way of *making* children do what the parents decide must be done. Developmental psychologists now perceive the situation differently: discipline is (or ought to be) a way of helping children to develop social skills, a conscience, impulse control, values, self-esteem, and a capacity for moral judgment and responsibility. The goal of discipline is ultimately *self-discipline*. I don't use this word in a rigid sense—to suggest that the child forces himself to behave in a certain way—but rather to imply an element of choice: the child evaluates alternatives and chooses to behave in ways that serve good purpose both for himself and for others.

It's likely that your child will be cooperative most of the time. However, even happy, well-adjusted kids will sometimes act out, hunker down, or grow defiant. The causes of these difficult or frustrating behaviors are numerous and varied. Your child may feel challenged by some aspect of his life. He may be testing the limits you've set. He may be declaring his independence. He may be trying to get your attention. He may be feeling unsafe or anxious. He may be feeling stressed out or tired. But in any case, how should you cope with your child when he misbehaves?

WHAT'S THE REAL ISSUE?

Whatever the situation, start by trying to determine the root cause of what's happening. Did your child have a bad day at school? Did someone hurt his feelings? Is he feeling pressured by a teacher or another child? Is he feeling depressed because he didn't do well on a test? Is he overwhelmed by the demands he's facing? Is he feeling overscheduled? Is he coping with sibling rivalry? Is he declaring his independence during a phase of puberty or adolescence? Is he signaling that you aren't setting enough limits or giving him enough attention? Kids' fussy, disruptive, or angry behaviors often reveal a symptom of an experience that's still under the surface. Jealousy, rivalry, tension, and anxiety frequently signal a deeper, more complex issue embedded within the more obvious behaviors.

In addition, many kinds of "misbehavior" or "acting out" indicate a positive event in a child's development. Perhaps your child is experimenting with autonomy and independence. For instance, a two-year-old may throw a tantrum because he feels torn between a desire to express his burgeoning abilities and a desire for structure and limits. Similarly, a teenager may rebel as a way of exploring the new possibilities of identity. Behavior that seems disruptive or infuriating may, in fact, indicate normal developmental progress. At the same time, your child needs to learn civility, self-control, and respect for others; chaotic or aggressive acts aren't acceptable. Finding the happy medium requires identifying the root causes of your child's behavior, determining what will help your child deal with the tasks he faces, and helping him learn age-appropriate self-discipline.

GENERAL PRINCIPLES OF DISCIPLINE

Whatever your child's age or developmental stage, here are the most important principles of discipline:

- Teach your child discipline through modeling and love, not dominance and submission.

- Stay in the present.

- Have high but not punitive expectations.

- Don't be judgmental—comment on your child's behavior, not his being or essence.

- Make the rules clear, consistent, and reasonable.

- Don't nag, scream, moralize, interrogate, or resort to name-calling.

- Avoid ridicule, sarcasm, or other indirect, ineffective forms of communication.

- Don't humiliate—validate.

- Avoid anger—be curious, not furious.

- Teach internal self-control.

- Encourage children to express their feelings verbally rather than lashing out physically.

- Don't spank your child—physical punishment humiliates and degrades children, and it teaches them to deal with frustration by being aggressive.

- Give kids lots of positive reinforcement.

- Don't overschedule children; kids need plenty of down time.

- Give children plenty of one-on-one attention so they don't have to act out negatively for attention.

- Negotiate, and help your child compromise on age-appropriate issues.

- Don't respond to every negative behavior; instead of saying no all the time, find ways of reframing the child's behavior.

In addition, each stage of child development involves specific issues that influence how you approach the subject of discipline.

TODDLERS

Until the age of about eighteen months, discipline is generally a nonissue; babies are simply too young to grasp the notion of "good" or "bad" behavior. Your goal as a parent during this stage should be simply to make sure that your child feels fully loved, accepted, and cherished. Keeping your child safe (from household hazards, from traffic, and so forth) means direct intervention to keep him away from danger. At the age of a year and a half, however, the early phases of discipline become appropriate. Here are ways to help kids deal with their frustrations and impulses during the toddler years.

JOIN FORCES

Join with them and help them deal with situations they find frustrating. Typical flashpoints involve sharing toys, cleaning up after play, and transition from one activity to another. Toddlers are just beginning to experience socially acceptable behavior and means of resolving conflicts, so they need to be guided through these social experiences. If you can offer choices or distract your toddler into collaborating with you, you'll get much further much faster than if you try to prod or coerce him.

EMPOWER YOUR CHILD

Toddlers often feel frustrated by their lack of power. Convincing a two- or three-year-old that he's partially in control can go a long way toward easing his anxieties and avoiding conflict. One method is to have him tell his body what needs to be done: "Tell your feet to walk." "Tell your hands to be patient." This technique is simple, but it empowers your child to be the boss over his own body; this in turn helps him to develop internal controls and strength.

PROVIDE EXTERNAL GUIDANCE

Books such as *Alexander and the Terrible, Horrible, No Good, Very Bad Day* and *Where the Wild Things Are* appeal to children because they allow kids to vent their aggression through a story. The result is twofold: one, your child can ease his tensions harmlessly; two, he can grasp that he's not "bad" for having angry or aggressive impulses. Some books (the *Berenstain Bears* series comes to mind) even show problem-solving techniques that children can emulate.

BLOW OFF STEAM

Encourage (and *monitor*) physical activities that let young children release their anger. Pound clay. Knead bread dough. Hammer wooden pegs. Physical projects vent tension and energy by creative means, and some of them also help children learn a skill. Allow your child to draw an angry picture, punch a punching bag, tear up pieces of paper or to throw soft cloth balls at bowling pins.

HELP TODDLERS IDENTIFY THEIR FEELINGS

If your child can label his emotions, he gains an important measure of control. Help him put words to his experiences: "Boy, that must have made you feel disappointed (frustrated, sad, angry)." Give him a positive vehicle for discharging tension, frustration, and anxiety.

PRESCHOOLERS

If you're consistent and patient in communicating your expectations to your preschool-age child, you can build a foundation for good behavior and cooperation that will serve you not only at the time but also during the school-age, preteen, and teen years. I recommend that you:

- *Look for the root causes of your child's behavior.* Almost everything a child does—even seemingly "pointless" misbehavior—has an underlying cause of message. Try to hear what he's telling you. Is he hungry? Tired? Scared? Feeling ignored? Wanting more independence?

- *Be empathic.* Childhood is often stressful. You face your own difficulties and demands, so does your child. If possible, push beyond your own concerns and empathize with his own. What may seem trivial or even comical to you about his worries may be greatly frustrating or traumatic to him. Support him verbally: "You're really having a tough time today," or "You seem worried (or frustrated) that Jake won't play with you."

- *Clarify the situation.* Ask questions about his day, his interests, his concerns. Listen to hidden messages. Try to understand and ask for more details. "So you're saying the teacher was in a bad mood?" or "So Martin tried to hit you? Can you tell me more about that?"

- *Paraphrase statements of emotion back to your child.* He may not even be aware of what he's feeling. If he says, "You're a dope," avoid taking this "insult" personally; instead, help him understand his emotional state. "You must be angry because I wouldn't give you more ice cream." Help him learn to understand his own feelings, and teach him the words that help him express his feelings clearly and directly without having to act them out.

- *Solve problems together.* Rather than imposing a solution, try to find one together. Children generally want to please their parents; if you can work out a mutually acceptable way of dealing with behavioral expectations, your child is more likely to go along with the program.

- *Make sure that consequences fit the problem.* Your efforts at discipline will be self-defeating if they're either too severe or too lenient. Moreover, discipline must be age-appropriate. When you specify limits and rewards, make sure that they're clear and concise *before* the child acts out.

- *Give warning in advance.* Make sure that cause-effect relationships between infractions and punishment are clear: "If you can't get ready for bed, you'll have to miss your TV show because there won't be enough time." Don't spring new disciplinary measures on your child out of nowhere. Consequences should be specified in advance: "If you do that again, you can't go to the movies."

- *Use "I-statements" to communicate how you feel about your child's behavior.* For example, state "When you won't help me pick up the toys, I feel frustrated" rather than "You're such a messy kid."

- *Don't berate your child or rattle on at great length.* Most children detest being lectured, nagged, or harranged; if you barrage them with too many words, they'll just tune you out.

- *Be clear about timing.* Even if your rules and cause-effect relationships are well-defined, you may confuse your children if you waffle about your expectations and the timing of what happens when. Give your child advance notice if possible: "It'll be time for bed after the story." If he isn't responsive, follow through with the consequences.

- *Be consistent.* There are certainly situations that justify making exceptions; overall, however, consistency will benefit both you and your kids. They'll know that you mean what you say, and they will be more likely to respond accordingly.

- *If all else fails, be categorical.* You are the parent; ultimately, you're in charge. Some aspects of family life aren't negotiable. There may be times when your child isn't responsive to rational persuasion; if so, gently but firmly exert your authority and indicate what must be done.

TIME OUT

One of the most popular methods for disciplining children is "time out." When used thoughtfully and sparingly, this method can be effective and useful. Time out offers several clear benefits. It's a safe way of expressing disapproval when your child misbehaves. It provides an opportunity for the child to see the connection between his behavior and your disapproval. It allows you to role-model a good attitude: calm and control rather than anger and lack of control. It allows your child a chance to calm down and to avoid "revving up" or spinning out of control. Just as important, it offers *you* a chance to calm down and to reduce the risk of protracted or no-win conflicts. In short, time out can offer some real advantages for parents to cope with issues of discipline.

I feel, however, that parents sometimes overuse or even misuse time out as a method. Here are some aspects of the subject to consider:

Age. Time out (or quiet time) is appropriate for preschoolers and perhaps kids in the early elementary school years—depending on your child's maturity—but it's less effective or counterproductive for older children. You can start using time out when your child is around two and a half years old; you should phase out and terminate use when he is in kindergarten or perhaps first grade. I don't recommend using time out at all past second grade. (Possible exceptions: if your child is developmentally delayed or socially immature—and even then only with great care, and perhaps with professional guidance.)

Location. Pick a safe, neutral spot that's close enough that you can monitor your child but far enough away that he's "out of the action." A corner of the living room or dining room may be ideal. Never confine him in a closet or utility room. Also, don't use his bedroom or bed as place of punishment: you want him to associate his room with safety and comfort, not with punishment and separation.

Frequency. If time out does not appear to improve your child's behavior, you may be dealing with a larger issue than normal misbehavior. The problem may be fairly minor, such as hunger or fatigue. It may be more substantial, such as a reaction to a school incident you haven't heard about yet. In any case, look beyond the immediate situation to what lies beyond it. There may be a developmental issue or an issue of family dynamics; if so—and if you're concerned about the situation—you should consider seeking the insights of a counselor, family therapist, or other professional clinician.

SCHOOL-AGE CHILDREN

Adjusted for age, the recommendations outlined on pages 95–7 (except for time out) will generally apply to school-age children as well. The specific situations will have changed, and the nature of parent-child interactions will have become more complex, but the same approaches that are creative for five-year-olds should be effective for ten-year-olds, including: looking for root causes of behavior, being empathetic, clarifying situations, solving problems together, negotiating clear limits together, and consistency in following through. My general recommendation is to "stay the course." In addition:

- *Keep developmental issues in mind.* As they change and grow, kids go through periods of organized behavior alternating with periods of disorganized or regressive behavior. Many of the difficulties and conflicts may result from changes in your child's emotional, social, motor, intellectual, and language development, or from disparities among these various aspects.

- *Monitor the limits you've set.* The expectations you have for your child's behavior may need to change more quickly than you think; what works at one developmental stage may be ineffective or counterproductive a few months later. Don't expect that you can "coast" for very long—if at all. Go with the ebb and flow of your child's development.

- *Stress* preventive *attention rather than* reactive *attention.* To put it bluntly, giving your child attention and TLC when he's behaving well is likely to pay off better than responding only when he misbehaves. In fact, close, caring time together will reinforce his good behavior, while reactive attention inadvertently gives the message that he needs to misbehave to be noticed.

- *Take advantage of older kids' more sophisticated skills.* Although some of the challenges you face may seem greater than before, dealing with the challenges may be easier. School-age children can often explain more clearly what's bothering them; encourage and cultivate their verbal sophistication. Foster and reward good negotiation skills. If you can stay calm as you deal with situations, and if you avoid responding to kids' efforts at provocation, you'll have much more abundant opportunities to solve the problems you face.

- *Remember that even the most verbal, accomplished, sophisticated children can regress to earlier developmental stages, and that they're most likely to do so in their parents' presence.* Your parental role—particularly your consistent, warm nurturance—makes you safe; your child can risk being immature, disorganized, outrageous, silly, and even babyish in your company. As frustrating as this situation may feel, it's a good sign, for it shows that your child can hold himself together elsewhere, then let loose *when he's with you in an environment he fully trusts.* Stay patient with these regressions; they're simply part of your child's gradual maturation.

TEENAGERS

For many parents, the teen years present numerous and often difficult challenges regarding discipline. Adolescents rightly gain more and more independence from the family as they mature; at the same time, teenagers are unpredictable, provocative, and often capable of major lapses of judgment. The result in most families is a tricky series of decisions about what constitutes acceptable behavior and what the consequences are for infractions. Chapter 50, "The Teen Years," discusses these issues in some detail, so I'll hold off from addressing them here. Many of the basic principles we've already discussed regarding discipline and younger children also apply (with some necessary modifications) to teenagers as well. What follows, however, are two issues that apply specifically to teens:

CURFEWS AND "GROUNDING"

One of the trickiest and most stressful issues for parents is coping with adolescents' growing independence in the outside world. Teens are notoriously social creatures; being out and about with their peers is the center of their lives. A degree of freedom is crucial to their happiness and development. *What* degree, though? That depends on their age and maturity. As your teen becomes more capable and responsible, he will warrant your trust by allowing him to be on his own. My own son, when he was a preteen, told me, "Mom, you're too easy. Teens will try to get away with whatever you let them get away with. You need to put your foot down sometimes." He's right; teens and preteens look to their parents for authority.

That being said, it's still appropriate for you to set clear limits on what is and isn't acceptable, both in terms of activities and the timing of those activities. Those limits should include clear curfews.

- Don't set curfews according to what your child tells you about other families' rules. Go ahead and check with other parents to verify the consensus regarding your child's peer group, but you should ultimately make your own decision.

- Starting at around seventh grade, a 9:30 to 10:00 curfew is probably appropriate on nonschool nights, depending on your child's maturity. (This situation assumes that activities are well supervised, such as school dances, gatherings at other families' homes, and so forth.)

- As your child earns your trust, you can extend the curfew.

- Insist on having a phone number where you can reach your child. If necessary, call the other parents to verify that the activities are as indicated and that they will include adult supervision.

- Don't back down from your decisions because of your child's claims or accusations: "You're the only parent who calls," and so forth. Your teen may object to your rules, but he'll know you care and will appreciate your concern, at least in the long run. Remember that your child will always love you *even if he doesn't appreciate your "strict" expectations.*

- In explaining the rules, focus on why you're setting them. "We trust you and care about you, but we do worry about outside influences, and we want you to be safe." The message: respect, love, and concern.

- Major infractions of the curfew should warrant grounding or other appropriate consequences, with the severity of the consequences dependent on the severity of the problem. However, try not to over- or underreact. Sometimes giving your teen the benefit of the doubt is effective; just pointing out his lateness will remind your teen and prompt his compliance in the future.

- When setting limits, be consistent with follow-through; don't threaten to ground him, then back off. Stand firm when setting limits, and follow through consistently. This is easy to say and tough to do, so find support if necessary, such as speaking with your partner, talking with a friend, or joining a parenting group.

THE CHALLENGE OF SERIOUS INFRACTIONS

What if your child isn't simply misbehaving in routine ways, but instead commits acts that are destructive, dangerous, cruel, or willfully antisocial? (Examples would include alcohol or drug use, skipping school, theft, vandalism, violence against others, or a pattern of lying, acting out, or violating others' personal rights.) What if your child doesn't respond to your best efforts to cope with his behavior? What if he reacts to your disciplinary measures by behaving worse and worse?

It's difficult to discuss these situations in the abstract, but in general I'd say that serious infractions may require a more intense approach. Let's say that your seventh-grader has been caught stealing another student's belongings. Stealing is ethically unacceptable in its own right; however, it's also a social problem (a violation of school rules and decorum), a potential legal problem (a violation of the law), and a psychological problem (a sign of emotional difficulties). Your adolescent child's theft of someone else's possessions goes beyond normal misbehavior. The disciplinary consequences of the act should be more severe than those warranted by a more trivial problem. Yet simply doling out a more severe punishment isn't likely to be an adequate response. Something more dramatic may be at work here; you need to step back, analyze the situation, and try to comprehend what's happening. There may be any number of contributing factors, including developmental issues, reactive problems resulting from home, school, and peer pressure. Less common but more extreme causes may involve depression or biochemical imbalances. What's crucial is to look beneath the surface rather than to react merely to superficial events.

In many cases, dealing with problems of this magnitude requires outside intervention. You know your child better than anyone else, but you're so close to the situation that you may not be capable of seeing the big picture. Moreover, assessing some kinds of problems may require professional expertise. Rather than attempting to manage the whole situation yourself, consider the option of others' insights. At times this means seeking the assistance of a school counselor or psychologist. At times it means private counseling, parenting classes, support groups, or therapy. You should evaluate the available resources as carefully as possible, then do whatever seems most effective to help your child and your whole family. Ignoring the situation or reacting angrily is almost certain to compound the problem in the long term.

A related possibility in some instances is a *parent-child contract*. This option is especially useful when a teen's behavior is problematic but not as worrisome as in the example just discussed. Typical situations would be when a child refuses to do homework, goofs off too much, bad-mouths the teacher, and so forth. If other disciplinary measures have failed, you might consider a parent-child contract that clarifies the behavior you expect and the consequences or rewards that will follow violation or compliance. Here's the standard process for establishing a written contract:

- Acknowledge and discuss the problem from your own point of view.

- Actively listen and discuss the problem from your teen's point of view.

- Negotiate together, compromise, and establish goals for mutually acceptable behavior.

- Create a mutually acceptable plan that your teenager will commit to for the purpose of achieving that behavior.

- Define both your own and your teen's responsibilities.

- Together, reach an agreement regarding the consequences (both rewards and punishment) for compliance or violation of the terms. Write this down in a contractlike format.

- Have your teen sign the contract, and sign it yourself.

A parent-teen contract isn't a foolproof method for solving disciplinary problems in older children; it is, however, a useful tool for clarifying expectations and setting up an unambiguous system for monitoring them. Many teens may initially resist the notion of a contract but adhere to it anyway. Teens often benefit from knowing exactly where they stand and what to expect from their parents. During the turmoil of adolescence, clear boundaries are—paradoxically—liberating.

MANAGING YOUR OWN FRUSTRATIONS

In conclusion, there's an issue that affects children but actually focuses on parents. This issue is the difficulty that you may face in managing your own frustrations. Children's misbehavior can intensify the stress you face, leading to frustration, exasperation, even anger. The situation is certainly hazardous for kids but almost as dangerous for parents themselves. It's hard to make good, creative decisions if your blood is boiling. To deal with your emotions, see chapter 33, "The Past," and chapter 49, "Taking Care of Yourself."

TEN

DIVORCE

- In the United States today, more than 50 percent of all marriages end in divorce.

- More than 50 percent of American children will spend at least some time in a single-parent family.

- Children in single-parent families are six times more likely to be poor than are kids in two-parent families.

- Research shows that following their parents' divorce, children do better if they maintain the same level of economic well-being they would have enjoyed if the marriage had remained intact; however, this stability rarely occurs, and the consequences for children are often negative.

DIVORCE IS ONE of the most stressful experiences that people can undergo. If you're going through a divorce, you'll be dealing with many dramatic changes, some of them involuntary. What I'll focus on in this chapter, however, is primarily how divorce affects children, and how you *as a parent* can help diminish the negative effects.

THE IMPACT OF DIVORCE

If you and your spouse are getting divorced, you are both understandably distracted, self-absorbed, and stressed. This state of mind is understandable; it's an enormous task to rebuild your life during and following a divorce. As a result, however, you may find that despite your best intentions, you're not as available emotionally to your children as you'd like to be. You may be putting your children and their needs "on hold" while you attend to your marital problems. Your child may not be as well supervised as usual, or you may hesitate to set appropriate limits. You may not be able to provide the same level of emotional and physical care that you'd like. Preoccupation with your own problems may leave your children feeling lonely, confused, fearful, and stressed. In short, divorce will probably hit you hard and may diminish your capacity to parent effectively.

Parenting is difficult enough under the best of circumstances; during the turmoil of divorce—and in its aftermath—parenthood is almost invariably harder still. But the truth remains: even as you go through the divorce process, you must still maintain your parental responsibilities and obligations. Research shows that children do better when the primary caregiver (usually the mother) is emotionally stable, and when there is a low level of tension between the parents. Maintaining your emotional equilibrium is clearly a tall order during and after divorce, yet close parental attention must somehow coexist with what's going on as you dismantle your marriage.

KIDS' RESPONSES TO DIVORCE AT DIFFERENT STAGES

A popular view holds that if you're feeling happy and less pressured because divorce has gotten you out of a bad relationship, your child will automatically feel happy, too. Sometimes this is true. However, your child will have her own experience of the divorce—an experience that's separate and different from your own, and which will vary depending on the child's age and relative maturity.

BABIES AND TODDLERS

The most important thing at this stage is consistency in scheduling. Make sure that you meet your child's needs for food, rest, play, and comfort on a regular basis. Toddlers will also need clear, simple information about what is happening, such as when the other parent will be around. Even very young children can respond intensely to changes resulting from a divorce, so it's crucial for you to monitor their behavior for signs of being tense, fearful, or anxious. Be open to changes in emotions, such as clinginess or signs of anxiety, and be as supportive as possible.

PRESCHOOLERS

A preschooler's biggest response to her parents' divorce is likely to be a sense of abandonment and a wish that her mother and father would stay together anyway. She is likely to experience separation anxiety during and after the divorce. She may worry that one or both parents will disappear from her life. As a result, you need to be clear and reassuring about your ongoing presence.

If she'll be living with one parent and visiting the other, be straightforward about the arrangements. Assure her that she'll see both parents (if that is indeed true) and that she'll still have a mother and a father. If, on the other hand, one parent won't be coming back, you need to tell the truth about what's happening. Don't dissimulate or pretend she won't be affected. The other parent's absence will create a deep sense of loss, but you can't avoid that by shoving your child's emotional reaction under the carpet. Help her grieve the loss of that parent. If necessary, find professional help to ease the burden.

EARLY SCHOOL YEARS

During ages five to eight, kids are often preoccupied with a sense of loss following a divorce. They are prone to feeling guilty, rejected, and angry. They may experience loyalty conflicts. Some children feel responsible for the parents' divorce or obliged to "fix" the problem. Others experience *parentification*—a tendency to assume a parental role and feel responsible for meeting the parents' needs. Children at this age also have a great need for wish fulfillment, so they may fantasize about reuniting the parents.

LATER SCHOOL YEARS

During ages nine to twelve, children depend tremendously on parents for a sense of stability. They may feel intense anger about the loss they've suffered, with especially strong anger at whichever parent they blame for the divorce. They're most likely to perceive the situation in black and white; they'll blame one parent or the other. They can suffer from intense grief and anxiety, too, and can feel an acute sense of loneliness or powerlessness. They are anxious about bringing the parents back together. They may act out to gain attention, but they are also more inclined to become caregivers, feeling responsible for the parents' happiness. They may complain of psychosomatic symptoms, headaches, or stomachaches. If one or both parents start dating, preteen kids can be overstimulated by the effects of the new love life they're witnessing. For this reason, it's important to avoid exposing your child to unpredictable relationships when they are so sensitive to abandonment; you don't want them to have to relive drawing close to someone, only to experience another separation. Keep your dating life separate from your kids unless your new partner is capable of making a long-term commitment in your life.

ADOLESCENTS

Although they may seem mature at this age, teenagers can be extremely fearful about the consequences of divorce. They need strong role models, especially for gender roles. The loss of a parent—especially the same-sex parent—can be disruptive, even devastating. Teenagers also need a strong sense of family structure to set limits for their own aggressive, sexual, and impulsive behaviors at this age. The lack of family structure can terrify them. Many fear that they'll repeat their parents' failures. They can become egocentric, self-absorbed, and angry at the parents. These emotions can show up as judgmental, critical attitudes toward the mother, the father, or both. Some girls experience what Judith Wallerstein calls the "sleeper effect"—acting out the loss of their father by becoming promiscuous during the teen years. Some worry about their future or develop an inability to make long-term commitments or intimate relationships. However, some may get involved in intimate relationships and may try hard to make them work. They may be overzealous about staying in relationships no matter what the circumstances. They may be angry about the abandonment, and they may act out or assume more responsibilities than they're ready to handle. They may feel responsible for a parent's happiness.

PARENTING TASKS DURING AND FOLLOWING A DIVORCE

I have no illusions that the following recommendations will make life easy. They may, however, help you avoid complicating your child's life still further at an already difficult time.

KEEP YOUR CHILD OUT OF IT

One of the biggest and most important tasks is to separate (to the degree possible) your child from your divorce experience. To put it bluntly: don't put the kids in the middle. Kids need to feel that they're allowed to love both their parents; they shouldn't have to choose one over the other. Putting kids in the middle is detrimental to their development and growth.

- *Try not to burden your child with unnecessary information about the divorce process.* Young children won't be able to follow legal or financial aspects of what's happening, and it's inappropriate to weigh them down with details; even older children don't need more than generalities. Don't expect your child to be your lawyer, accountant, psychotherapist, or confidant.

- *Don't bad-mouth your ex-spouse.* Doing so puts your child in an emotional bind: If she agrees with your criticism, she may feel she's betraying her other parent; if she rebuffs your criticism, she may feel she's betraying *you*.

- *Don't ask your child for information about your ex.* Requests of this sort put the child in a position of serving as a spy or messenger, which violates her bond with her other parent.

- *Keep your sense of balance about parenthood and divorce.* Even if your divorce is acrimonious, remind yourself that you love your child more than you resent your ex.

- *Don't pressure your child into not visiting the noncustodial parent.* Do not disrupt the visitation schedule. Be sensitive to your child's long-term emotional needs.

- *Whatever else, do what's in the best interests of your child.* Doing the right thing for your child is an enormous act of love and maturity, and it's difficult, but it will pay off in the long run.

REMEMBER THE IMPACT ON YOUR CHILD

Regardless of how the divorce has affected you, keep in mind that your child will be affected, too. Do whatever you can to stay tuned in to her. Listen to her without judging what she says. Validate what she's going through. Acknowledge her feelings. If she expresses anger or resentment toward you—even rage—don't take these outbursts personally. Reassure her that even though you're divorcing the other parent, you'll never divorce *her*. Lavish love and attention on her. Remind her constantly that you won't abandon her; you'll be there no matter what.

PROVIDE A STABLE HOME LIFE

Following the separation, do what you can to provide your child with a stable home life. Try to limit constant back-and-forth travel between households. Research shows that it's better for children to have one primary home rather than being constantly shuttled around. That doesn't mean that your child shouldn't see the noncustodial parent; the particular arrangement should be evaluated to determine what's best in each unique situation. Again, the central issue is the child's best interests. Sometimes that means that the child lives primarily with the mother, sometimes with the father. Whatever else, make a mature, adult decision, separating your own needs from what's best for your child. Devise a situation that's optimal for your child's emotional, physical, and spiritual growth. Whatever situation is agreed upon—even if it's not what you had hoped for—try to learn to live with it and accept it for your child's sake. As your child grows older, circumstances will change, and you and your ex should remain open and flexible in response to your child's changing needs. Try to do whatever is in your child's—not necessarily your own—best interests.

CLARIFY WHAT HAPPENED TO THE MARRIAGE

Exaggerating their own sense of power and struggling with feelings of guilt, many children feel that they are somehow responsible for their parents' divorce. They take responsibility for events that in reality have nothing to do with them. They berate themselves with an endless game of "if only." If only they'd behaved better. If only they'd paid more attention to their parents. If only they'd "fixed things" between Mom and Dad. As a result of these feelings of responsibility and guilt, it's important for you to clarify what really happened between you and your ex. Emphasize that the divorce isn't your child's fault. Stress the three c's: You didn't cause it, you can't control it, and you can't cure it. By the same token, don't blame yourself or your ex-spouse for everything. Try to explain that both parents tried hard to work things out, but that some things can't be fixed.

A related issue is the attempt that many children make to undo the divorce. Some will try to solve the problems that they perceive as being the source of their parents' decision to end the marriage. Others will act out in an effort to bring parents back together. If your child takes actions along these lines, it's important to let her know that she isn't responsible for the divorce, and she isn't able to reverse it.

DON'T MUDDLE THE ISSUE WITH MIXED MESSAGES

Despite the divorce, you yourself may feel ambivalent about whether it is a permanent reality. Some couples waver in their attitudes that the divorce is a true end to the marriage. Such ambivalence is understandable. The problem with it, however, is that your uncertainties may confuse your child painfully. How should you respond? Try to keep interactions with your ex-spouse polite but businesslike. Unless reconciliation seems certain, don't foster illusions that you and your ex might someday get back together. Keep the boundaries clear.

THE MYTH OF THE VICTIMLESS DIVORCE

Sad but true: there's really no such thing as a victimless divorce. And the person who suffers most in the divorce process is usually the child. Since parents are the bedrock of their children's lives, splitting up a marriage starts an earthquake that invariably frightens children and changes their lives. So if you can't avoid negative consequences altogether, what can you do?

- Try to minimize the fallout as much as possible. Keep your cool. Keep your frustrations in context; your child needs you to stay levelheaded.

- No matter how angry you feel toward your ex, don't turn your child against the other parent. Don't use your child as a weapon.

- Kids need the continued involvement of both parents. Ideally, both parents should keep interacting with the kids on a frequent, consistent basis. Both parents' presence is crucial for kids' cognitive, social, and emotional development, academic success, sex-role modeling, and overall self-esteem.

- A corollary to the above: Keep Dad involved with the kids. Children need their fathers. Men should take their responsibilities seriously and do everything possible to stay actively involved with their children.

- Keep routines as similar as possible in both households.

- Try to maintain similar values and routines in both households. The more similarities there are, the less instability there will be in routines, discipline, goals, and procedures. Consistency eases the stress on kids.

- Try to resolve your disappointment, sadness, anger, and regret by learning from your past mistakes, working through your feelings, and accepting the reality of what *is* rather than your desire for what *could have been*.

- If you feel you're floundering—or if you just need help—find assistance as soon as possible. Going it alone will make your own life—and probably your child's life as well—much more difficult. Join a support group or find a psychotherapist who specializes in divorce-related issues. Check the list of organizations in the Resource Guide to obtain information.

ELEVEN

DRUGS, ALCOHOL, AND TOBACCO

- A study of car-accident patients in a shock-trauma unit showed that 15 percent of drivers had been smoking marijuana.

- Even first-time users of cocaine and crack-cocaine can suffer cardiac arrhythmias, some leading to fatal heart attacks.

- Over four and a half million American teenagers have a drinking problem.

- Alcohol-related accidents are the leading cause of death among young people aged fifteen to twenty-four.

- Approximately half of all youthful deaths in drowning, fires, suicide, and homicide are alcohol-related.

- Eighteen percent of high school seniors are daily smokers.

- Young people who use cigarettes are also at greater risk for drug use.

- Four hundred thousand Americans die of tobacco-related illnesses each year.

MOST PARENTS NEED no reminders that drugs, alcohol, and tobacco present serious threats to their children's well-being. At the same time, many parents feel uncertain, even helpless, in countering the danger that substance abuse can present. It's easy to overreact and just as easy to deny the risks altogether.

But the risks are real. Hollywood and the pop music industry often tout alcohol and cigarettes as cool; street culture in many cities and suburbs promotes drug use; the tobacco industry, though in legal retreat, continues to pursue young people as the likeliest consumers of its products. Consumption of illicit drugs, alcohol, and tobacco remains a significant danger to children's health.

HELPING YOUR KIDS AVOID ALCOHOL AND DRUG ABUSE

In response to this situation, I recommend a calm, consistent approach that stresses these guidelines:

EDUCATE YOURSELF

The more you know about drug and alcohol use, the better you can help your child avoid their dangers.

Beware of the possibility that your child may experiment with cigarettes, alcohol, or drugs. Even children in elementary school may have access to these substances, and peer pressure can tempt even the best-intentioned, most obedient kids.

Keep the risks in proportion. Although many parents worry about their children's use of illicit drugs, alcohol and tobacco are generally greater long-term dangers. More children die from alcohol-related car accidents, for instance, than from all other kinds of injuries or illnesses combined.

Understand the specifics of alcohol and drug use. You should at least:

- Know the different types of drugs and alcohol and the dangers associated with each kind

- Be able to identify drug paraphernalia

- Be familiar with street names of drugs

- Know what the different drugs look like

- Know the signs of alcohol and drug use

- Know how to obtain help if you believe that your child is using alcohol or other drugs

The Resource Guide includes names of organizations that offer information on drug and alcohol use, prevention, and treatment.

BE A GOOD ROLE MODEL

What are your own beliefs about drugs and alcohol? What are your practices and habits? To what degree is your own behavior consistent with what you expect from your children?

Practicing one set of behaviors yourself while expecting your children to practice another is almost certain to backfire. Whatever you may tell them, your children will probably copy your actions. Children whose parents smoke, for instance, more frequently become smokers than do the children of non-smokers. Children whose parents indulge heavily in alcoholic beverages are more at risk for becoming heavy drinkers themselves. Even frequent use of over-the-counter drugs may send the wrong signal, since children may assume that popping pills is the solution for every discomfort. In light of these situations, one of the best approaches you can take is to size up your own attitudes and actions, change your behavior if necessary, and avoid hypocrisy.

COMMUNICATE OPENLY

Throughout this book I stress the importance of good communication. (See chapter 5, "Communication Between Parents and Kids," for a detailed discussion.) When dealing with issues of drugs and alcohol, warm and clear communication is especially crucial. This situation holds true both for the messages you give your child and for your willingness to hear what he's trying to tell you. Children should not be afraid to talk openly and honestly with their parents. Ideally, a child should have at least one parent who is psychologically tuned in to him, and with whom the child feels comfortable and free to say how he truly feels and what he is really experiencing.

The core issue is that if communication lines are open between you and your child, he'll be less likely to abuse drugs and alcohol in the first place. Parents who are involved, affectionate, and supportive provide a context in which children feel comfortable expressing all their feelings. This context is beneficial in its own right—it provides a much warmer, more embracing family atmosphere—but it's also important in helping to prevent kids from numbing or repressing their emotions. The result: your child is less likely to resort to alcohol and drugs as a consolation, and he's more likely to be honest and direct in speaking with you. By communicating attentively and honestly, you give the message that you love him, value his opinions, and want to hear about whatever concerns him.

Be a good listener. Help your child bring up problems or questions. Listen nonjudgmentally. Avoid accusations, sarcasm, and mockery. If something seems to be troubling your child, take the initiative to ask what's the matter. Be available to discuss even sensitive subjects. Be patient if the process of discussing a subject takes repeated conversations. Listen for hidden messages.

Offer lots of praise. Emphasize what your child is doing right rather than focusing on mistakes and errors of judgment. Help your child build his self-confidence and self-esteem.

Discuss the wider social issues. Talk about the damage that illicit drugs do, not just to individuals, but to entire communities. Point out how the tobacco and alcohol industries make billions of dollars on sales of their products despite the harm done to countless people. Discuss peer pressure and suggest ways to resist it.

Give clear messages. When talking about the use of alcohol and other drugs, make your expectations clear. Don't *assume* that he understands what you expect.

SET CLEAR, FAIR, SPECIFIC RULES

In setting rules about drugs and alcohol:

- *Be specific.* Explain the reasons for the rules. Set the rules and indicate the consequences of infractions—what the punishment will be, how it will be carried out, and what the punishment will achieve.

- *Be consistent.* Make it clear that a no-alcohol/no-drug-use rule remains the same at all times and places—in your home, in a friend's home, at school, etc.

- *Be reasonable.* Avoid unrealistic threats. React calmly if your child breaks the rule, and carry out the punishment that you have designated. Emphasize that although your child's behavior was unacceptable, you love him and accept him for who he is.

STAY AHEAD OF THE PROBLEMS

Many parents cope with drug and alcohol issues only when problems arise. This reactive approach often leaves them scrambling to catch up when the damage has already occurred. A better strategy: Stay ahead of the problems. Don't assume that your child won't be affected. Learn everything you can about substance abuse. Obtain informative booklets and other resources from the local schools, government agencies, and other sources. Don't overreact, but don't be caught by surprise.

To the degree possible, teach your children what they need to know about drugs and alcohol at each developmental stage.

Preschoolers

Even preschoolers can benefit from simple, straightforward information about these issues. Explain that each prescription medicine has its own proper use and, if misused, can be dangerous. Stress the importance of eating good foods and avoiding "yucky" things like cigarettes. Teach them that some things adults can do, such as moderate social drinking, are unacceptable for children. As when dealing with children of any age, be open-minded, patient, and kind.

If parents are more flexible and less authoritarian, a child is more likely to learn to make informed choices and, in the long run, is less likely to succumb to peer pressure.

Kids Ages Five to Eight
From kindergarten to grade three, children are generally trusting of adults and open to information. Depending on your child's developmental level, you can teach kids age-appropriate material and have age-appropriate discussions regarding:

- What illicit drugs are, why they're illegal, and what harm they can do
- How medicines and illicit drugs differ
- How medicines, though potentially beneficial, can be harmful as well
- Why alcohol can be dangerous
- Why rules and laws exist regarding use of drugs and alcohol
- Why alcohol and other drugs are illegal for all children

Kids Ages Nine to Twelve
By grades four through six, children start to question adults' authority and grow gradually more influenced by a peer group. This age is a crucial time for parents' involvement regarding drugs and alcohol. Peer pressure increases dramatically; contact with kids who are already drinking or using drugs grows more likely. The greatest risk for starting to smoke, for instance, occurs when children are in the sixth and seventh grades. The earlier kids start to use alcohol and other drugs, the more likely they will experience long-term trouble with substance abuse.

For this reason, it's crucial that you provide your child with straightforward information, including:

- How to identify specific illicit drugs
- How drugs affect the body, in both the short and the long term
- How drugs are especially dangerous to growing bodies
- How alcohol and drugs damage the individual, the family, and society

By discussing these issues and teaching techniques that allow kids to say no without losing face within the peer group, you can set the stage for your child to handle the high-risk teen years ahead.

Teens

Precisely because adolescence is a time of growing autonomy and diminishing parental influence, it's a high-risk stage. Strong peer affiliation leaves teens vulnerable to outside opinions and reluctant to take an independent stand. Many teens consequently use drugs simply because their friends do. Fortunately, teenagers develop greater powers of abstraction as they mature, so that discussing cause-effect relationships may grow easier over the years. You can help your teen deal with the risks of drug and alcohol use by these means:

- *Keep the lines of communication open.* Though parents often find adolescents moody and distant, it's a big mistake to take these emotional states personally. Stay calm and do what you can to remain in contact. Be patient and nonjudgmental. Listen carefully to what your child is telling you.

- *Counteract peer influence with parental influence.* Although your child may seem totally under the spell of his peer group, he's probably tracking your own opinions and beliefs anyway. Stay firm in upholding your values. Stress that your no-alcohol/no-drug rules are nonnegotiable. Counteract arguments that alcohol and drug use are "no big deal" or that "everyone else is doing it."

- *Practice what you preach.* Be a positive role model by observing, monitoring, and controlling your own use of alcohol and over-the-counter medication. Limit the amount of alcohol in your home. Try to use natural remedies rather than "quick fix" medicines for everyday aches and pains. This approach will model responsible behavior.

- *Get to know your child's friends and their parents.* Don't let your teen isolate himself within his peer group; invite the friends to visit your family. Develop mutually agreed-upon rules about activities, curfews, and communication. Check with other parents to get a sense of their own rules and curfews. By all means do what *you* think is right, but acquire a context for what's typical in your area.

- *Monitor your child's whereabouts.* Insist on clarification about where he'll be, who he's with, who's providing transportation, and a phone number where you can reach him, and so forth. Plan strategies to limit your teen's unsupervised hours at home.

- *Encourage creative activities.* Help your child join and take part in interesting clubs, sports teams, classes, or other pastimes. Plan alcohol- and drug-free parties, holidays, and outings.

- *Cooperate with other parents.* Work together to make sure that peer group social occasions are alcohol- and drug-free. Call ahead to make sure that there will, in fact, be a party or gathering, and make sure that a parent will be present.

- *Avoid scare tactics.* Trying to discourage drug and alcohol use by telling cautionary tales about grisly illnesses will probably backfire. Because teens can't clearly focus on the future, medical scare tactics aren't generally effective. Instead, emphasize short-term negative consequences that teenagers can grasp, such as bad breath, discoloration of teeth, and embarrassment from foolish behavior.

IF YOU SUSPECT YOUR CHILD OF USING ALCOHOL OR DRUGS . . .

It's not always easy to determine when a child is abusing drugs or alcohol. Though some parents discover persuasive proof—liquor bottles, drugs, or drug paraphernalia—the signs are often more subtle. You may need to track your child's behavior over time to spot indications of a problem. Here are some questions to ask yourself:

- Does your child seem withdrawn, depressed, tired, and careless about personal grooming?

- Has he become hostile and uncooperative?

- Have his relationships with other family members deteriorated?

- Has your child "dropped" his old friends?

- Is your child's academic performance deteriorating?

- Has he lost interest in hobbies, sports, and other favorite activities?

- Have your child's eating or sleeping patterns changed?

Positive answers to these and similar questions *may* indicate use of alcohol or drugs. To complicate the situation, however, positive answers to such questions may be consistent with normal (though potentially troubling) adolescent ups and downs. How can you determine what's going on? Again, it's important to keep communication lines open; raise your concerns with your child. If, after observing the duration and intensity of the problem, you're still uncertain, consider consulting your family physician. Have your doctor rule out illness or psychological problems that might explain your child's difficulties.

Should you search your teenager's room? Although I strongly believe that parents should respect their children's privacy, mothers and fathers dealing with extreme circumstances must make an informed decision based on the facts. Searching a teen's room should be an absolute last resort. Teens who use drugs will often hide the evidence, so even a thorough search isn't necessarily effective. A better approach: focus on your observations; communicate directly with your teen; stay closely involved. The picture will clarify over time regarding what's really happening. If your concerns linger even after following these guidelines, however, consult with your teen's physician or with a parent educator who specializes in adolescent development.

For information about books, hot lines, referral services, Web sites, and other sources of information, see the Resource Guide.

TWELVE

ENERGETIC CHILDREN AND HYPERACTIVITY

ONE OF NATURE'S great practical jokes is the disparity between adult's and children's energy levels. Here you are, a full-grown, competent, mature man or woman—thoughtful, accomplished, and committed to being a good parent—and your kids have you over a barrel. By the end of the day you're ready to drop and they're still going strong. Where's the justice?!

The truth is, most children are incredibly energetic. From an adult's viewpoint, even well-behaved kids often seem very active, and many appear "wired," "hyper," or "over the edge." Toddlers and preschoolers, no matter how delightful, are notorious for fatiguing their parents. During later years, too, children can engage in intense play or wild activity that leaves adults exhausted and dizzy. Parents often adjust and cope, though; kids' energy is just something to accept and deal with. Cycles of activity and fatigue are part of the rhythm of family life.

But what if your child seems more than merely active? What if his activity level seems frantic, disorganized, and impossible to channel? What if his energy isn't creative, but disruptive? What if his behavior becomes inappropriate at home, at school, or in other settings? In short, what if he's beyond active—he's *hyper*active? And if he's hyperactive, how should you respond?

WHAT IS HYPERACTIVITY?

First of all, let's clarify our terms. As John F. Taylor notes in his book *Helping Your Hyperactive/ADD Child*, hyperactivity is "a common syndrome with many names." Specialists and laypersons alike use a variety of other terms— some with technical precision, others more colloquially—to describe the com- binations of symptoms and behaviors that fall into the general category of hyperactivity. Noting the terms that fall under the rubric of hyperactivity, Tay- lor lists attention deficit disorder (ADD); ADD with hyperactivity (ADD-H); ADD without hyperactivity (ADD-noH); and a welter of other disorders, among them brain damage syndrome, dyslexia, functional behavioral problems, hyperactive child syndrome, hyperkinesis, hyperkinetic impulsive disorder, and many others. The abundance of these names and the overlap between their symptoms provide an indication of how complex the diagnostic issues really are.

For the sake of simplicity, I'll use the term *attention deficit hyperactivity disor- der* and its acronym, ADHD, as generic labels for what we're discussing. Please note, however, that *the problem itself isn't generic*. Each child is an individual, and ADHD affects children in highly individual ways. See the Resource Guide for a listing of books, Web sites, and other sources of information that can help you understand your child's specific needs.

NORMAL ENERGY AND HYPERACTIVITY

How can you tell the difference between a child who is merely energetic and one who has ADHD? This question is one of the trickiest involved in dealing with the issue of hyperactivity. ADHD has a great variety of symptoms, many of which occur in a range of severity; as a result, it's hard to determine whether a particular child is exhibiting ADHD symptoms or just ordinary youthful energy. There is no blood test or other clear-cut means for identifying ADHD. To date, diagnosis of ADHD relies on interpreting observations of the child in action.

To complicate matters, some aspects of diagnosing and treating ADHD appear to be subjective or culturally determined. Extroverted, physically active parents may be less likely to regard an energetic child as hyperac- tive, for instance, than are more subdued, physically retiring parents. Teachers who have sufficient time, abundant classroom space, and a rich variety of resources to devote to demanding students may be less likely to label a child as hyperactive than are teachers with tight schedules, limited classroom space, and scant resources. There may be an element of gender bias as well. Approximately 60 to 80 percent of children diagnosed with ADHD are boys. Although this statistic may well indicate that boys are simply more predisposed to hyperactivity, the preponderance of ADHD among boys may also suggest that boys are tagged as hyperactive partly because of adults' impatience or annoyance with otherwise normal high- energy behavior. (I discuss this issue later; see "The Boy Factor" on page 122.)

COMMON SYMPTOMS

Some common symptoms that *may* indicate hyperactivity or attention deficit disorder are:

- Difficulty making decisions, prioritizing, or focusing on tasks
- Difficulty tuning out environmental "static"—background noise, other people's activities, minor interruptions, and so forth
- Difficulty formulating ideas or thinking abstractly
- Inflexibility in dealing with choices or following directions
- Difficulty controlling impulses—touching, pushing, or hassling others
- Immature social skills
- Unpredictable behavior
- Difficulty learning from past errors or from cause-effect relationships
- A propensity for acting without thinking
- A propensity for self-centeredness, impatience, and recklessness
- Extreme emotionalism
- Difficulties with motor skills, coordination, or balance
- A tendency toward constant movement
- Other physical symptoms, including allergies and sensitivities, sleep problems, and food cravings
- Poor verbal skills
- Poor handwriting, including left-to-right progression
- Difficulty reading

THE AMBIGUITY OF DIAGNOSIS

As the number and variety of these symptoms suggest, many behaviors can indicate the *possibility* of ADHD. The sheer number and variety of symptoms, however, also suggest precisely why diagnosing these problems is so difficult. Most or all of these symptoms can also indicate issues far different from anything related to ADHD. Certain other physiological problems, learning challenges, mental and emotional difficulties, developmental changes, environmental stress reactions, learned behaviors, and fatigue can all produce symptoms similar to what I'm describing. As a result, even an abundance of these characteristic behaviors may or may not indicate ADHD. A child who seems "hyperactive" may be simply under external stress (as a consequence of his parents' divorce, for instance) or exhibiting symptoms of an entirely unrelated problem.

My personal opinion is that checklists and other diagnostic tools for assessing ADHD are often inconclusive. Until researchers discover a more reliable means for assessing ADHD—use of brain-scanning technology, such as MRIs, for instance—diagnosis will remain uncertain. What's most reliable at the moment is use of detailed interviews with children, their parents, teachers, and others involved with the family. This situation isn't ideal; however, it's what we have to work with presently.

THE NEED TO STEP CAREFULLY

Because diagnosing ADHD is so difficult, it's crucial that you step carefully before assuming that your child has developed this syndrome. I realize that reacting cautiously is easier said than done. If your child is disrupting your home or his classroom, you'll be eager—even desperate—to get a handle on the problem. Still, I urge caution. ADHD has become a convenient, socially acceptable way of explaining certain kinds of negative behavior among children. I'm especially concerned by the tendency among some school personnel to explain many or most children's behavioral problems as ADHD-related. In one area of New York City, for instance, a large number of disruptive students are diagnosed with ADHD, then put on medication. School administrators seem reluctant to acknowledge that other problems may account for much of the behavior these children exhibit. Some children are coping with abusive parents; some are suffering from inadequate nutrition; almost all of them attend schools that are overcrowded and understaffed. Labeling these kids as hyperactive is a convenient, cheap way to shove a host of problems under the carpet.

What other factors can account for hyperactive behavior? In many families, these are issues worth considering:

- The child may feel stressed by personal problems (the parents' marital problems or divorce, a new baby in the household, the presence of alcoholic family members, and so forth).

- He may be receiving insufficient attention because of the parents' absence, emotional indifference, or other reasons.

- He may have some other medical/behavioral condition.

- He may have a learning disability unrelated to ADHD.

During my work as a teacher, I knew children who were initially labeled as hyperactive but who ultimately received a diagnosis of some non-ADHD problem. Many conditions can cause distractibility, poor concentration, intense energy levels, emotional outbursts, and a short attention span. Family dynamics, biochemical changes, and even the overall classroom situation can all contribute to situations that appear to be ADHD. None of these possibilities should be ignored when trying to assess a child for hyperactive behavior.

THE BOY FACTOR

In addition, there's what I call the "boy factor." It's no secret that boys can be intensely energetic. Although there's always the risk of gender bias in generalizing about differences in male/female behavior, many parents and teachers state openly that boys often account for the largest proportion of children they regard as highly active. Does this mean that they're hyperactive? The answer to that question depends on the context. Throughout much of the past, boys' high energy levels tended to be regarded as part of their nature; in many cultures, this wasn't a problem. Historical periods and cultures that allowed boys to vent their energy through boisterous play or physical work may not have found this level of activity so problematic. But now children must sit still throughout long school days, and some school districts have abolished recess altogether. Teachers and administrators often resent children who are relatively less cooperative about sitting still. These conditions aren't healthy for boys *or* girls, and I'm sure that many children find them burdensome. A significant number of boys diagnosed with ADHD may be acting as they do at least in part as a backlash against their restrictive surroundings.

What's statistically clear is that boys are more likely than girls to be considered hyperactive. As noted earlier, John F. Taylor estimates that boys account for 60 to 80 percent of all ADHD diagnoses. William S. Pollack states in his book *Real Boys* that the ratio of newly diagnosed cases of ADHD is as high as ten boys for every girl. Pollack goes on to say, "[W]hen millions of boys are diagnosed as having [ADHD], and when far fewer girls are given the same diagnosis, I begin to wonder whether the diagnosis is sometimes being applied inappropriately to what are normal episodes of boy behavior." He speculates that what tends to be regarded as "hyperactivity" is instead a combination of boys' temperament combined with emotional resistance to certain social expectations and pressures. In general, Pollack feels that as many as 50 percent of boys labeled hyperactive have been misdiagnosed.

Pollack's opinions are likely to be controversial among ADHD experts. It's worth noting, however, that many of the standard assumptions about ADHD are controversial, too. My point is simply that if you're concerned that your boy is affected by ADHD, take the "boy factor" into account. (For discussions of related issues, see chapter 3, "Boys," in this book, and read Pollack's *Real Boys* and Michael Gurian's *The Wonder of Boys*, both listed in the Resource Guide.)

IF YOUR CHILD IS CLINICALLY HYPERACTIVE . . .

If you feel concerned that your child is hyperactive, how should you proceed?

FACE THE PROBLEM AS EARLY AS POSSIBLE

Many parents with a hyperactive child both want help and avoid seeking it. Because ADHD can intensely disrupt family life, everyone in the household may be tense and exhausted by the situation. This reaction is understandable. Some parents react by denying the problem or hesitating to take action. But there's little to be gained by stalling; you're far better off asking for assistance than muddling through. The earlier you have your child assessed and diagnosed, the better chances he'll have for coping with the problem and bolstering his self-esteem, self-confidence, and self-worth.

GET A PROFESSIONAL EVALUATION

The first step is to get a professional evaluation. Start with your pediatrician. If she feels there's reason to evaluate the problem further, consult with an expert on ADHD issues. Actually, proper evaluation may involve several experts, whether individually or working as a team.

The specialists who are most likely to be involved are physicians and mental health professionals.

Physicians. Because other health issues may resemble or contribute to ADHD, a physician should determine if other illnesses or conditions are affecting your child's situation. Issues include iron deficiency, lead toxicity, trauma to the brain, malnutrition, diabetes, thyroid dysfunction, side effects of medications, seizure disorders, and many others.

Mental health professionals. Psychologists, social workers, and other mental health professionals can help to assess behavioral aspects of your child's problems. This aspect of evaluation is important not just to help your child, but also to help other family members, who are affected by your child's situation. Issues under consideration include the child's personal development, family relationships, parents' concerns, available resources for treatment, and nature of psychotherapeutic treatment, if any.

CONSIDER THE POSSIBILITY OF MEDICATION

A significant number of children diagnosed with ADHD are treated with medication. As John F. Taylor states, "Of the biochemical approaches to treating ADHD, prescribed medication is the most popular, most researched, and best accepted within the medical profession." This method of treatment can benefit a significant proportion of hyperactive children. It is, however, controversial. Some clinicians feel that medication is potentially helpful but, given potential side effects, ends up used too often and without sufficient consideration of alternative therapies.

The most frequently prescribed medications for ADHD are stimulants (such as Dexedrine, Ritalin, or Cylert) and antidepressants (such as Elavil, Aventyl, and Tofranil). Many people ask why stimulants are appropriate when ADHD children are already so active. The reason is that these medications increase the child's ability to screen out extraneous thoughts and impulses, and to concentrate on the matter at hand. Both stimulants and antidepressants work by modifying complex biochemical reactions within the nervous system. (For a clear, brief summary of these medications and their effects, see John F. Taylor's book.) Taylor claims that "significant improvement occurs in about 70 to 75% of ADHD children treated with stimulants." However, both advocates and opponents of treating hyperactivity with medication note that children respond idiosyncratically to the kinds and dosage levels of medications; as a result, determining the ideal medication protocol may require a period of trial and error. In addition, most of these medications can have serious side effects. Working closely with an ADHD specialist is crucial.

CONSIDER THE FEINGOLD PROGRAM

An alternative to medication is the Feingold Program, a method of controlling ADHD children's exposure to chemical compounds that may intensify symptoms of hyperactivity. This method for treating ADHD was developed in the 1970s by pediatrician-allergist Benjamin Feingold. Based on the idea that the brains of ADHD children have a sensitivity to certain chemicals, the Feingold Program limits the kids' intake of certain foods and other substances. Typical target chemicals are synthetic food dyes, artificial flavors, flavor-enhancers (e.g., MSG), and certain preservatives. Typical target foods are certain fruits, chili powder, coffee, and certain vegetables.

Is this method of treating ADHD effective? John F. Taylor states that "Estimates of success rates by those familiar with the program range from 50 to 70% for children receiving a correctly enforced control of exposure to the suspected chemicals." Critics of the Feingold Program have derided it as a food fad and questioned its effectiveness. Whether you consider implementing it or not, keep in mind that both this method and other methods involve a commitment by the child and parents alike, and all methods, including medication, have some drawbacks. What ultimately matters most to your family in this regard is whatever helps your child. The Feingold Program is worth considering.

FIND THE RIGHT EDUCATIONAL PROGRAM

If your child has been diagnosed with ADHD, you should do whatever you can to find the right educational program for him. "Right" may mean a good special education program. Federal law (specifically, Public Law 94-142) mandates that public schools must provide special education for children who have specific problems, among them ADHD. (Note: The criteria for qualification vary from school district to school district; in addition, you must apply for most programs.) However, "mainstreaming" your child—having him receive an appropriate education in the same classroom setting as other students—would be optimal. Usually this arrangement means that an adjunct or special ed teacher takes your child out of the classroom from time to time, but he spends most of his day with his peer group. This situation has several advantages, the most obvious being that your child isn't sidelined or stigmatized; his classmates are more likely to accept him as part of the group.

One way or another, you need to be your child's advocate and work to get his needs met within the school system. Given all the competing demands on teachers and administrators, you may have to be persistent and assertive. I recommend a constructive rather than an adversarial approach: if you can be a team player rather than a nemesis, you'll accomplish far more for your child's sake.

FIND GOOD RESOURCES

Finally, I recommend that you work hard to find the resources you need. Raising a hyperactive child is a daunting task; you'll benefit from any good assistance you can find. Fortunately, national and local groups exist. Some offer informational literature about ADHD. Others organize support groups for parents of hyperactive children. In addition, there are Web sites with information about ADHD and related issues. See the Resource Guide for a selection.

THIRTEEN

Exceptional Children

PARENTHOOD IS HARD enough under the best of circumstances. How do you cope, then, if you have an exceptional child—one with physical or intellectual challenges, learning disabilities, or some other problem? How do you provide what a special-needs child will require to thrive and grow to his greatest potential? And how do you respond to those special needs while simultaneously honoring your commitment to your other children?

Generally speaking, you'll parent an exceptional child as you'd parent any other child—by simply doing the best you can. But parents of exceptional children have a complex, lifelong set of responsibilities that can make their tasks especially demanding. What follows is a sketch of issues and ideas about parenting the exceptional child. Most of this chapter focuses on challenged children; a brief final section concerns gifted children.

(When I speak of the "exceptional child," I'm borrowing a definition from Samuel A. Kirk's book *Educating Exceptional Children*. An *exceptional child* is one "who differs from the norm in mental characteristics, sensory abilities, communication abilities, social behavior, or physical characteristics to the extent that special education services are required for the child to develop to maximum capacity." I'm defining the *challenged* or *special-needs child* as one with special physical, intellectual, or emotional needs that are above or below the norm.)

HELPING A CHALLENGED CHILD

For parents, the most important issue is how you offer a challenged child the greatest support and opportunities for development, education, and happiness.

This is a big subject, but here are my initial recommendations. (See the Resource Guide for suggestions on locating more detailed information and support.)

ACCEPT YOUR FEELINGS

The realization that your child has special needs usually hits with a tremendous jolt. You may have had advanced notice of a problem through amniocentesis, blood tests, or ultrasound results, or you may have had no warning at all. In any case, the news of physical, emotional, or intellectual difficulties will leave you feeling shocked and unprepared. The elation you feel about the baby's birth may give way to ambivalence, sadness, or a sense of bereavement. Other emotional reactions may include numbness, disbelief, anger, and guilt, either in succession or (more likely) in a powerful, confusing mix of feelings.

If you're dealing with this situation, it's crucial that you allow yourself to feel what you're feeling. Don't deny your emotions. Discuss your feelings openly, but try not to put the blame on others—your spouse, children, or other family members. Don't bottle up your feelings or pretend they don't exist; find a trained ally to help you deal with what's happening. Locate a therapist or counselor who is experienced in helping parents deal with the emotional aspects of raising a special-needs child. Accept your feelings as normal and legitimate. Work through the frustration and sadness you feel. Then, with others' help, determine what you can do to help everyone in your family face the challenges ahead.

DON'T PROCEED ALONE

In later stages of coping with your situation, it's important to keep working with others. Counseling is only one such option. Parenting support groups are an excellent resource, too. Most hospitals or HMO programs can refer you to groups that can offer assistance to parents whose children have similar difficulties. By sharing problems with other parents, you can develop a helpful support network and sense of solidarity. You're not the only family that's dealing with this problem. Others can help you solve problems, cope with everyday challenges, plan for the future, and ease the weight on your shoulders.

PROVIDE FOR EVERYDAY CARE

One of the most daunting issues that parents of a special-needs child must confront is how to provide for everyday care. Depending on the challenges your child faces, he may not experience the standard sequence or duration of developmental stages. He may develop more slowly or in a different way. The demands on you may differ from those that parents ordinarily face. With children whose challenges are severe, the day-to-day demands of care may be stressful even in the short term and exhausting in the long term. How will you respond to your circumstances? Don't try to solve your problems alone. Find competent advisors to help you plan what needs to be done. Identify resources to assist you. Locate respite care—periodic help to "spell" you from the burden of being the primary caretaker.

EDUCATE YOURSELF

The more you know about your child's problems, the better you'll be prepared to help him and to pace yourself over the months and years. Obtain professional advice from pediatricians, specialists in child development, and ancillary professionals such as physical therapists, speech pathologists, and so forth. Contact the national associations that provide information and assistance regarding your child's difficulties. Just a few of the typical groups include the National Association for Retarded Citizens, the United Cerebral Palsy Association, the American Foundation for the Blind, and the Association for Children with Learning Disabilities. Almost every exceptionality has a national association that provides referrals, information, and advocacy.

MARSHAL YOUR RESOURCES

Once you better understand your child's situation, marshal your resources to provide for him medically, educationally, and in other ways. I'm not suggesting that you should (or can) map out everything you need long-term; however, it's important to get started as soon as possible. Working with the help of a social worker or other advisor, find out who can help you. Identify specific resources. Obtain referrals or recommendations. Gain control over the situation. Take an active role in doing whatever needs to be done. Don't be aggressive or threatening toward the people you interact with—you'll just put them off. A clear-headed, firm, assertive approach, however, will help you accomplish your goals.

UNDERSTAND YOUR RIGHTS

You should also educate yourself about your rights under federal and state law. For instance, federal Public Law 94-142 (enacted in 1975) requires every state to provide free appropriate education for all children with handicaps between the ages of three and eighteen. In addition, Public Law 99-457 Part H (1986) amended the Education of the Handicapped Act, mandating comprehensive, multidisciplinary services for infants and toddlers and their families. Public Law 101-476 (1990)—the Individuals with Disabilities Education Act, or IDEA—requires that schools provide transportation to all students with disabilities. In short, there's a lot of public assistance available for people who have children with exceptionalities. The better you know the laws, the better you can help your child.

WORK WITH THE SCHOOL SYSTEM

Since many educators are intensely committed to their students' well-being, your child's teachers can be valuable allies. Work with your school's principal and teachers to obtain the right education for your child. In addition to special education classes, your child may benefit from ancillary services such as speech therapy and counseling.

If you feel that your child isn't receiving the proper kind or level of education, press the point. Early intervention is crucial. Dyslexia, problems with motor function, and learning disabilities can all be treated more successfully if identified early. Request psychological testing, medical assessment, and any other appropriate diagnostic testing that can help your child.

PLAN FOR THE FUTURE

The day-to-day demands of parenting a special-needs child are often so strenuous that it's hard to plan ahead. To the degree possible, though, look beyond the near future and consider what your child may need in the medium and long term, such as:

- Day care
- Tutoring or other educational assistance
- Psychological counseling
- Vocational training
- Group assisted living
- Shared apartments with supervision

Some programs have long waiting lists, so don't assume that you'll have access to resources on short notice. Obtain as much information as possible, then map out a strategy. Look into arrangements with Social Security to verify guidelines and timing of applications. Investigate Medicaid policies and other means of financing medical care.

TAP INTO FINANCIAL RESOURCES

Raising a special-needs child often subjects parents to great financial stress. The situation is often difficult even if you have relatively good health insurance coverage; if you don't, the burdens can be devastating. To avoid short- and long-term problems, it's critical to find out what you can expect from Medicare, Medicaid, the Social Security Administration, and state or local agencies. In addition, you should identify any financial resources available from your church, synagogue, or other nongovernmental institutions. Don't assume that funds aren't available, or that you don't qualify. Do whatever is possible to ease the financial weight on your shoulders.

Many people hesitate to seek financial help. This is short-sighted and risky. Although funding for social service agencies is tight, you should seek access to whatever resources are appropriate to your child's needs. I know it's difficult to ask for assistance, particularly if you feel proud and independent, but do whatever is legitimately possible for your child's sake.

FOSTER GOOD SELF-ESTEEM

Many children with learning disabilities or physical challenges often feel frustrated or self-denigrating about their problems. Some tend to be socially awkward; feeling frustrated, they may act out negatively in class. Sometimes other children's taunting or scapegoating is a factor; at other times, emotional outbursts release internal frustrations. In these and other cases, make sure that you provide your child with as much emotional support as possible. Tell him that despite his physical or emotional challenges, he's still a wonderful person with his own genuine abilities. Above all, embrace your child with warmth, praise, and affection. Don't let his social frustrations chip away at his sense of confidence and intrinsic worth.

SUPPORT EACH OTHER WITHIN THE FAMILY

Special-needs children affect their families in a variety of ways. Depending on many factors—the parents' income, emotional cohesiveness, personalities, attitudes, religious beliefs, and so forth—the presence of an exceptional child can be a blessing, a challenge, an opportunity for growth, a jumble of problems, or a combination of all these effects. It's hard to generalize about how your special-needs child will affect your family overall.

That being said, it's true that having an exceptional child can be stressful. Research shows that the divorce rate tends to be higher among couples raising exceptional children than among couples whose children lack these challenges. Other children in the family, too, may find that the parents' preoccupation with a special-needs child causes frustration, resentment, and hurt.

You can strengthen your family and support your other children during the tasks of parenting an exceptional child in several ways:

- *Maintain stability.* Take advantage of any available resources to keep family life on an even keel. Depending on the severity of your exceptional child's needs, this recommendation may be a tall order, but it's important. Help your other children have a normal life.

- *Give your other children equal—or nearly equal—time.* Every child needs to feel that he's getting a fair share of his parents' time and attention. Sort out your schedule as well as possible to make sure that your other kids don't feel sidelined by your special-needs child.

- *Nurture your marriage.* Many parents of exceptional children find themselves devoting so much time to kid-centered activities that their marriage suffers. This is understandable. It's troublesome, though, since the parents' marriage is the family's foundation. When possible, find time (even a little) for you and your spouse to be together, have some fun, and look after one another.

HELPING A GIFTED CHILD

In some ways, gifted children present a much different situation from what parents face in raising a special-needs child; nonetheless, gifted children, too, present special challenges and problems. You may face significant emotional stress while parenting a gifted child; in addition, you may have to cope with special educational needs and expenses.

OBTAIN THE RIGHT EDUCATION

Many school systems have special provisions for accommodating gifted children; others don't. In schools that are relatively responsive to gifted children's needs, there's often no special curriculum for the gifted until around the third or fourth grade. This isn't to say that teachers at earlier grade levels aren't aware of gifted kids' presence in the classroom—only that the schools may not be capable of taking any action until later.

If you feel that your child is receiving a less-than-adequate education, given his intellectual or emotional needs, what should you do? On the one hand, gifted kids need to have their talents enriched; at the same time, federal and state laws don't mandate special programs in the ways that laws do for challenged children. You can't *force* your school to provide enrichment programs for your child. You may be better off trying to work within the system—perhaps by helping to set up an after-school enrichment program through the PTA or PTO—than by confronting it from outside.

Another possibility is to find local resources on your own. Clubs, classes, and private tutoring are all options. They have the drawback of costing money, but you have the trade-off of relatively greater flexibility as well. As always, the chief goal should be determining what serves your child's best interests. Consider the option of obtaining a private evaluation to assess your child and his abilities.

AVOID SOCIAL STIGMA

Ironically, many gifted children become underachievers. Why? Because our culture often stigmatizes kids who seem unusually talented, bright, or intellectually curious. This situation has changed somewhat over the past several decades, but many children still risk being mocked as "nerds," "geeks," "eggheads," or worse if peers feel threatened by their abilities. Your gifted child may resent being taken out of the class for special attention, for instance, or singled out as remarkable. The risks increase during the middle school years, when peer-group affiliation intensifies. Children of both sexes may feel stigmatized; overall, though, I'd say the risk is especially pronounced for preteen and teenage girls, given our society's tendency to value females more for their appearance and social skills than for their intellectual, scientific, or artistic gifts. (For a further discussion of this subject, see chapter 20, "Girls.") But for either sex, there's a potential downside to being gifted and talented.

My suggestions are to be supportive of your child without overemphasizing his giftedness. The risks involved in pushing your child toward precocious achievement are far greater than if you let your child seek his own level. At the same time, you need to support your child's interests and aspirations. This is especially true if your child's pursuits run contrary to gender stereotype. A girl who shows scientific talent, for instance, may need encouragement and emotional support as she pursues her studies, since American culture still tends to regard science as a predominantly "masculine" field. Similarly, a boy who shows gifts in some artistic fields, such as dance, may need heavy parental support to avoid feeling stigmatized by his pursuits.

PROVIDE A NORMAL CHILDHOOD

One of your biggest challenges as a parent will be to help your gifted child have a normal childhood. How do you encourage kids to believe that it's possible to be exceptional in several pursuits? That he can be a superb violinist and a great soccer player? That she can love both calculus and climbing trees? In some ways, these seeming contradictions are entirely artificial—and far more likely to reside in parents' imaginations than in kids'. Adults are much more inclined than children are to pigeonhole people for their abilities. For kids, there's really no reason not to love music *and* soccer, math *and* tree climbing. But this issue can still be tricky. Your ongoing challenge with a gifted kid will be to avoid making a big deal of what may, in fact, be a remarkable talent.

Another potential difficulty is that some gifted children can be impatient with peers who don't think as quickly as they do. For instance, a six-year-old named Sophie grew exasperated with her first-grade classmates' slow acquisition of math facts. Most of the kids in her class were just beginning to learn addition and subtraction; Sophie could already do multiplication and division in her head. As a result, Sophie became irritable and bored until her parents pressed the teacher to assign her additional math assignments. This situation was both an academic problem and an emotional problem. It's important in such instances to help gifted children stay excited about learning yet also accept other children for who they are.

Many gifted children figure out how to deal with these circumstances on their own. They may downplay some of their own abilities or mirror some of the other children's behaviors as a way of interacting on their level. Another child I worked with—a highly gifted four-year-old boy—understood that his verbal skills were much more advanced than those of his classmates. Rather than flaunt his vocabulary in all situations, though, he stepped carefully some of the time. "You know," he told me on one occasion, "they don't understand me when I talk, so I just talk like they talk. That way I have more friends." Gifted children can be observant and astute as they try to adapt socially. On the other hand, some aren't so adept at making those realizations, and they can have problems connecting with other children. If you sense that your child is experiencing social difficulties, consult with his teacher or, if possible, a thoughtful educational consultant or child psychologist.

SEE YOUR CHILD AS A CHILD

As remarkable as a gifted child can be, it's sometimes easy to forget that he *is* a child. There's a risk even among well-intentioned parents to end up so beguiled by their child's intelligence, talent, or other precocious feature that they lose track of his vulnerabilities and emotional needs. The most striking and even tragic examples of this phenomenon occur when a child-genius ends up a mere pawn of his parents' ambition. Wolfgang Amadeus Mozart, for instance—probably the most famous music prodigy in history—suffered greatly at the hands of his father, Leopold, who trotted the boy in front of kings and archbishops like a trained bear. What's more common, however, is a tendency for parents to treat their gifted child as emotionally more mature just because he's advanced in other ways. This is usually a mistake. Kids—even brilliant ones—need to be kids.

Keep in mind that within each person are differences in abilities and aptitudes. A seven-year-old who is capable of doing high-school math is still, emotionally speaking, a seven-year-old. A preteen piano prodigy will probably feel all the standard doubts and insecurities of any other adolescent. A chess genius may have shortcomings in motor skills, verbal skills, or social skills. In short, don't expect your gifted child's abilities to be consistent across the board. And, whatever else, treat him as a growing, changing, constantly developing individual.

FOSTER GOOD SELF-ESTEEM

As with special-needs children, gifted kids need constant reassurance and nurturing to foster good self-esteem. Children who perceive themselves as different *in almost any way* often struggle with a sense of self. Your child's aptitudes and accomplishments may sometimes strike him as much a burden as a gift. This situation can be especially difficult if he becomes the butt of taunts or jokes at school; at the same time, even positive reinforcement can sometimes feel oppressive. The core issue is that all children ultimately want to be loved for who they are, not for what they do. Here, as in so many situations, the greatest gift you can give your child is unconditional love. Let him know that although you appreciate his abilities, you cherish him first, last, and in every other way simply for being your child.

THE BURDEN AND THE BLESSING

Parenting exceptional children of any sort is both a burden and a blessing. The burden resides in the time, energy, and special effort that parents must put into the tasks of raising children with unusual needs. At the same time, the blessing is often undeniable. Many parents of exceptional children are adamant that they've gained at least as much as they've given throughout the course of their parenting years. They don't deny the difficulties, but they feel that they've gained immeasurably from the experience.

Here are a few such parents and their comments:

- Margo, forty-five, whose fourth child suffered brain damage as a result of a choking accident: "It's been a terribly rough five years, but seeing Ian's progress has been the greatest satisfaction I've ever felt."

- Jeff, thirty-eight, the father of an autistic daughter: "Of course I wish she were normal, but I still adore her. She has taught me to feel the purest love—something I never knew I had in me."

- Jane, forty-seven, whose son has severe dyslexia: "We've worked hard with the schools. Things were hard for a long time, but now Ted is making very fine progress, and he feels better and better about himself. We'll do whatever we can for him."

- Natalie, thirty, whose daughter is developmentally delayed: "There are problems of various sorts, but we just deal with them. What's satisfying is that Leigh is so happy. She's incredibly happy. And despite the problems, she makes the whole family happy, too. That seems to be her role."

FOURTEEN

EXPECTATIONS

Janet, a first-time mother, worries about her one-year-old son. "All my friends' kids were already talking by age one, but Scott says just a few words. I'm worried that he's developmentally delayed or something."

....

Before Samantha entered kindergarten, her parents had the girl tested by some educational consultants. The outcome: Samantha was well above average in intelligence. The girl's parents now worry that putting their daughter in kindergarten will slow her intellectual development; they want to enroll her in first grade instead.

....

Dale is twelve. Although intellectually capable, she doesn't pay much attention to her homework and prefers to socialize with friends. Dale's parents are disappointed by their daughter's academic performance but aren't sure if they should intervene, since the school counselor feels that Dale is simply showing an age-appropriate preoccupation with social relationships.

THE DANCE OF EXPECTATIONS

SOME PARENTS CLAIM that they have no expectations regarding their children. "I'll just let my daughter develop without my interference," they say, as if the child is a plant that only needs periodic watering. Other parents seem to have expectations of remarkable specificity: "I'm worried that my son turned eighteen months but still uses only a hundred words." The truth is that parenthood involves lots of expectations, and rightly so. The key question, however, is *which* expectations? It's proper to expect children to grow, change, and develop in certain ways, but the expectations need to be appropriate and realistic. And like so many other aspects of parenthood, finding that happy medium is easier said than done.

The good news is that your child will probably show you the way. There's a dance throughout the parenting years that is a give-and-take between what kids want and what parents want—a give-and-take, too, between what each partner in the dance is willing and able to provide. Initially, this dance is nonverbal—the baby's expression of needs and the parent's meeting of those needs—and later, as the child acquires the ability to speak, it's intensely verbal. Through words, body language, actions, behavior, and emotions, children tell us what they're ready to attempt, what they're reluctant to try, what they feel is the right thing at a given time. Parents, responding to the cues they see and hear, provide (or don't provide) the many forms of nurturance that make up parenthood. Throughout, there's a balance between expectations that are appropriate and expectations that are inappropriate. The whole process is complex, ambiguous, open-ended, and natural.

It's also often difficult. Just because this dance is natural doesn't mean it lacks a potential for conflict. Parenting a child is in many ways a tug of wills. You may expect one thing from your child, yet she may not be ready to do what you want, so she responds negatively to your expectation. Or she may expect something from you—a new level of independence, perhaps—that you're unwilling to provide. Parenthood proceeds in a complex sequence of conflicts and resolutions. But if you're tuned into your child, you can start to determine what she's trying to tell you.

Here are two examples.

First, the classic toilet-training scenario. Jack is two and a half years old. He's bright, capable, and independent-minded. Although he still wears diapers, he has developed enough sphincter control to time his urination and defecation to some extent. Meanwhile, Jack's mother, Mindy, feels that her son is ready to be toilet trained. But Jack is adamant: he wants to keep using diapers, so he resists his mother's efforts to make him use the potty. A standoff ensues. Are Mindy's expectations unreasonable? Probably not—but Jack's resistance isn't inappropriate, either. Mindy is right to raise the issue and start teaching her son to use the potty; at the same time, Jack isn't emotionally ready to stop using diapers, and he may not be quite physically ready, either. So the mother's expectations nudge her son, while the boy's reluctance allows him to fine-tune this particular developmental event.

The second scenario involves Bethany, a ten-year-old girl. Some of Bethany's fifth-grade pals are already hanging out at a local mall. The kids aren't entirely unattended; their parents run errands within the mall complex while the girls linger at a favorite ice cream joint. Bethany's parents aren't dead-set against this arrangement, but they aren't thrilled with it, either, and they regard it as somewhat premature for a ten-year-old. There's lots of tension between Bethany and her parents over this issue. At the same time, Bethany feels ambivalent: she worries about being in a public setting without her parents close by. In this case, the parents' reluctance to indulge their daughter coincides to some degree with Bethany's own mixed feelings. But within a year or two, the girl's expectations will require the parents to size up their own expectations and decide what's both safe and socially appropriate for their daughter.

THE INDIVIDUALITY OF DEVELOPMENT

Every child grows at his or her own rate. There are five different aspects of development within each individual: social, emotional, intellectual, verbal (language), and physiological (motor) development. Each child will develop in each of these ways at a different pace. As a result, there will be differences among an individual child's developmental aspects; and there will be differences among children, too—disparities between various children's development in relation to each other. Your child may have excellent fine motor development (she draws well, holds a pencil well, cuts paper well, etc.) while manifesting slower large motor development (she doesn't throw a ball as well as she performs other tasks). Your child may also be intellectually curious and have wonderful verbal skills but doesn't excel at putting words to her feelings. In short, development isn't a synchronized event even for an individual child.

What's important here? First, keep in mind that individual children develop at different rates *in relation to each other.* And second, children develop different skills or abilities *in relation to their own skills and abilities.* This is significant because it underscores what we all know intuitively: each child is unique. There may be norms or standards for every age group, but within that age group individual children fall above or below the norms. After all, norms are only averages. The tables and descriptions of developmental milestones for a given age group reflect statistical compilations.

The implications are important. It's difficult for you to know exactly what to expect from your child at a given time. More to the point, it's crucial not to be too specific in your expectations. Flexibility is paramount. If you learn that your child is performing tasks at a level different from the norm—whether higher or lower—it's worth keeping an eye on the situation. You may even need to intervene at some point; you don't want to neglect an emerging problem. Carefully observe what's happening. Obtain good advice if possible. Step in if you sense that your child is having genuine difficulties of whatever sort. At the same time, don't overreact. Many children have inconsistent development; intellectual growth may be out of sync with verbal or physical growth, social growth may be out of sync with emotional growth, and so forth. You don't want to jump to conclusions that your child is "behind" in some way simply because the statistical norms prompt certain expectations. Here again, parenthood is a delicate balance between having appropriate expectations and unrealistic expectations.

THE INEVITABILITY OF DEVELOPMENT

Here's another important issue to keep in mind: kids develop. Parents often worry that their children aren't developing fast enough, or developing right, but almost all children go through all the phases of development in spite of us, in spite of their own occasional periods of resistance, and in spite of the difficulties in our society. Kids have an inborn drive to grow, change, and develop. Even children living in difficult conditions tend to develop normally. (One of the most amazing examples of this fact is conspicuous in Anne Frank's famous diary, which shows a young girl experiencing the normal ups and downs of early adolescence despite the horrendous circumstances of her long confinement in Nazi-occupied Holland.) In short, children are resilient. With the ordinary encouragement, support, and educational opportunities, kids generally attain a large measure of intellectual unfoldment, personal satisfaction, and maturity.

What does this mean for parents? Once again, the core issue is simply to give your child as much support and unconditional love as possible. Providing a rich environment—interesting surroundings, a variety of friends and family members, good exercise, and aesthetic stimulation—is certainly worthwhile as well. But if you let your child simply explore her world and, over the years, acquire a greater and greater degree of autonomy, you have set the stage for optimal growth and development.

The issue of expectations is hard to avoid. You may have read, for instance, that intense stimulation benefits infants, and you may worry that you're doing too little for your child. Should you enroll her in a "baby enrichment" class? Should she start a foreign language when she's a toddler? Are math and language computer programs useful during the school years? How many playdates per week will foster good social skills? The answers to most such questions are complex.

In addition, your own personal experiences may intensify your concerns. If you had difficulties learning math as a child, you may feel anxious in ways that pressure your child to acquire these skills earlier than seems necessary or advisable. Your own parents' expectations about you during your childhood may influence what you want for your child. To cope with these situations, you'll do yourself a favor if you can stay aware and insightful about what expectations you feel, where they're coming from, and whether they're truly appropriate for your child.

THE BALANCING ACT

Parenthood is a delicate balancing act between too few and too many expectations. If you have too few expectations, you may not provide your child with certain developmental nudges that she needs; on the other hand, too many expectations may needlessly pressure your child. How can you decide what's right?

Here's a rule of thumb. If you feel fundamentally uncomfortable about a specific expectation, or if your child is uncomfortable or resistant, that may be a warning sign. If, on the other hand, you and your child feel comfortable with and relaxed about the expectation, you're probably on target. In short, trust your instincts when you're evaluating expectations for yourself and your child.

Outside views are worthwhile in evaluating the situation. Ask your child's pediatrician and teacher to offer their opinions. You can read up on many of these issues, too, in parenting or child development books. The information you find can be reassuring. At the same time, here's a caveat: child development researchers have a variety of theories, some of which contradict each other. It's easy to end up confused by the welter of ideas that experts advocate. So by all means do your homework. But always keep in mind that every child will develop at her own pace. There may be norms for children in general, but *these aren't exact predictions for any one child.*

Ultimately, you are the expert on your child. Keep an open mind, watch your child change and develop, and consider what you see and hear as thoughtfully as possible. If in doubt, trust your own judgment.

FIFTEEN

FAMILY LIFE

CONSIDER THE RELATIONSHIP between the words *family* and *familiar*. It's no accident that *familiar* derives from *family*, since *familiar* means well known, close, intimate. Ideally, family life is the basic source of what you find familiar—what's most comfortable, best known, meaningful, normal, and intimate about your daily routines, rituals, activities, structure, traditions, beliefs, values, roles, and relationships.

THE FAMILY AS A SUBCULTURE

In a sense, each family has a culture of its own that imparts the family's values, ways of doing things, belief systems, and ideas about relationships, roles, gender issues, decision-making procedures, and priorities. As is true for the larger surrounding culture, the family defines practical goals, spiritual and religious values, interpersonal relationships, decision making, and communication. Children also learn about kindness, generosity, respect, sharing, and reciprocity—or their absence—within the family setting.

What has changed within American society, however—and changed rapidly—is the sheer variety of different *kinds* of families. No matter how much some religious and political groups protest, the Mom-stays-home-while-Dad-goes-to-work type of family is now a distinct minority. Relatively few American households have a stay-at-home mother and a full-time–breadwinner father. Most family households have either two breadwinners or a single-parent breadwinner. There are single-parent families, gay and lesbian families, families with grandparents raising the grandchildren, and families with aunts and uncles raising nieces and nephews. Regardless of this diversity, however, many common elements exist from one family to another, elements that can add up in many different ways to create either a healthy, flexible family, or else a less healthy, rigid family.

THE COUPLE AS THE FAMILY'S FOUNDATION

In any family that includes a couple relationship—whether heterosexual or homosexual—the bond between the partners will form the family's foundation. Everything else will be built on this base. If the couple's relationship is strong, with a high degree of compatibility, self-esteem, and mutual respect—then the family will be much stronger than if the relationship is weak, conflicted, or ambivalent. Each partner comes to a relationship with his or her own memories, values, beliefs, customs, and traditions; how these aspects of individual background mesh or conflict with the other partner's background greatly influences the harmony or disharmony within the family.

The partners' harmony or disharmony will have an intense effect in at least two ways. One way is the couple's (and each individual partner) own states of mind. Sexual attraction, emotional chemistry, shared values, mutual acceptance, and communication style are all crucial factors in determining how well the partners get along throughout their daily lives and the journey of parenthood. To the degree that the partners can accept each other—including their differences—they will be that much better off in managing all their tasks together.

The couple's relationship also has dramatic effects on how the children perceive intimate relationships. The parents' bond will provide the kids' first basis for understanding relationships both during childhood and in the future. That is, you will be your children's primary role model for how intimacy works or doesn't work. Children who see positive, healthy, committed relationships have a better chance of transferring their sense of intimacy, compromise, and communication to their own relationships later in life. Children who witness constant bickering, competitiveness, anger, and hostility will probably have more trouble establishing a framework for communicating openly, honestly, and directly with other people. Either way, the parents' relationship sets the stage for family life both in the present and in the future.

FLEXIBILITY AND CONSTRICTION

As a therapist, I observe families of many different kinds. Some are clearly flexible and relaxed, with a great deal of spontaneous affection evident between the members; others seem tense and rigid, with unreasonable expectations and guardedness. Examining the characteristics of these two basic groups can help us see what makes family life either a nurturing or a depleting experience.

THE FLEXIBLE FAMILY

What I call the flexible family shows a high level of self-esteem and spontaneous, direct, honest, open communication. The family members express love and affection. Members in these families don't expect others to know automatically what they need or feel. They're able to ask freely for what they need, without fear of being judged or punished, and individual needs aren't considered antithetical to family needs. The family serves not only the family as a whole but also supports and encourages the individual members' development. Members are allowed and encouraged to become autonomous and to develop their own interests.

In short, there's a feeling of give-and-take within these families. The rules are flexible and fair. Family members participate in family meetings or discussions, and the children are allowed to have voice in these settings. They also listen closely to each other without interruption, and they take turns when speaking. Members can express all sides of their personalities and their feelings, including anger, resentment, disappointment, and joy. The parents don't dampen the children's spirits, and individuals can hold differing opinions, which are accepted rather than rejected. They aren't perfectionists, they can accept their imperfections and flaws and laugh at their mistakes. They accept human complexity. There's a feeling of joy and playfulness in such families. The family members feel sufficiently loved and cared for that they can share with others, and in general they support and cherish each other, truly like each other, and enjoy each other's company.

THE INFLEXIBLE FAMILY

By contrast, the inflexible family often has an imbalance of power within the couple's relationship—a me-against-you competitiveness that can undercut the members' confidence in each other. Family members talk but don't listen to each other, and they only grudgingly give each other turns to speak. Many inflexible families give the impression of unfulfilled expectations, resentment, regret, and guilt. Members frequently seem frustrated by unmet needs.

In inflexible families, there's often a stated or unstated belief that children should be seen and not heard, and that individual members are present to serve the family rather than the other way around. Rules tend to be numerous and strict. Attitudes are often black and white—there's a right way and a wrong way—without shades of gray. There's little or no room for tolerating individual experiences, complexities, or ambiguities. The most common communication style tends to suggest either open hostility or cold detachment. In such families, self-esteem tends to be low. Communication is often unclear, indirect, and manipulative. Name calling, blaming, and threats are common, with much behavior suggesting that members are avoiding, distracting, or

manipulating each other. There's a lot of meticulous analyzing and intellectu-
alization, too; family members are often out of touch with their feelings and
have difficulty expressing needs. Many emotions tend to be repressed or
avoided. Love isn't expressed warmly, openly, naturally, or spontaneously.
Family members often spend very little time together as a family; when they
do, they present an impression of a tense, uneasy, pent-up, or indifferent
group.

STRIVING FOR GENUINE HARMONY

One of your most important responsibilities as a parent is to monitor the
overall tone of your family's interactions for signs of distress, tension, resentment, or other difficulties. To do this you'll need to find a balanced approach.
On the one hand, you don't want to be overly scrupulous, finding problems
where only the normal ups and downs of family life exist; on the other hand,
you don't want to miss a chance to identify a real problem before it worsens.
The normal human desire to see the bright side further complicates the task.
Even so, it's crucial to keep an eye out for developments that warrant intervention. Typical issues of the sort I'm referring to include intensely reactive parent-child power struggles, acute sibling rivalry, a scarcity or excess of rules,
developmental issues affecting individual children (toddlerhood, school transitions, puberty), and so forth. Alert parents can intervene in these situations in
ways that make the difference between a flexible, happy family and an inflexible, unhappy, rigid one.

If you sense an issue that's burdening your family, confront it as soon as possible. Pretending or hoping that the problem doesn't exist almost never solves
it, but only makes it worse instead. Family life is so complicated that there's
nothing to be gained by wishful thinking or neglect. Besides, many relatively
small problems are easy to solve, and shoving an issue away may leave you with
a much worse problem down the line.

Another consideration: You don't have to face these difficulties alone. A
well-trained counselor, family therapist, or parent educator can help your family cope with the challenges you face. Although private therapy is expensive,
lower-cost resources exist: pastoral counseling through churches and synagogues; city- or county-subsidized counseling; counseling through some university and hospital training programs for therapists; and parent-education
classes through nonprofit organizations (which may also offers parent consul-
tations for gathering information, offering suggestions, and making referrals).

In addition, the following are some suggestions that can help you make family life as cohesive and creative as possible.

FIND TIME TO BE TOGETHER

The demands and stresses of contemporary life make it difficult for families to have relaxed, uninterrupted time together. All too often, parents and children don't even share meals as a family, and congenial time to play, talk, or do activities is increasingly hard to find. As a result, many parents lack opportunities to hear about their children's interests and concerns in detail. "Quality time" is no substitute for the less structured situations that often prove more satisfying and informative. I'm aware that current work schedules (as well as obligations to family and friends) often complicate the task that parents face when trying to spend time with their children; in some families, it's hard to find more than a few minutes each day when everyone is in the house at the same time. Still, it's important to try. Even a few shared meals per week are better than none at all. If relaxed family time requires some planning ahead, then planning is worth the effort.

FIND TIME TO DO ACTIVITIES IN DIFFERENT COMBINATIONS

At the same time, you shouldn't feel that all family members must do everything together. It's fine to honor the different relationships and individuals in the family; kids need time to pursue their own interests both alone and in conjunction with other family members. There's no reason that people shouldn't join together in different combinations for different purposes.

It's particularly important for the parents to have time to be alone with each other. Parenthood is so stressful that spouses or partners need opportunities to reenergize their relationship. Although children often protest when their parents go away, spouses shouldn't feel guilty for taking a sensible amount of time to be together. An evening date now and then is ideal; if that's not feasible, however, you should at least take time to go on a walk or have a cup of coffee together.

FIND TIME TO BE ALONE

You also need time for solitude. For many parents, time alone is the scarcest resource of all. One child or another always needs your attention; you never have a moment's peace. But the heavy demands on your time are all the more reason to schedule some time for yourself. Whether this means that the parents take turns "spelling" each other or that you find an outside sitter, you should work out some kind of arrangement to get away from time to time. Here, too, this arrangement isn't self-indulgent; it's a necessary way of easing tension, getting away from the hurly-burly of family life, and recharging your batteries.

FIND TIME FOR ONE-TO-ONE PARENT-CHILD ACTIVITIES

It's important that children have time with each parent alone as well as having time together as a family. Unless you have occasional "alone time" with each child, you can never really have a window into your child's soul or enough intimate conversations in which a child feels completely attended to, cared for, and loved. Children at different developmental stages need different kinds of attention; a twelve-year-old, for instance, may have concerns about preteen social issues or bodily changes that he or she wouldn't want to discuss in the presence of younger siblings. Similarly, a younger child may want a rowdier or sillier kind of playtime than what an older sibling would enjoy. The best way to address each child's needs is to set up at least sporadic opportunities for focused one-to-one interaction.

If your partner is available, take turns so that each spouse can take part in these activities. Your children may have specific needs for one parent or the other depending on their gender and developmental stage. Boys and girls will each go through stages when they need a close relationship with the parent of the same sex; at other stages, it's the parent of the other sex whose company is crucial. Be flexible about how you match the child's needs with the parent's attention.

BE FLEXIBLE REGARDING AGE-RELATED NEEDS

When your child reaches adolescence, he or she will probably prefer not to spend as much time together with the family. Many parents find this transition disappointing, since there's usually a marked decline in parent-child contact; however, this phenomenon is a normal part of a teenager's progress toward separation and independence. Your child's social life will become the center of his existence. The change will probably feel like a loss, but don't take the situation personally. If you allow your teenager enough time with friends, he or she will be much more receptive when you request participation in family activities. Similarly, asking for your teenager's opinion regarding trips and vacations will help him or her feel included in the process, hence less resistant to the notion of family travel.

FOCUS ON AGE-APPROPRIATE ACTIVITIES

When you try to meet every child's needs in a family of varied ages, it's hard to please everyone. A particular activity may delight some kids while frustrating others. You can deal with this situation by using an approach discussed earlier: each child gets special one-to-one time with a parent. Other arrangements require more compromise, since pleasing one child may mean disappointing another. The goal in any case is to focus on what your child may prefer, depending on his or her interests and age. Differences of opinion are almost inevitable. If you can stay consistent in letting children take turns, however, most kids aged five or older will realize the advantages of staying patient rather than trying to call all the shots. Also, expressing empathy when your child is frustrated may ease the child's concerns. Compromise of other sorts may help, too. For instance, many teenagers who may protest participation in family outings will agree more congenially if they can bring a friend along.

THE FAMILY IN TRANSITION

Families today are changing rapidly. Many pressures and stresses confront parents nowadays, but creativity and flexibility can help many people adapt to these changes.

If you live in a family that is different from the statistical norm, your child may face challenges from people's attitudes in the outside world. This issue frequently turns up for children with gay or lesbian parents; it's also common for children from ethnically diverse or interfaith families and even for families in which the parents are divorced. (This last situation is ironic, since such families are now almost more statistically normal than two-parent families.) In any case, your main task in these situations is to avoid taking outsiders' responses personally. Validate your child's feelings even if there's no way you can "fix" the situation.

If, for instance, your child comes home from school after having heard derogatory comments about your being a single parent (or gay, or lesbian, or whatever), try not to react to those statements. Simply listen to your child's feelings, take his concerns seriously, and don't blame or shame him if he makes negative statements about the family. Empathize with your child; validate his feelings, but don't feel that you have to defend the situation. Be straightforward and accepting: "Yeah, our family is different, but we're proud of who we are." Try to show your child that there's no right or wrong way to be a family. Families come in all sizes, shapes, and kinds. You have a right to be who you are.

THE FAMILY FOLLOWING DIVORCE

For options that can help a family in the aftermath of divorce, see chapter 10, "Divorce."

THE GAY OR LESBIAN FAMILY

If you and your partner are gay or lesbian parents, consider two factors that can help you cope with family life.

First, try to include members of the other sex in your extended family—your parents, grandparents, uncles and aunts, or friends. Make sure that your child has access to at least a few adults of the same sex as he is, whether as family or friends, since all children need these role models as they grow and develop.

Second, build an alternative family or community of friends if your own families of origin are hostile to your lifestyle choices. You may feel able to thrive without this more extended clan, but your children will need the support that a wider web of relatives or "relatives" can provide.

THE INTERFAITH FAMILY

If you're in an interfaith marriage, consider locating an interfaith group for support. Many spouses in interfaith marriages end up feeling isolated from or rejected by their families of origin; it's crucial that you find people who are sympathetic to the choices you've made. If you can associate with other interfaith families at least some of the time, your child won't feel so alone or so "different." In addition, having a community of interfaith families can, under some circumstances, provide opportunities for shared worship services, holidays, and other occasions.

In addition, you should have ongoing discussions with your spouse about your religious beliefs and practices well in advance of specific decisions. This process is important partly so that you and your spouse can understand what your preferences and goals are, but also so that you can work out a means of making decisions about holidays, rites of passage, and home life, and you can present a united front when you discuss these issues with your child.

Keep in mind, too, that spirituality isn't restricted to what takes place in formal institutions. Your spiritual insights and experiences can occur in nature, in an art gallery or concert hall, in your interactions with members of the wider community, and in the ordinary events of raising children. For a more detailed discussion of spirituality and family life, see chapter 45, "Spirituality."

THE IMPORTANCE OF ROLE MODELING

One of the most important dimensions of family life today is the opportunity for children to see their parents in nongender-oriented roles—for children to see their mother and father perform many or all parenting duties without "pegging" the roles according to gender. Dad has a career but also shops, cooks, does laundry, and takes care of the children. Mom goes to work, too, but also does many of the same domestic tasks as Dad. Given the pressures on parents, some division of labor is probably inevitable, but your children will benefit if the division is fairly equitable. When children see that roles are largely interchangeable—that Moms and Dads are flexible and willing to do whatever needs to be done for their families—the kids benefit greatly. What they perceive widens their perspective about their own particular mother and father, and it opens their minds about what being male or female really means.

The issue isn't a fifty-fifty split in who does what. A truly precise division of labor is rarely possible; each family will have its own struggle with practical realities and will reach its own conclusions about what works best. What matters most isn't attaining the ideal fifty-fifty; rather, the core issue is simply cooperation. What works best for your family? What can you work out with your spouse that meets your needs, expectations, responsibilities, and schedules? If you can support each other, doing what seems fair and attentive to everyone's needs, you're giving a great gift not just to yourselves, but to your children as well.

SIXTEEN

FATHERS

THE TITLE OF a recent article in the *New York Times* asks an odd, provocative question: "Daddy Dearest: Do You Really Matter?" Summing up the article's substance, the subtitle notes that "Everyone Agrees You Do, but So Far No One Has Established Why." The issue at hand is this: which attributes of fatherhood really make a difference to children's development, happiness, and well-being? Throughout history, people have recognized that fathers make a significant contribution to their sons and daughters, but there's widespread disagreement about what, exactly, fathers are (or ought to be) contributing. Should a father try to be his family's "leader"? Is it preferable for the dad to have a quasi-maternal role—Mr. Mom? Is day-to-day contact with children as or more important than an authoritative paternal presence?

It appears that even social scientists who specialize in studying families can't agree on what function fathers play in their children's lives. One researcher quoted in the article, Frank Furstenberg of the University of Pennsylvania, suggests that fathers' importance may be marginal: "My own theory is that once you have one good parent in place, having another . . . doesn't have a huge effect on children. It helps, but it's a subtle effect." Other sociologists and psychologists have their own theories, many of which contradict each other.

What's the upshot of all this disagreement? Does it imply that fathers *don't* matter? Not at all. As the article's author, Patricia Cohen, summarizes: "It seems self-evident to just about everyone who has ever had a father that a caring, involved dad is good for a child."

What also seems evident is that the *absence* of fathers is destructive. In 1960, fewer than eight million American children lived in families in which the father was absent. Nowadays nearly twenty-three million American children do not live with their biological fathers, and 40 percent of the children of divorced parents haven't interacted with their fathers in the previous twelve months. What are the implications of these statistics? As always, there's an enormous variety to the human experiences behind the numbers. Some children who live only with their mothers nonetheless have warm, sustaining relationships with their fathers. Other children—including those whose fathers have been physically abusive—benefit from having no paternal contact. On the other hand, many children clearly suffer the economic and emotional consequences of their fathers' absence from the home. Those consequences are alarmingly widespread:

- Compared to children living with both parents, fatherless children are five times more likely to live in poverty.

- Households with a father present have seen a steady rise in income from 1960 to 1990; during that same time span, households without a father experienced a decline in income.

- Fatherless children are at a dramatically greater risk of drug and alcohol abuse, mental illness, suicide, poor educational performance, teen pregnancy, and criminality.

- Children who exhibit violent behavior at school are eleven times more likely not to live with their fathers than are children whose parents are married.

- Fatherless children are twice as likely to drop out of school as children who live with a father, have contact with their biological father following a divorce, or live with a stepfather.

- Seventy percent of kids in state reform institutions grew up without their fathers.

I could quote one statistic after another. The pattern would state—would shout—the same message: *fathers matter.*

THE MYSTERY OF FATHERHOOD

Throughout most of human history, motherhood has involved a predictable series of biological events. A woman conceives a child; she carries the child to term; she gives birth to the child; she nurses the child; she nurtures the child during infancy and toddlerhood. Different cultures have perceived mothers in different ways and have defined their tasks by means of varying roles, but the basic events of motherhood have been consistent for thousands of years. Only within the past twenty years, with the advent of in vitro fertilization and other forms of advanced reproductive technology, has the physiology of motherhood started to change.

By contrast, the nature of fatherhood has been somewhat varied throughout human history. Some cultures have granted men a central place in the nurturing of children; others have offered men only the most peripheral of parenting roles. Biologically, the only act necessary to define a man as a father was for him to impregnate a woman. (Now even fertilizing an ovum doesn't require a man's physical participation.) One of the ironies of fatherhood is that a man can be a father without ever knowing it.

Despite the malleability of fatherhood as a role, however, almost all cultures have defined fathers as more than simply the impregnators of women. A father provides for his children, protects them, teaches them, or performs other duties involved with their upbringing. No culture—at least none that has survived—can dispense with fathers as a creative presence in its children's lives. In short, it's clear once again that fathers matter.

Why, though? In present-day America as in the past, one of the reasons is economic: children in two-parent households have a higher level of financial well-being than children in single-parent families, which lowers the stress on all family members and increases opportunities. But the higher income of two-parent families isn't the whole explanation. Children from low-income two-parent families, for instance, academically outperform students from high-income single-parent homes. Boys between the ages of one and two whose fathers are suddenly absent often experience sleep disturbances (trouble falling asleep, nightmares, and night terrors) within one to three months of the father's departure. Other aspects of behavior verify that the presence of a father is ideal for healthy child development. The variety of roles that fathers perform for their children doesn't deny their importance.

What Do Fathers Do?

Both anecdotal evidence and formal research show that fathers and mothers have somewhat different ways of parenting their children. My own personal sense is that many mothers—even those who seem strict with their children—are more embracing and consoling than most fathers; fathers, by contrast, often have specific external standards that they expect their children to attain. This situation suggests that mothers tend to offer kids a more nearly unconditional form of love, while fathers stress that their children should meet designated expectations. Both ways of being a parent can be nurturing and creative. It's possible that when thoughtfully combined, these differences prompt children to feel both fully accepted and progressively challenged toward greater and greater achievement.

FATHERS AND SONS

In addition, fathers have significantly different roles in relation to their sons and daughters. This is true even though many of the benefits that a father brings to his family hold true for children of either sex. Being present, providing a safe environment, preparing food, offering consolation and reassurance, monitoring countless changes, teaching what needs to be taught—these and other parenting tasks aren't gender-specific. Fathers can rest easy that most of what they provide their children will work equally well for boys as for girls. In addition, evenhandedness along gender lines is preferable to a more gender-specific approach. (For a discussion of gender bias and its risks, see chapter 19, "Gender Bias.")

It's also true, however, that fathers have some particular responsibilities and opportunities regarding their sons. The most significant issue is that a father's relationship with his son includes being a good gender-role model. At every developmental stage, a boy can gain from his father's presence. Babies benefit from having another adult who can lovingly nurture, protect, comfort, and play with them. Toddlers benefit in similar ways; in addition, they gain from a second firm, caring presence as they explore the world and test the limits of what is and isn't acceptable. Preschool- and school-age boys benefit from having a man to help teach them new skills, show them right from wrong, explore their own interests, and experience the world. Preteen and teenage boys need a male figure both to distinguish themselves from and simultaneously to look to for guidance, advice, and insight. During all stages, a father's stable, loving presence is invaluable. A boy may or may not ultimately choose to emulate his father's personality, follow his career, or accept his values, but he will generally end up better off if he has experienced a father's caring presence.

FATHERS AND DAUGHTERS

Similarly, fathers can have a unique and creative influence on their daughters. One significant role that a father plays in his daughter's life is psychosexual. That is, a father is crucial in a girl's developing her sexual identity from girlhood all the way to womanhood. The relationships that a child of either sex experiences with each parent will influence how that child perceives himself or herself; for a girl, the relationship with her father will shape her sense of herself in relationship to men. A warm, trusting, nurturing father-daughter bond will set the stage for positive relationships with male friends, colleagues, and potential mates. A cold, uneasy, debilitating, or demeaning father-daughter bond will set the stage for negative relationships in the future. In many respects, what a girl experiences with her father will, for better or worse, influence how she perceives every other man throughout the course of her entire life. The implication for her father is both a huge responsibility and a huge honor.

A FATHER'S TASKS

The most important action that a father can take is to be there on his children's behalf. In stating these words, I'm not invoking the cliché that "simply showing up is half the job." A cruel or abusive father is usually worse than none at all. What I mean is hidden in the words *on his children's behalf*. Love your kids. Be present in their lives. Look after them. Give them whatever gifts you have to offer. To put it simply: your children need you. The day-to-day, often tiny events of family life—dressing kids, fixing meals, playing games, telling stories, helping with homework—matter greatly. Big events—giving presents, showing up at birthday parties, taking major trips, attending special ceremonies—matter as well, but less so than the ebb and flow of little tasks and interactions.

I realize that being present for the day-to-day events isn't always possible. Divorce often separates fathers from their kids. (Family courts in some states treat fathers in ways that prompt them to feel like the "second parent," and some fathers end up sidelined, unable to spend routine time with their kids.) Even liberal custody arrangements can mean that dads don't have enough time to take part in the daily duties that matter so much. Work obligations (for both married and divorced parents) can also keep fathers away from their children far more than they'd like. So, yes, the day-to-day is often a luxury that people can only sporadically afford. In dealing with the limits that custody arrangements impose or that work schedules demand, you should simply do the best you can. There's often no alternative, and browbeating yourself won't help the situation. My point is simply that ordinary kid-centered activities often make more of a difference than grandiose gestures intended to "make up to the kids" for time away from them. Frequent, relatively brief occasions of hanging out, playing games, or helping with homework may prove more satisfying than rare, if protracted, fancy outings and special occasions.

Following are some suggestions for specific ways that fathers can support and nurture their children.

GET SAVVY

Perhaps you've already had some experience dealing with younger siblings, cousins, or nieces and nephews; if so, you're ahead of the game. But don't feel concerned if you're a first-time father. Many American men haven't taken care of children before they become fathers, yet they learn fast and do well once their own kids arrive on the scene. The key is to open your mind and get savvy. Some sources of information:

- *Your wife.* If your wife is experienced in caring for children, she's your best source of information. Best of all, you are parenting together, so you have the ideal situation for sharing her accumulated lore and advice. You may have differences of opinion—that's inevitable—but keep an open mind and learn as much as you can.

- *Friends and relatives.* Most relatives and good friends will happily offer their opinions about parenthood. Although they may give you an earful, don't dismiss their insights out of hand.

- *Books.* This country is awash in parenting books. You can find hundreds about babyhood and scores on other subjects. Take your pick. I recommend focusing on good overviews of child development (see books by Penelope Leach and T. Berry Brazelton in the Resource Guide) rather than "cramming for the final" through specific care-and-feeding manuals.

- *Classes.* Especially for first-time parents, good parenting classes can be invaluable. Some hospitals offer classes that go beyond prenatal training to provide a background in baby-care skills. Your local adult education program or community college may have offerings. Other classes focus on toddlers, preschoolers, and adolescents. Such information can be valuable; the companionship and accumulated advice of other parents can be still more so.

TAKE IT AS IT COMES

As you begin the great voyage of parenthood, you'll encounter many rough patches. Rest easy—the bumps are simply part of the terrain. One of the things that children do best (and often!) is to confound your expectations. If you want everything to go according to your plans, you're certain to feel frustrated. A wiser strategy: don't push the river.

One man described his experience to me as follows: "Before I had kids, I told a friend of mine—the mother of three teenagers—that I questioned my ability to go with the flow. She said, 'Well, if you don't know how to do that yet, your kids will teach you.' And they have."

So by all means learn everything you can ahead of time, plan well, and do what you can to keep family life organized. At the same time, be ready to scrap your assumptions and improvise. This advice holds true on everything from weekend plans to vacations to the whole of life itself. Parenthood is nothing if not unpredictable. Don't expect otherwise.

ACCEPT IMPERFECTION

There isn't a parent alive who doesn't mess up. You'll mess up, too. Like most American men, you'll feel terrible about it simply because our culture teaches you that guys should be cool, competent, and always in control. Here's a great parenting secret, though: it's generally okay to mess up. I'm not talking about major safety issues or serious lapses of judgment, just the regular daily mistakes. Rest easy. Everyone's parenting years are full of mistakes. Your children will survive, forgive you, and proceed to grow and develop regardless. Forget about cultural expectations of mastery and finesse. Just love your kids, do the best job you can, accept the imperfections of everyday life, and proceed.

LIGHTEN UP!

Last but definitely not least, don't forget to laugh. Parenting your kids may well be the most important thing you ever do, but it doesn't have to be serious. Accept the silliness and looniness of raising kids—*they* will, certainly. Maintaining your sense of humor will help you survive any number of crises.

HOW MOTHERS CAN HELP

If you're like many women, you may find it difficult to watch your husband sort out his role as father. Most American men have minimal experience caring for kids until the birth of their own children; as a result, wives often feel frustrated by their husbands' uncertainty and awkwardness. In other instances, women simply disagree with their husbands on how to perform certain parenting chores. Fair enough. If you find yourself dealing with these issues, however, it's worth stepping carefully to avoid undercutting your husband's good intentions and growing abilities.

GIVE YOUR HUSBAND TIME TO GROW

Fatherhood, like motherhood, involves enormous change. Few people of either sex understand the magnitude of how having children will alter their lives. If your husband feels confused or ambivalent, it's entirely understandable. Confusion and ambivalence don't necessarily indicate a fundamental doubt about parenthood. Give your husband time and support to sort through his feelings. Talk things out. By recognizing your own strengths and weaknesses as a parent, you can embrace the differences in parenting styles. One style isn't better than another, it's just different. And remember—children need *both* parents' styles for optimal growth and development. Stay open to the emotions that each of you will experience during the course of your years as parents.

Many men—sometimes even those who initially resist the notion of having children—end up becoming passionately devoted fathers. One man I know expressed his feelings this way: "I wanted to get married but never really wanted to have kids. Over the years, Sandy and I talked over the possibility and went around and around. I just couldn't imagine that kids would be more than a burden, and I didn't think I'd be a good father. Eventually I decided, Okay, we'll have a kid, but only one. And I wouldn't guarantee how good I'd be as a parent. But the moment Sandy gave birth, everything changed. Rachel came out and stared at me and I just melted. I fell madly in love. I knew right then that I'd do anything for my daughter. And I will. And the same goes for our son, Brandon, who was born three years later. I've had to learn while doing the job, but that's fine. My kids are great teachers."

In short, much of parenting involves on-the-job training. Many men I know find this surprising. In a culture where men often feel that they ought to know everything, it's a shock—and in some ways a relief—when they discover it's fine to learn as they go.

In addition, many men (not to mention women) are surprised how frequently they gain crucial hints or directions from children themselves. Kids often tip parents off about what they need—yet another reason we don't need to know everything. Both of these issues underscore the fact that many parenting tasks are acquired skills. If men haven't had early opportunities to acquire knowledge about child care, it doesn't mean they won't pick up what's necessary. Even the most insecure new dad can be a quick study.

GIVE YOUR HUSBAND *ROOM* TO GROW

Your husband and your child will have their own relationship, one that is inevitably different from what you have with the child. Whether your husband is familiar with child care or totally inexperienced, give him enough space to figure out his own ways of performing child care tasks. If you persistently criticize his methods or style, you may undercut his willingness to take part in what needs to be done. A dad named Jake told me, "I take care of our kids a lot, but every time I dress our daughter or fix her a meal, my wife steps in and does it over. She puts Samantha in a different outfit or fixes her a different meal. I end up feeling I'm not doing things right—my work isn't up to standards. It's depressing when I'm trying so hard." There's a risk in such cases that the husband will simply give up. This is a regrettable development for everyone concerned, but it's not entirely surprising. Yet as noted in part 1 of this book, mothers and fathers often parent differently; it's important that spouses respect and provide each other with enough leeway to do things in their own individual ways and at their own pace.

TAKE THE LONG VIEW

Becoming a skilled parent is a long process for everyone. Many men struggle with contradictory cultural messages before deciding the kind and level of involvement they want as the father of their children. In addition, practical considerations (among them the statistically likely role as primary wage earner) may complicate a husband's ability to be as involved with the kids as he'd like to be. All of these issues put both of you under pressure. How should you respond? That's a question that no one outside of your marriage can answer. But my recommendation applies to most couples: take the time you can—and offer each other the time you both need—to grow into the tasks and roles of parenthood. In the long run, working together can only serve you well.

SEVENTEEN

FINANCIAL PLANNING

MOST OF THE topics discussed in this book focus on the heart of parenting—the complex, ambiguous, unquantifiable decisions that affect our relationships with our children. I believe that these topics are what matter most about parenthood. There's another topic, though, one that deals with some of the practical means to these matters of the heart and spirit. This topic is money. And although I believe that money is greatly overstressed in our culture, money remains important, if only because it is part of the practical system by which we get things done.

What follows is a brief overview of financial aspects of parenthood. Since this book doesn't have space for a detailed discussion of this complex subject, I'm going to touch on a scattering of issues, primarily focusing on financial planning. This book's Resource Guide lists books and computer services useful in exploring these issues further.

ONE INCOME OR TWO?

One of the biggest decisions facing parents today is whether to earn one income or two, for the choice affects not only the family's overall financial well-being but also the division of labor and day-to-day logistics. Earning one income will mean less money to spend and save, but this arrangement frees one parent to look after the kids. By contrast, earning two incomes means more complex decisions about child care, transportation, and other practical matters, but it usually leads to higher gross earnings.

Which choice is preferable? That's a difficult question, one with no across-the-board right answer. But here are three factors to consider.

INTRINSIC SATISFACTION

For many couples, two careers make sense for nonfinancial reasons. Each partner wants his or her own job because the work is interesting or fun; it allows a sense of community; it leads to professional advancement; or it provides intellectual or emotional satisfaction. In short, work matters in its own right. Money isn't the main issue. If this situation applies to you, then two incomes will be only one aspect of a more central career decision. Similarly, you may find one income more acceptable if a career isn't so personally compelling.

THE HIDDEN COSTS OF A SECOND INCOME

Most parents, however, find the financial issues central to their decisions. They simply need the money. Raising a family is expensive—current estimates for bankrolling ages zero through twenty-two hover around $150,000 per child *not counting college costs*. Earning one income often isn't an option. And for most couples, net income will probably increase if both spouses work outside the home. You're probably better off financially if you are both wage-earners.

However, you should consider some hidden expenses that many people ignore when they assume that a second income will pay off as much as they expect. Being employed is expensive. Here are some of the additional costs that many couples face when both spouses are employed:

- Transportation (gas, parking, tolls, carfare, auto maintenance, etc.)
- Child care (day care, after-school care)
- Work clothes
- Domestic help (such as housekeeping services)
- Food (meals at work, take-out food because of limited cooking time)
- Tax withholding and FICA

THE TWO-INCOME TAX BITE

The final item listed above—tax withholding and FICA—takes many couples by surprise. No doubt you've figured that the second spouse's gross income will be reduced by federal and state income taxes. But that's not the only tax bite. In addition, FICA or self-employment taxes will further reduce your take-home pay. Keep in mind, too, that Social Security regulations may ultimately disrupt your ability to benefit from the second wage-earner's FICA payments.

What's the best way to proceed? Once again, nonfinancial considerations may swing a lot of weight. My point is simply that if you regard two incomes as a *guaranteed* means of raising your net income, think through all the implications first. Consult a financial advisor well before committing yourself to a specific decision.

A FINANCIAL CUSHION

Having a family means you *must* have a good financial cushion. You simply can't risk your children's well-being—not to mention your own sanity—by failing to sock away sufficient emergency funds. "Sufficient" generally means an amount equivalent to at least three to six months of your fixed and variable expenses. This financial cushion should be in a liquid account (that is, with easily accessible funds) without risk of losing your principal. Many people use money market funds for this purpose.

In addition to this financial cushion, you should consider having a second tier of contingency funds available. These could include:

- A line of credit (such as a home-equity loan)
- Credit cards
- Your 401(k) plan
- Loans against cash-value life insurance policies

The catch with all of these sources is that you must arrange them well before any emergency occurs; if you wait until you're financially pressed, many lending institutions will consider you a bad risk and may deny your request. In addition, you must maintain enough financial discipline to use credit only for true emergencies.

THE IMPORTANCE OF A BUDGET

Another crucial aspect of financial planning for families is a budget. Even if you're careful about how you spend your money, the costs of raising children will probably take you by surprise. This is especially true when your kids reach adolescence: teenagers are notoriously covetous and fashion-conscious; their schooling often requires expensive purchases such as sports gear, high-tech calculators, and computers; and their extracurricular activities may involve spending money on travel and special projects. Anticipating and funding all these costs requires as much financial planning as you can tolerate. And the bedrock of such planning is a budget.

To learn the standard methods for creating and following a budget, you should consult any of the standard financial planning reference works. (See the Resource Guide.) Another possibility is to use a computerized financial planning software program, such as Quicken or Microsoft Money. As you proceed, keep in mind that raising children will involve expenses in addition to the items listed in many personal budgets. Here are just a few possible categories that you should take into account:

- Child care (nanny, au pair, baby-sitter, child care center)
- Private schooling, tutoring, or lessons (music, art, etc.)
- Children's extracurricular activities (sports, Scouting, clubs)
- Moving to a bigger or better house (to gain access to better schools, etc.)
- Adding on to your current house (to accommodate more children)
- Travel (visiting relatives, taking family vacations)
- Medical expenses
- Dental care and orthodontia
- Increased insurance coverage
- College savings

INVESTMENT PLANNING

Concern over how to pay for all these expenses strikes terror in most parents' hearts. Unfortunately, there's no simple answer, and this book isn't a place for a detailed response. However, I can offer some initial ideas to get you going.

START EARLY

Financial planning is scary. To take control of the situation, you have to face difficult and often alarming issues. It's easy to sidestep the whole tangle of issues and hope for the best. That's courting disaster, though—first, because bad things really do happen even to nice people; and second, because there's nothing to be gained by stalling. In fact, stalling will complicate your problems. So tackle the issues head on. The earlier you start, the better off you'll be. What I'm saying is more than just a truism. Starting your financial planning early will pay off in the most tangible way, since any money you save will benefit from compounding of interest.

SEEK ADVICE

Financial planning is complex and often technical. Are you confused? Fair enough. But that's no excuse for ignoring the task or, on the other hand, for carrying the burden alone. You can find help from many sources. If you can afford it, obtain the advice of a financial planner—ideally, an independent financial planner who can offer you advice on a variety of methods and planning procedures rather than representing specific financial products. If you can't afford professional assistance, seek help from financial planning books and software products. You can learn a great deal from easily available resources.

EDUCATE YOURSELF

The more you learn about financial planning, the less anxious you'll be about the issues facing your family. You don't have to earn an MBA to get a handle on the situation; just start reading, ask questions of knowledgeable authorities, and go from there. Accept the fact that you'll make some mistakes along the way. As with every other aspect of parenthood, family finances are complex and often confusing. Don't berate yourself if you miss some opportunities or take a few gambles that don't pay off. The main thing is to take control of the situation.

INSURANCE PLANNING

One of the most important ways in which you can safeguard your family is through insurance planning. No matter what you decide to do regarding retirement accounts, the stock market, and other aspects of finances, it's a huge risk not to have enough insurance.

LIFE INSURANCE

I never cease to be amazed by how many people speak of death as an optional event: "If I should die . . ." Unfortunately, this kind of denial often expresses itself in ways that could be calamitous for these optimistic souls' families: many Americans have little or no life insurance. What's the outcome? Too often it's a surviving spouse who must struggle with financial hardship as well as personal tragedy.

How can you become well insured? First, realistically assess your current financial needs. Using a financial planning guide or software program, list your fixed and variable expenses for a given month, then multiply by twelve. Then list the sources of income (salaries, interest and dividends, existing life insurance, etc.) that your family would receive upon your death. Now compare the sources of income with your annual needs. The difference—and there probably will be a difference—is your *capital gap*. This is the shortfall between the amount of money you will have and the amount of money you need to provide for your family. Shocking? It usually is. The question now is how to close the gap.

There are, of course, many ways to close a capital gap, and the answers will vary for one couple to another. But for most people, life insurance is one of the easiest and most affordable ways to do so. Here again, you can gain an excellent overview of insurance issues from the standard financial planning guides. You can also obtain good advice from many independent financial planners. To the degree possible, avoid dealing with insurance agents who represent only one company, since most of them have no incentive to sell you anything but their own products. Finally: as with many other investments, start early. Premiums will be lower, and restrictions because of health issues will be fewer and less stringent.

OTHER KINDS OF INSURANCE

In addition to life insurance, you should carefully consider your needs for health insurance, disability insurance, and property/casualty insurance.

Health insurance is one of your most critical investments. If you're lucky, you'll have good coverage through your employer. If not, don't sidestep the issue. Even a brief hospitalization can cost tens of thousands of dollars, and a major accident or illness can easily bankrupt you. Do whatever you can to obtain good coverage.

Disability insurance is a form of coverage that many people neglect. For people in good health, it's difficult to imagine the possibility of a disabling illness or accident. Many young people, especially, see the situation as all-or-nothing: "Either I'll die or I'll survive." But there are many gray areas between perfect health and outright death. Even something as simple and survivable as a broken leg may leave you temporarily unable to support your family. Keep in mind that Americans between the ages of twenty and forty are statistically much more likely to suffer disability than a fatal accident or illness during that stage of life. Although disability insurance is expensive, consider the costs of leaving your family unprepared for months or years of unemployment.

Property/casualty insurance is coverage that protects you and your family against economic loss if your property is damaged, or if someone sues you because of injury or damage to their own property. The most common kinds are homeowners' insurance and auto insurance. You probably have both. But do you have enough? Here, too, you may discover you have a capital gap. Whether on your own or with professional assistance, run the numbers and define your actual needs.

ESTATE PLANNING

Like insurance, estate planning requires you to think about calamitous events, so it's understandable if you avoid the issue altogether. This is a big mistake, however—one that can cause untold heartache and hardship for your spouse and children. You owe it to them to face the situation and make careful decisions.

The standard advice regarding estate planning follows these general steps:

- Calculate the size of your estate.

- Decide on your estate planning objective.

- Make a realistic plan.

- Provide for financial liquidity (that is, easy access to cash).

- Minimize taxes.

- Review the plan over time and make changes when necessary.

Using the financial planning resources I've mentioned, you can gain an overview of your needs and sketch your options. Ultimately, however, you'll probably need legal advice to help you with the specifics. The most common outcome of such advice is a will. (Other options exist, however, including various kinds of trusts.) I can't overstate the importance of having a will or some equivalent document to define your wishes following your death. If you die *intestate*—that is, without having a valid, up-to-date will—your assets will be distributed according to state law regardless of your wishes. Other crucial aspects of estate planning for parents include:

- Designating a guardian for your children

- Specifying a trustee to manage any trusts you set up

- Writing a testamentary letter—a handwritten letter setting forth how you wish your personal belongings to be allotted

FINANCES FOR SINGLE PARENTS

The issues we've discussed in this chapter apply as much to single parents as to couples; the difference is simply in degree. It's difficult to face all these complex financial matters alone. I know that all too well—I've been a single parent myself. But there's no alternative to tackling the issues. No one else can make these decisions for you. And since you're raising your kids alone, any misfortune that befalls you, whether major or minor, can have huge consequences. Weave the best safety net you can, and make it strong.

TEACHING KIDS ABOUT MONEY

One last issue: financial education for your children, which is almost as important a topic as those we've discussed so far.

Here as in so many other aspects of parenthood, you have a fine line to walk. On the one hand, you don't want to make your kids anxious about money; on the other, you want to teach them financial responsibility. American culture, with its emphasis on consumerism, will constantly barrage your children with messages that acquiring stuff—*more more more!*—is what matters. How can you help them see that money and possessions are only a small part of what makes life satisfying and meaningful?

Here are just a few suggestions:

- *Set a good example.* Make a budget and keep to it. Show that it's fine to enjoy the good things in life, but only in proportion to what's financially sensible. Don't go on spending sprees. Save money. Give to charity.

- *Give your kids an allowance.* Let children over age five have a small allowance, then earn more money for chores. Use incentives to teach responsibility. At the same time, make sure that everyone in the family tackles some duties for free *simply because you're all working together.*

- *Teach your children to save.* Let young children open a savings account. Allow teenagers to learn about other investments—stocks, savings bonds, etc.—by making small investments.

EIGHTEEN

FOOD

PARENTS OFTEN FACE power struggles with their children over food, and at inopportune times—when you're busy, when you're getting ready for work, or when you're hoping for a relaxing family meal at the end of a stressful day.

Food is a loaded issue for several reasons. Among young children, one reason is that eating is one of the very few aspects of their lives that they can control. (Another such aspect is elimination.) Older children, too, may use food to exert power over their parents. A common situation is wrangling over rules—for instance, how much nutritious food a kid must eat before indulging in dessert. A less common but more worrisome example is the increasing incidence of eating disorders like anorexia and bulimia, which often exemplify parent-child power struggles. Unfortunately, these struggles mean that mealtimes, which should be times to relax, are often stressful experiences.

EASING THE STRESS OVER FOOD

How can you avoid battles over food issues? Precisely because food is so important to children (and parents!), there's no simple solution to the problems that arise. To complicate matters, children's nutritional needs change as they grow and develop, which means that you must respond in different ways over the years.

BE A GOOD ROLE MODEL

If you eat a healthful diet and aren't obsessive about food, your child will be predisposed to eat well, too. On the other hand, if you indulge in a high-fat, salty, sugary diet, if you engage in faddish dieting, or if you have a weight problem, your children will be inclined to imitate your behavior. Children will generally develop nutritional tastes similar to their parents'. So by all means give your children information about food and nutrition, but focus on being the best role model possible. Particularly around the middle school and teen years, kids won't pay much attention to your words anyway; it's all the more crucial to practice what you preach. Arguing will only create the power struggles you want to avoid.

PLAN AHEAD

In the feeding of kids, as in other situations, good planning will contribute to sanity. Stock your cabinets and fridge as fully as your budget and kitchen space allow; plan meals in advance; think through your logistics. But remember, Murphy's Law definitely applies to cooking for kids, so be ready to change your plans when necessary. Your child will suddenly refuse what he's insisted on eating for years. He'll bring home two friends for dinner. You'll discover that you forgot to buy the food you planned to fix. There's always some kind of hitch.

Eating together as a family is important (more on this point shortly) but you'll often need to work around family members' schedules. In larger families, it may work well for one parent to feed one or more kids while the other parent helps other children with homework, baths, or school-related activities. Insisting on a fixed schedule has its merits, but only up to a point; if in doubt, be flexible.

AVOID FOOD FANATICISM

Although I strongly believe that children need and deserve a nutritionally sound diet, I also recommend that you avoid food fanaticism. Pushing any one set of dietary beliefs almost always backfires. I have a friend who was so strict about her son's nutrition, for instance, that she forbade the boy to eat any dessert of any kind. Sweets were *out*. When her son went to birthday parties, he'd eat a special organic fruit salad while the other children ate birthday cake and ice cream. This little boy grew up intensely obsessed with food—but not the health foods his parents advocated. I've never seen a child more fixated on cakes, pies, candies, ice cream, icing, and everything else that's sweet. Small wonder. Anything taboo will become what your child wants most. My recommendation? Be moderate. Let your child explore different foods. A balanced diet is the goal, but most kids will go through phases, even crazes, that eventually pass if you don't object to them too hard.

Two other recommendations: Don't make your child eat foods that he truly dislikes, and don't use food as a reward or as something to replace or substitute for your love. Eat-this-or-else situations set up power struggles down the road.

If you insist on your child eating a particular meal or food, he's almost certain to reject it. Keep in mind as well that children's taste buds are so sensitive that many foods appealing to adults are overwhelming, even repulsive, to kids. Just ask your child if he'd like to try a certain food. If he says no, back off. Wait till he's somewhat older, then try again. Give him a degree of control. If you don't insist on calling the shots, he's more likely to be flexible and curious about food in the future.

INCLUDE KIDS IN KITCHEN DUTY

Some food issues focus on preparation rather than eating. It's hard to cook when your kids are around, especially if they're toddlers or preschoolers. Distracting them with TV only goes so far and has built-in drawbacks. Besides, children sometimes just want to be with their parents. How do you cope with this situation?

- Let toddlers "cook" nearby with toy utensils while you do the real thing. Many young kids happily occupy themselves by imitating Mom or Dad.

- Set up preschoolers to stand at the kitchen sink and do water-play while you work nearby. If you provide them with soapy water and nonbreakable dishes and utensils, they can have safe fun while you're cooking.

- School-aged children can perform actual cooking duties. If you tolerate some initial messiness while they learn, even kids as young as five or six can help out productively and often delight in the responsibilities of real work.

- Other children can do other useful tasks such as bringing you ingredients and utensils, mixing, stirring, and setting the table.

- Many kids also enjoy helping to plan meals—playing "chef," deciding on menus, looking up recipes, and so forth.

- Consider using a children's cookbook occasionally rather than relying only on standard adult recipes, or create a cookbook for your child that contains his or her favorite recipes.

Even if your child helps out now and then, his assistance will ease some of the pressure on you. Helping out in these ways can also teach responsibility and encourage participation in preparing food, which can heighten eagerness to eat what you've prepared. A child who really enjoys cooking can benefit from kid-friendly classes, too, such as those offered by many local YMCAs and YWCAs. The most important goal, however, is simply to encourage your child to be part of a group endeavor—each member of the family helping the others—rather than to assume that you're there simply to wait on him. This attitude encourages independence and responsibility, which will serve him well in both the short and the long run.

SERVE KID-FRIENDLY MEALS

Children sometimes feel that food isn't kid-friendly even when they're eager to eat; portions are too big or difficult to pick up with conventional cutlery.

- For babies and toddlers, eating is an intensely sensory experience; let them mush and squash the food if necessary.

- Young children often like smaller portions than adults serve. A few spoonfuls of peas are sufficient, for instance; a full serving seems too big to be appealing.

- Special plates and kid-sized cutlery can ease the task for younger children.

- Most children eat quickly, but some are simply slower and, if possible, shouldn't be rushed; be flexible about the pace of meals.

- Although it's important not to overreact to concerns about sweet foods, you can simplify your life to some extent by timing snacks properly. If you can, avoid giving your child sweets late in the day, especially right before bedtime. Indulging a desire for sweets at less disruptive times—after lunch or on weekends—may limit the temptation to be rigid about treats and may help to keep your child relaxed and calm at these times.

BE READY FOR AGE-APPROPRIATE SHIFTS

Children go through major physiological changes that affect their appetites. The most predictable shifts occur during toddlerhood and puberty, when kids often eat voraciously. Other shifts are more idiosyncratic. To the degree possible, be ready for these age-appropriate surges in appetite; don't limit your child's intake at a time that's simply a growth spurt. (When my son reached adolescence, I used to joke that if I hooked a conveyor belt from the grocery store straight to my son's mouth, I still couldn't feed him fast enough.) Note also that these surges of appetite differ depending on children's body type, genetic predisposition, metabolism, and so forth.

WIDEN THE KIDS' HORIZONS

To the degree possible, widen your child's horizons regarding food. He'll benefit from experiencing even a few different cultures' culinary traditions. Beyond the aesthetic dimension, though, these experiences will help prepare your child for meeting people with different tastes and customs. The easiest way to approach this goal is simply to eat out occasionally at different kinds of ethnic restaurants. You don't have to get fancy or spend a lot of money. Just take your kids out now and then to places that serve foods from other countries. There are lots of inexpensive ethnic restaurants. Alternatively, you can experiment by cooking ethnic foods at home or by visiting street fairs that sell food from different lands.

EAT TOGETHER AT LEAST SOME OF THE TIME

Many parents I know complain that their family members are too busy to eat together. This is understandable, given the schedules that we all face these days. Still, sharing meals as a family is crucial for a sense of connectedness to each other. I feel that a family should eat together at least once or twice a week, more if possible. Sports schedules, lessons, work obligations, and social commitments all complicate the opportunities; with a little patience, foresight, and planning, however, you may be able to work out more family meals.

To the degree possible, make meals relaxing and comfortable. It's good to hear everyone's stories about their activities and experiences, but try not to bring up stressful issues that can create conflicts. If arguments arise, acknowledge that they are important, but address the problems later.

TAKE OCCASIONAL SHORTCUTS TO SAVE YOUR SANITY

The *Leave It to Beaver* era is long gone. Few families have a stay-at-home parent who can prepare fancy, elegant meals on a routine basis. Although I strongly feel that family meals are important, I don't advocate extravagant cooking for its own sake. Excessively high standards can aggravate the already abundant stresses of family life. Likewise, although I urge an overall emphasis on good nutrition, an occasional meal at Friendly's or McDonald's won't kill anyone. Sometimes you need to take shortcuts to save your sanity. This route is far healthier in the long run than being obsessive and perfectionistic. Check around to see what options you have. Some local restaurants have special nights when children eat free. The goal is to ease stress when possible, both for yourself and your kids.

AVOID POWER STRUGGLES OVER FOOD

There's a fine line between giving kids too much choice over food and giving them too little. If you're careful, you can avoid most power struggles.

- For younger children, give them a choice of one or two things to eat. Don't allow more than a couple of options.

- Try to prepare at least one food that you know your child really *does* enjoy, as this allows a built-in fallback.

- For toddlers and preschoolers, don't get too worried about the child's insistence on one food over all others. Kids usually eat a variety of foods over a period of time. All carbohydrates for a full day or week, or all proteins for a full day or week, won't hurt them; nutritionally, things will balance out eventually.

- Don't get too hung up on having a precisely balanced meal every single time. Just let them enjoy the food and not make a power struggle out of it.

IF YOU'RE CONCERNED ABOUT EATING DISORDERS . . .

Many parents ask me how to determine if their child has an eating disorder. This is an important question. More and more American children are manifesting signs of eating problems, and it's important to keep an eye out for telltale signs. That being said, it's also true that relatively few children are afflicted. All children have ups and downs in their eating patterns; many children focus occasionally on a single food to the exclusion of others. Children's appetites also vary widely—from voracious to indifferent and back again—as they grow and change.

However, eating disorders can be a serious problem. Some children tend to use food as a way of comforting themselves, punishing themselves, gaining power and control, or repressing their feelings. As a parent, you should avoid doing things that reinforce that sort of behavior. If your child needs a hug or feels sad, don't give him food as a substitute for your love. Ask him what's bothering him; offer comfort—time, attention, and emotional support—but don't use food as consolation. This response can set the stage later for habitual use of food as a substitute for love or comfort. So by all means talk to your children about their feelings, but don't encourage relying on food as compensation for fear, self-doubt, or anxiety.

Anorexia and bulimia are significant issues that warrant professional help. Is it possible that your child has a problem with one of these conditions? (Note: 90 percent of children with eating disorders are girls.) The standard warning signs for anorexia and bulimia are listed below.

Anorexia:
- Persistent refusal to eat, or to eat abundantly enough in relation to the child's size and age

- Relentless dieting, even when the child is obviously underweight

- Insistence on eating vegetables or other low-calorie foods to the exclusion of other foods

- Use of appetite suppressants

- Compulsive exercise with intent to burn calories

- Recurrent or compulsive need to vomit

- Inappropriate use of laxatives

- Cessation of menstrual periods

- Failure of adolescent "growth spurt" to begin, perhaps including absence of secondary sexual characteristics (breasts, pubic hair)

- Severe fatigue, depression, and inability to concentrate

Bulimia:
- Binge eating, especially of high-calorie foods such as ice cream, candy, etc.

- Severe, repeated weight gain and weight loss

- Recurrent or compulsive need to vomit

- Inappropriate use of laxatives

- Severe fatigue, depression, and inability to concentrate

Trust your instincts about what's happening. Tune in to your child to get a sense of what your child is feeling. If you need an outside opinion, ask your pediatrician for her insights. You can also find useful information in the Resource Guide.

Whatever you do, don't jump to conclusions and start your child on a diet. Dieting of any sort deserves careful scrutiny; most diets have significant physiological and psychological effects, especially on children, and some will aggravate rather than ameliorate any underlying emotional conditions. A joint approach—combining a physician's recommendations and a therapist's insights—is crucial.

NINETEEN

GENDER BIAS

WHEN I ASK parents about gender differences, most state that boys and girls behave differently in some respects. Many parents assert that these differences exist even at a very early age. Some believe that they can see the differences from the time of their children's birth. "Boys and girls are so *different*," many parents have told me, at once emphatic and bland. One father phrased his perception with cosmic exaggeration: "Boys and girls come from different galaxies." A friend describes her daughter and son in all-or-nothing terms: "Sally is 100 percent girl and Damon is 100 percent boy."

While there may or may not be substance to these claims, one thing is clear: every culture has some biases about the "nature" of males and the "nature" of females, and American culture is no exception. As a result, our society expects at least slightly different behavior from girls and boys; we respond to the behavior of boys and girls differently; and our expectations in turn affect how our sons and daughters respond to us. One result of this chain of expectations is gender bias.

ARE THERE INNATE MALE/FEMALE DIFFERENCES?

Some innate male/female differences do exist. Males and females are slightly different in their genetic makeup. The two sexes have different reproductive organs and urinary anatomy. Males' and females' endocrine systems, including the nature and levels of hormones at various developmental stages, are markedly different. There also appear to be subtle but significant differences in brain structure, as well as in some neurological functions, though these differences are only now beginning to be identified and understood.

What does this indicate about the differences between boys and girls? Recent studies may suggest that baby boys as a group are more emotionally expressive, while baby girls as a group are more reflective. When unhappy, baby boys tended to cry more; in the same emotional state, girls tended to suck their thumbs and comfort themselves in a quieter way. What do these patterns of behavior tell us? As always, that's open to interpretation. One possibility is that girls may be more consistently able to control their emotions, while boys vent their emotions outwardly. But the implications of these findings are unclear.

Scientists have known for some time that even very young boys have higher levels of testosterone than girls do; in addition, researchers know that boys have lower levels of seratonin, a neurotransmitter that inhibits aggression and impulsivity. These differences may help to explain why boys are often less complacent and cooperative than girls, and why they tend to be more aggressive and more impulsive than females. One implication: when teachers observe boys and compare their activity level to that of girls, they may tend to interpret the raucousness as indicating pathology, when in fact the high level of activity may be normal for male development.

RESPONSES TO THESE DIFFERENCES

By the time children go off to school, both biology and culture ("nature" and "nurture") are shaping both boys and girls. The kind and degree of influences are complex and intertwined, and they are often hard to separate. In any case, the result tends to be a disparity in children's behavior and in the responses that others make to the behavior:

- Boys generally manifest a greater abundance of physical energy.

- Boys generally are more physically assertive and outgoing.

- Boys tend to be reprimanded more often than girls in the classroom.

- As a consequence, boys receive more of the teacher's verbal attention than girls do.

- Boys tend to overestimate their academic skills.

- Boys tend to be reinforced for their independence.

- Girls are generally quieter and less strident in school settings, hence less likely to be reprimanded as often.

- Girls tend to be praised for their neatness, politeness, quietness, and cooperativeness.

- Girls tend to underestimate their academic skills, especially after age nine and older.

- Girls tend to be praised more often for cooperative behavior—being calm and quiet, being the teacher's helper, staying close to the teacher.

- Girls tend not to get as much attention, at times as a side effect of teachers' concentrating on managing the boys.

ACADEMIC SIDE EFFECTS

Although the tendency toward gender stereotyping may vary, the consequences of these differences—whether they result from nature or nurture—are often troubling. And one of the most difficult and contentious areas that gender differences affect is the academic arena.

Over the years, social scientists have noted some gaps in how male and female students perform in certain academic areas. Boys *as a group* often outperform girls *as a group* in math, science, and social studies. Girls *as a group* often outperform boys *as a group* in reading and writing skills. In addition, researchers have found that when girls enter middle school, at around age nine or ten, they start to lag behind their male counterparts in several areas, and they lag distinctly behind boys in the areas of math and science by the time they reach high school.

What do these differences in academic achievement mean? One explanation—more often implied than stated outright, and always hotly disputed—is that girls as a group have less aptitude than boys do in math and science. Another explanation is that social pressures, including widespread cultural messages that math and science are "male turf," influence girls into expressing less interest in these subjects, studying less rigorously, and perceiving themselves as less competent.

In response to these issues, many parents and educators have attempted to address the situation. Teachers have tried to encourage girls' efforts in math and sciences. Educational advocates have urged schools to let girls be more outspoken and more assertive in the classroom. In addition, teachers and counselors have tried to help boys learn to be more accommodating and group-oriented. Both responses serve to address fairly common shifts that children undergo during the middle school years.

It's important to note the psychosocial aspects of what is happening. Starting in the middle school years, girls are going through puberty and often focus less on academics than on social concerns, including winning boys' approval and attention. At the same time, boys tend to become more stereotypically macho and often repress their "softer" sides, squelching emotions such as tenderness, affection, and sensitivity. In short, both girls and boys tend to exaggerate identification with rather extreme stereotypes of femininity and masculinity. This exaggeration is normal to some extent, part of the ordinary processes of self-definition during puberty. To a great degree, however, it is learned behavior. Children are unwitting recipients of a barrage of messages—from society, from teachers, from the media, and from parents—regarding gender roles in society. Small wonder, then, that pubescent boys end up more and more "boyish" and girls end up more and more "girlish." The vague but powerful influences of culture are difficult to resist.

GENDER BIAS IN SCHOOLS

To complicate matters, most teachers bring their own sociocultural biases, beliefs, and values into the classroom. In the early years, this may stack the deck against boys. Later, girls are more likely to suffer the consequences.

Early childhood education is a predominantly female profession. An energetic boy who has difficulty sitting still isn't likely to be considered one of the teacher's little darlings. On the contrary, such a child may end up labeled a disciplinary problem—an unruly child, a disruptive student, or a child with attention-deficit and hyperactivity disorder (ADHD). There are, in fact, more boys than girls who are clinically hyperactive or affected by ADHD. However, many boys are currently being misdiagnosed with ADHD when they are really just normal, energetic boys. (See chapter 12, "Energetic Children and Hyperactivity.") It's often difficult for female teachers to understand a young boy's behavior. (See chapter 3, "Boys.") We need to start appreciating, understanding, and accepting that boys and girls manifest some significant behavioral differences. These differences shouldn't be used as reflexive, across-the-board judgments about all boys and all girls. They should be considered, though, in defining expectations.

As we've already noted, the middle school years begin a phase during which girls may be more consistently shortchanged at school. Assertive boys may overwhelm some girls' classroom participation. Previously confident girls may withdraw to some degree from academic pursuits as they struggle with issues of self-image, values, and social expectations. Curricula may be out of sync with girls' educational needs. Even fairly progressive schools may shortchange girls' needs for mentoring, collegiality among peers, and differing educational interests.

PARENTS' EXPECTATIONS

Last but certainly not least, parents' own attitudes and actions about gender differences help to form each child's sense of self, self-esteem, and confidence. We want to help our children become the best people they can be. If we have parental expectations, these can influence how far a child will go in reaching his or her greatest potential. Either set of expectations can become a vicious cycle.

Low expectations can lead to indifference, discouragement, and limited success or endeavors. High expectations can lead to confidence, pride, and greater success. (However, high-pressure or unreasonable expectations can be as harmful as low expectations.) If we have certain preconceived ideas of what constitutes a boy and what constitutes a girl—if we have a predefined sense of what interests are appropriate and what behaviors are permissible for each sex—then we risk limiting the child. We're not really looking at the child as a whole person; we're placing our own gender biases onto the child. This, too, can create a vicious cycle that alters the child's self-image.

HOW TO DIMINISH GENDER BIAS

Given what we've been discussing, how can you protect your child from gender bias? How can you help your son or daughter to develop without the pressures of restrictive expectations?

Look at Your Own Roles, Relationships, and Behavior

Consider your values and beliefs about gender roles.

- How traditional are your views of male and female abilities and interests?
- How polarized is your sense of masculine and feminine "nature"?
- How open-minded are you willing to be about what both boys and girls can achieve and become?
- What are your expectations and attitudes?
- Do you treat your sons and daughters differently?
- In what ways do you treat them differently?
- In what ways do you treat them the same?

Be Flexible About Gender Roles and Behaviors

Allow your son—in fact, encourage him—to be empathic and to express all his emotions, including his fears, doubts, and insecurities. Let him engage in caregiving roles. By all means encourage his interests in traditionally "masculine" pursuits (math, science, sports, etc.) but support his interests in literature, art, music, and other traditional "feminine" subjects.

Likewise, encourage your daughter's interests in all studies, disciplines, and activities. Give her strong reinforcement as she studies math and science. Encourage her interests in sports, travel, and so forth. Allow and encourage her to express her competitive and assertive sides, as well as her feelings of anger and frustration.

BE PATIENT

These tasks will be especially difficult during the middle school years, when social pressures to conform are greatest. My experience, however, is that after those early teen years—once children have gone through puberty and have established a clearer sense of identity—they don't have to adhere to such exaggerated images of male and female. Be patient. This phase, like all others, will pass.

DON'T BE ALARMED BY EXPERIMENTATION

Children who manifest traditional gender norms—the all-American boy, for instance, who loves sports and rough play—may eventually start to explore other roles and interests. This is a good development. Encourage it by being open-minded. On the other hand, some independent-minded kids may suddenly grow more conventional. One example is the athletic girl who suddenly becomes preoccupied with hair, nails, and makeup. This may strike some parents as retrograde motion, but here again you should be patient. She is probably just trying out new roles and self-images. At some point it will all balance out. The same holds true if your son, who has been affectionate, suddenly pulls back emotionally.

Children can, in fact, become extremely conservative, even small-minded, despite what they know about reality. When I was head teacher in the nursery school at the Duke University Lab Pre-School, one of the little girls, Darla, insisted that girls couldn't be doctors, only nurses. "But your mommy is a doctor," I told her. "No, no, no!" Darla insisted. "Mommies can only be nurses!" This assertion totally ignored the fact that her own mother was a doctor! Such is the power of sexual stereotypes that during certain developmental phases, children will rigidly adhere to certain criteria for what is feminine and what is masculine. Fortunately, this rigidity often diminishes as children begin to feel more comfortable within their own gender identification.

TAKE ACTION

Do what you can to overcome gender bias directly.

- Encourage girls in technological studies and pursuits. Do science, math, and computer activities with your daughter.
- Teach girls practical skills—carpentry, house painting, car repair, or any other skills you possess. Encourage interests in a full range of disciplines, sports, trades, and professions.
- Sign your daughter up for a science lab or a computer course.
- Encourage boys to express themselves verbally.

- Encourage boys to be open to their own feelings. What disappoints them? What makes them feel vulnerable? What scares them?

- Give boys the vocabulary and communication skills to verbalize and identify what they're feeling. Let them know that expressing emotions is a strength, not a weakness.

- Stress to both boys and girls that every person has the right to express his or her own personality.

- Reassure your daughter that girls have the right to express anger, to speak out on issues, to have opinions, to stand up for themselves, to be assertive, to be counted on and valued.

- Give boys an opportunity to take care of and nurture other people.

- When boys act in egocentric or noncommunicative ways, encourage them to get more involved with people and relationships.

- Express affection through hugs, etc., to both boys and girls.

- Stress to boys that it's okay to get mad, but help them develop ways of expressing themselves in nonphysical ways. Create opportunities that help boys to communicate.

- Parents need to be role models for nonstereotypic behaviors, since their example is the most powerful force that children will emulate.

EMOTIONAL LITERACY

One of the biggest tasks involved in overcoming gender bias is emotional literacy. Gender bias in our culture limits the ways in which both boys and girls learn to express themselves. To some degree, emotions end up parceled out as relatively masculine or relatively feminine. Certain feelings are allowed or disallowed to members of each sex. Anger is often considered fine for boys but unseemly for girls to feel and express. Similarly, hurt and sadness are regarded as acceptable for girls but pathetic or contemptible in boys. This dividing up of the emotional spectrum is a loss for everyone. As a parent, do what you can to allow your children—boys and girls alike—to feel what they're feeling. Feelings aren't right or wrong; they just *are*.

The issue of emotions may be especially restrictive for boys. On an emotional level, boys often struggle with the desire to be close to people and to have warmth, affection, and intimacy. At the same time, they tend to pull away from intimacy because they're socialized to believe that interpersonal warmth isn't manly—that boys and men should be strong, tough, and disengaged. American culture gives the message that boys should suppress their feelings. Another message is that the only socially acceptable emotion for boys and men is anger, and that assertiveness and aggression are the best ways to get things accomplished. There are obviously individual differences. Each boy has his own inborn temperament, and each family will influence each child. Not only families, but peer pressure and socialization as well, exert a great deal of pressure over each child's gender development.

A final suggestion: Don't pull away from your children physically. Children need demonstrative affection. They sometimes bellyache about it, protest, and holler "Yuck!" Still, they need to be hugged and kissed. Physical affection is important for long-term development of intimate relationships—for the ability of men to stay involved and connected in an intimate relationship and for women to trust men. They need to have healthy, strong, nonconflictual, trusting relationships with their parent of the other sex to help set the stage for intimacy down the road.

TWENTY

GIRLS

"Chloë was absolutely fearless up till age ten. Nobody could tell her what to do. Then she hit puberty and **bam!** *everything changed. She worried constantly about messing up or saying the wrong thing, and if you asked her to make a choice, she'd just stand there quivering and whine, 'I don't know what I want!' "*—Cecelia, 38

....

"I told myself my daughter wouldn't get yanked around like other girls. She'd choose whatever profession she wanted, then go out and do it. She's been a great student all her life. But she's almost done with high school now and not doing well. Her grades are terrible. The teachers think she's on drugs or something. She's not—she's just kind of adrift. It's like she's had a personality transplant!"—Martha, 44

....

"I ask Janice [who's five years old], 'What are you going to be when you grow up?' She says, 'A flight attendant.' I say, 'A flight attendant. Why's that?' ' 'Cause I like to fly in airplanes.' So I say, 'Like your aunt Judy?' 'Yeah, like Judy.' So I say, 'But Judy's a pilot. Why don't you want to be a pilot like your aunt?' And Janice says, 'Bobby at school said girls can't be pilots.' "—Jared, 37

THE CHALLENGES GIRLS FACE

IN TERMS OF early child development, girls as a group advance more rapidly than boys as a group. Girls generally start talking, reading, and counting earlier. Girls between the ages of two and five generally attain higher scores on IQ tests than boys do. Later, as children enter elementary school, girls earn better grades than boys of the same age. In addition, most girls' social skills consistently develop faster than those of their male peers—girls tend to be more cooperative and more capable in resolving conflicts—so that most teachers find girls more congenial than boys in the classroom. It's not an exaggeration to say that on average, girls outpace boys according to most developmental criteria.

However, the situation changes significantly when girls reach age ten or twelve. Around the start of middle school, even the most talented and accomplished girls run the risk of losing their academic momentum, especially in math and science. Some girls slump academically; others continue to perform at high levels but less confidently than before; many enter a phase of severe personal uncertainty. The reasons for these changes are uncertain. One explanation is that because boys tend to be more demanding and unruly in school, teachers may often focus preemptively on boys—calling on them more frequently and attending more closely to their interests—as a means of controlling their behavior. A side effect of this situation may be that many girls wither academically from lack of attention. Another explanation is that societal expectations of girls (with an emphasis on looks, sexuality, and conventional behavior rather than intellectual accomplishments) pressure girls into neglecting their academic pursuits. In any case, the results are striking. By adolescence, the large majority of girls experience a crisis in self-confidence, some of which shows up in attitudes toward schoolwork.

The phenomenon I'm describing has been extensively documented. A report called *Shortchanging Girls, Shortchanging America*, released in 1990 by the American Association of University Women, provided disturbing insights into contemporary girlhood. Based on research and interviews of three thousand boys and girls aged nine through fifteen, this report verified a situation that many parents already recognized: girls often experience a pronounced decline in confidence during adolescence. The AAUW report revealed that self-esteem undergoes an especially steep decline during girls' preteen and teen years. Boys at that age are much more likely than girls to regard themselves as "pretty good at a lot of things"; they are also twice as likely to state that what they most appreciate about themselves is their talents. By contrast, girls tend to cite an aspect of their physical appearance as most appealing. Teenage girls also tend more often than boys to describe themselves as "not smart enough" or "not good enough" to reach their personal goals.

During the years since the AAUW issued its report, other analyses have attempted to explore and explain the situation. Peggy Orenstein, for instance, a journalist concerned about the AAUW findings, wrote *Schoolgirls: Young*

Women, Self-Esteem, and the Confidence Gap, a detailed anecdotal account of adolescent girls in two California schools. Orenstein found that despite improvements in girls' and women's overall situations, "many of today's girls fall into traditional patterns of low self-image, self-doubt, and self-censorship of their creative and intellectual potential. . . . They emerge from their teenage years with reduced expectations and have less confidence in themselves and their abilities than do boys." In 1994, Mary Pipher wrote *Reviving Ophelia*, a psychologist's study of the same issue. *Reviving Ophelia* became a national bestseller and further heightened concerns about girls' crises of confidence.

According to the AAUW's updated research, typical signs of the problem include these manifestations:

- High school girls and boys take similar numbers of science courses, but boys are more likely than girls to take all three core science courses—biology, chemistry, and physics—before graduation.

- Girls take fewer computer science and computer design courses.

- Girls use computers less than boys do outside of school settings.

- Although girls have narrowed the gender gap in math and science over the past eight or ten years, they often lag in studying technological subjects; technology has become the new "boys' club."

- Girls cluster in traditionally female occupations in School-to-Work and vocational education programs.

- While boys generally use computers for programming and problem solving, girls use computers mostly for word processing.

- Girls continue to experience significant risks to their health and development, such as sexual harassment and abuse, pregnancy, and substance abuse.

- Boys repeat grades and drop out of school at a higher rate than girls, but girls who are held back are more likely to drop out.

The developmental situation for girls in early twenty-first–century America now seems fairly clear. Most girls thrive until around puberty. During the early teens, however, something occurs that consistently undermines the self-esteem and self-confidence of almost all American girls. What triggers this crisis remains unclear. Social pressures toward conformity appear to explain much of the phenomenon. In any case, many if not most girls suffer the consequences; an appalling majority never fully regain the easygoing self-assuredness they felt before reaching adolescence.

HOW TO SUPPORT AND NURTURE YOUR DAUGHTER

One of the biggest and most important tasks facing a girl's parents, therefore, is how to counteract the effects of the factors that tend to jeopardize female confidence. How do you support and nurture your daughter at around the time of adolescence so that she stays open to her own abilities and strengths? In emphasizing this aspect of girls' development, I'm not suggesting that younger girls don't need their parents' supportiveness and nurturance, too; on the contrary, raising a confident girl requires her parents to be supportive and nurturing throughout her development. But the crisis that adolescent girls routinely face requires particular vigilance and attention.

BE A SUPPORTIVE, LOVING PARENT

Nothing will contribute more positively to your daughter's growth and well-being than your support and love. If she feels confident that you love her and stand ready to assist her when she needs you, your daughter will gain a depth and breadth of confidence that will help sustain her for a lifetime. She will still have to fight some strenuous battles—everyone does— but she'll be better prepared for what she faces than she would be otherwise.

In many ways what I'm saying is far more general than specific. Simply love your daughter unconditionally. Go ahead and have high expectations, but love her because she's your daughter. An equivalent recommendation holds true for boys, too, of course, but in some respects it's even more crucial for girls precisely because the world judges girls and women harshly in so many ways. Anything you can do that communicates your steadfast, unwavering love for her will reinforce your daughter's image of herself as a good, strong, creative person.

For a mother, offering unconditional love is a way of strengthening one of the most powerful bonds possible between human beings. Your love also presents you as your daughter's primary role model, someone whose opinions, whether favorable or unfavorable, will generally influence a girl more than anyone else's. Your daughter may tend to discount or even mock your influence during the adolescent years, but your ability to affect her beliefs and behavior will remain powerful in the long run.

For a father, offering unconditional love is a way of strengthening your daughter's image of herself in relation to men. If your affection for her is strong, unwavering, and sensitive to her need for freedom, you will encourage her to feel confident with males yet confident enough to define herself in her own terms, stand by her opinions, and expect kindness and respect. This kind of love, too, is crucial for her development.

A related issue: sibling relations. As a parent, you have to balance between, on one hand, letting your children work things out among themselves and, on the other hand, providing guidance. You need to allow your kids enough leeway to establish their own relationships, define the terms of their own ways of getting along, and work out their conflicts. At the same time, you need to intervene when there are major problems, and you need to clarify expectations for sibling behavior. One aspect of this situation concerns standards for sons and daughters. In many (if not most) human societies, boys' well-being takes precedence over girls. Even well-loved girls in these cultures learn that they matter less than their brothers. Americans claim to be more equitable in the treatment of boys and girls, but the reality of the situation has much to be desired.

- *Pay close attention to any double standards for boys and girls.* "The boys can go dig in the backyard now, but you girls shouldn't get so dirty."

- *Keep an eye on hidden messages.* "It's okay if you want to take trombone lessons, but don't you think a girl should play a smaller instrument?"

- *Counteract any sexist assumptions your sons may subject your daughters to.* "Jake told me girls can't program computers as well as boys can."

PROVIDE GOOD ROLE MODELS—AND BE ONE

In addition, it's crucial that you provide your daughter with good role models. The best way to do so is, of course, to *be* a good role model. Regardless of what you do in terms of work and family life, you have the ability to shape your child's perceptions like no one else. The goal is simply to demonstrate the values and beliefs that matter most to you by living them yourself. You can also reinforce whatever you personally offer your daughter by bringing her into contact with intelligent, accomplished, generous-spirited women who can demonstrate the huge variety of roles that girls can aspire to.

One of the best ways to accomplish what I'm suggesting is by participation in Take Our Daughters to Work Day. Started in 1993 by the Ms. Foundation for Women, Take Our Daughters to Work is a special day when girls ages nine to fifteen can accompany their mothers to their jobs and observe (or even participate) in what they do. "TODTW" Day occurs on the fourth Thursday of April every year. The goal, according to the Ms. Foundation, is "to focus attention on the needs and concerns of girls and to help them stay focused on the future during adolescence."

Some other goals to strive for include:

- *Avoiding stereotypes.* Resist using language that pegs either males or females in traditionally gender-based roles.

- *Suggesting nongender-stereotyped activities.* Encourage girls to explore traditionally "masculine" fields of interest.

- *Encouraging opinions.* Support your daughter when she takes a stand, resists conventional wisdom, or demands her rights. Give her the freedom to explore possibilities and make mistakes.

- *Avoiding "rescuing" your daughter intellectually.* Let her find her own answers and reach her own conclusions. Intervening may jeopardize her confidence in her abilities.

- *Resisting praising her for conventionality.* Offer her praise for her skills and ideas, not for tidiness, quietness, or cautiousness.

PROVIDE A REALITY CHECK AGAINST THE MEDIA

Many parents feel rightly disturbed by the power that the media exert on their children. Television, movies, the Internet, magazines, and other media—traditional and innovative alike—influence kids more than ever before. The pervasiveness of the media is one aspect of the problem; another is that the media often model behaviors or teach values far different from what parents want their children to acquire. (For a discussion of the media, see chapter 29; for a discussion of computers, see chapter 7.) What compounds the problem for parents of girls is the frequently negative portrayal of girls and women.

There are two basic ways to deal with this issue. One involves rejecting movies, TV shows, or other media that you find offensive. This approach is legitimate and important; producers and distributors of media products need to feel the full blast of consumers' anger and contempt. Some years ago, for instance, a software developer released an outrageously racist, sexist Wild West video game: players who succeeded in shooting a certain number of on-screen Indians were "rewarded" by letting their digital cowboys rape a digital squaw. The outcry against this game resulted in its immediate recall. Consumers don't often win such a clear-cut victory, but it's worthwhile to try. In any case, you can "vote with your feet" and avoid any movie, TV show, magazine, or Web site you find offensive.

An important approach, meanwhile, is to raise your daughter's consciousness about the media. Talk with her about the books and magazines she reads, the movies and shows she watches, the Web sites she visits. What does she find interesting and appealing? What does she find unpleasant, worrisome, or scary? To what degree does she understand how the commercial aspects of the media determine what gets published and produced? In discussing these situations with an adolescent girl, it's not necessary—or even desirable—to convince her to share your precise opinions; on the contrary, the goal is to help her think for herself, make her own decisions, and stand by her own beliefs. But open discussions about the media are critical in reaching this goal.

Some typical media issues that warrant attention:

- Images of girls and women in TV, movies, and popular music

- Images of girls and women in the advertising media

- Corporate pressure on girls and women to meet ideals of beauty, sexiness, etc., by acquiring goods and services

- Portrayal of violence against women in TV, movies, and popular music

- The manufacture of fads and fashions

REINFORCE THE RIGHT TO SPEAK OUT

Whether regarding big issues (the media, the arts, politics, and culture) or little issues (a favorite color, a taste for chocolate rather than vanilla ice cream) reinforce your daughter's right to speak out. Preadolescent girls can be wonderfully opinionated. They know just what they believe and don't mind setting the whole world straight. By the early teens, however, many girls grow more cautious and conventional. They check to see which way the wind is blowing; they worry about "saying the wrong thing"; they embarrass easily. Parents can compound the problem by being too pushy about their own opinions or by scolding their daughters for being "sassy." It's appropriate to expect civility from girls—and from boys as well, of course—but you should allow your daughter to state what she believes. Encourage her to stand by her beliefs, too. To the degree possible, prepare her to face society's double standard: while many people regard an opinionated man as "willful" or "authoritative," an opinionated woman is considered "strident," "shrill," or "uppity."

ENCOURAGE LEARNING

Girls, like all children, are naturally curious. From babyhood onward, they have an inherent human drive to explore the world and make sense of it. Individual girls have individual interests and individual abilities, but there's nothing about being female that necessarily limits their ways of learning or the degree to which they can learn. Only later in life, as society enculturates girls, do they start to believe that certain subjects, intellectual disciplines, or methods of inquiry are "masculine" or "feminine." This process almost inevitably occurs, however, narrowing what girls perceive to be their proper spheres of learning.

To counteract this process and help your daughter stay open to exploring the full range of human experience, I urge you to take these steps:

- Support her right and need to ask questions.

- Encourage her to take risks, challenge herself, and explore new interests.

- Support her right and need to speak out, even when doing so seems risky, unconventional, unpopular, or uncool.

- Encourage her to strive for leadership roles—student government, extracurricular activities, sports teams, etc.

- Provide opportunities for her to play sports or take part in other physical activities.

- Encourage at least some girls-only activities—Scouts, sports, camp, etc.

- Read your daughter's textbooks to see if they represent women abundantly, insightfully, and favorably.

- Volunteer at your daughter's school, both to observe classes and to make your presence known to the teachers and administrators.

- Encourage your daughter's teacher, the principal, and other staff members to honor women's and girls' accomplishments.

- Support your daughter's interests in math and science, and encourage her studies even if she complains that math and science courses are "hard."

- Provide opportunities for home-based projects in math and science, such as math software, chemistry experiments, and backyard astronomy.

COMBAT GENDER BIAS IN THE SCHOOLS

I believe that American schools aren't sufficiently supportive of either boys or girls. Despite the best intentions of many teachers and administrators, our schools lack sufficient resources to attend properly to our children's needs. Many observers rightly note that girls often get the "short end of the stick" in public education; the AAUW's studies, as well as those by psychologists like Carol Gilligan and writers like Peggy Orenstein, have documented this disturbing situation. However, I believe that boys, too, are inadvertent victims of our culture's limited attention to educational issues. (For a discussion of boys in this regard, see chapter 3.) The solution: a renewed nationwide focus on educational issues affecting *all* children.

In the meantime, how do you deal with the situation if you're raising a girl? First of all, be supportive of your daughter's efforts in school, and encourage her to pursue subjects that are generally considered boys' turf. To the degree possible, lobby your school district to take these measures to diminish and discourage gender bias in the schools:

- *Reinforce girls' individuality.* Provide programs and classes that boost girls' lagging self-perception in areas such as math and science.

- *Foster girls' involvement.* Eliminate competitive classroom practices that alienate or marginalize girls.

- *Provide girls with mentors and role models.* Recruit paid staff or volunteers with backgrounds in math, science, technology, and other fields who can teach and inspire girls regarding the range of skills, activities, and professions they can choose to pursue.

- *Give girls equal access to learning.* Guarantee that girls have enough hands-on experience with computers, lab equipment, and other technology often dominated by boys.

- *Empower girls to achieve goals.* Coordinate efforts with community groups and businesses to provide girls with routes to success other than traditional measures such as testing, grades, and class participation.

REJECT GIRL- AND WOMAN-BASHING

I am frequently horrified by the girl- and woman-bashing still widespread in our society. Men utter much of this abusive and dismissive language, but an amazing amount of it comes from the mouths of girls and women themselves. Either way it's a threat to girls' self-confidence, and you should reject it.

Of course, you can't silence more than a few of the voices that demean girls and women. You can't plug your daughter's ears with wax to diminish what she hears. You can, however, model respect for girls and women yourself; you can comment on the thoughtlessness of people who subject girls and women to gibes, jokes, insults, snide remarks, and slurs; you can insist that your daughter speak respectfully of others, too. This approach doesn't solve the whole problem. What it does accomplish, however, is to set high standards for your daughter's ability to communicate openly, directly, and civilly. And it also encourages her to perceive herself as worthy of open, direct, civil communication.

REJECT BOY- AND MAN-BASHING

Similarly, I urge you to reject boy- and man-bashing. There's already enough tension and acrimony between the sexes; we don't need more. Although I believe that one of the world's greatest problems is the disparity of power between men and women, I'm not convinced that personal attacks on boys and men will help solve the problem. More to the point, you can't really build your daughter's self-confidence and self-esteem by teaching her to mock, deride, tease, or abuse other people, whether male or female. Her growth and strength as a human being will evolve primarily as she perceives her own abilities and accomplishments.

DE-EMPHASIZE PHYSICAL APPEARANCE

Our society, like most, greatly overemphasizes the importance of female beauty. Girls and women are subject to scrutiny of their physical appearance unlike anything that boys and men must tolerate. In the long run, it's possible that this problem will diminish; in the short run, you have better chances raising your own daughter's awareness than combating this obsession in the culture as a whole.

- Increase your daughter's awareness in media images of women.

- Discuss the ways in which commercial interests (the fashion industry, makeup companies, etc.) gain from women's concerns about their appearance.

- Encourage an interest in health, fitness, and physical activity as good in their own right, not because they lead to a fashionable appearance.

- Avoid focusing attention on weight issues and dieting.

- Tell your daughter she's beautiful just the way she is.

TEACH FINANCIAL RESPONSIBILITY

Although our culture is far too materialistic, I believe it's important for girls to learn as much as possible about financial responsibility. Am I contradicting myself? Not at all. In fact, I'm convinced that financially responsible behavior is a way of combating rampant consumerism. Many girls and women grow up convinced that they can't master even the basics of responsible financial behavior and that they live at the mercy of the urge to spend. "When the going gets tough, the tough go shopping"—this is a clever, jokey slogan, but it's also a sign of how willingly women submit to consumerist propaganda. As a result, many girls and women are subject to pressures to buy, buy, buy and to define themselves substantially in terms of what they own.

What I suggest is that from an early age, teach your daughter as much as possible about good finances. A number of good books exist now that explain financial planning for kids. In addition, you can teach your daughter many things yourself, including the importance of saving and the nature of various kinds of investments. (For a selection of materials on financial planning, see the Resource Guide.)

TWENTY-ONE

HEALTH

"I jog, play tennis, and swim at a local health club, but I can't get my children to do any kind of exercise at all. Their idea of a strenuous workout is clicking the mouse when they play computer games!"

....

"My daughter eats a pretty good diet—lots of different foods, mostly healthy stuff. But my son is a disaster. He's never met a junk food he doesn't like, and I can't remember the last time he ate a vegetable. How can I keep him healthy if he eats like that?"

....

"Three weeks ago Ryan, my two-year-old, started choking on a bead he found on the floor. Luckily he coughed it up, but the incident scared me half to death. What can I do to prevent that sort of thing in the future?"

....

"I want to keep my kids as healthy as possible. I read whatever I can about medical breakthroughs, diet, fitness, and so forth. But I feel more and more confused—there's so much contradictory information out there. No matter what I do, someone somewhere has an opinion that makes me feel I'm messing up."

THESE STATEMENTS REFLECT just a few of the concerns that parents express about health-related issues. Parents want to protect their children and help them thrive, but they worry that they're not doing enough—or else they're doing the wrong things despite their best intentions.

There's no doubt that health issues worry many parents. The world often seems like a dangerous place, with all sorts of risks—pollution, drugs, car safety, diet, and medical problems, to name just a few—hanging over everyone. Looking after their children's health is certainly among parents' biggest responsibilities. So how do you keep your kids healthy in an often unhealthy world? How much concern is appropriate, and how much is too much? What are the best sources of information about health? How should you sort through conflicting claims about what to do and what not to do?

PRACTICE WHAT YOU PREACH

I never cease to be amazed by some parents' expectations that they can deliver one message about health while ignoring it themselves. One mother, Marie, came to me for advice about her daughter's troubling health habits. "Linnea eats nothing but junk food," Marie complained, "and she never gets any exercise. She's a total couch potato!" When I asked Marie about her own health practices, she got defensive. "Look, I know I should be more active, too, but my work schedule is totally nuts." Her own diet? "I have to eat on the run." Exercise? "I belong to a gym, but it's hard to find time to go there." The situation was just as I suspected. Don't misunderstand: I sympathize with Marie's dilemma. She's coping with the same pressures that all of us face. The problem is that her mixed messages to her daughter are confusing the child.

The solution is to start by sizing up your own attitudes toward health-related issues. Are you eating healthful foods? Are you getting enough exercise? Do you smoke or drink alcohol in excess? Next, keep in mind that your own behaviors will powerfully influence your child. If you feel you're setting the wrong example, do whatever you can to change your own behavior—if not for your own good, then for your child's.

DO YOUR HOMEWORK

People often complain to me that when it comes to health issues, it's hard to know what's right. The newspapers, magazines, and television programs are full of contradictory reports. First comes the news that high levels of cholesterol harm the heart and arteries; then researchers find that only certain kinds of cholesterol are damaging; then we hear that *low* cholesterol can be damaging, too. What should we believe? It's true that information about health issues comes at us in confusing abundance. It's also true that even as educated laypersons, we can't follow all the issues or understand the implications of each new discovery. Still, it's important for you to educate yourself on health-related topics despite the complexities and frustrations of the task.

Here's what I suggest. Keep an open mind. Follow the news on health and medical topics to the degree possible. Be curious about developments and breakthroughs. Ask questions of knowledgeable people—doctors, nurses, medical technicians, and other professionals who understand the issues that concern you. At the same time, stay skeptical. Although medical researchers are gaining valuable insights into many issues, these people are ultimately just human beings and fully capable of making mistakes, exaggerating claims, or being influenced by political aspects of a highly competitive endeavor. In short, learn what you can but don't believe everything you read. Do what feels intuitively right for you and your family.

PRACTICE GOOD HOME SAFETY

I visited a friend of mine recently and noticed that the soap in her kitchen was antibacterial. "Oh, yeah," she said when I commented. "I'm not taking chances. With so many weird bugs out there, I figure I shouldn't gamble on my kids' health." She has stocked her bathrooms with strong antibacterial soap as well. What surprised me, though, wasn't these precautions; the shocker was that despite her worries about dangerous microbes, she had ignored far greater risks. Her house had no smoke alarms. She had also installed deadbolts on the doors which required a key to unlock—but the key was nowhere in sight. With a household fire much more likely than an outbreak of salmonella, were these oversights really so wise?

Some families are penny-wise and dollar-foolish when it comes to household safety. It's easy to assume that no harm will come to you and your kids, but the risks remain.

SMOKE DETECTORS

These are an absolute must. Ideally, you should have one in each room (except in the kitchen, where cooking fumes will trigger the alarm too easily). Test batteries once yearly.

CARBON MONOXIDE DETECTORS

Carbon monoxide gas (CO) is a significant threat in many households. Even a well-regulated furnace or water heater can malfunction, and some stoves or space heaters give off dangerous amounts of CO. Colorless, odorless, and tasteless, CO can kill you easily before anyone in your family knows there's even a problem. Check with your local fire department about recommended types of CO detectors, which are increasingly available in hardware stores.

SECURITY SYSTEMS

Though not necessary in most communities, you may feel greater peace of mind if your house contains some sort of electronic security system. One common mistake, though: installing a security system, then growing lax about ordinary household safety, such as locking windows and doors.

CHILDPROOFING

Depending on your child's age, you should determine what safety hazards exist, then correct or compensate for them as well as possible. The most crucial general issues occur during the toddler years and focus on:

- Stairs, porches, and windows
- Electrical hazards (cords, outlets, appliances)
- Fire and burn hazards (matches, fireplaces, radiators, flammable fabrics)
- Water hazards (tubs, toilets, ponds, swimming pools)
- Kitchen hazards (stoves, toasters, knives and cutlery)
- Access to poisons (cleaners, automotive supplies, lawn and garden chemicals, lead paint)
- Pets (unpredictable dogs and cats, rodents, "exotic" animals [alligators, snapping turtles, etc.])

FIRST AID AND CPR

Many people feel squeamish about dealing with even minor health emergencies. This is understandable, but as a parent you have a responsibility to help your children regardless of any nervousness about blood, cuts, or other injuries. I strongly believe that every parent should learn basic first aid and cardiopulmonary resuscitation (CPR). Even in communities with good emergency medical response teams, you may be the first person to help your child, so you shouldn't assume that professionals will arrive fast enough to take you off the hook. Here are the most minimal skills you should acquire:

- *Basic first aid*—early treatment of cuts, burns, and other trauma; emergency responses to shock, drowning, poisoning, and electrocution
- *CPR*—cardiopulmonary resuscitation of adults, children, and infants
- *Heimlich maneuver*—emergency removal of obstructions of the airway

In addition, you should stock and maintain a first aid kit sufficient for treating minor emergencies, and you should learn how to use the contents safely and confidently. Call your local chapter of the American Red Cross for information about first aid classes in your area.

PRACTICE GOOD CAR SAFETY

Auto accidents are one of the leading causes of death in this country; according to the National Highway Traffic Safety Administration, almost 42,000 American lost their lives in car crashes in 1997 alone. Among children, death from car accidents occur at a rate of about 9,000 per year, with tens of thousands of other kids injured as well. It's hard to overstate the risks that children face simply from going place to place in automobiles. Yet given the nature of American culture, most families have little recourse but to rely on cars for transportation. Here's how to minimize the risk to your kids.

DEFENSIVE DRIVING

Statistically speaking, it's hard to say whether driving is more dangerous "out there" than it used to be, but many people believe it is. A certain number of drivers in most parts of the country appear to be driving more recklessly than in the past. "Road rage" seems to be spreading. More and more people act as if they regard obedience to traffic laws as optional. As a result, many parents fear for their own and their children's safety. Defensive driving seems a minimal response to this situation. You don't have to assume that every other driver is a homicidal maniac; consistent, thorough caution is adequate.

STATE-OF-THE-ART EQUIPMENT

If you can afford the cost, certain features in your car may be lifesavers. By this I refer to antilock braking systems (ABS), air bags, side-impact air bags, and other safety devices. ABS in your car is especially crucial.

Two caveats, however:

First, don't assume that high-tech gear allows you more leeway to stretch the rules. I see many drivers whose well-equipped cars lead them to a foolish sense of invulnerability and from there to inconsiderate, even aggressive driving. Don't let all that equipment tempt you to succumb to carelessness or road rage.

Second, air bags are potentially a mixed blessing. No child under ten or twelve should ride in the front passenger seat of a car equipped with an airbag on that side.

CAR SEATS

All children should use an adequate restraint system when riding in a car. Seat belts alone aren't adequate until children reach middle school age. (A parent's refusal or unwillingness to use car restraint systems is, in my mind, gross irresponsibility.) No infant in a kiddie seat should ever be strapped into the front passenger seat. Ideally, children should ride only in the back seat—or, in vans, in the middle seat. All children should have well-fitting, age-appropriate restraints. For infants, this means a rear-facing bucket-type kiddie seat; for toddlers, a front-facing bucket kiddie seat is adequate. A preschool-age child should have a booster seat that keeps the shoulder belt off her neck. Check all restraint systems for proper fit.

SUPPLEMENTAL TRAINING

Can you handle automotive emergencies? Are you sure you can respond properly to a bad skid? Do you know what to do following a car accident? Is your car stocked with an emergency kit? If you can't honestly answer yes to these questions, consider getting supplemental training. AAA and other automotive clubs offer classes for people who want to augment their driving skills. The main goal is simply to prepare for the unexpected events that can easily occur on the road; one additional benefit is that some auto insurance companies grant discounts to drivers who complete these courses.

DON'T SMOKE

One of the best things you can do for your children is not to smoke. By now the evidence against smoking is overwhelming; few common habits can do more to jeopardize your health. So if you smoke, you risk your children's well-being indirectly by damaging your own health. In addition, you risk your children's health directly through the effects of secondhand smoke. Asthma, ear infections, and even cancer are possible consequences for kids if they're exposed to significant amounts of cigarette smoke. The consequences for fetuses are also substantial and may include low birth weight, circulatory problems, and failure to thrive. In addition, parents who smoke set a poor example for children, who may be more likely to smoke during their teens or adulthood.

EXERCISE

Many parents don't pay enough attention to exercise as a health issue. To the detriment of their own health, many adults get little or no exercise. What shocks me even more is that even adults who pride themselves on their own fitness activities—jogging, bicycling, swimming, or working out at a gym—do little to encourage their children to get enough exercise. In fact, American kids as a group are often less physically fit than American adults as a group. The result: a growing population of couch potatoes.

Exercise is important not only for physical health but for emotional health as well. Vigorous physical activity releases chemicals called endorphins that affect the body as natural antidepressants; consistent exercise can lead to a wonderful sense of well-being. For this reason, you should encourage your children to take part in kid-friendly sports, participate enthusiastically in gym class, and join you in vigorous activities as a family. Doing so doesn't necessarily mean elaborate, equipment-intensive sports. Rather, the goal is simply to get out and get moving. Chapter 46, "Sports," includes a more detailed discussion of related issues.

DEAL WITH MOOD ISSUES

Life is so strenuous that all of us sometimes feel stressed, burdened, or drained. Occasional low moods aren't usually a problem. This holds true for children as well as adults. No matter how much adults assume that childhood is carefree, kids have their own burdens, too, and sometimes feel deep sadness. It's important to regard such moods as well within the normal range of human feeling.

If low moods are more intense and long-lasting, it may be quite another matter. If you have more intense symptoms—or if you note these symptoms in your child—you should consider finding professional assistance from a counselor or therapist:

- Total lack of motivation

- Withdrawal from life

- Inability to concentrate or make decisions

- Feelings of hopelessness or helplessness

- No interest in everyday activities

- Inability to get out of bed

- Recurrent inability to sleep at night

- Loss of appetite or tendency toward compulsive under- or overeating

- Suicidal thoughts or feelings

THINK POSITIVE

Although this chapter touches on many troubling possibilities, please don't get the wrong idea. You'll probably navigate through the parenting years without experiencing any but the most ordinary accidents and illnesses. Children do get sick a lot, but most often without major consequences. Your family may well go years and years unafflicted by serious problems. The truth is, kids are amazingly hardy. They're biologically programmed to grow, change, and develop in fundamentally sound ways. As a parent, your main job is simply to assist in a process of unfoldment that usually takes care of itself. In short, be prepared for problems and emergencies, but be ready for the likeliest scenario—your kids growing on schedule without major problems.

After centuries of denying the connection between mind and body, Western medicine has come to acknowledge the importance of this link. Your state of health clearly affects your state of mind; similarly, your state of mind can affect your state of health. Stress, tension, and worry all contribute to how well (or poorly) your body functions. It's true that some holistic practices now overemphasize the mind-body relationship—assuming, for instance, that every concern you feel can contribute to a specific malady—which I find as counterproductive as a refusal to see the connections. However, I believe it's important to recognize that your overall attitude can affect your state of health. A positive attitude is more likely to foster positive health; a negative attitude is more likely to burden your physical well-being.

What are the implications? First of all, being healthy means to be alive, and life includes a measure of pain. This is simply the nature of reality. Generally speaking, pain won't destroy you. If you tend to disregard it, however, pain can build up, increasing tension, and tension in turn can intensify physical ailments. At times it can also lead to psychogenic ailments such as headaches, stomachaches, backaches, neck aches, and so forth. In addition, tension can aggravate loneliness and depression.

One interesting discovery: medical researchers have established that people who have better support systems (friends, relatives, acquaintances, business associates) tend to get sick less often than people with less substantial support systems. It appears that an abundance of warm, sustaining relationships can actually strengthen your immune system. It's hard to know whether it's possible to draw further conclusions from this information. Can a good, close circle of friends foster health in other ways? Maybe, maybe not. One way or the other, though, it's not hard to figure that having a good balance in your life, including an abundance of friends and family, tends to be emotionally satisfying, and that such satisfaction is salutary.

TWENTY-TWO

HOLIDAYS

PART OF THE American Dream is an idealized image of holidays. We expect holidays to be times of merriment, joy, and renewed family closeness. Unfortunately, there's often a big gap between the ideal and the reality. Holidays often fall short of our expectations—sometimes far short. In fact, with dual-career and single-parent families now predominant, holidays can be the proverbial straw that breaks the camel's back.

THE BURDENS OF HOLIDAYS

The main reason that holidays end up burdensome is that these special occasions add stress to our already hectic schedules. The result: instead of the holidays becoming a dream, they often feel like a nightmare. With frazzled nerves, time constraints, and high expectations all around, disappointment is almost inevitable. In addition, kids spend more time at home during holidays, which adds to the logistical and emotional burdens already weighing on parents' shoulders.

Holiday tasks can be enjoyable, but they are often stressful and time-consuming as well. Shopping for food, decorations, and other supplies; ordering, buying, and wrapping gifts; and cleaning and decorating the house are obvious examples of that double-edged sword. In addition, calling and visiting friends and relatives and entertaining guests can also wear us out even as they give us pleasure. Here are other potential stress intensifiers.

KIDS' TENSION LEVELS

During holidays, children feel understandably excited about what's to come. Fair enough—these are special occasions. But kids are often overstimulated by their own expectations and by holiday-oriented advertising on TV and else-where. In addition, the disruption of normal routines can add to the crescendo of excitement.

FAMILIAL EXPECTATIONS

Whose relatives should you visit this year? Your spouse's? Your own? Maybe some from each side? Sorting through these commitments can trans-form even the happiest holidays into a tangle of obligations. Even if you man-age to meet everyone's expectations, does that leave you any time to do simply what *you* want to do? And will you have any energy left even if you find the time?

DIFFERING TRADITIONS

Some families celebrate multiple cultural traditions. Not only must they cope with two or more sets of relatives, they must also meet expectations regarding the "right" way to celebrate. This situation occurs even when both spouses are Christian, both are Jewish, or both are of some other background, since holidays are often celebrated differently within the context of various subcultures. Family and individual differences complicate the situation further. Couples in interfaith marriages face an even more complex set of decisions and familial expectations. I know one family that juggles three different major hol-idays each December: Hanukkah, Christmas, and Kwanza. This holiday merry-go-round can be delightful and fun, but the demands also create more work and more expectations.

WHAT TO DO

There's no single, simple solution that will ease all the pressures, but here are some strategies that can help to diminish the toll that holidays can take.

PLAN AHEAD

Anticipate what's coming. Talk to your spouse and coordinate your plans. Sorting through your options will require some effort, but forethought and planning will pay off in the long run. This is true of logistics—shopping, trans-portation, cleaning, etc.—but just as true of decisions on visits.

CLARIFY YOUR VALUES

Determine which values you want to stress. What do you want your children to learn from the holiday? What aspect of the holiday is most important to you? What is the real meaning of your celebration? Is the significance in the gifts—material things—or is it in the traditions and the family time you spend together? Children often model what they see in their parents' behavior; they'll acquire those values and beliefs simply by watching your behavior. It helps everyone if you can focus on what you're really doing. If holiday time is a stressful, tense time, your kids will associate these occasions with Mom and Dad being frazzled, on edge, and nervous. This will really dampen their enthusiasm and throw a shadow over the holiday. If holidays are a time of sharing and serenity, your kids will pick that up, too.

Another way to teach children morals and values at holiday time is to do some volunteer work. Drop off clothes for the needy. Participate in a food drive. Have the whole family volunteer at a soup kitchen. Unrealistic? Not at all. Let the kids participate so that they can see that holidays aren't just about getting; they're also about giving. Of course volunteerism is ideally something to be done throughout the year, not just at holidays. Still, it can be especially important at holiday times.

There comes a time when every couple—particularly couples with young children—must break with family tradition. You may have to decide what's best for your family rather than going along with what relatives prefer. Consider the issues carefully; try to reach an agreement with your spouse in advance of contacting your parents, in-laws, and others.

KEEP THINGS SIMPLE

Once you define what the holiday means to you, figure out which activities best fit your family's beliefs. Choose among those activities; select several that express your values. However, don't try to do everything. Even if each possibility seems important, attempting to do too much can backfire as badly as doing things that feel inappropriate. Be flexible. Although tradition is important, flexibility is crucial, too. Stay open to new possibilities; don't get too fixated on every little detail. If a tradition or a custom doesn't fit your family lifestyle or situation, create new ones.

One low-stress option for visiting is to host an informal open house. Invite guests to visit throughout the day or evening. Prepare a simple buffet or brunch—bagels, sandwiches, coffee, pastries, soup, or chili. You can also ask people to bring a dish. Nowadays, people don't resent this kind of arrangement; on the contrary, most welcome the chance to get together without anyone feeling obligated. With a potluck, there's no burden on anyone. People can visit without feeling stressed or guilty.

If there are too many obligations, communicate with your spouse, friends, and family. Let them know that you're anxious, stressed, or frustrated, and that they shouldn't take it personally. You love them very much but you're going to have to cut back on some of the commitments for the holidays. Look at your schedule; it's probably overbooked. Simplify things. We generally do more than our kids—especially young kids—really need. They get disoriented and overstimulated by too many activities. Keep the number of visits low, at most two per day.

LOWER YOUR STANDARDS

If you are stressed out and don't have time to do everything, just do what you can.

- *Try not to put so much emphasis on perfection.* What matters most is your generosity and love, not how things look or how much money you've spent.

- *Cut corners.* If you're stressed, take easy shortcuts to decorate and cook. Buy prepared deli platters or store-baked cookies. Don't try to do everything—or anything—from scratch. No one will think less of you. You will enjoy yourself more and will accomplish your goal feeling much more relaxed.

- *Get domestic or child care help if possible.* Too expensive? Maybe, but the emotional payoff may far exceed the dollar value. And you may have low-cost alternatives to commercial services. Ask a neighbor to help watch your kids while you're doing these extra tasks. Offer to reciprocate at a later date. Or indulge yourself in occasional hired help.

- *Share the burdens.* Take turns with your spouse so that no one is burdened all the time. Divide up the holiday tasks. You don't have to be Super Mom, Super Wife, Super Dad, Super Husband. Pitch in, have fun, and enjoy the holiday experience.

INCLUDE THE KIDS

Include your children in planning and preparations. Encourage them to make gifts, write notes, and think about the holiday in a less commercial way. Help them think about what kind of gift a person might like to receive, and why. It helps children to define who they are, and it strengthens their character to give in a much more meaningful way.

ATTEND TO YOUR NEEDS

Take care of yourself during holiday times. This is easy to forget when you're devoting yourself so thoroughly to others' needs. In addition to keeping things simple, try to maintain a consistent schedule. Eat regular meals. Get enough rest. If you can, get some exercise. A steady, balanced schedule will help to decrease the stress for both you and your kids. Try to enjoy your friends and family as much as possible. Ultimately, that's what the holidays are about. Forget the fringe benefits—the frills, the food, the gifts—but try instead to have more time with your spouse, kids, and friends.

KEEP THE KIDS BUSY

Children often feel keyed up and "hyper" when major holidays approach. The holidays themselves can be a challenge, even an ordeal, for parents. Keeping the kids busy can ease the pressure on everyone. However, choose the activities carefully. Try to limit your kids' viewing of commercial TV. It's true that TV may provide a welcome respite when the children are home, but there's no reason not to use it judiciously. Also, keep in mind that advertising increases dramatically during many holidays—especially in December—and the barrage of ads may agitate your kids and make them covet toys and special foods. Carefully chosen videos may better serve your purposes. Ideally, keep kids busy with other activities. Playing games, making decorations, and playing outdoors, if possible, are all preferable to vegging out in front of the tube.

EXAMINE YOUR OWN EXPECTATIONS

It may sound odd, but what stresses many people during the holidays isn't the present but the past. Expectations from long ago exert a tremendous pull on our perceptions in the here-and-now. For this reason, try to readjust your expectations to fit your present situation. You may want to relive some of the traditions you celebrated during your childhood, but it's difficult to do so nowadays because circumstances have often changed. You're an adult now; you're not a child. From a child's viewpoint, the holiday may have been more magical then than it seems now, but that's understandable. You have many more responsibilities now, including financial duties. Life has changed. If you expect to have the same magical experiences that you had when looked after by your parents, you'll set yourself up for disappointment.

HOLIDAYS IN THE AFTERMATH OF DIVORCE

If you're a single parent, you probably face additional stresses during holidays. Being with your child for a protracted period may be difficult; similarly, *not* having time with your child (if custody arrangements dictate) may also prove stressful. If your separation or divorce are recent, memories of past holidays can be burdensome. You may feel a great sense of loss of extended family as well as a loss of the relationship with your former spouse.

PRACTICAL ISSUES

If you are divorced, plan ahead to coordinate the kids' activities and logistics. You and your ex should work together as much as possible. Make sure that the children know in advance what the plans will be. As with intact families, let the kids take part in the planning. Children who feel they're central to the occasion will handle the stresses better than those who feel they're merely being bounced from one household to another.

EMOTIONAL ISSUES

Protect your own emotional state during these special occasions. Holidays are "loaded"; it's easy to feel burdened by your memories. To avoid complicating your life at an already stressful time, plan your activities and celebrations to minimize emotional stress. Don't go back to your old haunts. Don't do the same things you did when you were married. Don't fall into patterns that evoke your former life. You may or may not miss married life, but conjuring the ghosts of holidays past will probably leave you grappling with emotions that limit your enjoyment of the present. Instead, try to create new traditions and new holidays. Go to new places. Make it fun and enjoyable for both yourself and your children.

PEACEFUL COEXISTENCE

Another important issue concerns how you coexist with your ex-spouse during holidays. To the degree possible, put your grievances aside. Do what's in the best interest of your children. My motto is: Love your child more than you dislike your ex. This isn't easy, but it's crucial. How?

- *Keep things in proportion.* Holidays tend to magnify emotions, so stay level-headed about what's really happening. If your ex drops off or picks up your child an hour late, is that really such a calamity? Or is your annoyance out of keeping with the event's significance?

- *Try to make the holidays as pleasant and as conflict-free as possible.* Let things go to ease your children's stresses. This isn't the time to sort through financial or legal matters; let those wait till after the holidays. If you have "bones to pick" with your ex, avoid raising those issues, too. You'll have many other opportunities to sort through your differences.

- *Beware of holiday-inspired dreams of reunion.* During holidays, children in divorced families sometimes imagine that they can bring their parents back together. This is understandable, since the underlying theme of several holidays—Christmas, Thanksgiving, Passover, and others—is family unity and continuity. But don't be swayed by holiday sentiment. Size up the situation in the clear light of normal post-holiday reality.

- *Keep the boundaries clear.* Some people feel that the children will inevitably benefit if their divorced parents share holiday festivities. In fact, these otherwise good intentions can confuse children and give them false expectations. It's best to keep celebrations separate.

- *Keep gift-giving in proportion.* Divorced parents tend to compete, each attempting to buy bigger and better gifts than the other. Don't fall into that trap. Ask your child what he or she might like. If you can discuss this issue with your ex, talk about the situation, consider the risks of a gift-giving battle, and divide up the kinds of gifts you're giving. You can also simply ask your child to request different gifts from each parent. If they get a gift that is similar, don't make a big deal out of it. Try to keep your ego out of the situation as much as possible.

- *Anticipate feelings of sadness, loneliness, and isolation during holidays.* You may feel even more overwhelmed being a single parent. If you struggle with these emotions, talk to a friend, relative, or therapist to get the support you need. The sense of isolation and sadness may be especially acute if this is one of the first holidays you've spent alone. Be reassured: it does get easier with the passage of time.

DEALING WITH THE LETDOWN

Expect and anticipate that after the fantasy of a holiday passes, you may feel a letdown. This is common and understandable. Precisely because holidays are special, returning to normal reality can hit with a jolt. You can't match that level of excitement and anticipation long-term. A sense of disappointment and sadness may be inevitable. Rather than ignore the possibility, try to anticipate it. Plan for some fun activities after the holidays if possible.

TWENTY-THREE

JUGGLING WORK AND FAMILY LIFE

GIVEN TODAY'S HECTIC, overscheduled, goal-oriented lifestyle, many observers have compared the American family to a minicorporation. This analogy isn't altogether complimentary, but it's not far off the mark. Balancing and juggling all the demands of family life are genuine management issues. It's a major logistical effort to get everything done and solve all the problems that parenthood entails. The basic question is this: how do you meet everyone's needs without succumbing to the resulting stress? The truth is, you can't completely do away with the rigors of trying to balance everything, but you *can* simplify your life in ways that will make tasks flow more easily and less stressfully.

THE BURDEN OF EXPECTATIONS

One of the biggest problems in managing family life is expectations. Many of us were raised in families for which TV programs like *Father Knows Best, Ozzie and Harriet, The Waltons, The Brady Bunch,* and *Happy Days* created unrealistic images of both parenthood and childhood. For better or worse, those images are no longer valid. Most families today are either dual-career or single-parent families. It's rare that families today have a full-time stay-at-home parent. As a result, we all have to avoid transferring our expectations from the past to the present.

THE POINTLESSNESS OF GUILT

In parenting, guilt comes with the territory. Children have more or less infinite needs; parents have more or less finite energy. Luckily, most parents at least do an adequate job of raising kids, and many do far more than that. The catch is, we still feel we ought to be doing more. The result: lots of guilt.

But guilt is a waste of time. It doesn't solve any problems; it merely bogs you down in feeling bad. This isn't to say that you shouldn't acknowledge your mistakes or limitations, but you should focus on doing what needs to be done rather than on regretting errors or lost opportunities. Parenthood is a messy, imperfect process. Even so, you're probably doing a better job than you think.

How can you disengage from guilt? Maintaining a sense of humor helps. Learn to laugh at the everyday capers in your house. Make a list of goofy incidents that have happened to you and your children. Don't take parenting too seriously. If you need inspiration, read Erma Bombeck's books about family life or rent Steve Martin's movie *Parenthood.*

Another aid in controlling guilt is to maintain good boundaries. Keep your work at work and your family life at home. Carve out no-work times each day when your children are likely to need your attention. Put on the answering machine. You'll have to acknowledge the world's demands soon enough, but don't apologize for the importance you place on parenthood. In my opinion, you can't do anything more meaningful than raise children.

IS YOUR LIFE IN BALANCE?

Draw a circle on a piece of paper. Now consider how much time you spend on family activities, how much on work, and how much on yourself. Divide the circle into three sections proportionate to each topic. The reality of parenthood is that time to yourself may be represented by the smallest wedge. There's no question that raising children—especially during the early years—involves a great deal of outright self-denial. Even the later years demand enormous patience, stamina, and generosity of spirit. That being said, it's true as well that some degree of balance is crucial. You can't attend to others' needs long-term without recharging your batteries now and then. You need at least some sort of pursuit that's relaxing, sustaining, and self-nurturing.

Look at the circle again. If you're lucky, the circle may have fairly equal wedges. If you find that most of your pie is consumed by work and family activities, however, you may need to compensate in some way. You (and your children, too) may benefit by your reevaluating the degree of balance among work, family, and personal time in your life. There are no easy answers to the concerns I'm raising, but thinking them over may help you assess the issue of balance in your life.

The issue of "downtime" is particularly easy for parents to ignore. Do you do at least one thing a day that you enjoy *in its own right?* Can you incorporate some leisure into your daily activities? Can you find at least thirty minutes a day to do something that's relaxing and enjoyable for yourself? Research shows that personal interests are crucial for your sense of inner peace and contentment. Keeping your equilibrium and combating stress by this means, and those discussed below, will help you in many ways. Ironically, giving yourself a break will help you attend to your children's needs as well.

- *Do you get enough sleep?* Most people need at least eight hours of sleep nightly. Unfortunately, most Americans get only six or seven.

- *Are you able to leave work issues at the workplace* and be present emotionally for your family members when you're with them? The importance of this ability to pigeonhole activities should be self-explanatory.

- *Are you able to set boundaries against outside demands* such as work-related entertainment or community volunteerism? Such commitments can be important. If your schedule is already full, however, can you delete some items from the agenda or diminish certain nonessential activities?

- *Do you have a vacation* at least once per year for five to seven days? Although popular wisdom states that the phrase "family vacation" is an oxymoron, getting away from work is crucial.

- *Do you exercise* at least two or three times per week? This level of exercise is the minimum necessary to maintain good overall physical and emotional health.

- *Do you see friends or engage in some social activity* at least once per week? Aside from the psychological benefits, a good network of friends can lead to overall better health.

- *Are you able to take time to be alone* at least fifteen to thirty minutes per day? This, too, is crucial for maintaining your psychological stamina.

GETTING YOUR (JUGGLING) ACT TOGETHER

Depending on how you answer the preceding questions, you may find that you're juggling the demands on your time and energy well enough. You feel stressed but not to a degree you can't handle. Your children seem fairly well adjusted to the demands on them, too, and they feel you give them enough attention. As you go about the business of family life, you're reasonably content. If so—congratulations!

It's also possible that you feel intolerably stressed. If life is a juggling act, maybe you feel you're about to start dropping the balls, bowling pins, swords, and flaming torches. How, then, should you respond to the dilemma facing you?

Don't Try to Be Perfect

Adjust your expectations. Go easy on yourself. Decide what's really important. Don't worry so much about external things—fancy cars, clothes, electronic gadgets, and other consumer goods—that may force you to overwork rather than being available to your kids and tuned in to their emotional needs.

Get Better Organized

Make sure you prioritize. Do advance preparation whenever possible. As Walt, the father of two boys and a girl, says, "You can do almost anything with kids that you can do without them. The catch is, it just takes a lot longer." When children are around, give yourself at least fifteen to thirty minutes more for each individual task. Allow plenty of transition time, too, particularly for getting from home to work, from work to the day care center, or from your child's school to home again. These transitions make life easier and less stressful. Prepare meals ahead of time, or buy prepared or carry-out food from time to time. Get your child's clothes ready the night before school.

Spread the Weight of Parenthood

Encourage your partner to share domestic responsibilities. Try to avoid clear-cut divisions of labor, especially along traditional gender lines. There will be less stress and more mutual understanding if both parents in a two-parent family can each do some of the various tasks. If you do split duties, don't insist that your partner perform tasks exactly as you do. Encourage him to do it in a way that's comfortable for him, and don't criticize his methods or results. Be flexible. The goal is to spread the work around and get the job done.

Avoid Unnecessary Errands

Many Americans spend far more time driving around than is necessary. Some of the chauffeuring and errand-running is unavoidable, but why do more than the absolute minimum? Try to consolidate errands. Avoid any that lack a tangible payoff; determine what must be done and what can wait. Skip "nuisance" errands, such as driving across town for a single pint of ice cream.

Get Help

Don't try to do everything yourself. Hire some kind of domestic help. I don't mean having an expensive full-time au pair or nanny. Even a neighbor of middle school age assisting you a few hours a week after school as a parent's helper can be a huge boost. While you cook, a parent's helper can play with or read to your kids so you're not overwhelmed by several domestic duties at once. Even limited housekeeping help can make a difference, too.

BE CREATIVE ABOUT CHILD CARE

If you can't afford child care, trade baby-sitting services with friends or neighbors. (Predictably, this arrangement works well only if the other family's child is compatible with your own—and not too demanding!—and if this situation doesn't leave you with yet another set of obligations to struggle with.) Some families arrange child care cooperatives. Explore what services your workplace offers. Although many corporations provide only limited assistance, others have benefits that you may not know about. Sociologist Arlie Hochschild writes in *The Time Bind* that many American families are actually underutilizing corporate resources, such as flextime, parental leave, day care, and after-school care that might otherwise help them balance work and family responsibilities.

DO "NOTHING"

At least now and then, disengage from everything. Do something that has nothing to do with duties, expectations, or goals. Take time for yourself. Go for a walk *just for the walk*. Listen to some relaxing music. Read the paper. Do a crossword puzzle. Soak in the tub. Stare out the window. Do some things that give you pleasure or help you relax.

IS ONE INCOME A POSSIBILITY?

Finally, here's an issue that's difficult to raise and complex to evaluate. It's more and more common for American families to earn two incomes. Many couples have no alternative to both spouses working outside the home. However, some families currently relying on two incomes may, in fact, be able to live on one. Each couple must consider if this possibility is desirable or even feasible. And of course there are many reasons other than financial need that can justify pursuing a career. I'm *not* necessarily advocating a Dad-goes-off-to-work-while-Mom-stays-home-with-the-kids scenario; in fact, what I'm suggesting *could* mean that Mom goes off to work while Dad minds the home and hearth.

Here's the core issue: you should periodically analyze your financial situation and clarify your goals regarding who earns the income, and how much. The financial payoff from both spouses working may not be what you imagine. In a recent book, *Shattering the Two-Income Myth*, Andy Dappen notes that for every three dollars of gross income that a couple earns, the second income may actually net only one dollar. Why? Ancillary costs such as child care, business meals, work attire, and taxes eat up most of the difference. The core issue: look at the whole financial picture, particularly when your children are ages one to six, since child care expenses at that time can be the highest you'll ever face. Assess what's really causing you stress, then consider if you should change the source of that stress or perhaps your attitude and response to the stresses instead. (For a further discussion of this issue, see chapter 17, "Financial Planning.")

TWENTY-FOUR

LATCHKEY KIDS

PEOPLE OFTEN ASK me at what age children can be left alone. There are two answers to this question—one legal, one developmental. Each state has guidelines from its Department of Social Services that mandate the legal age for leaving children alone. The age varies from state to state. Some states don't even have these regulations on the books. Nonetheless, you must consider the legality of leaving children alone in your community. (To learn the laws in your area, call your state's Department of Social Services.)

Whatever the legality, at what point is it *developmentally* appropriate for kids to be alone? My belief is that children really need a parent around, or at least they need to be in a situation where they're not alone. Even preteens and early teens benefit from having an adult present or conveniently nearby. A sixth-grader might be fine if left alone for a half hour to an hour but probably not for longer. It's not that kids can't be independent or self-sufficient under these circumstances; rather, the problem is that they feel lonely. When I cohosted a radio call-in show for kids recently, children repeatedly told me how scared they felt when home alone. This response varies from child to child, of course, but kids generally need to feel safe and well looked-after. They want an adult present to talk with them, to ask them about their day, to find out what happened in school, to hear about bad, happy, or funny experiences. They don't need the company just to create a safe environment; they also need communication, intimacy, and guidance about life issues, homework, and other personal needs.

THE RISK OF "PARENTIFICATION"

A school principal once told me that by making children into latchkey kids, we tend to parentify them—we make them into adults at an earlier age than is developmentally suitable. To complicate matters, we put children in an odd double-bind. On the one hand, we give them authority and autonomy; then we come home and expect these same pseudo-adults to revert to being kids again. We want them to listen to us and do as we say despite our having put them temporarily in an adult role.

What's the response? Kids often resent the switch. It confuses them. It also complicates the task for both parents and children to navigate the parent-child relationship. I'd suggest that if your child is younger than eleven or twelve, he or she shouldn't be left alone at all. Kids in their early teens can be left alone for up to an hour if you can call them (and they can call you) once they're home (assuming, of course, that this arrangement is legal in your state). In any case, I wouldn't leave children in this age group for more than an hour. Teenagers can be left alone for longer periods of time if their coping skills and overall responsibility warrant your trust.

OPTIONS FOR PARENTS

What if you simply can't be present during the after-school hours? Given parents' high-pressure schedules, this dilemma is becoming more common.

STRUCTURED AFTER-CARE

Many communities have "after-care" programs at schools or other locations. The best of these programs offer a combination of sports, playtime activities, and adult supervision that give kids a sense of security and guidance.

HOME CARE

On a fee basis, a trusted neighbor might take in your child for an hour or two following school. This arrangement is especially suitable for elementary school children, but even middle school kids may be amenable if the neighborly relationship is right.

TEEN BABY-SITTING

Is there a responsible high school student in the area who might briefly look after your child each afternoon? Teenagers today are less interested in baby-sitting than in earlier decades, but this possibility isn't out of the question. Under the right circumstances, this arrangement may be congenial for everyone involved.

SIBLING CARE?

One situation that tempts many parents is to have an older child look after younger siblings in the family. This arrangement has been common throughout human history and remains so throughout much of the world. However, I strongly advise against it. At least in contemporary America, it can be a recipe for trouble: once again it parentifies the older child, which can lead to the same difficulties discussed earlier, and it can easily lead to resentment by the younger children, thus intensifying sibling rivalry.

IF THERE'S NO ALTERNATIVE . . .

If your child absolutely must be left alone, make sure that emergency phone numbers are next to the telephone. You might also consider purchasing a cell phone. They aren't very expensive, and with one your child can reach you at a moment's notice. Regardless of your telephone arrangements, however, you should arrange for your child to have access to a responsible neighbor. Other preparations include rehearsing these emergency and nonemergency scenarios:

- Unknown visitors
- Uninvited children/teens/neighbors
- Fires or other household emergencies
- Accidents or medical problems
- Anxiety or loneliness
- Conflicts between children

Many parents assume that once children reach middle school, they can be left to their own devices. Frankly, older children often need more guidance, not less. They're more stressed by school pressures; they need more help with homework; they need more guidance about peer pressure, social problems, decision making, and physical and psychological changes. So it's important for you to be around for your kids. It's important to stay involved in their lives. The more involved you are in your children's life, the more you know what's going on. The more you know what's going on, the more you can help them with all the changes facing them. Your kids may balk at your involvement, but underneath they feel cared about, cared for, and loved.

TWENTY-FIVE

LETTING GO AND HOLDING ON

SOMEONE SAID LONG ago that parents give their children two great gifts: roots and wings. Roots provide the sense of connection that keeps children close to their parents and allows the parents to nurture their children. Wings allow the children to separate from the parents and eventually to move off into their own realm. Parents know that both roots and wings are important. Yet many mothers and fathers find it more difficult to give their children the wings than the roots. The fact remains: for kids to grow up, they really need to test their wings. This process can be scary for both parents and children. But it must happen.

Letting go is one of the most important tasks for parents, yet it's also a most difficult and emotionally charged process.

DEVELOPMENTAL STAGES

As with many other aspects of life, the timing involved in this issue is crucial. Rushing a child into inappropriate independence can cause great anxiety; thwarting a child's drive toward self-sufficiency can create tensions and resentment. It's important to sense what your child needs and respond with nurturing encouragement. I'll have more to say in a moment about how to determine "what your child needs." First, here's a useful overview for sizing up what children are going through at different phases of life.

Erik Erikson, a prominent psychological theorist, developed a theory that provides a good overview of children's social development. These stages aren't ironclad predictors of what your child will experience; however, Erikson's theory can give you a better sense of what's appropriate as children start to let go at different ages.

The first five stages that Erikson described are:

- Stage One (Birth to 1 Year)—Basic Trust versus Mistrust
- Stage Two (1 to 3 Years)—Autonomy versus Shame and Doubt
- Stage Three (3 to 5 Years)—Initiative versus Guilt
- Stage Four (5 to 10 Years)—Industry versus Inferiority
- Stage Five (10 to 20 Years)—Identity versus Role Confusion

Let's have a look at each stage, its characteristic features, and ways that parents can respond to children's needs.

STAGE ONE—BASIC TRUST VERSUS MISTRUST

Starting at birth and ending at about one year of age, stage one is the period during which infants develop trust for others and a feeling of security and well-being. This stage is when children are most fully dependent. They rely on parents for sustenance, shelter, comfort, hygiene, safety, and emotional well-being. Soon they start to explore the world physically, linguistically, and emotionally, yet they remain greatly reliant on others. Language creates some of the greatest developmental leaps at this stage, since babies begin to acquire the skill to indicate what they need from their caregivers.

Children at stage one feel simultaneous drives toward dependency and independence. On the one hand, they crave the safety that nurturing adults provide; on the other hand, they push outward to achieve new levels of autonomy. They often feel a developmental yearning for more space, more freedom, and more independence even at the same time that they want protection and nurturance. They need to explore, yet they also need their parents for grounding and for security. Babies at this stage often venture outward, then return to the parents when tired or scared—a process that some developmental psychologists call *refueling*.

What children need most at this time is acceptance and unconditional love. For most of the first year of life, dependency on others is almost total. Consequently, your role remains one of nurturance, patience, and guessing what the baby needs. You may find that even a baby can start to assert his will and begin to explore what he can accomplish with it. One example is the child who, seated in his high chair, repeatedly throws his bottle onto the floor. This may seem like mere aggravation to a parent, but it can suggest a pivotal change at work. Your child is grasping that his own choices can alter events. No longer a passive recipient of others' actions, he is discovering that he, too, can *act*. This sort of incident is the bedrock on which so many other behaviors are built.

STAGE TWO—AUTONOMY VERSUS SHAME AND DOUBT

The next stage covers ages one to three years, or roughly from the end of infancy through toddlerhood. During this stage, children start exploring the world. The more freedom a child has to be independent, the more he will begin to sense that the world is a good, safe place, which will set the tone for a positive attitude later in life.

The toddler years are usually the time when the child begins to explore his surroundings most energetically. As any parent knows, this process is often strenuously physical: crawling, walking, climbing, looking into cabinets and boxes, taking things apart, testing the environment with all five senses, and generally checking out everything in sight. At the same time, the exploration is emotional: saying no, making demands, trying out different feelings, and testing the limits of independence. Toddlers need to venture outward in all these ways; like babies, though, they need the security of knowing that their parents are available and ready to help if needed. Hence the child's progress during this stage is generally two steps forward, one step back.

At this stage of development you can give your child:

- Unconditional love

- Good, sensible limits on behavior

- Choices for age-appropriate activities

- A safe, childproofed environment for maximum freedom of movement

- Parental participation in peek-a-boo and hide-and-seek games, which help reassure the child that the parents will always come back

- Close parental attention, including listening, talking, singing, reading, and playing

- Reading aloud of books like *The Runaway Bunny* and *Goodnight Moon*, which stress parental love and reliability

STAGE THREE—INITIATIVE VERSUS GUILT

During this stage (coinciding more or less with the preschool period, or ages three to five), your child will continue exploring his environment. The scope of these explorations widens constantly. A positive school experience will help him develop feelings of trust, self-esteem, and internal confidence. These internalized feelings of safety and security encourage the child to take chances, progress in his development, and become more and more independent.

Stage three children generally want to start preschool but also experience separation anxiety. This ambivalence is hardly surprising. Preschool is often the child's first venture into the outside world, away from Mommy and Daddy and the home environment. Any concerns about the newness of departing from the known surroundings may be compounded by magical thinking—in this case, a feeling that the parent's absence from view means that the parent has ceased to exist. To ease the negative consequences of magical thinking, a child needs a repetitive experience of seeing Mom and Dad leave him at school but always coming back.

- Be as secure as possible with your choice of the program and teacher.

- Visit the school with your child to look around *before* the first day of school.

- To the degree possible, don't reveal your anxieties about your child's going off to school, since your concerns will almost certainly heighten his own, thus increasing separation anxiety.

- Go through your child's schedule to reassure him of what will be happening during the day, and when.

- Respect your child's dignity regarding drop-offs and pickups—some children want kisses and hugs, while others want to leave and arrive with a simple good-bye or hello.

- Consider the possibility (if the school permits) of a "gradual intake"—a decreasing amount of time during which parents can remain at school over a period of the first few days.

- Don't be overly alarmed if your child cries at drop-off time, as this response is common and generally stops soon after you leave.

- Put a picture of yourself and your family in your child's cubby at school to remind him of you.

- Make sure you're not late at pickup times, especially early in the school year, as this can intensify your child's anxieties.

- If possible, volunteer at school, which can help your child establish a connection between school and family.

- To the degree possible, invite one or more of your child's classmates over to play at home, since this also helps him connect home with the outside world.

The grades following kindergarten involve a huge cognitive and behavioral leap for most children in school. Teachers expect the students to do many more tasks and to have better impulse control than in preschool and kindergarten. There's more structure to the curriculum and more limits on the freedom to explore the classroom. Children must take turns, follow directions, and turn in homework. Some kids thrive on structure; others find these expectations stressful. How should you respond? The most important part of your role as parent during these transitions is to be supportive. Don't be surprised if your child vents his frustration at home, especially on first returning from school; this reaction is the equivalent of an adult letting off steam after a hard day's work. Don't take the situation personally. Your child is caught between the tug of contrary impulses: on the one hand, the drive for independence; on the other, the desire for nurturance and closeness with you, the parent.

STAGE FOUR—INDUSTRY VERSUS INFERIORITY

Ages six to ten years—the middle-to-late period of childhood—involves mastery of skills. Children need positive support and love from adults and peers to foster even greater independence. This is a significant period for helping a child develop high self-esteem and confidence, which can be paramount for success in later years. Children will try new things, master new skills, and work hard on projects. Competition with peers (academic, athletic, artistic, social, etc.) becomes more pronounced, since the child now endeavors to learn skills crucial to success during adulthood. This is a critical time: mastering skills leads to further confidence and self-esteem, while failure to master skills can lead to feelings of inferiority.

HOMEWORK-RELATED ISSUES

Homework is a big issue at this stage, since most schools increase the number, complexity, and difficulty of assignments. As a parent, part of what you face is the task of being available to help without intervening too much, which can jeopardize your child's ability to acquire independent learning skills.

WALKING HOME FROM SCHOOL

For many children, the drive for independence can manifest itself as a desire to walk to school or walk home after school lets out. You have to evaluate your own situation. My own feeling is that kids shouldn't walk to or from school unaccompanied until about third or fourth grade. I suggest that you wait until your child is truly comfortable and secure; then walk with him a time or two to make sure he understands the route and the rules. Never allow your child to walk alone. Don't scare your child about personal safety, but make sure he understands the safety issues involved.

PEER AND PARENT PRESSURE

Don't allow peer pressure or other parents to call the shots. Just because other parents in the neighborhood allow their children to do something doesn't mean that you should comply with your child's requests or demands. Some parents expect their child to be independent too quickly. Others go along with children's preferences too easily.

Trust your instincts. You know your child better than anyone else. Determine what you feel is appropriate, given your child's abilities, interests, and development.

STAGE FIVE—IDENTITY VERSUS ROLE CONFUSION

Finally, from ten to twenty years of age, children tackle the task of deciding who they are and what they want from life. They start to perceive themselves as more fully separate from their parents and other children. As part of this process, they examine their psychosexual identification. Peers have enormous influence during this period of your child's development. Exploring the world, evaluating likes and dislikes, and experiencing new emotions are all part of separation and individuation.

Children undergo enormous changes during this stage, and many of these changes have to do with issues of independence. Parents' overall influence starts to wane; peers become more and more important. This shift in affiliation is inevitable. What differs enormously is whether a fundamental trust exists between parent and child. If you have a good, strong relationship with your child, you'll work your way through even the most complicated changes during adolescence. If you don't, life will be much more difficult than it could be otherwise. (For a more detailed overview of this situation, see chapter 50, "The Teen Years.")

The truth is that during stage five, your child will be fundamentally ambivalent. He desperately wants to separate from you, but he also wants you to remain available to him. To complicate matters, he will probably refuse to acknowledge any emotional reliance on your perceptions, opinions, etc. Yet even when he won't talk to you—when he's feeling arrogant or moody—he's much more secure knowing you're there. Kids at this age balk at having parents around, but they feel loved by having you in the background. Ironically, the chief goal at this stage of parenthood is to become obsolete: to provide your child with what he needs to take the necessary steps toward autonomy and then move on into young adulthood.

PREPARE TO BE TESTED

Preteens and teenagers often subject their parents to seemingly gratuitous tests of independence. They may come home late after school. They may or may not phone when asked to do so. They may be uncooperative or noncompliant in pointless ways. Why? Mostly to test your will. Do you really mean what you say? Will you stand up to them if they violate the rules? Such behavior isn't necessarily "bad" behavior; it's no more "bad" than a toddler's behavior is "bad" when he refuses to put on his shoes or eat his vegetables. It's often just another way of exploring a sense of self and the distinction between self (the child) and the other (the parent).

GO EASY

Children are very tender-hearted at this age, and even the slightest criticism wounds them terribly during stage five. Seemingly harmless comments you make may cause deep offense, embarrassment, or anger. For this reason, it's important for you to go easy in your comments and criticism. This isn't to say you shouldn't speak your mind; rather, you should step carefully and avoid provocative phrasing. Comment objectively on mistakes or errors of judgment rather than making more personal attacks. Phrase criticism gently. Above all, avoid correcting or criticizing your child in the company of his peers, which most kids this age will regard as the most hurtful cut of all.

NEVER UNDERESTIMATE THE IMPORTANCE OF PEERS

Peers are ascendant at this phase of life. It's not overstating the situation to say that peers matter almost more than anything else. In fact, children in stage five largely define themselves in terms of their peers. Don't take this state of mind personally; it's simply the nature of adolescence. Peer pressure is a constant factor to consider as you view your child's behavior. Acknowledging the situation doesn't mean that you capitulate to your child's desires to comply with peer expectations; on the contrary, you have to stay steady and resolute. But don't lose track of the central place that peers hold in your child's life. If you stay calm, and if your child's self-esteem is high, the situation will stabilize in time.

TRUST BUT MONITOR

Teens and preteens start to have sleep-overs and other peer-oriented get-togethers that warrant the parents' vigilance. It's important for kids to have leeway in their social gatherings, but a careful parental eye is appropriate. You have a right to double-check about the nature of your child's plans. If he's heading over to a friend's house, feel free to call that friend's parents to make sure that this arrangement is acceptable. Your child may find your double-checking intrusive; however, you still have a right and a responsibility to monitor the situation. In fact, your child may appreciate that you care enough to make sure that he really is safe.

INSIST ON INVOLVEMENT

The trust-but-monitor approach also holds true for transportation or time limits on activities. Your child may want to go where he wishes, when he wishes, as he wishes, but you still have a right to clarify the situation and influence the plans. If travel plans sound vague ("Joe's friend is driving us in some other guy's car") you can press for details. Close parental involvement leads to a higher margin of safety. Don't threaten your child or make the situation sound too scary; just point out in a nonthreatening way that certain situations warrant your concern.

IGNORE ACCUSATIONS

So many parents are *un*involved with their children that kids may resent one who's engaged to a sensible degree. And many teens and preteens aren't accustomed to having an attentive parent on the scene or checking up on things. You don't have to be Parent of the Year—just be involved and feel confident that even if your child resents your involvement on the surface, he will feel taken care of and loved regardless.

CONSIDER THE ISSUE OF A CURFEW

As teens start dating, driving, and working, you'll have to face the issue of a curfew. Some parents have a curfew; some don't. I suggest a middle way:

- First, decide how mature your teenager is.
- Second, stress group activities rather than solo dating.
- Third, maintain the same lines of communication and safety precautions as during the middle school years.
- If your teen's behavior seems noncompliant, proceed to a more structured set of expectations, perhaps including a curfew.
- Whatever you decide, hold firm to your guidelines, because equivocating will allow your child to up the ante.

Be Unrelentingly Vigilant About Car Safety

Car accidents are the leading cause of death among teenagers. Although many states are tightening regulations for teen driving, the overall situation remains extremely dangerous. The older kids are when they drive, the better the odds of their reaching adulthood alive and uninjured. Statistically speaking, there's a high incidence of accidents among teens because they're less experienced; greater age correlates approximately with maturity and experience.

THE PARENT'S DILEMMA

The fundamental dilemma facing parents is the same regardless of the child's developmental stage. When do you hold on? When do you let go? There's no general answer—only specific answers for specific children. And to complicate matters, there's always the delicate balance of when to encourage dependency and when to encourage independence.

Ultimately, what I recommend is an odd blend of two suggestions that seem contrary but aren't. On the one hand, follow your child's lead. Watch him closely; sense what he's doing; try to determine what he needs. How will you know? Whenever there is stress or conflict between parents and children, there's often a hidden message that it's time to let go a little. An early instance of this tension is when a toddler, long accustomed to being carried, insists on being allowed to walk. His unstable gait may slow you down, but his fussiness about being carried can reveal a crucial push toward independence. A later, more complex example: an eight-year-old who demands the privilege of walking home from school. Is this appropriate? Only you, the parent, can decide.

Which brings me to the second suggestion. If you follow your child's lead, you may discover what he needs to gain greater autonomy and move toward the next stage of maturation. At the same time, you have to call the shots. Following your child's lead doesn't mean that you capitulate to anything; rather, it means that you size up the situation and make the decision that seems right. Letting go isn't a passive act, but is instead an active response.

Does this all sound difficult? In some ways it is; parenthood is often strenuous. But as with so many other aspects of parenthood, you'll find your own path. Letting go is hard in many respects, but it's easy in at least one: your child's whole being is full of the strange, grand drive toward self-sufficiency. Even at the moment of his birth he is pushing toward change and autonomy. The process is difficult for everyone involved, but it's wired into every cell, and it happens so gradually that both parents and children respond to the call for independence even when they aren't quite sure what it is they hear.

TWENTY-SIX

LET YOUR KID BE A KID

WHY DO WE pressure kids to hurry and grow up? One reason is that we adults often project our anxieties—economic problems, social pressures, competition between parents, and needs to succeed—onto our children. If we're on the fast track, we often expect our kids to join the rat race, too. Sometimes we expect children to acquire an unstated value system. We don't say anything outright, but we transfer our behavior, tensions, and expectations onto our kids as a result of what we do: how we dress them, what activities we choose for them, how we expect them to behave. We want the best for our kids, and we think that's what we're giving them—more material things, more activities, more encouragement to achieve—but in fact what we often do is rush kids into looking and acting like little adults.

The truth is, your child needs time to develop emotionally and socially. You can't rush her. You can't pressure her into faster development or greater achievement without the risk of harming her. As she gets older, she'll have plenty of time to acquire adult roles, behaviors, and expectations. Until then, let your kid be a kid.

One of the most worrisome ways in which adults pressure kids is through an obsession with academic achievement. There's nothing wrong with academic excellence, of course; the risk is in focusing too much on externals. Many parents are obsessed with grades, SAT scores, and honor rolls. Yes, these indicators have their place. But they are only *indicators* of scholastic growth, not the growth itself. They certainly aren't the same as intellectual development, imagination, or creativity. An obsession with these outward measures can stunt rather than foster a child's development.

In our culture, we're inundated with advertisements of programs guaranteed to accelerate children's growth. Teach your child to read at two! Start math lessons for your preschooler! In fact, any bright child can memorize words or math facts at an early age. But if you focus too early on reading or other cognitive skills, your child may miss an opportunity to develop social and emotional skills—skills she needs to develop before she's ready to go on to the larger academic tasks. A high-pressure approach can backfire. Sometimes kids who have been pressured into reading and writing too early can rebel at a later age.

THE DIFFICULT ART OF LEAVING WELL ENOUGH ALONE

Let your child develop at her own rate rather than imposing inappropriate expectations. Don't push your child simply because you yourself feel hurried. Don't transfer your own anxieties onto your child. Sometimes we push our kids because our own self-esteem is low. If our children look good and achieve great things, then we must be wonderful, too. Unfortunately, kids—particularly young kids—perceive this pressure as a form of rejection. If they need to change so much, then they may feel they're not good enough *as they are.* Their achievements must be more important than their being, their soul. This situation can be extremely stressful.

THE TYRANNY OF SCHEDULES

Our schedules are the antithesis of what's good for kids. Because children play in part to discharge tension and explore the world, they need lots of unstructured time. We overschedule them because our own lives are overscheduled. In addition, we don't want our children to miss out on any exciting opportunity or extracurricular opportunity after school.

Why are kids' schedules so packed these days? One answer is what I call the "guilty working parent syndrome." Because we have complex, demanding work lives with lots of time away from home, we often compensate by overindulging our kids. We try to make up for the fact that we're not at home by enrolling our kids in all sorts of fancy after-school activities, camps, or extended-day programs. To some degree this is appropriate. We do need child care. It's better to put your child in a high-quality program than in something less adequate. Still, children really like to hang out. They like to get together with other kids after school. They need large blocks of unstructured time just to be creative, to use their imagination, to discharge tension and stress through play, to *be.*

THE BURDEN OF ANXIETY

Another risk is in being weighed down by anxieties. Modern life *is* stressful. Still, don't weigh down your family by worrying too much. Curb your own fears, doubts, and insecurities. Don't transfer these onto your children.

Similarly, it's important that you fulfill your own dreams and ambitions rather than transfer them onto your children. Be the best person you can be, but don't expect your children to make you feel good about yourself. If you always wanted to be a dancer, singer, or baseball player but never had the opportunity, do what you can for yourself. *Don't pressure your children to do it for you.* Go out there and find something to do. Join a local baseball team. Get voice lessons. Take a dance class. But try to see your child as a separate, unique person. Separate her from your own goals so that you're encouraging her talents and gifts rather than projecting or transferring your own unfulfilled dreams onto her.

TIPS FOR LETTING KIDS BE KIDS

How can you combat a tendency to push your child to grow up too soon? How can you let your kid have a childhood? Below are some suggestions that can ease the pressures on parents and kids alike.

- *Find the balance between holding on and letting go.* Help your child find the happy medium between dependence and independence.

- *Allow your child to develop at her own rate.* Don't put too many inappropriate expectations on her.

- *Be attentive to your child.* Try to tune out the static of your life. Tune in to who your child really is and what your child's interests really are.

- *Limit the number of activities for a young child.* One activity after school—two at most—is plenty. More can leave her too tired to focus.

- *Leave plenty of time in your child's everyday schedule for unstructured time* to hang out, relax, and play in the yard or house. Free play reduces stress.

- *Allow your child to create, to use her imagination, to engage in fantasy.* This lowers her stress level and helps her discharge tension after a busy day at school.

- *Allow for "lazy time" on weekends.* Kids like to stay at home in their pj's, watch cartoons, hop in your bed and cuddle, or have a pillow fight.

- *Don't focus on big-buck activities.* A few major excursions are fun, and children appreciate them, but in the long run what they need are abundant, low-key, home-centered activities.

- *Play with your child in noncompetitive ways.* Let her choose the activity and lead the way. This is crucial. Many times adults think it's their role to teach their children. Quite the opposite. Parents are guides to their children but parents should give their children that unconditional love that says they're cherished just for being who they are. Don't get into a tug of wills with your child. If you're playing a game, let your child win some of the time, especially if she's younger than six or seven, and let her lead and control the game as much as possible.

- *Be a child yourself.* Forget now and then that you're the parent. Empower your child—let her believe that she has some control in her life. During most of a child's life, she's told what to do, how to do it, and when to do it. It's important for her to learn how to make decisions.

- *Keep activities simple.* Read books. Bake bread. Paint pictures. Go for a walk. Collect leaves. Look through a telescope. Fly a model airplane or kite. Assemble a scrapbook.

Remember, the goal is progress, not perfection. Your child will grow up in the fullness of time. Forcing her to grow up too soon risks a regression or a backlash, which can come back to haunt you. You may end up with a pseudo-mature child on your hands who's actually very insecure, lacks confidence, and has many fears, doubts, and insecurities. Instead, develop her sense of maturity from the inside by letting her grow at her own rate.

Finally, keep your sense of humor. Learn to laugh with your child—and at yourself. Take things one step at a time. Before you know it, your child will be grown up. Don't miss those precious, magical moments by forcing your child to hurry and grow up.

TWENTY-SEVEN

LOSS, BEREAVEMENT, AND GRIEF

Adele, age three, had just heard the news of her grandmother's death. Her initial response was to sob in her father's arms. Then, perking up, she asked, "Well, when Grandma's done being dead, can I go visit her?"

Martin had turned fifteen shortly before his father died. After some months of intense grieving, Martin seemed to accept the loss and proceed with his life. Tess, Martin's mother, felt reassured at first, then worried. Martin never spoke of his father and avoided the subject of his death. Tess decided at first to leave well enough alone, then pressed the issue with her son. What was he feeling? Martin responded with a tantrumlike outburst of rage that left Tess reeling. Stunned, she didn't know how to respond.

When Janice was ten, her best friend, Katie, died in a car accident. Janice took the loss hard: her appetite diminished, her grades fell, and she stopped taking part in activities she enjoyed. Her parents worried intensely about her state of mind. "It's been three months already," they complained to a friend, "and she's still in mourning." Janice's intense grief reaction continued for several months more, then started to ease. By about a year after the accident, Janice seemed more accepting of Katie's death and returned to her normal activities.

Monica's son Jake was four when he acquired a gerbil. For two years afterward, he paid little attention to his pet; he ignored it and avoided even the simple chore of feeding it. Monica felt astonished when, following the gerbil's death, Jake cried intensely, bemoaning the loss of his friend.

WHAT ARE BEREAVEMENT AND GRIEF?

"BEREAVEMENT IS THE reaction to the loss of a close relationship," according to Beverley Raphael, an Australian psychiatrist who is an expert on the subject. Dr. Raphael and other experts believe that this reaction helps human beings adapt to loss. If two people have a significant relationship and one of these persons dies, the survivor usually experiences some form of bereavement. This experience is as likely in children as in adults, though the nature of bereavement will vary according to the child's age.

Although bereavement is a reaction, what follows it is a *process*. This process involves a variety of emotions—sadness, longing, bewilderment, and so forth—collectively referred to as grief. When someone you love has died, you need a period of time to adjust to the loss. The grief process doesn't happen all at once, and it shouldn't be rushed or compressed. Grief has its own internal logic, and it almost always resolves successfully.

THE NORMALITY OF GRIEF

Although grief is painful in many ways, it is normal. A good comparison might be your body's response to a broken leg. The trauma to the bone is clearly harmful. You're in pain. If you ignore the injury or expect to heal overnight, you may do yourself much worse damage than what you have already suffered. But if you let your body's capacity for self-healing do its work, you will recover. The broken bone may end up stronger than it was before the injury.

The grief process is more complicated than the healing of broken bones, of course, and subtler as well, but the basic analogy is appropriate. Bereavement is the human organism's adjustment to major loss. This adjustment, as well as the grief you feel as part of it, is a sign of health, not a sign of its absence.

GRIEF AT DIFFERENT DEVELOPMENTAL STAGES

Children perceive loss in different ways at different stages of their intellectual and emotional development. When helping your child deal with loss and grief, keep in mind that his perceptions of loss will dramatically influence his emotional response.

BABYHOOD THROUGH AGE THREE

Very young children have little understanding of death. Toddlers may perceive that older children and adults find the concept of death upsetting and scary, but they don't understand why. They don't grasp the permanence of death.

AGES THREE THROUGH SIX

Preschool-age children start to understand death as the cessation of life, and they begin to perceive that every animal and plant will die someday. The concept of death as irreversible still eludes them.

AGES SIX THROUGH TWELVE

As kids reach school age, they increasingly understand the inevitability and permanence of death. Such understanding may lead to deeper anxieties, including a fascination with ghosts and new worries about the transience of life, but it coincides with a greater ability to express concerns and discuss the issues with adults.

THE TEEN YEARS

Teenagers have a dramatically increased ability to discuss many subjects, among them complex, ambiguous subjects like illness, death, and spiritual concerns. At the same time, teens' emotional reactions to these issues remains intense; there may be a gap between intellectual grasp and emotional understanding.

INDIVIDUALITY OF GRIEF

No matter how consistently grief may follow certain age-related patterns, it's important to remember that personal experience of grief is highly individual. One person's experience doesn't necessarily resemble that of someone else. What your daughter feels at the time of a grandparent's death may differ dramatically to the grief that your son feels. Some people grieve quietly, others more expressively. Children, especially, may show emotions that adults consider "inappropriate" to grief, such as giddiness, wild activity, or aggressiveness. There may also be abrupt shifts of mood. What's important to remember is simply that each child will respond to loss in his or her own way, and that a parent's calm, accepting attitude toward grief will have a beneficial effect.

THE GRIEF PROCESS AND EMOTIONS

The grief process usually includes intense emotions. The particular emotions, their intensity, and their duration will vary from one person to another. In adults, the most common emotions during the grief process are shock, sadness and depression, relief, regret and guilt, anger, and longing. Young children are most likely to experience shock, sadness, and longing, though outbursts of anger aren't unlikely, and expressions of guilt—at times an almost magical feeling that the child has caused the death himself—are certainly possible. Teenagers' emotions may include the full gamut typical of adults; expression of these feelings may be very intense.

Many people feel afraid of their own or others' emotions during the grief process. This fear is understandable: grief can be an intense experience, sometimes an almost altered state of consciousness. As much as possible, it's important to stay open to the experience of grief, since squelching it will only delay coming to terms with loss. The challenge of dealing with bereaved children (especially when you yourself are also bereaved) is often daunting. It may be advisable not to travel this path alone; thoughtful guidance from a counselor or therapist can be invaluable.

THE PHASES OF GRIEF

During recent decades, social scientists have identified several phases that people typically experience during the grief process. These phases make it easier to understand what formerly seemed a shapeless, confusing jumble of experiences.

The most persuasive theory of phases during grief is that formulated by the late John Bowlby, an English psychiatrist. Writing in *Loss*, one of the fundamental books on the subject, Dr. Bowlby states that people experience four phases of grief: 1) numbing, 2) yearning and searching, 3) disorganization and despair, and 4) reorganization. Most people, including children, experience all of these phases in one way or another. Dr. Bowlby warns, however, that "these phases are not clear-cut, and any one individual may oscillate for a time back and forth between any two of them." In short, the grief process rarely proceeds in a smooth flow from one experience to another. The erratic nature of the process is probably even more typical of children's responses to grief, given their intense emotions and sudden changes of mood.

If you have heard that grief occurs in a fixed set of "stages," it's worth noting that social scientists have developed their theories about the grief process as theoretical models, not as precise guides for what any one person will experience. The most important response you can make to your child's emotions following a major loss is to observe his behavior closely and to be emotionally available yourself.

DIFFERENT CRISES

In some senses, grief is grief. The nature of grief is fairly fundamental, and the process of dealing with it follows some consistent patterns regardless of its origin. That being said, it's also true that grief differs—at times dramatically—in accordance to the loss someone has suffered. Here again, this is true for both children and adults.

The following kinds of losses are the likeliest for most children:

DEATH OF A PARENT

From a child's perspective, the most traumatic loss is usually the death of a parent. The severity of the consequences will vary according to the child's age, the nature of the parent-child relationship, and the nature and duration of the parent's death (that is, whether as a result of accident or illness, slow or sudden death). It's risky to underestimate the impact of this event on any child. Under the best of circumstances, it's a significant loss; under the worst conditions, it's a calamity.

SEPARATION FROM A PARENT (FOR REASONS OTHER THAN DEATH)

Similarly, separation from a parent is almost certain to be traumatic even if it occurs for reasons other than a death. The most common cause for this event is divorce. Precisely because of the parents' central place in a child's world, such a separation is still a loss even if the child will stay in contact with the parent. (This is why it's essential, ideally, for the child to be allowed to love both parents and to have equal access to and involvement with them.)

DEATH OF A GRANDPARENT

Some children have only sporadic contact with their grandparents. The relationships between many children and their grandparents, however, is often extremely close and intense. The death of a grandparent is therefore a major loss for many children and shouldn't be considered insignificant. In addition, children who have never known their grandparents may mourn their absence anyway, given all that kids hear from friends about their own child-grandparent activities.

DEATH OF A SIBLING

Predictably, another difficult loss is the death of a sibling. This can be a double blow: first, because the child loses a peer, friend, and equal within the family; second, because the death may strike closer to the child's own sense of safety than would other deaths. The death of a sibling may leave a child feeling vulnerable, concerned that he or she is no longer safe in the world, thus intensifying a sense of loss.

DEATH OF A FRIEND

Depending on the nature of the relationship, other losses, too, can lead to intense grief. Parents should pay as much attention to the details of closeness as to the bond. For instance, the death of a cherished playmate may have much more impact than the death of an uncle that the child scarcely knew.

DEATH OF A PET

Parents sometimes underestimate how intensely children grieve the death of a pet. It's understandable that a dog's or a cat's death might inspire a sense of loss; it's harder to fathom how a hermit crab or a goldfish could prompt sadness and tears. The truth remains that children develop strong bonds to animals and often project profound emotions onto the least likely objects of affection. Just as children can deeply love inanimate creatures—stuffed animals or other toys—they can become attached to all manner of pets and feel bereft when they die.

HELPING YOUR CHILD COPE WITH LOSS AND GRIEF

You will almost certainly feel concerned about your child following a death in the family or within your family's circle of friends. Such concerns are understandable, and certain actions may help your child cope with grief. However, it's important to stress that you can't spare your child from the pain of grieving. The best you can do is to be supportive, loving, and attentive, as your own stable presence will assist your child in dealing with his own grief.

TAKE GOOD CARE OF YOURSELF

Perhaps most important, take care of your own well-being. This may be a tall order if your grief is intense. For instance, the death of your spouse will almost certainly leave you shaken, depleted, and disoriented—all understandable reactions that will complicate your ability to respond fully to your children. There's no simple way to meet the challenges you face. If you attend to your own health, however, you're much more likely to attend fully to your children's physical and emotional needs. Do whatever you can to keep your financial and practical circumstances under control. Marshal your resources. When possible, ask for help from relatives and friends. Seek support from competent counselors to the degree that seems useful.

DON'T ASSUME A CHILD UNDERSTANDS

Following a loss, children may or may not understand what has happened. A child younger than age six, for instance, may have only a vague notion of what death means. When you explain the situation to your child or discuss its aftermath, make sure that you're not using terminology that your child finds confusing. Complex medical information may be bewildering and scary. Financial discussions may also prove upsetting. If you need an outlet for your own frustrations and concerns, find it among trusted adult friends, relatives, and advisors; don't rely on your children for the support you need.

GIVE HONEST ANSWERS

We Americans tend to be squeamish about death. We have a tendency to avoid the subject, and we talk around it even when its reality stares us in the face. Bluntness about death may be uncomfortable, but honesty in this regard is crucial, especially when speaking with children. Vagueness ("Grandma has passed away") will only lead to confusion. Certain euphemisms can even cause children profound anxiety. For instance, comparing death to "falling asleep and never waking up" may prompt kids to fear going to bed at night. Don't explain too much about death, but don't sidestep the issues, either.

In a related vein, be open about what you don't know. The death of someone close to your family often prompts children to ask fundamental, often difficult questions. Typical ones include, "What happens when someone dies?" "Will I die, too?" and "Will you die?" It's important to answer (in an age-appropriate way) as fully as you can; it's equally important to admit the limits of your knowledge. Be honest about your religious/spiritual beliefs without pretending that you know everything.

STEP CAREFULLY REGARDING FUNERALS AND OTHER SERVICES

Make careful decisions about when and how children take part in funerals and memorial services. On the one hand, participation in these ceremonies can help kids accept the reality of death; it's important not to exclude them out of hand just because they're children. On the other hand, some kids may feel overwhelmed by what happens at funeral services. Toddlers, especially, may be unable to cope with the complexity and intensity of the occasion. Age isn't the only factor; individual differences are significant. Listen carefully to what your child says about what she's feeling. Decide what's right based on what you know about your child, not according to others' expectations or social customs.

CONSIDER YOUR OWN BELIEFS

To the degree possible, think through your beliefs before a crisis occurs. What you believe about death and loss will influence your own state of mind, which in turn will influence your children. Do you regard death as a cessation of all being? Or is it a transition to a different state of existence? What are your preferences about marking a death and celebrating a life? Knowing the answers to these and other questions will simplify your tasks when dealing with a death in the family, thus helping you help your kids at a stressful time. An emergency isn't a good situation for "winging it."

INCLUDE AND INVOLVE CHILDREN IN YOUR GRIEF

Be honest about what you yourself are experiencing. You have a right to your own emotional response to loss. Don't overwhelm your kids, but don't suppress your emotions, either. It's true that your children need you to be stable in times of loss, but they also need you to be open about your own experience. This is a good situation for modeling behavior that you consider appropriate to the intensity of life.

DON'T EXPECT A SET PATTERN IN CHILDREN'S GRIEVING

Just as children are intense, often effusive, and sometimes unpredictable in how they can react to other events, they can have intense, effusive, and unpredictable ways of expressing grief. They may be wracked by sobs one moment, giddy with laughter two seconds later. Don't be surprised if their grief is tumultuous, shifting abruptly from one emotion to another. Stay as steady as you can and go with the flow.

BE WILLING TO SEEK PROFESSIONAL HELP

Grief is normal, and most people cope with it well enough. However, some situations warrant concern. If you worry that your child's bereavement (or your own, for that matter) seems too protracted or too painful, consider finding help from a therapist, counselor, or member of the clergy. An increasing number of mental health professionals understand the issues related to bereavement; they can help you and your child adjust to loss more easily and less painfully—even though the grief response is normal.

LIFE GOES ON

Death strikes a terrible blow, and dealing with loss and grief is difficult. As if it isn't hard enough to cope with your own bereavement, parenthood sometimes includes the strenuous experience of consoling others while struggling with a personal sense of loss.

At the same time, helping your children deal with loss can be a consolation in itself. Children are full of life. Children are a sign of how life rejuvenates and renews itself. As in so many other ways, children—whom we claim to teach—are often our greatest teachers, and one of their constant, unspoken lessons is that life goes on.

TWENTY-EIGHT

LOVE

IF I HAD to name the single factor that's most important in developing a child's well-being, I would say unconditional love. Your child needs your love. More than that, however, she needs you to love her without conditions—looking pretty, getting good grades, winning at soccer, studying ballet, or even behaving well all the time. If your love depends on what she produces, she won't develop a truly solid sense of confidence. She won't feel fundamentally good about herself. Her confidence and self-love will last only as long as she keeps winning prizes, earning good grades, or feeling your pats on the back. If, on the other hand, your love doesn't depend on her accomplishments—if it's simply what you feel because she's your child—her confidence and self-love will thrive, grow, and become a source of strength she'll carry within her no matter what challenges she faces later in life.

THE STARTING POINT: YOUR OWN SELF-LOVE

As a parent, start by loving yourself. Some people object to this notion. Self-love is selfish, they say; it's immature and self-centered. Well, that isn't necessarily true. There's a big difference between narcissism—a distorted sense of oneself as the center of the world—and healthy self-love. Self-love doesn't mean that you think only of yourself; rather, it means that you acknowledge your own goodness and worthiness. Here as in so many other ways, balance is crucial. If you feel a balanced sense of self-love, you'll feel good enough about yourself to attend to others' needs, including your child's. You'll be more alert to what your child feels. You'll have more energy, patience, and imagination as you deal with the tasks of parenthood. If you feel hostile or indifferent to yourself, you're actually more likely to neglect your child or express negative emotions toward her, since you'll be more preoccupied with your own internal discomfort.

SIX EASY TIPS FOR LOVING YOUR CHILD(!)

I know it sounds ridiculous for me to offer tips to help you love your child, but certain actions you take or attitudes you maintain can make a big difference.

SEPARATE BEHAVIOR FROM BEING

Despite our best intentions as parents, we sometimes damage our children's sense of self by criticizing or punishing their being rather than their behavior. (By *being*, I mean who they are, as opposed to *behavior*, meaning what they do.) An example: you discover that your daughter's room is a mess. "What a pigpen!" you exclaim. This kind of utterance can wound a child to the core; she may interpret your words to mean not only that the room is a pigpen, but that she herself is a pig. A less provocative comment would be simply, "It's time to clean up your room." In short, you should separate your child's behavior from her being. Be aware of how your words may affect her self-esteem.

WATCH YOUR NONVERBAL CUES

Children can also be strongly affected by nonverbal cues. If you're supposedly playing with your daughter but not really engaged—reading a magazine, for instance, or talking on the phone—you send a message that being with her isn't important. Kids notice body language and gestures with astonishing acuity. Your words may say, "I love you," but your nonverbal message may be "I'm bored," "I wish you'd go away," or even "I don't like you very much today." We all have rough days; we can't be energetic and outgoing all the time. You have a right to your own feelings. If you're feeling irritable, though, it's best if you say so outright, since your child is likely to take your moods personally. Indifference, coldness, or the "silent treatment" can do a real number to a child's self-esteem. You don't have to be in high spirits to love your child; just let her know what you're feeling to provide a context. Tell her, "I'm sort of grouchy right now, but it's not because of anything you've done," or "I'm happy to be with you but I'm really tired," or whatever fits the situation. Otherwise your mixed messages may prompt her to feel hurt or not cared about.

SET RULES AND LIMITS

Throughout this book I discuss the importance of rules and limits, which children need in order to learn safe, good behavior. The issue of rules and lim-

LOVE   241

its is complex; what's most important is to walk the fine line between strictness and laxness. Excessive strictness can break a child's spirit; excessive laxness can be overindulgent. My impression is that nowadays, few parents set rules and limits that are too strict. (There are some parents, however, whose overall style is too authoritarian.) Many parents establish too few, inconsistent, or unenforced rules. The result, ironically, is that some children end up feeling that their parents don't really care what happens to them. After all, rules and limits are a sign that parents are concerned about the child's well-being. For this reason, I urge you to think carefully about the rules you establish and the limits you set; be consistent and have high expectations for compliance.

At the same time, make sure that you're fundamentally supportive of your child's efforts to meet your expectations. Rely on praise, not criticism, to reinforce behavior. Don't just note mistakes or bad behavior; stay alert to good behavior as well. As a rule of thumb, praise your child when she accomplishes a goal or meets your expectations. Criticize the behavior (not your child) when she makes a mistake or lets you down. If you praise your child more often than not—realistically, about 80 percent of the time—she'll make progress in developing her self-confidence and self-love.

GIVE YOURSELF SOME LEEWAY

How critical are you of your own behavior? How much do you attend to your own needs? To what degree do you let yourself make mistakes? Can you laugh at yourself? Do you accept your own foibles? Can you accept your imperfections?

These questions all touch on an important issue. Even if you try to be patient and accepting of your child but you don't give *yourself* any leeway, stress and frustration will increase. You need to be patient and accepting of your own shortcomings and imperfections. If you can love yourself and tolerate your own limitations, you'll be that much more loving of others, including your child.

INDULGE YOURSELF A BIT

Being the best parent possible, loving your child, and helping her feel that she's the most important part of your life does, in fact, require that you focus primarily on her. Parenthood unquestionably involves a lot of self-denial. At the same time, you need to accept yourself as a priority, too. You need to take care of yourself both because you have a right to be healthy and happy and because that way you'll be the best parent for your child. Be gentle with yourself, be good to yourself, indulge yourself a bit, and get the help you need to support your efforts as a parent. Parenting is full of rewards, but it's also challenging and stressful. For specific recommendations on how to meet these challenges and deal with the stress, see chapter 49, "Taking Care of Yourself."

EXPLORE THE PAST

The ways in which you were nurtured or neglected as a child will almost certainly affect your ability to nurture others; your past experiences set up patterns that influence your behavior as a parent. You may or may not be aware of these patterns, but they exist. For this reason, it's important to gain self-awareness and insight into your past. How did your parents treat you? How did they treat one another? How well did you and your siblings get along? What were the expectations in your family? Who made the decisions? (Chapter 33, "The Past," considers these issues in more detail.) If possible, explore your past and constantly keep in mind how the past affects the present, including your ability to nurture and love your child.

If you felt loved as a child, for instance, you probably feel secure enough to open your heart to your own child. If your parents prompted you to feel that love was contingent on performance, however—if love felt unstable or inconsistent—you may feel obstructed in some ways as you try to express the love you feel. You may fear becoming intimate with your child or with other people. These situations are understandable. But if you feel that you're blocked in any of these ways, consider speaking with a counselor or therapist to deal with the pain from the past. There's a risk otherwise that you'll transfer this burden to your child rather than break the cycle of distrust and hurt.

THE CHALLENGE OF OPENHEARTEDNESS

Loving with an open heart—unconditionally—is much easier said than done. We all have certain expectations. It's easy to feel frustrated when the people around us, including our children, fall short or let us down. Precisely because children are constantly developing, parents tend to look at them not just as people in the here-and-now, but as the people they will be. This attitude is understandable. Yet it's potentially problematic, too, for it focuses mostly on what is yet to come. Since children live primarily in the present, looking to their future runs the risk of missing the heart of their being. This is why loving children for who they are now—faults, limits, potentialities, and all—is so important.

Ultimately, this is my advice: accept yourself, and accept your child. You can accomplish both of these deceptively simple goals simultaneously. If you accept yourself—if you feel good about yourself and who you are—you'll be content, happy, and relaxed. You won't set your children up for unrealistic expectations. You'll be able to separate them from your own sense of self. You'll be able to avoid the temptation of projecting your own feelings onto them in a negative way, which will give them the best opportunity to thrive and succeed as young adults in the future. You'll be able to love them unconditionally.

Even the most nurturing mothers and fathers sometimes find their children exasperating or wearisome. No one (at least no one I've ever met) feels flaw-lessly loving all the time. Just about every parent I know sometimes says, "I love my children, but I don't always like their behavior." Children are wonderful but demanding, frustrating, and at times even infuriating. There's nothing wrong with discovering that the well of affection within you doesn't overflow from dawn to dusk. So if you sometimes feel less than enthralled with your child, and you find yourself tense, anxious, and ready to scream, join the club. Don't beat up on yourself. We all have those moments. Just take it easy, accept yourself as imperfect, and do the best you can.

TWENTY-NINE

THE MEDIA

- Is TV a parent's enemy, or can it be an ally?
- Will TV stunt your kids' intellectual development, or can it heighten their curiosity and ability to think?
- What are TV's physiological effects on children?
- Will watching TV and movie violence prompt your kids to act aggressively?
- What, if anything, should be done about violence in the movies, on TV, and in video games?
- Are children affected by other media, too, including newspapers, magazines, video games, and computer on-line services?

THESE ARE JUST a few of the questions that parents ask about how the media influence children. It's hard to answer these questions definitively. Movies, videos, computer games, and other media have strong but ambiguous effects on children. Even those old standbys, newspapers and magazines, warrant some parents' concern in an unpredictable and often violent society.

TV VIOLENCE—PARENTS' BIG WORRY

When it comes to concerns about the media, parents probably worry most about TV violence. This concern is appropriate: violence is epidemic on television, and some evidence suggests that frequent viewing of TV violence harms children's well-being and psychological development. It's important to note, however, that violence isn't the only important concern regarding TV; it may not even be the factor that's most damaging to children. But since violence comes to mind first for many parents, let's start with that issue.

First of all, the raw statistics about kids and TV aren't encouraging. On average, a five-year-old American child watches more than twenty-five hours of TV per week. That's the *average*. By implication, some kids watch more, while others watch less. After age five, children watch still more TV. These numbers are in themselves discouraging. To complicate matters, a violent incident is shown on TV, on average, approximately every six minutes. By seventh grade, an average child will have seen eight thousand murders and more than ten thousand other acts of violence on television.

However, formal studies of the *effects* of TV violence have been inconclusive. Various commentators, educators, social scientists, and other observers of the contemporary scene offer conflicting interpretations of cause and effect on this subject. Some feel that there's no clear correlation between violence on-screen and violence among children and teenagers; others claim that a connection is undeniable. It's true that you can find a study to support any theory you care to advocate. The bottom line is still unclear.

Skeptics claim that there is no scientific evidence that TV violence leads directly to violence among children. In fact, there may be no direct connection. However, there remains abundant anecdotal evidence concerning this issue; many teachers, clinicians, and parents feel strongly that there's at least partial causality between TV violence and children's violent behavior. If you observe preschool-age boys karate-chopping one another—perhaps in the style of *Teenage Mutant Ninja Turtles* or *Power Rangers*—it's hard not to conclude that something has influenced their behavior.

THE BIGGER CONCERN

The wider issue, however, goes well beyond the specific subject of television violence and its consequences: that is, the general influence of TV in American culture. Television has an enormous power to shape children's thinking processes, opinions, worldviews, habits, and beliefs. Commercial television is ruled largely by advertisers. As one TV executive stated years ago, "Television isn't an entertainment medium, it's a marketing medium." Forget about aesthetics and education—the TV companies certainly do. Forget about entertainment for entertainment's sake; that's secondary, too. What matters most to commercial TV companies and their affiliates is selling merchandise.

The clients who pay for commercial airtime are the businesses that the TV stations cater to. Children and families are mere consumers. Conveniently, children are easy targets for exploitation. Children don't easily separate fantasy from reality, and they are easily seduced by the fast-paced magic of TV wizardry. Advertisers know how vulnerable young children are, and they often prey on their vulnerabilities. As a result, it is difficult to change the morals and ethics of commercial broadcasting precisely because the industry is so dependent on advertising to pay the bills. Advertisers choose which stations to work with according to the station ratings. What are the chances, then, that TV executives will focus on children's needs?

In 1996, the U.S. government prodded the broadcast industry into airing at least three hours of "educational" programming each week. But the TV companies themselves had wide leeway to decide what constitutes an educational program and what doesn't. As a result, the standards are predictably dismal. When forced to justify specific programs' educational content, television spokespersons have provided far-fetched, even laughable rationalizations, such as the claim that old Road Runner and Wile E. Coyote cartoons instruct children on the importance of desert ecosystems.

Below are more issues relevant to children's TV viewing.

DISTRACTION AND DISPLACEMENT

As a former day care center director, as a teacher, and as a mother, I believe that protracted TV viewing leads to a reduced attention span, an inclination toward frantic activity, and a loss of creativity. It can also lead to poor reading habits and a limitation of artistic abilities. Kids tend to be mesmerized by TV; their minds go into neutral. They also get less exercise if they're constantly in front of a television set. In short, TV often displaces other activities, such as playing with blocks or other construction toys, role playing, doing sports, designing and building projects, and experimenting with materials and artistic media. In addition, family members don't interact as much or converse when they're glued to the tube.

EFFECTS ON HOMEWORK

One study indicates that TV may reduce the time that children spend on homework. Other studies aren't as clear-cut in showing this effect. However, I find it hard to imagine that there isn't a correlation between watching television and avoiding homework. Almost any kid would rather watch TV than do her homework.

REENGAGEMENT WITH THE WORLD

Some research indicates that even after viewing television for only fifty minutes, it takes a child about five to ten minutes to become actively engaged and communicative again. TV has a hypnotic effect on children and adults alike. There's nothing wrong with feeling engrossed in an interesting program; the problem is that the dazed state that many children enter while watching TV persists after the program ends. Kids sometimes act irritable, even disoriented, following long periods of viewing television.

REDUCED ATTENTION SPANS

Some studies suggest that TV can increase a child's attention span; others indicate that TV definitely reduces children's attentiveness because it's so quick-paced and often contains minimal content. Perhaps the reality of this situation depends on the kind of program. Other factors include the number of commercials and the show's pace, content, and overall mood.

DESENSITIZATION

In my practice and teaching, I sense that children can become desensitized by what they see on TV. Observing fights, rapes, murders, explosions, and lots of mayhem leaves children numb to human suffering. People become objects instead of human beings. Children begin to disengage from what's really happening, and they objectify what they're seeing on television and disassociate from it.

TV IMAGES OF WOMEN AND MEN

The images of women and men on TV are often a distortion of reality. The complexities of human personalities are often reduced to stereotypes. Sex roles, too, are often presented stereotypically. Although the majority of Americans (51 percent) are women, most prime-time TV characters are men. Few male characters on prime-time TV ever do household chores, while in real life men nowadays are helping out more at home than in the past. Although men and women are going into professions in roughly equal numbers, only a small minority of female characters on TV work in a professional role.

WHAT A PARENT CAN DO

Despite its numerous, profound limitations, television has the potential to help children learn and grow. It can provide children with important information about the world. However, making constructive use of TV requires parents to be strong-minded guides. You should monitor the TV scene, guide your child, and set clear limits.

SELECT PROGRAMS CAREFULLY

Don't let your children simply surf the channels. Explore what is available. Pick carefully. Even some of the so-called "family-friendly" channels offer programming of questionable value.

Rent Videos

Again, you have to pick carefully, but videos at least allow you more discretion than being at the mercy of broadcasters' schedules. Preview what your children will see, or watch with them.

Ensure Balance

Provide plenty of other activities—games, sports, cooking, art, music, and outdoor explorations. This approach will require more of your time and effort. Still, it's preferable to letting your child's mind marinate in the often toxic brew of commercial TV.

It's not necessarily the government's role to monitor television; parents should accept the lion's share of responsibility. If you're unsure about a particular show's appropriateness, watch it and decide for yourself. If you find it inappropriate, don't abdicate your responsibility and let your kids watch it anyway. Many parents feel a temptation, of course, to use TV as a baby-sitter. This is risky but not entirely inappropriate. Letting your kids watch a show can allow you a break from looking after them, or it can let you focus on an older child's homework while a younger child is occupied. These are legitimate uses of television. But these choices assume a willingness to assess the shows and make decisions about what's acceptable. Use TV carefully for this purpose.

- *If a particular show is inappropriate, stand firm in declaring it off limits.* Whether "everyone else gets to watch it" or not isn't the issue. Is the show something you want your kids to watch? Make your decision and be firm. Ideally, you should offer an alternative you prefer.

- *If a show is borderline—not ideal but not completely inappropriate for your child's age level—consider watching it with your child.* Use the show as a vehicle for discussion. Ask your child to explain whether the events portrayed on the show seem real or unrealistic. What does she think of the characters' behavior? What is good or bad about the show? Do the characters manifest stereotypic thinking? Take the negative effects of television and transform them into a positive experience. The show itself may not be educational, but your child can learn something from your discussion of the issues involved.

- *Help your children distinguish fantasy from reality.* Ask if they consider TV situations realistic or not. Start at an early age so that your children really begin to become reality-based and understand what's entertainment. Let them tour a television station or a movie set to see how shows are made.

TEACH YOUR CHILDREN ABOUT ADVERTISING

Are the products in a store as pretty as what they see on television? Do they do what TV ads have claimed? Will those tennis shoes, for instance, really make your child invincible, as the advertisements would have kids believe? Help children become smart, critical consumers.

THIRTY

MOTHERS

FOR MANY WOMEN, motherhood is the single greatest transformation of adulthood. It's not just the breadth of their new responsibilities that changes their lives; it's also the *permanence* of being responsible for a new life. Once a mother, always a mother.

I want to say outright that becoming a mother has been one of the most blessed, miraculous experiences of my life—one that I couldn't imagine despite having spent my whole professional life around children. I had been a kindergarten and nursery school teacher for many years, and I had been the director of a day care center. I had helped other people to raise their children, and I had enjoyed working with kids so much that I very much looked forward to raising my own. I felt well prepared and eager. But working with children and parenting children are fundamentally different. If you go home and don't have kids to deal with, it's simply not the same experience as having a parent's round-the-clock responsibilities. Being a parent all day seven days a week is both a challenge and a delight that nonparents can't really understand. Fortunately, the delights are abundant and the challenges are mostly manageable. But the tasks are still demanding, often difficult, and never-ending.

To complicate matters, there's great tension within our culture regarding what motherhood ought to be, and this tension complicates the task that all of us face as mothers.

THE MANY VISIONS OF MOTHERHOOD

Until recently, few aspects of human life were more predictable than the biology of motherhood. A woman conceived a child, carried him within her womb, gave birth to him, and nursed him. However, even before the development of reproductive technology—in vitro fertilization, surrogate pregnancy, and so forth—the biology of motherhood was only one part of the story. Other aspects of being a mother varied enormously throughout history and from one place to another. As Shari L. Thurer, a psychologist at Boston University, states in her book *The Myths of Motherhood*, "Motherhood—the way we perform mothering—is culturally derived. Each society has its own mythology, complete with rituals, beliefs, expectations, norms, and symbols. Our received models of motherhood are not necessarily better or worse than many others." That is, the expectations of what mothers ought to do, as well as the specific child care duties that mothers perform, have varied from place to place and through the passage of time.

During the past few decades, perceptions of motherhood within American society have changed in many ways. As Thurer goes on to write: "The briefest glance at history will dispel any notion that there is but one correct way to mother." Yet mothers feel (as they have probably always felt) both external and internal pressures to do everything "right." This is understandable; most parents intensely desire to serve their children well, to help and protect them, to teach them what they need to know about life. It's easy to imagine that there's a clear-cut path, the Proper Way, to accomplish these tasks. Doesn't an experience as ancient and as intrinsically human as motherhood embody some sort of fundamental common sense? To some degree, that's probably true. There are elements of common sense: feeding your child, keeping him warm, avoiding accidents, and so forth. But the details of child care have differed so vastly over the millennia, and from culture to culture, that it's impossible to argue that one single way is correct.

Simply put: There's no one Motherhood. There are millions and millions of mothers, and there are many ways to be a mother. You can benefit from the collective wisdom of individual mothers; you can find solace in your own culture's traditions, suggestions, advice, and expectations about motherhood; but you still have a right to walk your own path. By all means consider what other parents believe and what parenting experts advise. That being said, however, take outside opinions (mine included!) with a grain of salt. Only you can decide what it means to be a mother.

THE POLITICS OF MOTHERHOOD

Motherhood is so crucial that during certain stages of history, cultures have suffered great hardships—have even vanished altogether—because women didn't give birth to enough children. Famines, wars, or plagues sometimes killed so many women or rendered so many of them infertile that the tribe or clan couldn't reproduce. Even today, when disruption of these sorts seem unlikely in most of the world, people in certain countries express deep concern about their own viability: falling birthrates in Italy, for instance, have led to fears about that nation's long-term economic health. Every society has an enormous stake in its mothers' survival and fertility. Even those cultures that are most neglectful or abusive of women can't endure unless the women of childbearing age are sufficiently numerous and healthy. In addition, mothers have always had a primary role in transmitting the culture's values to the young. To quote the ancient adage: The hand that rocks the cradle rules the world.

Motherhood isn't just a personal, biological event. It's also a value that various forces within a culture will define in different ways and struggle over. The political consequences of this situation affect all mothers.

One example is the current squabble over working mothers. Some people within American culture feel that a mother's place is strictly in the home. Only mothers (these people say) can provide what children need; although women may be fully capable of working elsewhere, their duty and greatest fulfillment lies in caring for the young. Encouraging women to work outside the home will not only complicate the tasks of parenting; it will also risk jeopardizing the well-being of countless children. Meanwhile, other people within our society reject this line of reasoning. They argue instead that mothers can be good, responsible parents while simultaneously attending to their children and pursuing outside work. Full-time, stay-at-home mothering isn't necessary for children's safety, happiness, or proper development; on the contrary, women who find fulfillment at home *and* in the workplace may foster rather than jeopardize their families' well-being.

This is a battle that's raging with great fervor on the contemporary scene, and I'm certain that the arguments and counterarguments will continue for a long time to come. I've certainly reduced the two sides to simplistic terms; there are numerous variations spanning a wide spectrum of beliefs. My point is simply that motherhood generates intense passions, and many of these passions are political.

The most important dimension of what I'm describing is that what you face as a mother isn't just the physiological issues—nutrition, elimination, growth, health—of child care. It isn't just the psychological issues—attachment, separation, identity, self-esteem. In addition, there are the political issues, many of them far more complex than the question of stay-at-home versus go-to-work mothers I've sketched above. Part of what you'll face, unfortunately, is what I call the politics of the Perfect Mother.

As Shari Thurer states, "[I]n the current mother mythology, children are seen as eminently perfectible. There are no bad children, only bad parents. . . . This wishful idea . . . keeps parents permanently on the hook. Parenting is a precarious business. Do it wrong, suggest the advice columns and child-care manuals, and your child will be warped." As she rightly implies, this is nonsense. Children tend to thrive. Provided with love and an acceptable level of reasonably consistent care, most children will grow, develop, and reach competent adulthood. But current standards for good mothering are, according to Thurer, "so formidable, self-denying, elusive, changeable, and contradictory that they are unattainable. Our contemporary myth heaps upon the mother so many duties and expectations that to take it seriously would be hazardous to her mental health."

THE GOOD-ENOUGH MOTHER

In truth, you don't have to be the Perfect Mother. You don't have to be all-loving, all-knowing, all-giving, all-accepting, all-forgiving. You don't have to be infinitely selfless. In the words of the great psychologist D. W. Winnicott, all you have to be is a "good-enough mother." Does this mean indifference, sloppiness, or mediocrity? Not at all. Being a good-enough mother means simply that you accept your own imperfection and proceed do the best you can caring for your children. Parenthood is by nature uncertain. It's not always possible to know what your kids want, much less what they need. Even your best efforts are subject to outside influences—everything from the laws of physics to the will of society to plain old luck. You can't accomplish everything that needs to be done in a single day, much less throughout the whole span of the childhood. Given the complexity of parenthood, how can you be perfect? It's simply not a possibility.

It's not necessarily even desirable. If you were the Perfect Mother, you might actually jeopardize rather than foster your child's successful development. Here's a small example. During infancy, children need a parent to provide complete physical care. A baby must be fed and kept warm and clean. A parent's proper role during this stage of development is to attend to the infant's every need. During toddlerhood, however, a child enters a stage of more complex needs: on the one hand, toddlers still require considerable task-by-task attention; on the other hand, toddlers feel a new urge to assert their independence, and they start to acquire skills that will eventually allow them to care for themselves. But toddlers are ambivalent. They want to be cared for *and* to care for themselves. One of the reasons that toddlers can be frustrating is that they are caught between contrary drives. They don't know what they want—or they want two or more things (often contrary things) simultaneously. Hence the enormous frustration they feel and express through nay-saying and throwing tantrums. The role for parents is therefore difficult as well.

In response to this kind of situation (not just relatively straightforward issues like dealing with toddlers, but more complex parenting tasks as well), I urge you to be a good-enough mother. By all means do everything you can for your child. Love him. Look after him. Perform the tasks that are appropriate to his stage of development. At once nurture him and challenge him. But accept the finite limits of your own abilities, energy, and imagination. Tolerate the possibility—the certainty—that you will make mistakes, fall short of his expectations, and sometimes let him down. I'm not suggesting that you should *seek* human imperfection as an excuse or as a refuge, only that you should acknowledge your own as well as other people's limits. Imperfection is as fully a human attribute as the desire to overcome it.

THE NITTY-GRITTY FOR MOTHERS

When I consider the complexity and vastness of motherhood, I feel supremely challenged to provide useful guidelines, suggestions, advice, and tips. I am a mother myself. I know how difficult parenting can be. I understand both the immense scope of the responsibilities and the sense of helplessness that being a parent can bring. I also feel frustrated by the intricacy of American culture, by the contradictory nature of the messages that it barrages parents with, and by the ambivalence that it expresses toward parents in general and toward mothers in particular. Given this situation, what kind of recommendations can I offer to mothers? How can I dare to offer any at all?

I'm going to acknowledge the challenge and simultaneously admit to my own qualms about it. This chapter can't address all the particular difficulties that mothers face during the parenting years. However, I can offer some ideas—derived both from my own experiences as a mother and from my clinical practice—that may prove helpful.

TO WORK OR NOT TO WORK?

One of the most contentious questions within American society is whether mothers should work outside the home. There's nothing I can do to resolve this argument. Here are two aspects of the situation to consider, though.

First, there's no possibility that American women will stop working outside the home. Outside income is simply too crucial for most families to allow the option of a strictly parenting role. According to the *New York Times*, 77 percent of all married women with school-age children were employed or looking for work in 1996. The figure was 63 percent for women with preschool-age children—a figure five times higher than the equivalent statistic in 1950. Moreover, American women frequently pursue careers, often waiting until their thirties and forties to start their families. Working women have been major participants in the world of work since the late 1950s, and they'll continue to join the work force for the foreseeable future. Current divorce rates will reinforce this situation. More than 50 percent of first marriages end in divorce, as do around 55 percent of second marriages. In the majority of these divorces, children will live with their mothers, who will become the custodial parents. Some of these women will remarry, but many will not, placing great economic pressure on mothers to work outside the home.

Working mothers are now the norm. This may or may not be an ideal situation—many women would rather have less financial weight on their shoulders—but it's certainly not an anomaly. Cultural critics of working mothers simply ignore the fact that a very low percentage of American families are currently composed of a breadwinning father and a stay-at-home mother. So if you feel that you're somehow deviant by deciding both to work and to raise children, rest assured. You're in the majority.

The second issue concerns whether children can fully and happily develop despite their mothers' less than full-time presence in the home. The evidence here offers a clear-cut yes. Again, this isn't to say that most mothers wouldn't rather have more time with their children. But as regards the ability to thrive under these circumstances, there is qualified but genuine evidence that children manage fairly well. If I sound hedgy, I am. The reason: it depends on the child's stage of development. Studies by John Bowlby, Mary Ainsworth, and other researchers suggest that to thrive emotionally, infants need the focused care of either a loving, attentive parent or else a loving, attentive parent-surrogate. Toddlers and older children require consistent affection and care from a parent or parent-surrogate as well, but they gradually acquire the ability to thrive when looked after by one or more other caregivers. School-age children continue to broaden their scope of acceptance. The most important factors throughout are the warmth and consistency of care.

The implications are that if your child has close, competent, one-to-one care during infancy, he will develop normally. The mother does not need to be the sole source of this care. A loving father is perfectly acceptable; the same holds true for a loving grandparent or other relative. The key issues are affection, competence, and consistency. In the best of all possible worlds, you wouldn't have to choose between nurturing your child and nurturing your career. Given obvious and abundant shortcomings in the world we inhabit, though, you may be forced into situations that aren't what you'd otherwise accept. But doing so doesn't mean you'll jeopardize your child's health, happiness, or development.

CHILD CARE AND "MOTHERCARE"

Once you have a child, your life will never be the same. There are ways in which the changes you experience will be unalloyed delight; some changes will lead to complex frustrations; some changes will create a mix of emotions that can be hard to understand, much less describe to others. Whatever else, though, motherhood will open up an entirely new phase of your development as a person. This is true for fatherhood as well, of course—or ought to be. Parenthood more than any other role demands that you see the world anew and make decisions thoughtfully. Your life is no longer solely your own. You can't make many choices on the spur of the moment. You have responsibility to nurture a helpless new human being, and everything you do now counts even more than before.

Many mothers feel exhausted by the burdens they carry. This exhaustion can occur regardless of how much you love your children. Motherhood is incredibly demanding. Under these circumstances, how can you pace yourself so that you don't burn out, lose patience, or feel resentful of the children in your care?

Some suggestions:

Take Care of Yourself

You can't maintain your stamina if you attend solely to others' needs. Somehow you must recharge your own batteries. This can take any number of forms; pick and choose among them as your circumstances, including time and financial resources, allow. But by all means find something that allows you to pace yourself and avoid physical and emotional depletion. For further suggestions, see chapter 49, "Taking Care of Yourself."

Explore the Past

Your relationship with your own parents will have an enormous influence on how you feel about being a mother. If you're like most people, your family of origin provided you with both positive and negative images of parenting. You may feel that your own parents offered you enough love and generosity that you want to emulate them as you raise your own child; on the other hand, your parents may well have made mistakes that you wish to avoid. Both reactions are common and understandable. To understand the situation better, you may find it useful to explore the past even as you focus on the present. The thoughtful guidance of a trained therapist or counselor may help you understand your own upbringing in ways that enrich your own experience of motherhood.

Listen to Your Children

In some ways parenthood isn't only about child development, but about parent development as well—not just child care but also "mothercare" and "fathercare." I mean simply that it isn't just the children who do the developing as family life unfolds. Parents, too, find themselves transformed. Parenthood is a kind of dance, with both parents and children guiding and changing each other as the dance gets under way. As one mother described the situation to me, "I don't know who's learning more from this experience—my kids or me."

To benefit fully from this dance, you need to stay as alert to each other as possible. Listen to what your children are telling you. Listen not only in terms of the words they say—their expressions of frustration when you feel you're doing things right, their expressions of love when you feel you've failed—but listen also to the subtle, even silent cues they give you. One of the truly remarkable things that happens during the parenting years is that children often alert parents to what they need, or even to what the parents themselves need. (A stark but amusing example of the latter is when a teenager, exasperated by his mother's constant hovering, told her, "Mom, you really need a hobby.")

BE A GOOD ROLE MODEL (BUT DON'T SWEAT IT TOO MUCH!)

Mothers are significant role models for their children—for daughters chiefly in terms of same-sex identification, for sons chiefly in terms of male-female relationships. Both aspects of being a role model are substantial, but in many ways the issues tend to take shape on their own. If you are comfortable with yourself and warm toward your children, there's not a whole lot else you need to do other than be available to them. The process of role modeling will take care of itself.

Regarding daughters, mothers are important not just for manifesting the so-called feminine attributes (caregiving, nurturing, creating a warm domestic environment) but also for so-called masculine attributes like strength, assertiveness, and independence. The best way for a mother to manifest these attributes is to be a whole person herself, in touch with all sides of her personality and accepting both the "masculine" and "feminine" sides. (For a further discussion of these issues, see chapter 20, "Girls.")

In the meantime, sons benefit greatly from being able to stay connected to their mothers in a warm, loving way. Having a close relationship with his mother can allow a boy to develop a fundamental sense of intimacy and communication and closeness with others. Some mothers worry that nurturing this kind of closeness can make their son a wimp or a sissy; on the contrary, boys need this sort of close bond with their mother, including an openness for expressing a full range of emotions, not just the so-called masculine emotions of aggression or anger. (For a further discussion of these issues, see chapter 3, "Boys.")

As with other dimensions of human experience, action speaks much louder than words, so make sure that your values, beliefs, and morals are part of your everyday life. I'm aware that this is a huge responsibility; your kids will be watching every move! At the same time, it's a tremendous challenge and a joy to be that kind of mentor. So if you want a child who is focused, attentive, relaxed, nurturing, kind, gentle, and patient, those are the behaviors that you must have within yourself first and demonstrate to your child.

FINDING YOUR OWN PATH

Although many people tend to assume that motherhood is predetermined—a clear-cut, fundamental set of expectations, actions, and values—it isn't. Mothers have raised their children in different ways over the whole span of human history, and somehow the species has survived. It's presumptuous for anyone to claim that he or she has a definitive sense of what mothers ought to do, feel, or be. I'm not saying that motherhood is simply whatever you want it to be. If you feed your children nothing but turnips, dress them in aluminum foil, or teach them always to speak backwards, they (and no doubt you) will suffer the consequences. Like all of us, you stand to gain from delving into the acquired knowledge of the human race and discovering what is useful, good, and wise. But I do believe that doing so is ultimately an individual quest.

I urge you not to let others (either individually or collectively) dictate what it means for you to be a mother. I urge you to avoid letting others prescribe how you ought to raise your children. I urge you to explore the possibilities, consider your options, trust your intuitions, seek good advice, weigh it carefully, and ultimately, find your own way.

THIRTY-ONE

PARENTING STYLES

TO BE A good parent, you have to be in touch with yourself as an adult and be a fully mature, well-rounded person—having good self-esteem, being reasonable and flexible. That being said, parents raise their children in different ways.

How you raise your children invariably reflects several aspects of how your own parents raised you. Each parent learns from his or her own mother and father. Your parents were your first role models; it's impossible for you *not* to be influenced by what they did or didn't do when you were a child. The influence may be relatively straightforward or complex. If you found your parents nurturing and supportive, their nurturance and supportiveness will almost certainly prompt you to act in similar ways toward your own children. If, on the other hand, you had an unpleasant or conflicted relationship with your parents, you may react against their behavior and work hard to do the opposite of what they did. The daughter of inflexible parents, for example, may swear she'll never boss her own kids around, thus becoming a more permissive parent. This response may be appropriate and beneficial; on the other hand, there's always the risk of overreacting.

DIFFERENT PARENTING STYLES

Despite the huge variety of human beings, there are four fundamental parenting styles: flexible, inflexible, permissive, and disengaged. Any one parent may manifest a combination of these styles; however, one style may predominate. In addition, your child may respond to your personal parenting style, which may predispose him to manifest certain patterns of behavior. Note, however, that neither your predominant parenting style nor your child's responses to it are cast in stone, and many factors—not just your parenting style—will influence your child's personality, development, and behavior.

FLEXIBLE

The flexible parent is warm, affectionate, reasonable, capable of good listening, and neither neglectful or too indulgent. Although confident of his or her authority, this kind of parent isn't strident or rigid. The flexible parent helps the child to feel good self-esteem, includes the child in negotiations about behavior and activities, fosters collaboration in problem solving, and is open-minded but not overly permissive.

Generally, researchers have found that children of flexible parents have high self-esteem; they're good problem solvers; they're achievement oriented; they are often leaders and excellent students; they tend to be cooperative, creative, and basically happy kids.

INFLEXIBLE

By contrast, the inflexible parent is controlling, rigid, strict, and overly concerned with maintaining control over children. The inflexible parent doesn't allow children to make mistakes; he or she expects perfectionism and has inappropriate expectations about children's abilities at various developmental stages. The inflexible parent can't adjust his or her parenting style to the child's changing developmental stages. These parents tend to be those who say (or at least believe) that "children should be seen, not heard." Their rule of thumb is, "It's my way or the highway."

The children of inflexible parents tend more often to be moody, anxious, and characterized by lower self-esteem. They can be well behaved, but they are basically followers and tend to be average-to-good students.

PERMISSIVE

Another basic parenting style is that of the permissive parent—the indulgent parent who allows his children an excess of control and decision-making power. They are anything-goes, nondemanding parents who don't set limits or guide their children adequately. Because of issues stemming from their own childhood, they may be afraid to set limits, and they may feel an inordinate need to be loved.

Their kids tend to be whiny, egocentric, self-centered children with relatively low self-esteem, or they may appear grandiose (which is often the flip side of low self-esteem). They may not achieve their full potential and tend to be followers more than leaders, or else bossy leaders.

DISENGAGED

The disengaged, uninvolved parent is emotionally detached. Disengaged parents don't set a lot of limits and may be less available to their children. Their kids tend to be needier, more aggressive and rebellious, with low self-esteem and an increased tendency to get in trouble.

WHY THE FLEXIBLE STYLE IS BEST

Many experts on child development agree that the ideal parenting style is the flexible style. Here are several reasons why.

It helps a child gain confidence in his judgment. You are basically saying, "I believe in you." Allowing your child an age-appropriate degree of autonomy boosts his trust in his own abilities. Instead of ordering him around, you're showing that you believe in his growing capacity to make decisions. The issues may be as simple as helping to select clothes to wear at school or deciding when to clean up the playroom, but the effects go far beyond these simple tasks.

It fosters growth in problem solving and decision making. By saying, "We can work this through together," or "I can give you some suggestions, but you need to be part of the decision," you are challenging your child to use his best judgment, to be resourceful, and to be responsible. This process requires great patience—it's often easier to make the decisions by parental decree—but involving your child will pay off in the long run.

It diminishes stress. Children, like adults, resent being ordered around; it's frustrating to be told constantly what to do. At the same time, children feel anxious having little or no structure in activities; they need guidance. The flexible parent is more likely than the inflexible or the permissive parent to find a happy medium between bossiness and a hands-off attitude.

You're teaching negotiation and compromise. You're not saying, "You're out there all alone." At the same time, you're not saying, "Do it my way or else." Rather, you're saying, "Let's talk about all the options here, let's sort out our feelings, and let's work together." The skills your children acquire in sorting things out will serve them well throughout their lifetime.

THE GOAL OF GOOD PARENTING

Ultimately, the goal is to be as effective and as creative a parent as possible. You should respond to your child's individual needs. Kids need good limit-setting *and* freedom to grow. Try to find a good balance. Don't feel that you must either imitate or reject everything your parents or anyone else does. Consider various courses of action and choose carefully by learning from anyone around—friends, siblings, acquaintances, anyone and everyone who shows you what to do (or avoid doing) as you tackle this most difficult of tasks. Read books about parenting. Take parenting courses that offer new ideas about raising kids. Above all, be flexible and patient. Don't expect perfection from yourself or from your kids. Parenthood, like life itself, is an ongoing process, so you'll cause yourself a lot of needless grief by expecting to master all the necessary skills at once.

THIRTY-TWO

PARENTING AS PARTNERS

EACH MOTHER AND each father comes to the job of parenting with a different family background, different childhood experiences, different perspectives from being female or male, and different personal beliefs and attitudes. Given so many variables, it's remarkable that parents manage to coordinate their parenting efforts at all. Still, some couples work more closely together than others. Some are natural partners. Some inadvertently work at cross-purposes. Some are willful rivals. Overall, however, I'd venture to say that most couples can benefit from evaluating their goals, values, skills, and styles, and doing whatever they can to parent more effectively as partners. (For a related discussion, see chapter 31, "Parenting Styles.")

The goal isn't necessarily to have precisely the same parenting styles or practices. Parenting your children in exactly the same way isn't ideal, since kids often gain different benefits and insights from each parent. Rather, the goal is to minimize conflict, tension, and any actions that diminish your spouse's effectiveness as a parent.

WHY PARENTING AS PARTNERS IS SO IMPORTANT

To the degree that you can work with your spouse as a parenting partner—coordinating and harmonizing your efforts to raise your children—you will benefit yourself, your marriage, and your family.

PARENTAL CONFLICT STRESSES THE KIDS

Children are highly sensitive to their parents' disagreements. Precisely because kids depend on adults in so many ways, they feel disoriented and even scared to hear their parents argue. The effects differ according to the child's age, of course, but the overall nature of spousal conflict is stressful for kids. They pick up on the parents' tension and often internalize it. Does this mean that you should never disagree in front of your child? Not at all. But if possible, keep conflict—especially conflict regarding major issues—out of your child's awareness.

PARENTAL CONFLICT STRESSES YOUR MARRIAGE

Disagreements over parenting issues are a source of conflict in many marriages. At times, the "lightning rods" are major philosophical differences over religious, cultural, or political aspects of parenthood. Such disagreements can also occur regarding parenting practices—discipline, feeding, schooling, and so forth. Many couples squabble over the fine points of parenting, too: whether a five-year-old must dress himself entirely without assistance or not; whether applesauce counts as a fruit or a dessert; whether Legos belong in the bathtub or not. Here as in other ways, conflict is inevitable. A willingness to sort through these issues, however, eases pressure on the marriage, while an unwillingness to do so raises the tension level and increases the tendency to overreact. It may also increase the risk of putting the child in the middle of your conflict.

CHILDREN LEARN TO MANIPULATE PARENTS

An unfortunate side effect of parental disagreements is that your child may learn to play one parent against the other. To some extent this is a normal process. If a child wants something that one parent denies him, it's not surprising that he'll check with the other parent just in case. Even a few successes in discovering inconsistency can lead to remarkable sophistication in "playing the system." In short, your child may learn to manipulate you and your spouse. This is a risky situation; it encourages your child to be indirect rather than direct in gaining what he wants, and it may encourage dishonesty rather than honesty. In addition, it diminishes either or both parents' authority, which, at least in the long run, can harm the whole family.

HOW TO RESOLVE PARENTAL CONFLICT

Because parenting as partners is so important and beneficial, I strongly urge you and your spouse to coordinate your efforts in child-rearing practices. It's not an easy task, and it won't happen all at once, but it's well worth the effort.

IDENTIFY COMMON GROUND AND OBVIOUS DIFFERENCES

If possible, sit down with your spouse and sort through the issues systematically. I'm not saying that you should try to plan every aspect of parenting; rather, you should examine the beliefs, values, and attitudes that may be helping or hindering your efforts as parents. This task is a means of identifying both common ground and obvious differences.

Sit down with your spouse and ask yourself these questions:

- What does family mean to you?

- What do you want for yourself and your family?

- How can you balance the demands you face individually, as a couple, and as a family?

- How can you balance work life and family life?

- How can you find time for each child individually and for the whole family?

- How do you believe children should be raised?

- What are your beliefs about discipline?

- About a child's social life?

- About education?

- About ideal family life?

- What do you believe is essential for the optimal growth and development of your children?

- What lifestyle do you feel is healthy for nurturing a family?

- What aspects of your current lifestyle would you like to change?

- What do you find favorable about your own parenting skills?

- What do you find favorable about your spouse's parenting skills?

- What do you find unfavorable about your own parenting skills?

- What do you find unfavorable about your spouse's parenting skills?

- What would you like to remember as being the most wonderful times of your family life?

- What issues, problems, or conflicts would you like to avoid in the future?

- What would you like to achieve as a family?

- What makes a wonderful, nurturing, healthy family?

- How can you and your spouse prevent family conflict?

- What are some good ways to avoid arguing or sorting out problems in front of the children?

Keep in mind that when answering these questions, there are no "right" or "wrong" answers; there are only differences of opinion. If you and your spouse can accept one another's differences and work to find more common ground, you can make a great contribution to your children's well-being.

ACCEPT THE INEVITABILITY OF DIFFERENCES

It's fine to have differences. They are inevitable anyway. The key questions are: 1) How serious and abundant are the differences? and 2) How will you deal with them?

Couples with numerous, severe differences can benefit from outside guidance. Again, it's not an issue of resolving all differences or of convincing one or the other partner to drop his or her beliefs. Rather, it's a question of understanding where you stand and deciding how to deal with the situation. A couple may disagree, for instance, about how to discipline their child. This issue involves a major aspect of parenting, and it can have real impact on a child's development. Ignoring the issue doesn't serve anyone well. At the same time, attempting to sort out every aspect of the situation—your past experiences, your grasp of child psychology, your parenting strategies—can be daunting. The assistance of a counselor or family therapist can be helpful in sorting through this kind of situation.

In addition, it's important for spouses to avoid resorting to male/female stereotypes in working through their differences. There may or may not be clear patterns of how men and women parent their children; if there are, however, they're as likely the result of cultural influences as of innate tendencies. But many couples argue about parenting styles as if gender determines everything. "He's such a typical bumbling dad," a young mother told her friend as they sat near me on a park bench one afternoon. And I've heard many men make comments like, "Wives just can't seem to discipline the kids." In these and other cases, people ignore the individuality of parenthood and focus primarily on stereotypes. But parenthood is almost always an expression more of personality or learned behavior than of gender.

WORK OUT MAJOR DIFFERENCES IN PRIVATE

One of the most important ways in which you can parent as partners is to work out your differences in private. This advice may or may not hold true regarding minor differences—who picks up the pizza this afternoon, who gives your child a bath tonight, and so forth. You can sort out those smaller issues as you go. But if the issue is a major decision or conflict, it's best to discuss the situation out of children's earshot.

If you realize that an argument is brewing or a big problem needs solving, stall for time. Circumstances won't always lend themselves to this option, but grab it when you can. Reach some sort of temporary agreement with your spouse: "Okay, let's drop the subject for now." Then figure out when you can get back to the topic and deal with it when you can.

- Pick a relatively stress-free time.

- Avoid arguing when you're exhausted.

- Make sure your child is elsewhere, well looked after, or sound asleep.

- Make sure you have enough time to cover the subject and resolve your disagreements.

- Discuss the situation openly, without rancor or efforts to score points.

- Avoid letting the discussion "spill over" to when your child is around again.

Some parents I know maintain a troubling let-it-all-hang-out attitude. "We have no secrets in this family," an acquaintance boasted to me once. In fact, kids don't need to be involved in every discussion, and they shouldn't be involved at all in issues that aren't age-appropriate. Topics such as finances, job stress, sex, marital conflicts, and major life decisions (such as moving, health crises, and parenting issues) should be off limits. In short, don't bring your child into adult discussions. Don't expect your child to take an adult role in the family. Don't burden your child with practical or ethical decisions that exceed his abilities to cope.

DEMONSTRATE HEALTHY DISAGREEMENT

Many people ask me if it's okay for their kids to see parents disagree. The answer can be either no or yes. As noted earlier, it's not healthy for children to observe parents arguing angrily, and it's not advisable to include kids in high-stakes discussions even if the tone is less emotional. However, it may be a positive experience if your children see you and your spouse working through ordinary day-to-day issues in a constructive manner. Healthy disagreement, negotiation, and compromise can offer kids an excellent role model for resolving their own problems later in life.

CHOOSE YOUR BATTLES

Some couples squabble over every difference of opinion; others are more selective. If you can, ignore issues that don't really matter. Is it really important if your spouse uses brown sugar instead of honey in the kids' oatmeal? Is it really a big deal if the sheet of paper towel comes off the top or the bottom of the roll? Try to size up the basic substance of what you're discussing. If it's not of major consequence, try to compromise. If it's trivial, drop it altogether. Save your energy for the big issues in life.

ADDRESS BASIC MARITAL PROBLEMS

Some couples, however, find every issue beyond compromise. This attitude subjects their kids to pointless stress. And in marriages where everything is a point of contention, there may be much more going on than disagreements about sugar or paper towels.

If you and your spouse are experiencing frequent, protracted conflicts over parenting issues—or other issues—you should take time to uncover the root causes. What couples often fight about are really deeper, more complex issues that lie beneath the surface. Ask yourselves what you're really fighting over. Is the conflict what it seems—or is something else bothering you? Is the problem an issue within your relationship with your spouse, or could it even have its source in your own childhood experiences? Try to determine the real cause of the problem rather than just squabbling over its manifestations in daily life.

If you find that you're struggling as a couple with issues that seem beyond your abilities to resolve, don't give up or take out your frustrations on each other. Seek help. Find a family therapist, marital counselor, or pastoral counselor who can help you put your problems into clearer perspective.

DON'T USE YOUR CHILD AS A PAWN

Whatever you do, don't pull your child into your marital struggles. Don't compete with your spouse for your child's affection. Putting your child in this position can make your child feel unsafe, and it jeopardizes his confidence in you. It also places too much responsibility on your child, as if he were a partner in your marriage. Making your child choose loyalties is guilt-provoking and stress-inducing. Your child needs to love both parents and feel loved by both as well.

COORDINATE YOUR RESPONSES

On a day-to-day level, one of the most common occurrences is that a child wants something—to eat another Popsicle, say, or to watch another TV show—which one parent agrees to and the other denies. This situation is often a setup for conflict and tension. It's particularly tricky if your child claims that the other parent already okayed his request.

- Try to sort out issues in advance so that you have agreed-upon responses.

- When new situations arise, coordinate your responses if possible.

- Double-check with your spouse to make sure your child really got the message he claims he did.

- Try to resolve the issue as a team; show your child a unified front.

- Use statements like, "Mom (or Dad) and I will talk that over" to make it clear that you work together.

- Confront your child if you find that he's playing one parent against the other.

- If you and your spouse find that your responses are out of sync, avoid undercutting your spouse; go along with the arrangement for the short term but work out issues between you in private and coordinate your responses for the future.

THIRTY-THREE

THE PAST

Cheryl, age twelve, was upset with her mother, Morgan. After a long discussion of homework issues, the conversation collapsed, and Cheryl wouldn't even speak with her mom. It was then that Morgan started to cry. "I can handle the arguments," she told me. "What I can't stand is the silent treatment. I don't know why, but it drives me crazy. As long as we're still arguing, I know we'll sort things out, but when Cheryl shuts me out I can't quite believe she still loves me."

....

"I was fighting with my son," says Frank about his nine-year-old, "and Ned was really getting my goat. 'I'm not cleaning up,' he said. 'Yes you are,' I told him. 'I'm not.' 'Yes, you are.' 'You can't make *me.' 'You wanna* bet?' 'You can't,' he said, 'and you know why? 'Cause you're a* wimp!' *'Who are you calling a wimp?' 'You!' I was furious. Then suddenly I realized why this whole argument was so upsetting. Not because I shouldn't have been arguing with my son like this. But because this was just how I sounded with my* brothers!"

....

Maureen, the mother of three girls, prides herself on her dedication to her daughters. She is intent on being more nurturing and supportive than Maureen's mother was during Maureen's own childhood. "Mom was distant toward us kids," Maureen explains. "She didn't do anything bad—she just acted like she was someplace else. She wasn't expressive." Parenthood has provided Maureen with an unexpected insight, however. "Raising my girls has helped me understand my own childhood. The longer I'm a mother, the more I realize what Mom was up against. Raising five kids alone. . . . I've started to realize it wasn't that she didn't love us—she was mostly just exhausted."

THE BURDEN OF THE PAST

A S A PARENT, you want to do everything possible for your child. You want to nurture him, protect him, and teach him. You want to love him with all your heart. You want to give him any gift that's within your ability to offer. And in all likelihood, you probably do a good job of parenting, yet you may end up feeling (as so many parents do) that you're falling short. Despite your good intentions and best efforts, you act less generously than you intend, you say things you don't mean, you do things you've tried to avoid, or you sabotage your best efforts to be nurturing. Forces beyond your control seem to be influencing your capacity to be a good parent.

What's going on here? Why do good parents sometimes act selfishly, thoughtlessly, clumsily, even cruelly? The short answer is trite but true: nobody's perfect. All parents fall short because we're all imperfect human beings. But there's another reason for our fallibility as parents, one that's hard to face, easy to deny, but crucial to accept, perceive, and understand. That reason is the burden of the past.

To put the issue succinctly, much of what you know about parenting you've learned from your own family of origin. It's true that raising children involves some innate abilities—what we tend to call maternal or paternal instinct—but most of what takes place during parenthood *isn't* instinctual. It's learned. Your first and most powerful relationships were with your parents, and it's from them that you learned much about the nature of parenthood. The effects of these early relationships will linger within you for the rest of your life. The nature of family life, the ups and downs of interpersonal communication, the strength or weakness of trust, even the durability of another person's love—all of these aspects of parent-child interaction will derive from your own experience of family life.

This doesn't mean that the past will *determine* what you do as a parent. Many other aspects of your being—your personality, your state of health, your values and beliefs, your strength of character, your ability to make rational decisions, and your education—will combine with effects of the past to determine how you respond to the demands of parenthood. The past, however, will *influence* your response. The influence may be relatively great or relatively slight, but some degree of influence is inevitable. Some of these influences are:

- Expectations about the nature of family life—is it happy/sad, collaborative/divisive, harmonious/fractious, etc.?

- Expectations about the nature of the good mother, good father, or good child

- Expectations about the nature of good and bad behavior

- Experiences of feeling loved or unloved; accepted or rejected; nurtured, merely tolerated, or thwarted

- Experiences of communitarian or individualistic family life (that is, with family members supporting each other or looking out only for themselves)

- Experiences of economic well-being or hardship

- Experiences of sibling rivalry or solidarity

- Experiences of being rewarded or punished

Given these influences, here are some of ways in which you may see the past erupting into your present-day efforts as a parent:

- Saying things "just like what Mom and Dad used to say" when speaking with your child

- Feeling hurt or losing your temper in response to your child's seemingly trivial comments, gestures, or other actions

- Falling "into a rut" of certain behaviors—irritability, depression, scolding, punitiveness—despite your efforts to behave in a different way

- Acting out of control when scolding or punishing your child

- Feeling depressed or blue at certain times of year or during certain kid-related events, such as holidays, birthdays, the start of school, family trips, vacation times, and so forth

- Feeling that you're letting your child down despite fundamentally competent, well-meaning actions as a parent

Depending on the intensity and duration of these incidents, they may suggest that some aspect of your past is welling up into the present and influencing what you do or say as a parent. In some instances you'll find yourself doing or saying things that seem an obvious repetition of what you experienced as a child; in other situations, what happens is more subtle. The experience can be unsettling either way. You may treat your child in ways that contradict your preferences; you may hurt your child's feelings; you may simply end up feeling as if you've acted foolishly. In any case, what's happening is that some experience in your past—often one that you don't rememember clearly—is influencing your actions in the here-and-now. The result may or may not do real damage. However, influences of this sort can limit your control over the choices you make as a parent, and until you understand the nature of the past and its power over you, you will lack a degree of freedom in your thoughts and actions. You will be less likely to perceive your children for who they are rather than through the veil of your own experiences. You will be less likely to be emotionally available, responsive, and empathic to them.

THE BLESSING OF THE PAST

What I've said so far may suggest that most people feel painfully haunted by the past—by their parents' shortcomings, by experiences of loss or deprivation, by negative recollections. That isn't what I mean to convey. In fact, most people recall the past in both positive and negative ways. The negative ways do, indeed, often linger with great intensity. But the past isn't just a burden; it's also a blessing. Many of the memories you have of your childhood may be suffused with great warmth and sweetness. These, too, will influence your feelings toward yourself, toward parenthood, and toward your children. And here as elsewhere, understanding your past can illuminate the present and allow you a greater degree of choice over the decisions you make and the actions you take.

Ironically, you may find that your children become your best guides in this regard. Martha, the forty-four-year-old mother of two school-age children, had long resented her parents for having favored Milly, her older sister. When asked whether her parents had really favored their other child, Martha could never really articulate the situation. She would respond with vague comments like, "They just seemed to like her better." Milly was, in fact, quite in tune with her mother and father; both parents and their older child were gregarious people who enjoyed singing, acting, dancing, and other theater arts. Martha was quieter—scholarly and introverted. Martha felt excluded by the rest of the family's theatrical inclinations.

Only once she started raising her own daughters did Martha understand the situation more clearly. Her son, Jared, was bright but subdued from the start. Her daughter, Sarah, was much more outgoing. Martha loved both children deeply and felt shocked when Sarah made an accusation at age eight: "You love Jared better than me!" When Martha asked what could have prompted the girl's claim, Sarah explained. "He's just like you, so you love him more." One insight led to another until Martha gained a better understanding of how the "fit" between parents' and children's temperaments can influence a sense of belonging and acceptance. Her own parents didn't love Milly better than Martha; they just understood her and related to her more comfortably. What had seemed a burden from the past became—no matter how delayed and roundabout—a blessing.

In short, one of the benefits that understanding the past can bestow on the present are insights like these:

- Your parents weren't necessarily so bad after all.

- Much of what they did wasn't entirely willful, but was ordinary do-the-best-you-can, get-through-the-day, fly-by-the-seat-of-the-pants parenting.

- The nature of parenthood is to be fallible.

- Your childhood was more complex (and maybe less terrible?) than you recall.

- Some of your negative experiences (getting grounded, losing a contest, feeling embarrassed, etc.) weren't really such a big deal.

- Your own efforts as a parent are just as fallible.

- Your own children will probably feel hurt and resentful, too, despite your own do-the-best-you-can, get-through-the-day, fly-by-the-seat-of-the-pants parenting.

- Everyone in your family—parents and children alike—will probably emerge from the experience to tell the tale.

To sum things up in a more psychological way: the more insight you gain into your past, the less opportunity you'll have to transfer or project unresolved conflicts from your past onto your children. If you can resolve these old conflicts—if you can understand some of the root causes and their influence on the present—you'll have a much greater chance of gaining control over the situation. You'll be less likely to:

- Live primarily through your children

- Pressure them into being something other than who they really are

- Love them for their accomplishments rather than for their being or soul

- Expect them to meet your emotional needs

- Attempt to control them rather than let them unfold as individuals

- Treat them as possessions rather than as beings

- Manipulate them for your own needs

- Subject them to anger, envy, or vilification

- Conflict with your spouse, friends, and other adults

Understanding both the positive and the negative aspects of your past will grant you a degree of freedom you'll otherwise lack, and these benefits will help you and your children alike.

COPING WITH THE PAST

If you feel a willingness to explore your past and its influences on the present, here are some specific practical methods to consider.

PSYCHOTHERAPY

Most people can benefit from having a guide to help them explore their personal and family past. A trained psychotherapist or counselor can ask you appropriate questions or help you see patterns that clarify your behavior now and during your childhood. While right in the middle of family life, you may find it difficult to make those connections precisely because the task is often emotional; it's hard to be objective and see the puzzle in its sheer complexity. A skilled therapist can help facilitate insights into both your past experiences and your present behavior. In addition, a therapist can reassure you about difficult aspects of this task as they occur.

Psychotherapy can even provide a second chance at being "parented" by someone who is consistent, nonthreatening, and perhaps more understanding than your own parents were. Obviously, individual therapists' skills vary; however, a good psychotherapist can provide you with the chance to perceive your life in a new light. If you tend to form dependent or symbiotic relationships, psychotherapy can help you transfer that need to a consistent, kind person—the therapist—who in turn can ultimately provide a different vision of intimacy with another person, one that differs from what you experienced in your family of origin. Therapy can help set the stage for more nurturing, more loving, less dependent interactions within your own family.

The main drawback to psychotherapy is the cost. Especially in this era of managed care, therapy isn't cheap. Many insurance plans offer only limited benefits for psychotherapy treatment, so size up the situation carefully before you start treatment. In addition, it's also true that therapy is almost always hard work. Exploring your past, delving into long-past events, and making sense of ambiguous situations takes great effort and courage. As a result of these two "costs"—financial and emotional—many people say that they can't really afford therapy. That's each person's decision to make. I believe, however, that the financial cost and emotional costs of therapy are often far lower than the cost of ignoring the past and its influence on the present.

KEEPING A JOURNAL

You can also explore your past by keeping a journal of thoughts, feelings, memories, and experiences. In some respects, journal keeping is a kind of private psychotherapy: both methods involve digging into the past and bringing long-hidden experiences to light. You can keep a journal in any way you wish. What's important to keep in mind is not to censor what you write. Write by free association, noting whatever thoughts or feelings you experience. Try not to inhibit what you think or feel. Write as honestly and as clearly as possible, without feeling that you have to hide anything, or that your emotions are embarrassing or shameful. Note any feelings of rage, anger, desire, or destructive impulses. Anything that you feel you *don't* want to write is probably something that needs to go into your journal. Don't censor any of those primal feelings, particularly the ones that make you feel uncomfortable.

Keeping this kind of uncensored, uninhibited journal is a way of releasing your most intimate emotions in a nonthreatening, safe, nondestructive way. If you're worried about someone finding your journal, make provisions in advance to maintain your privacy. Once you've written your entries, you may end up having a cathartic experience that crystallizes your insights; later, you may decide to destroy or discard the journal. That's fine, too. You don't have to consider the journal a permanent fixture in your life. Think of it as a *process*, not a *product*.

USING A TAPE RECORDER

A variation on keeping a journal is using a tape recorder. I recommend this method to people who feel more comfortable talking than writing, and sometimes it's less time-consuming. Tape recorders are interesting, too, because you'll hear your tone of voice and any inflections of fear, longing, or anxiety. Certain situations may reflect a younger stage of your development. Perhaps you sound childish. Perhaps you sound angry or confused. Tone of voice can reveal much about your state of mind. One way or another, the experience can provide a window into what you're experiencing when you speak about your childhood or other aspects of your past.

LETTERS

You can also write letters—either letters you'll send or letters you have no intention of sending—as a means of releasing thoughts and feelings about your past.

Writing but not sending these letters is, ironically, often especially useful. The object is to write to a specific person (your mother, father, siblings, or whomever) and to say whatever you may have left unsaid. The "recipient" of your letter doesn't even have to be alive; in fact, this exercise can be especially powerful regarding someone who is deceased. In any case, it's another opportunity for catharsis—a way of releasing anger, expressing disappointment, and airing confusion. Here again, write in an uncensored way, without the other person's feedback to inhibit your feelings or thoughts. The anxiety and fear you've experienced can now surge outward rather than remain submerged. It's a way of getting pent-up feelings off your chest.

THE RISKS INVOLVED

A few caveats, however.

First, think carefully about proceeding with any of the alternatives I've sketched. They may seem easy and harmless, but they can trigger surprisingly intense reactions. Writing a letter in which you blast your long-dead mother for her mistakes and shortcomings, for instance, may unleash far more powerful emotions than you anticipate. The same holds true for writing entries in a journal or dictating remarks into a tape recorder. Step carefully. Above all, maintain your privacy, since the words you write may be harmless when restricted to your eyes alone but profoundly destructive when allowed to fall into the wrong hands.

Second, consider combining the journal/recorder/letter approach with psychotherapy. Any of these methods can be productive when pursued alone, but the experience will be less stressful and lonely if you have a guide along the way.

AN ASIDE ABOUT DEPRESSION

Because parenthood is so stressful and demanding, some parents respond to the rigors involved by becoming depressed. This response may be understandable; that being said, I need to emphasize that depression should *not* be ignored and simply shoved under the carpet. Depression takes many forms. Some are a short-term reaction to a finite problem—job stress, family difficulties, contradictory expectations, marital disagreements—but still warrant attention. Others are long-term, often biochemically based problems that need immediate attention. It's not uncommon, too, that earnest efforts to deal with the past can trigger feelings of confusion, sadness, or depression. In each of these situations, however, it's important to seek outside help. A psychotherapist's helpful guidance may help you gain control of what you're feeling. In some cases, antidepressant medication is helpful, too. These are the most common signs of depression:

- A marked sense of low energy or fatigue

- A constant feeling of sadness or the blues

- The loss of a sense of who you are, what you need, what you want, and what you're feeling

- A need to repress or deny your emotions

- Raging or lashing out irrationally at others

- A deep sense of shame, insecurity, and guilt

- A sense of emptiness, loneliness, or worthlessness

- A feeling of being overwhelmed by life

- An inability to get up in the morning and cope with everyday life

- Recurrent suicidal thoughts or actions

WOUNDS FROM THE PAST

By its very nature, parenthood means making mistakes. No one can go through the rigorous parenting years without making one mistake after another. Your parents made plenty; you will, too.

It's true, however, that some of the mistakes your parents made have hurt you, and the wounds can linger through a whole lifetime. This is true even for seemingly trivial childhood wounds—the thoughtless words spoken, the wrong gift given, the recital forgotten—and it's certainly true for the more willful, angry, cruel wounds that parents sometimes inflict on their children.

But the truth remains: wounds can heal. Even some of the oldest, deepest, most painful wounds can stop festering and cease to hurt. How? By bringing the pain to the surface. In dealing with the past, it's the hidden wounds that do the most damage, while those that we expose to the light of day usually (though sometimes gradually) cease to trouble us. Is this process foolproof? No. Can you accomplish it without great effort? Almost certainly not. Still, coming to terms with your own past is one of the best ways ever found for soothing the pain that's an inevitable element in being human.

It's not easy. It's not always pleasant. But facing the past will help you to understand yourself better and, in so doing, to open yourself more fully to your children. If you can accept the complexity of your own past, you'll see your kids with open eyes, with new respect, with deeper understanding, and with empathy for what they feel, experience, and hope for. You'll perceive your children not as extensions of yourself, but as separate from yourself—a realization which, ironically, will allow you to embrace them and love them even more fully than before.

THIRTY-FOUR

PLAY AND LEARNING

Parents sometimes refer to their children's activities as "just play"—or even as "goofing off" or "wasting time." On the surface, that's what it appears to be. The truth, though, is that children learn about themselves, about the world, and about many skills through play. Play is how kids interact and explore their environment. As a result, one of your tasks as a parent is to understand the significance of play in your child's life.

Observing your child at play will give you a window into the world of his personality, character, and level of self-esteem. If you observe closely, it will also give you an idea about all areas of his development, since you can gain insight into character, social skills, communication, and empathy through watching a child play.

CHILD-CENTERED PLAY

Some parents believe that they must teach their children when they're playing with them. The resulting anxiety over making play constructive and educational, however, is unfortunate for several reasons. First, it ignores the fact that for children, almost *all* play is educational. Second, this anxiety can lead to stress for both children and parents. Third, it's an attitude that may even disrupt children's creative impulses.

PLAY EQUALS LEARNING

Play is a natural way to learn. It's no exaggeration to say, in fact, that for children, play *equals* learning. Through play, children acquire and master a huge array of skills, including:

- Language development
- Large motor skills
- Fine motor skills
- Intuitive thought
- Grasping of concrete operations
- Learning rules
- Abstract reasoning
- Taking turns and sharing
- Awareness of others' feelings
- Role playing
- Competition
- Honesty

PLAY AS STRESS RELIEF

Play is also a way in which children discharge stress and tension. It's their downtime. When kids don't have enough unstructured free time to play, they tend to be more anxious, frazzled, and agitated. They cry more easily and make more demands on those around them. This is especially true for children who are between toddlerhood and ages four or five. Older children need less unstructured time; even so, children as old as ten to thirteen need lots of time to try new roles, to experience their environment, and to develop relationships with peers and adults.

THE IMPORTANCE OF INDEPENDENCE

Children—especially very young children—have very little control over their lives, and one of the few realms in which they do have control is through play. When they choose, direct, or lead the play—and when adults follow along—it allows kids an opportunity to be in charge. This is particularly important for children ages five or younger.

THE STAGES OF CHILD'S PLAY

It's important to note that children play in different ways at different developmental stages.

BABYHOOD THROUGH AGE TWO

Babies and children in pre-toddler stages play mostly by themselves. They're much more egocentric and isolated than older kids. Their main focus is on manipulating the environment, which they do mainly by means of solitary experience. They may notice other children at the playground, but they are basically involved in their own world.

TODDLERHOOD

By the start of toddlerhood, children are more sophisticated, but they still play mostly in isolation. Communication with other kids may occur, but it's often ego-centered—grabbing a toy from another child, asking for a toy, or reaching out to hug another child or hold another child's hand. During late toddlerhood—around age three—children begin to do what's called *parallel* or *associated play*. This is a form of play in which children near one another in a particular setting (such as a sandbox or a playroom) will engage in the same activity but without communicating or interacting. They are literally playing side by side, yet there's not a lot of interaction on any higher level.

THE PRESCHOOL YEARS

Between about three and a half to four or five years of age, children begin to play in more communicative ways. If they're in a playroom, they'll assign roles and develop relationships. "You be the daddy, I'll be the mommy." "You be the nurse, I'll be the doctor, he'll be the patient." "You be the teacher and I'll be the student." Play becomes much more sophisticated. Learning is creative, fun, and relevant to the child's appropriate developmental level. Such play provides opportunities for children to try on real-life roles, relationships, and activities.

During the preschool years, children learn by exploring their environment and by manipulating didactic materials. The types of learning activities that a child experiences add enormously to his intellectual development and growth. When children do a cooking project, for instance, they're learning a multitude of skills: counting, using their hands, and experiencing tastes, textures, and scents of the ingredients. As outlined by the Swiss developmental psychologist Jean Piaget, play is instrumental in these aspects of children's physical, cognitive, and emotional growth.

SCHOOL-AGE CHILDREN

As the child reaches the start of the school years, around age six, play grows more complex and focuses more often on social interests. Children are less egocentric at this stage. They have more empathy for others, and they communicate better than before. Their games become much more sophisticated. To some extent, gender differences emerge in boys' and girls' play styles. (I discuss these differences in chapter 3, "Boys," and chapter 20, "Girls.")

At around school age, children also start to take more initiative in asking others to play with them. They also become highly imitative at this age, which can lead to a love of repetition, including songs or jump rope games. They are learning how to master social relationships and all kinds of cognitive skills. They learn how to sort out arguments and to resolve conflicts, too, in more socially acceptable ways than before.

THE PRETEEN YEARS

During the preteen years, your child continues to develop his personality, his voice, his values, and his beliefs. His self-esteem begins to develop as well. As all of these changes occur, play is an essential part of his ability to build confidence, master skills, and learn about himself and the world around him. Play increases his self-esteem through positive interactions with other children. In addition, structured activities such as team sports, drama clubs, school newspapers, and so forth give your child other kinds of activities through which to develop his personality and learn about others.

At the same time, this communicative stage of play can become a time of increased sensitivity, especially regarding rejection. Your child may need some guidance for dealing with specific situations, such as how to avoid taking things too personally. Most often, these interactions have nothing to do with your child, but instead are a consequence of social context or other children's personal frustrations. Other issues may include how to share, how to avoid being bossy, how to listen to other children, how to be empathetic, and how to have balanced social relationships. This stage may also be an important time to address issues of aggression, assertiveness, submissiveness, and other aspects of relationships.

THE TEEN YEARS

During adolescence, children's play emphasizes the mastery of skill—often through sports and games—and focuses heavily on peer-group interaction. Play becomes an arena both for perfecting abilities (athletic, academic, linguistic, etc.) and for engaging in social relationships. Teenagers' play also allows a safe setting for venting high energy levels and aggressive impulses. (For further discussions of teens, see chapter 50, "The Teen Years.")

PLAYING CREATIVELY WITH YOUR CHILD

Parents often ask me how they can play creatively with their children. Once again I need to stress the importance of going with the flow. Spending time together and following your child's lead are the most crucial things to do. The rest will follow. In addition, here are some tips for playing creatively with your child:

- *Understand your child's developmental stage* and the skills your child needs to learn at this time. Many parents push too hard or take play too seriously, thus frustrating the child.

- *Introduce age-appropriate activities and materials* for your child to explore in a safe environment. Childproof your environment so that you don't have to say no too often; especially for younger children, a relatively childproof environment means more freedom to explore the world.

- *Allow your child to select the activity that he finds most interesting.* Follow his lead in child-centered, child-directed play; avoid calling the shots. Allow your child to be in control during playtime. Let him tell you what to do, what he finds interesting, exciting, and fun. Be flexible.

- *Be patient with your child's weaknesses and praise his strengths.* Praise your child 99 percent of the time, particularly when he's younger.

- *Challenge your child but don't be overzealous*, pushing activities that may be too difficult.

- *Be spontaneous and uninhibited.* Laugh with your child and at yourself. Reexperience your own childhood. Remember what was fun when you did things as a kid. Try not to repeat negative experiences with your child. Enjoy playing and being playful with your child.

THIRTY-FIVE

RACISM AND PREJUDICE

A FRIEND TOLD me this story:

"I once had an awkward, embarrassing experience on a plane. En route to a conference, I ended up sitting beside a talkative man from Los Angeles. His endless chatter annoyed me, but it wasn't the number of words so much as their content that caused the problem. This fellow was an equal-opportunity racist. He hated *everyone*. All Asians were inscrutable little Orientals. All Latinos were sneaky illegal aliens. All African-Americans were welfare cheats. All Arabs were Islamic terrorists. All Jews were members of a Zionist conspiracy. He didn't have a kind word for any human being on earth. And his diatribe against humanity—everyone except himself—went on and on and on.

"Now, I knew this guy had a problem. *My* problem, though, was surviving a two-hour flight right next to him. What should I have done? The flight was packed, so moving to another seat wasn't an option. Arguing with him was a possibility, but my initial efforts only threw gasoline onto the bonfire of his prejudices. Trying to ignore him proved fruitless. I was trapped. Never in my life have I endured such a tedious, exasperating diatribe. I didn't know what else to do, so I kept quiet to the degree possible, mumbled a few halfhearted challenges to his assumptions, and just tried to shut him out.

"The worst part of the whole incident, however, happened as we deplaned. I couldn't wait to get out of there—I was free at last! But when all the passengers stood to leave, a woman in the seat ahead of me turned and glowered. She was African-American and stared with a laser gaze that she directed not at the bigot I'd tolerated for two hours, but at *me*. And I understood at once that I deserved her contempt. 'That man,' her eyes told me, 'is a lost cause. He's totally bogged down in his bigotry, and he'll never leave it. But *you—you* know better. You know what rot he's talking. You know how dangerous these attitudes are. Yet for two hours you've done nothing to contradict him!'

"That woman was right. I'd totally wimped out. Not because I agreed with him—I disagreed with everything he said. But because I just kept my mouth shut.

"I've never forgotten the intensity of her contempt. And it constantly reminds me of something someone once said: 'All that must happen for evil to triumph is for good people to remain silent.' "

THE STRUGGLE AGAINST SILENCE

I pride myself on my lack of prejudice. I am open-minded and openhearted to people of every background. But like my friend, I am aware that when dealing with racism and prejudice, there's a constant struggle against silence. This struggle—like so much else in life—is central to parenthood.

Racism and prejudice are born of fear and ignorance. Precisely because we live in a world that, for all its beauties, is often risky, it's easy to be on guard and cautious about the people around us. For this reason, it's also easy for parents to communicate their fears to children—the feelings that We are the known and good and safe, while They are the unknown and bad and dangerous. And so racism and prejudice are something that our children learn, whether from the larger society or from us, the parents, regardless of our intentions.

In this sense most of us are guilty of racism and prejudice. Most of us have, at one time or another, prejudged someone else unfairly. This prejudice doesn't have to be intentional or malicious to be damaging; it simply has to exist. And because kids are acutely aware of their parents' attitudes toward other people, we must all be cautious—in fact, constantly aware—of the messages we're intentionally or unintentionally teaching our children.

HOW TO RAISE PREJUDICE-FREE KIDS

There's no easy way to raise prejudice-free kids, especially in a country whose past has scarred many ethnic groups and left a complex legacy of racial misunderstanding.

EXAMINE YOUR OWN BELIEFS, ATTITUDES, AND BEHAVIOR

Start by taking a hard look at your own reactions toward other people.

- What do you believe about the differences and similarities between people?

- Do the differences outweigh the similarities?

- Are individual characteristics more or less significant than ethnicity or group affiliations?

- To what extent does your behavior suggest racist or nonracist attitudes?

- Are you comfortable with people of other ethnic or religious backgrounds?

- Does your group of friends include people of various backgrounds?

Asking these questions can be disconcerting. Few of us are as pure-hearted as we'd like to be. I'm not suggesting that you conduct a harsh self-interrogation, simply that self-knowledge is the key to understanding others.

MODEL NONPREJUDICIAL ATTITUDES AND BEHAVIOR

The best possible way to raise nonracist children is to have genuine friendships with people of many different ethnic and religious groups. I am *not* advocating that you "collect" friends simply on account of their racial backgrounds; that's prejudicial in its own way. Rather, I'm suggesting that you open your heart (and your home) to people who appeal to you as friends regardless of their ethnicity. Your warmth, acceptance, and openness for others will be something that your children take for granted. You won't have to teach them anything specific; your actions will do it for you.

By contrast, your children will notice any fear or discomfort that you exhibit toward others. If they hear you expressing hostility or derision toward other ethnic or religious groups, they'll pick up on it. Worse yet, they'll imitate you. Any lip service to equality ("We're all created the same") will strike them as hypocritical and pointless. This is true even if you are fundamentally nonracist but indulge yourself in "harmless" jokes and epithets in your child's presence. Whatever behavior, attitudes, beliefs, and values you manifest, your child will start to internalize.

The bottom line: You can't just talk the talk—you have to walk the walk. Be genuinely compassionate and nonprejudicial toward others. Respond to people as individuals, not merely as members of groups. Teach your child to be curious about other people, to ask open questions about their backgrounds and beliefs, to avoid making generalizations about people based on stereotypes.

PROVIDE MULTICULTURAL EXPERIENCES

No child is born prejudiced. In fact, children are prejudice-free until taught otherwise by adults. But parents and other adults often start to instill prejudicial attitudes by the time kids reach preschool age. This isn't to say that parents are overtly racist—though such attitudes are lamentably common. Rather, parents often unconsciously create a sense of us-versus-them that children pick up all too easily. Or else the de facto segregation of many American communities deprives children of experience with people of other ethnic and religious backgrounds, which in itself tends to reinforce stereotypes.

How should you respond? One of the best ways is to seek opportunities for contact with a diverse range of people in your community. Some of these opportunities seem artificial or limited in scope, but they're better than nothing. Attend ethnic fairs. Visit cultural festivals. On trips within the United States, visit cities and towns that provide contact with other ethnic groups. If you can afford the expense, travel to other countries. Almost any opportunities that you can provide will broaden your children's horizons.

SUPPORT A MULTICULTURAL CURRICULUM IN THE SCHOOLS

One of the most important means for diminishing fear and ignorance about ethnicity comes from the educational system. Although the American public schools are under siege in many ways, they remain one of this country's most democratic institutions. Children have a chance at school to work side by side with members of other backgrounds and, ideally, to grow comfortable with people who are unlike themselves.

(By the way, this situation holds true not just for ethnic and religious issues, but also for children with physical, intellectual, or emotional challenges. There remains a tremendous amount of prejudice and discrimination toward people with physical, emotional, visual, auditory, or learning challenges, and school policies that stress mainstreaming can help children to accept others for who they are.)

For these reasons, I urge you to support a multicultural curriculum within your local schools. This situation has become increasingly controversial over the past few years; currently, there's a backlash under way against multiculturalism. But I personally see no alternative to an approach that educates American children about the diversity in our past, present, and future. We live in a rainbow culture. That's not about to change. It's crucial for children to understand the huge variety within our country and to see that no group should have more privileges than any other. Reading, writing, and social studies are central to this curriculum. Language study is paramount. There are significant extracurricular elements, too—cultural arts festivals, food fairs, book fairs, and celebrations of many different holidays.

USE MOVIES AND TV SHOWS TO TEACH TOLERANCE

You can also use movies and even TV in age-appropriate ways to help your child understand the importance of tolerance. Precisely because children are so visual, movies and shows offer a powerful tool for parents to educate their children. Movies such as *Schindler's List*, *Amistad*, and *Beloved* bring home the reality of human suffering and longing for freedom in ways that few other media can equal. Beyond the powerful impressions they create of the Holocaust and of slavery, however, there's an equally crucial element at work here: to an important degree, these movies portray not just *ethnic* experience, but *individual* experience. We get to know the characters as people. Seeing up close what people have experienced, we can enter their lives and learn empathy.

My only caveat is that as a parent, you should select the right time, age, and place for your child to experience these movies. As I've indicated elsewhere (see chapter 36, "Scary Experiences and Childhood Fears"), it's important to size up your child's maturity so that the viewing experience isn't overwhelming. First, read the ratings for parental guidance. If possible, see the movie yourself before letting your child see it. Then ask your child beforehand if she wants to see the movie in question. Explain what it's about. Listen closely to her verbal response, but also observe her nonverbal reaction. If she seems reluctant to proceed, honor her hesitance; or, if she wants to see the movie, allow her the leeway to stop at any time. Also, make sure you're available to answer your child's questions about what she sees.

My personal opinion is that most children aren't ready to see movies like *Schindler's List* until high school age or older depending on your child. One child I know viewed *Schindler's List* at age eight and felt upset for months until her parents discovered the girl's concern: she worried that Nazis would come and haul her family off to a concentration camp.

In short, help your child understand why certain ethnic and religious groups have suffered discrimination and why this treatment is unfair. Ask her what she thought of the book or movie and how she sees the events portrayed there. Help your child develop a conscience and sense of empathy from the inside out.

THE VALUE OF COMMUNITY

One of the great legacies we have received in America is our celebration of individuality. More than the citizens of almost any other nation, we have great leeway for deciding how to live, what to believe, and what to value. In celebrating individuality so highly, though, we run the risk of ignoring or even denigrating certain other values. One such value is community spirit. We Americans still give lip service to a sense of community, but we often ignore it in practical terms. There's a tendency, for instance, for many of us to feel so comfortable about our own personal circumstances that we're willing to ignore the hardships of others within the wider group. Why should I worry about anyone else if I'm safe and affluent? As a recent article in the *New York Times Sunday Magazine* put it, we run the risk of becoming the government "of the comfortable, by the comfortable, and for the comfortable."

Teach your children a sense of fairness, of working together, of looking out for others. Avoid any kind of us-against-them attitude. Don't look at others as opponents struggling for dominance, but as people who can work together. Show your child how to share not just with people of your own ethnic background and social class, but with everyone. Stress that the problems we face—prejudice, crime, pollution, economic injustice—affect all of us, and that we must all find the solutions together.

Avoid the danger of merely falling silent.

THIRTY-SIX

SCARY EXPERIENCES AND CHILDHOOD FEARS

Ned, who's two years old, worries about ghosts in the attic. "I hear them up there," he tells his mother, Cindy. Cindy reassures her son that ghosts don't exist. Ned protests, "But I still hear them!" and he has more and more trouble sleeping.

Nine-year-old Jake doesn't worry about ghosts, but someone else is haunting his life: the local bully. A big, aggressive kid named Theo teases and hassles Jake almost every day. So far Theo hasn't done any physical damage, but Jake dreads going to school and fears that Theo will beat him up.

At seventeen, Alicia is a confident and high-achieving young woman. She is responsible in most respects. Now that she has reached driving age, however, her parents worry about her safety. Alicia is bright but somewhat "ditzy," as her mother puts it, and often oblivious to the aggressive drivers around her. Alicia's parents don't want her to be a fearful driver, but they feel that she should be far more cautious.

HELPING KIDS DEAL WITH THEIR FEARS

THE WORLD IS dangerous enough that it's appropriate for kids to learn well-placed concern about many things. Yet many children's fears exceed the risks involved, and some fears focus on completely imaginary problems. As a parent, what can you do to teach your children sensible ways of dealing with what they fear?

TAKE CONTROL OF YOUR OWN FEARS

Although your child's well-being is at stake, it's important to keep your concerns in proportion to reality. There are several ways to understand the situation. One is to learn about children's specific fears at specific developmental stages. Another is to sort through the issues with someone else—your spouse or partner, your child's teacher, or a pediatrician. Yet another is to learn more about child development through a parenting support group, a parenting course, books, or videos.

The most important single issue you should know is that kids struggle with both real and imagined fears throughout their development; different fears trouble children at different ages. (I'll discuss age-appropriate fears later in this chapter.) It's also important to realize, however, that how you handle your own worries will make a big difference in your child's state of mind. Your ability to cope with stress, your resilience, and your attitudes will influence whether your child sees the world through anxious or confident eyes. The goal is to be concerned but calm—aware of risks but comfortable with the task of dealing with them—so that your child accepts your fallibility but feels confident you'll always stand up for him.

DON'T INTERVENE TOO MUCH

One of the hardest tasks of parenthood is letting your child take risks. Parents have a reflexive tendency to intervene, sparing their children from any danger, discomfort, pain, or uncertainty. This tendency is crucial: it's a moment-by-moment necessity in caring for babies and toddlers, who can't survive without their parents' constant intervention, and it's an important task, though less constant, in later stages of child development. But as children grow, develop, and begin to separate from their parents, they need opportunities to explore the world. Even young children need to take risks, test their skills, and learn from experience.

The core issue for parents is to weigh the risks and the consequences. There's a big difference between letting a two-year-old run around close to a busy street and letting him run across an enclosed playground. The first requires immediate intervention; the second, despite the risk of a skinned knee, deserves a more judicious response. If you step in too quickly at noncritical times, you may limit your child's ability to acquire and perfect his skills. The key is to provide a safe-enough environment to allow your child to test his wings. If you childproof a room so that he can explore freely with minimal risk, you decrease both your own fears and your child's as well. You also give him a message that you have confidence in him, which will help him master his own insecurities in the long run.

LIMIT THE MEDIA'S INFLUENCE

Most young children can't differentiate easily between reality and fantasy. Their grasp of the difference develops rapidly after about age five, but fanciful events in books, movies, and TV programs may seem frighteningly realistic even to older children. This situation has been compounded by the vividness of cinematic imagery. Films are now so graphic and vivid that they terrify even sophisticated children. Even family fare like *The Lion King* can upset some kids. I see many children in therapy whose minds are buzzing with violent or fantastical images that disturb their sleep or haunt their waking hours.

- *Don't assume that your child is ready for a particular movie or TV show.* Kids are highly individual in what affects them, and the emotional effects may be much stronger than you anticipate.

- *Follow your own hunches about what sorts of entertainment are appropriate.* Many parents are incredibly lax about what they let their kids watch; don't let other people determine your choices.

- *If your child insists on seeing a particular movie that you feel may frighten him, consider the option of watching it on video rather than in a theater.* The smaller screen and familiar surroundings may make the imagery less frightening.

- *Be alert to seemingly unrelated anxieties.* Your child's reaction to a movie or show may reflect something far different from what it seems; a child's worry about ghosts, for instance, may stem less from worries about death than from a concern about separation from his parents.

- *Keep your child's viewing of TV and movie violence to an absolute minimum.* Many parents tell me "My kids can handle it," but the stories I hear in therapy sessions suggest otherwise.

BE PREPARED FOR FALLOUT FROM REAL-LIFE CRISES

If your child is going through a real-life crisis—your separation or divorce, an illness in the family, or the death of a grandparent or other relative—the crisis can exacerbate seemingly unrelated fears. He may regress emotionally while facing these external pressures. He may act more immaturely, need more reassurance, complain of physical symptoms (headaches, stomachaches, etc.), or show signs of anxiety or depression. He may also worry about risks you consider unrealistic, such as animal attacks, strange diseases, space aliens, and so forth. Stay sensitive to what you see and hear. Your child may not be able to describe his core anxieties in rational terms; what he really fears may manifest itself more indirectly.

In any case, times of crisis should prompt you to be as supportive as possible. A lot of physical comforting is appropriate. Verbal reassurances, too, are important. Give your child many chances to express his worries in whatever way seems to work best—by describing his fears outright, by telling stories, by acting out scenes, by using dolls or stuffed animals to act out his fears by proxy. To the degree that your child can express his concerns, he will master his fears. If you find it difficult to be supportive during the crisis, find resources—a relative, a close friend, a member of the clergy, or a therapist—to help yourself cope.

The message throughout should be that you believe in your child; you're present to do whatever you can for him; you're a calm harbor in any emotional storm. This is a tall order for anyone. It's difficult to stay stable if you're going through hard times. But if you can be steady, open-minded, and expressive, you'll provide a safe place in which he can deal with his own fears.

BE ALERT TO YOUR CHILD'S TEMPERAMENT

Some children worry more than others. For instance, some children are terrified of thunderstorms, while others react to the noise and light with amusement and delight. Other kids feel anxious around animals. Others worry about improbable events or nonexistent creatures. To some degree, these anxieties may be a learned response—a fearful reaction to storms or animals in the past, for instance—but they also may suggest an emotional predisposition. Anxiety may well be a feature in a child's overall temperament.

If your child is anxious, the most important response is to acknowledge his fears. Don't belittle him. Making fun of his worries or humiliating him for having such fears will only intensify his anxiety. What's most important is to assure him that you love him and you'll do everything you can to protect him.

AGE-RELATED FEARS

As I mentioned earlier, children fear different things at different developmental stages. There are always individual differences; at the same time, there are some basic patterns. You'll help your child a lot by knowing in advance what's likely to scare or worry him.

BABIES

Although babies do express fear—at scary faces, at loud noises, etc.—they are often notable for their unawareness of risks and dangers. Perhaps the most striking fear that babies exhibit is fear of strangers, which is a major developmental milestone at about nine months. Your main task as a parent during this stage is simply to do what you're already doing: keep your child out of danger. In addition, try to limit the number of caregivers and strangers that come into your baby's life. Try to be present and emotionally available as often and as consistently as possible.

TODDLERS AND PRESCHOOLERS

The situation for toddlers and preschoolers becomes much more complex. On the one hand, children between two and four worry about many dangers, both real and imagined; on the other hand, they step forth brazenly and often believe that they're totally in command of the world. You're not likely to know which attitude your toddler will display from one moment to the next.

For a toddler, one big goal is to help him master his fears. You can't take away your child's fear, and you can't make the whole world perfect for him, but you can help him to cope with what frightens him. One way of helping him grow is to paraphrase what he expresses to you. If your toddler says, "Scared of doggies!" you can acknowledge that he's scared of the dog he saw, reassure him that the dog didn't hurt him, and promise to protect him from dogs in the future. Such words will help him feel accepted yet simultaneously increase his sense of safety. Similarly, if your preschooler tells you about his nightmare, you can say, "That ghost must have been scary" but also explain that the ghost was only part of a dream. "You are more powerful than the ghost in your dreams." Over a period of time, this approach will help your child feel stronger, more confident, and less fearful.

By contrast, pushing your child too quickly—telling him there's nothing to fear, or that he's being babyish—will only demoralize him. This approach will make it harder for him to build his sense of self-confidence, which can only backfire in helping him master his fears.

SCHOOL-AGE CHILDREN

By the time kids reach school age, their fears tend to be more concrete; they focus less on monsters and ghosts than on social situations. School-age kids often worry if the teacher likes them and if they'll find new friends. Other typical concerns are winning at sports and getting good grades. They have a better idea of what's real and what's pretend. Although TV and movie violence can be disturbing, kids at this stage can distinguish between fantasy and reality.

What's appropriate for helping a school-age child deal with his fears? First of all, there's a question of degree. If your child has particularly intense or numerous fears, you should consider getting an outside opinion. All children struggle with anxieties and fears, but protracted or debilitating fears are unusual. Contact your pediatrician to discuss the situation. You might even consider consulting with a child psychologist. Typical fears that warrant this sort of concern are personal loss (death of a parent, sibling, grandparent, or even a pet), the parents' separation or divorce, or physical disability. Another consideration is the possibility of a biochemical imbalance, since some children have fears, anxieties, or panic reactions that can be physiological in nature. Although this issue may be worrisome, denying the possibility won't help your child.

During some stages, children may experience rapid mood swings. This state is typical during the preteen and teen years but can occur much earlier. One moment your child seems confident; the next moment, he dreads everything. Parenthood can feel like a roller coaster at such times. You can respond by staying calm, by not overreacting, and by being as thoughtful as possible; don't take everything your child says at face value. This holds true for your parent-child interactions (e.g., he may scream at you one moment, then be all hugs and kisses the next) and for external events, such as what you hear about school or social events. School-age children can be so sensitive to others that they perceive problems ("Susie hates me" or "The teacher's gonna flunk me") that have little or no basis in reality.

During this stage, you have to listen closely and speak openly with your child. Validate his feelings again and again. Be a walking reality test for your child. An example: your child is pushing hard to be a good soccer player but clearly dislikes the sport. Under these circumstances, you may have to present a view of the situation that's considerably at odds with what he perceives. "Are you having fun playing this sport?" you ask. He answers, "Well, yeah—all my friends play soccer." You ask, "But is soccer what *you* want to play?" At a stage when children begin to feel the peer group's influence, your role may include being a "devil's advocate" in ways that jolt his sense of things. Here, too, you need to be supportive—children always need to feel that their parents are on their side—but the support may be more challenging than in the past.

Some school-age children also fear their parents' reactions. Let's say that your child is worried about telling you that he had to stay after school. He was talking in class, got punished for it, and now dreads your response. Under these circumstances, it's important to size up what's happening. Is he worried because you really did react angrily in the past? If so, can you take responsibility for how you spoke about the prior problem and stress that you'll work to support each other in the present? If your response has been thoughtful in the past, ask him why he's convinced you'll be angry now. The goal is to build long-term sense of trust; avoid putting barriers between you.

PRETEENS AND TEENS

The situation for adolescents gets both simpler and more complicated: simpler, because preteens and teens are increasingly confident and capable; more complicated, because the risks they face rise dramatically. During this stage, kids increasingly deal with the world. Parents have less direct influence. When it comes to fear and worry, adolescents present a contradictory situation: the biggest risk they face is often not what they fear, but rather it's their absence of fear.

Here's a fairly stark example: driving. Most teenagers eagerly await the day they're able to drive. Having access to a car means freedom, status, and fun. Most teenagers know that driving is dangerous, yet few, if any, can imagine the calamitous consequences of an accident. By nature adolescents feel invincible. This delusion of invincibility—combined with untested, unpracticed skills, and relatively limited judgment—leads to the highest accident rates for any age group. In this case, teenagers don't fear too much, but far too little.

Here and in other situations, parents face difficult challenges. As a mother or father, you have fewer outright controls over your child, and you probably have him in the house less than ever before. How can you address both your child's fears and his lack of fear?

- *Keep the lines of communication open.* If you keep talking openly, you'll at least know what's on his mind, and to some degree you can help him think through his choices.

- *Avoid judgmental attitudes.* You have a right to state how you see a given situation. Until your child turns eighteen, you also have the legal right to make certain decisions whether your child approves or not. But if you judge your child (as opposed to disapproving of his behavior) you'll probably alienate him.

- *Be supportive.* Whether you regard your child's worries as excessive, appropriate, or insufficient, never stop supporting him as a person. Let him know you're concerned. Never criticize him in public. Make sure he knows you're available.

- *Allow both independence and freedom.* Preteens and teens resent the restrictions on their lives yet need to feel connected regardless. It's a long-term, ambiguous struggle to find the right balance between independence and freedom. Here as in other ways, the answer is constant, open-minded communication.

For further information on related issues, see chapter 50, "The Teen Years," and chapter 5, "Communication Between Parents and Kids."

THE CONSOLATIONS OF REALITY

In reality life is full of hazards, and children must eventually reach this insight along with the rest of us. At the same time, it's true as well that life is full of delights, pleasures, and consolations. This, too, is something that your child needs to learn.

One of the most important ways to alleviate children's fears is to stress a sense of community. We're not alone in the world—and neither are they. Many people care for them and stand ready to help them: not only parents but also teachers, friends, neighbors, relatives, and a whole community of people. Children find this realization enormously comforting.

In addition, your child needs to learn that he's his own best resource. Growing, changing, and learning, he can always turn inward to find the answers he needs. Mastering that truth is a long-term task, but it's at the core of growing up. And herein lies one of the great goals of parenthood: to love your child so fully that he'll learn to trust himself and his sense of things, and he'll know that he can deal with any problem he must solve and any fear he must confront.

THIRTY-SEVEN

SCHEDULES

Jenna, thirteen, is a busy girl. In addition to attending middle school, she plays in an all-city orchestra, takes modern dance lessons, competes in her school district's intramural soccer league, and studies art with a local artist. She enjoys these activities but complains to her parents that she never has time to play or hang out with her friends.

Bruce and Mandy are concerned that Pete, their seventeen-year-old, won't get into a top-ranked college. Pete is a good student but lacks the sterling credentials that might guarantee admission to the schools that he and his parents have targeted. To increase his chances, Pete has agreed to take on a grueling schedule of high-pressure classes, private tutoring sessions, and extracurricular activities. Both the boy and his parents are convinced that no effort is too great for Pete to attain his academic goal.

Although only eight years old, Theresa complains of vague but physical discomforts. She suffers from frequent headaches. She experiences intermittent bouts of flulike symptoms. She often feels exhausted. Medical tests and examinations have revealed no identifiable problems. When confronted with the possibility that Theresa's problems may be a side effect of the girl's highly scheduled, almost incessant athletic and cultural activities, her parents dismiss the idea out of hand.

BOTH AS A clinician and as a mother, I see more and more children with stress-related ailments. Sometimes the complaints are relatively benign:

fatigue, crankiness, or inability to focus. Sometimes kids describe more substantial symptoms: headaches, gastric upsets, rashes, asthma. Now and then I encounter children with significant but undiagnosable physical complaints, or else depression serious enough to require treatment. There are, of course, many individual explanations for these problems. What concerns me is that among the explanations is the suggestion that these are stress reactions to high-pressure schedules even before kids reach middle school. The phenomenon is all the more common in preteens and teenagers.

Childhood is no longer the relatively unstructured experience that it used to be. From toddlerhood on (sometimes even earlier) American parents schedule their children's time. Play groups, gym classes, enrichment programs, and other organized activities are increasingly common. School-age children have most of each day's events specified hour by hour. After-school activities are often planned, monitored, even regimented. Parents set up and supervise playdates rather than letting their children entertain themselves. As a result, kids have little autonomy over what they're doing. These children may, in fact, enjoy their activities. And in a risky, unpredictable world, it's understandable that the circumstances of play have changed. Yet many parents go too far in organizing their children's lives, and the side effects are unfortunate. When adults have too many expectations and exert too much pressure on children for performance through organized activities, the opportunities for kids to relax and decompress often evaporate. The result: more stress on children.

THE BENEFITS AND RISKS OF SCHEDULES

Depending on your child's personality, temperament, and interests, there are definite pros and cons to scheduled activities. Some children need more structure; some need more leeway to do as they wish. Some kids are ambitious about mastering sports, arts, or other pursuits, while others prefer to dabble and explore the world more casually. There's no right or wrong way, and parents must determine their children's needs individually. Age, developmental stage, and specific interests are all important factors in sorting through this issue. In addition, the overall question of how much of a schedule is good or bad will depend on the realities of the parents' work schedules; moms and dads who must spend longer hours away from home understandably have to schedule more activities for their children.

YOUNG CHILDREN

For toddlers and preschoolers, schedules can be highly beneficial. Young children often thrive in a consistent routine: they feel secure in a dependable schedule, and they like knowing what comes next. A clear schedule is probably appropriate for your child during the early years. This is true whether you care for your child on your own or rely on child care or preschool some of the time.

I believe that extra activities can be an important part of younger children's lives. Play groups, toddler gym classes, preschool art classes, and other activities can offer new experiences to children, allow kids to vent their energy, and give moms and dads a chance to interact with other parents. I'd suggest, however, that you avoid overstimulating or fatiguing your child. One or two activities per week is quite sufficient. Make sure you leave plenty of downtime for children after their activities; let them discharge tension and stress through free play.

A relevant issue for young children is separation anxiety. Many kids between the ages of two and six are cautious about engaging in activities away from their parents. The most difficult transitions occur when leaving for school, starting activities away from home, and at bedtime. These are all times when the child is physically and emotionally separating from the parent; as a result, various anxieties and fears surface, creating an emotional reaction and sometimes slowing down the child's shift into the new activity. That's why you should allow plenty of extra time before any transition. Don't rush your child. If possible, adjust your timing to what I call Kid Standard Time. This slower pace frustrates many parents, but pushing too hard can frustrate your child and quickly backfire. If you expect a toddler or preschooler to meet your pace, you'll set yourself up for greater difficulties. Worse yet, you'll pressure your child with unrealistic expectations.

SCHOOL-AGE CHILDREN

Your child will probably be more organized and compliant about transitions by the time she starts elementary school. The shift into other activities, including classes, lessons, and team sports, will probably be smoother. Even so, it's important to recognize that even children ages five to ten have their own sense of timing about these activities, including the shifts necessary to move from one to another.

We adults often pressure kids into following adult schedules. To some degree this is understandable: Things simply have to get done, and we can't always go with the flow, much less allow children to call the shots. Even so, we should always keep in mind that adult schedules are usually at odds with kids' internal clocks. Children's abilities to get moving and respond to external schedules tend to be slower. Even school-age kids struggle to keep pace with the parents' demands. The tension between adults' and children's sense of timing accounts for a lot of the squabbles in otherwise congenial families.

- *Discuss the schedule in advance.* Make sure that everyone knows what's coming next and who's responsible for what tasks in order to meet each individual's and the family's various needs.

- *Help your kids get organized* (finding equipment or supplies, getting dressed, and so forth), but encourage personal responsibility and autonomy. If each child tackles a portion of what needs to be done, there's that much less pressure on any other individual member of the family.

- *Indicate in advance when a transition is coming.* Remind kids about upcoming activities. For toddlers and preschoolers, you'll have to give them a concrete reference point: "We're going when this show is over," or "We'll be leaving after your bath." For older children, you can refer to clock time: "We'll be leaving the house in half an hour, okay?"

- *If necessary, use a gadget* (such as an egg timer) to keep children "with the program." This will nudge them without constant nagging. Younger children, especially, may be more attentive if their role includes taking care of the timer during the countdown.

- *Give a final alert.* "Got your gear? We're out of here in five minutes."

Using one or more of these methods may ease the stress on everyone in the family. I should underscore, however, that these tips are almost beside the point if your family has an overloaded, stress-inducing schedule. If there's simply too much happening, you'll pay the price. Half the battle in maintaining family sanity is won by not overscheduling.

PRETEENS AND TEENAGERS

Many parents complain that their biggest logistical problem with adolescents is mobilizing them. If preteens and teenagers have so much energy, why is it so hard to get them moving? The truth is, kids this age are often exhausted. Their bodies are doing double duty; they're growing like crazy and often intensely active. In addition, teenagers' hormones often create intense surges of energy followed by deep fatigue. Recent physiological research into child development suggests that adolescents sleep a lot partly because of profound changes taking place in their brains and nervous systems. The result is that teenagers often run out of steam. In short, what often appears to be teens' laziness or poor motivation may well have a biological basis.

Yet the reality remains: teens are busy. They have demanding academic schedules, multiple activities after school, and complex social lives. Regardless of feeling tired, teenagers somehow have to keep moving. How do you, the parent, nudge your child along at this stage without creating resentment or adding to the existing pressures? Some of what I've outlined regarding school-age children is appropriate here. Outline the schedule in advance; encourage autonomy; provide medium- and short-term "alerts" about what's to come. You can't resort to egg timers with a teenager—and you shouldn't have to—but you can suggest self-monitoring to children this age that serves the same purpose. A personal calendar or a date book may be useful. Some computer-oriented kids will benefit from using a notepad computer or similar high-tech personal organizer.

But none of these strategies will solve the bedrock issue: too many activities can be stressful. No "fix" involving external solutions can easily relieve the pressure of a tightly packed schedule. My opinion both as a parent and as a clinician is that too many children are simply doing too much. Three, four, even five or more extracurricular commitments on top of heavy homework assignments are increasingly common. No wonder kids feel stressed out!

This situation is absolutely epidemic among high school students, and it's getting more and more common among kids in middle school. It's true that many children take on activities themselves, but sports and cultural pursuits in addition to teachers' expectations quickly add up. In addition, many teenagers have high academic standards and professional ambitions. These goals are admirable in many ways. However, it's important for parents to size up the situation and make sure that the level of activities isn't excessive.

SOUL-SEARCHING

How you respond depends on the details of your child's schedule, but a good place to start is by pondering your own contribution to the dilemma. Although many factors prompt children to end up overextended, the first step to solving the problem is some good old introspection.

Start by answering these questions:

- To what degree are you pressuring your child to take on more activities than is healthy or productive?

- To what degree is your encouragement that your children take on activities an effort to compete with other parents? Is this a kid-oriented equivalent of "keeping up with the Joneses"?

- Are your child's activities a reflection of her own personal interests, or do they express *your* needs, hopes, dreams, and expectations?

- Is a stress on organized activities an expression of fears you feel about the riskiness of contemporary life? That is, are you afraid that your child isn't safe enough simply playing in a less structured environment? If so, is it possible that your concerns are out of proportion with the realities in your area? Could you provide a less organized setting for your child, one that allows easygoing, kid-driven play rather than parent-supervised activities?

- Is it possible that you're pushing your child to acquire skills earlier than seems appropriate? Certain sports may demand greater strength, stamina, or coordination than your child can manage at a given age; certain arts (music, visual arts, etc.) may require greater motor skills than young children can muster. Is it possible, too, that by starting later, your child will do better than by risking the frustration of premature commitment?

YOUR CHILD'S STATE OF MIND

One of the patterns I see in my clinical work is that children worry about disappointing their parents. Kids fear that they'll somehow fall short of their parents' high expectations. In some respects, these kids are right. Sometimes they *are* falling short—but not through any real lapse of their own. These aren't underachieving children; on the contrary, they're usually bright, thoughtful kids who do well in school, get along with others, and behave well. Why should they feel as if they're letting anyone down? As often as not, the problem isn't with the kids' actions, but with the parents' high-pressure goals. The moms and dads simply expect their children to do too much, too often, and in an overly scheduled way. It's as if the parents feel that children should emulate the frantic, goal-obsessed lifestyle typical of so many adults nowadays.

One side effect of this situation is that children often worry about drawing the line. They're afraid to tell their parents that they don't want to take part in team sports, formal lessons, or other organized activities. They worry that they'll disappoint Dad or Mom. Worse yet, kids internalize their parents' anxieties that doing fewer activities will doom them to academic and professional mediocrity, so they go along with what their parents suggest or request. They hesitate to say, "I'd rather just hang out in the backyard instead," or "Can't I just do my own art projects at home?"

Don't get me wrong. Art, sports, and other extracurricular pursuits are often wonderful. Kids can learn enormously from exploring these different activities. New abilities, better social skills, and greater confidence can all result from such pursuits. It's important for children to try out different disciplines, and sometimes organized classes and teams are the best way to accomplish this goal. But if possible, try to see the situation less generally and more in light of your own child's interests and needs. Just because your child may be good at a particular activity doesn't mean that he or she will necessarily enjoy a group activity. And even if your child enjoys the activity, it doesn't mean that you should have a few more of them under way at any given time. Track the situation carefully.

It's also extremely helpful to assess your child's state of mind:

- *Is your child not enjoying the activities you've planned?* Does she speak of the lessons/sessions/practice with enthusiasm—or with indifference, even dread? Is she taking part willingly or just going through the motions?

- *Does your child seem unusually tired following the activity?* Obviously most sports are physically demanding, and practicing many arts (music, dance,

etc.) can be strenuous as well. Is your child's participation disproportionately draining or disruptive?

- *Does your child drag her feet before scheduled activities?* Does she make excuses
  about why she can't make it this week or stall unnecessarily before leaving
  for a particular class, meet, or session?

- *Does your child suffer from inexplicable symptoms* (headaches, stomachaches,
  rashes, etc.) in general or right before a scheduled activity?

- *Does your child seem uncharacteristically subdued, depressed, or burdened,* and
  can you attribute her state of mind to expectations or pressures related to
  her scheduled activities?

- *Does your child's academic performance seem negatively affected by extracurricular activities,* whether through fatigue, depression, somatic symptoms, or
  inadequate time to study?

- *Does your child show signs of "rebelling" from a certain activity?* (Example:
  expressing contempt or anger toward the child's chosen sport, art, etc.;
  refusing to practice; neglecting or willfully damaging equipment; and so
  forth.)

- *Does your child complain of lacking enough time to play,* hang out with friends,
  or spend time with the family?

Answering "yes" to any one of these questions is cause for concern. Answering "yes" to two or more should prompt you to evaluate the situation as soon
as possible. If these questions suggest that your child is under stress because of
scheduled activities, don't panic. Even several "yes" answers doesn't necessarily
mean that you have a long-term problem—simply that your child may be coping with too much pressure. In most instances, you can ease the pressure simply by thinning out the schedule. In other cases, the solution is to pick a
different activity.

LIVING IN THE MOMENT

One of the true glories of childhood is that kids have the ability to live in the
present. They enter the here-and-now and, losing awareness of external expectations, do what they've doing with great intensity. If you watch your child
doing an art project, seemingly at one with the paper and the crayons or paints,
you know what I mean. The same holds true if you eavesdrop on your child as
she pretends to be a doctor, an astronaut, a mother, a gardener, a dog. The
same is true if you listen to a toddler sing a song or play with clay. Children
have a remarkable capacity for being at the heart of their own existence. When
they're in that state of mind, they don't feel the pressures, anxieties, and ten-

sions that often accompany more organized activities. They don't worry about schedules, deadlines, or tangible outcomes—the timetables followed, the games won, the artworks created—that adults so often value. They just enjoy being alive.

As adults, we should value kids' abilities to savor existence in ways that we ourselves often tend to forget. It's not always necessary to *do;* sometimes it's enough—perhaps even better—simply to *be.* That level of being often can't take place in an overly scheduled environment.

It's true that organized activities can allow for moments of great insight, delight, even exaltation. Kids love sports because when mastered well, making the right moves can liberate the body and the spirit. The same holds true for children acquiring the discipline to practice an art—painting, singing, dancing, drawing, or playing an instrument. So what's the solution? By all means give your child the opportunity to learn new things through classes, lessons, and activities. At the same time, allow her the freedom to explore on her own. Children need time to exercise their creativity and imagination. They need time to play in solitude and with their pals. They need opportunities to discharge tension and stress. They need chances to develop an internal sense of self—to look within and know who they are.

THIRTY-EIGHT

SCHOOL CONFERENCES

WHATEVER THE STRENGTHS and weaknesses of your local school system, there's one especially important dimension you'll face: your child's relationship with one or more specific teachers. This relationship may be creative and congenial or negative and tense, but in any case it's a reality you can't ignore. Dealing imaginatively with teachers will be a task you'll confront for many years to come. Dealing successfully with this situation will serve you and your child well. Dealing unsuccessfully with it may complicate your child's education. And the crux of your interaction with teachers will be the ritual of the parent-teacher conference.

MAKING THE MOST OF
PARENT-TEACHER CONFERENCES

To make the most of a parent-teacher conference, you should think about your goals, questions, and concerns before the meeting. These conferences are generally brief; even if it's a responsive teacher facing you across the table, you may not be able to cover every issue on your mind. To complicate matters, the teacher may have his or her own agenda.

PRIORITIZE

What are the most important matters you wish to discuss? Be specific. Don't feel pressured to address all issues at a single conference. If you feel that this occasion hasn't answered your questions or met your needs, you can always meet again at some point to continue the discussion. The best strategy is to choose the most crucial concerns first and tackle them at your conference. Schedule a follow-up meeting later, if necessary.

BE OPEN AND FLEXIBLE

Don't be rigid, with only one specific approach to the issues at hand. By all means have an agenda, but stay open-minded. Listen actively to what the teacher says about your child. This open, flexible approach makes for a team effort between parent and teacher. Remember: Most teachers desire the same thing that parents do—to resolve problems and to keep the child's best interest at heart. An adversarial approach will shut doors from the start.

TUNE IN TO YOUR OWN FEELINGS ABOUT SCHOOL

School is an intense experience for everyone. You surely had some ups and downs during your own school years. As a result, it's important to examine your feelings about school and teachers. Is it possible that your experiences in the past are affecting your communication with teachers in the present? What images, thoughts, or emotions come to your mind when you think of teachers? Do you feel competition, jealousy, or a fear of authority figures? If so, you're not alone. But no matter how common, these reactions can complicate your child's current situation.

The best way to overcome negative feelings from the past is to become aware of them, understand them, and let go of them before they obstruct your ability to engage in trusting, cooperative, open-spirited communication in the present. By initiating good will and by staying involved with and supportive of your child's teacher, you can establish a positive team approach between home and school. This will help your child far more than an aggressive, demanding attitude—one that's sure to put the teacher on guard.

AT THE PARENT-TEACHER CONFERENCE

Once you're actually conferring with the teacher, be organized, respectful, and clear-headed. Your main responsibility is, of course, to serve your child's best interests; at the same time, it's important to acquire information without prejudging the situation. Why have you been asked to attend the conference? What's really going on? How can you help your child? These three questions are at the heart of the matter.

GO TO THE MEETING PREPARED

Jot down key points on the issues you want to discuss. Don't waste the teacher's time (or your own) by struggling to formulate concerns on the spot. Take samples of your child's work in case you need material to illustrate questions or comments.

LISTEN WITHOUT INTERRUPTING

Attend the meeting with an open mind. Hear the teacher; focus on what she's telling you without getting defensive. Paraphrase out loud what she has said to clarify your understanding. Make sure you aren't misconstruing her statements.

ASK FOR SPECIFICS

If there's a problem, or if you're not clear about the situation, ask the teacher for specific examples. There's a difference between clarifying and being defensive.

REQUEST AN ASSESSMENT OR RECOMMENDATION

Ask the teacher what she recommends about the situation and what the school is doing to address the problem. Then ask her suggestions for how you can help at home. In so doing, you join the teacher on the same "team," rather than accusing her and making her feel defensive.

PROVIDE YOUR OWN OBSERVATIONS

Indicate how you perceive your child's situation. Suggest what seems to work well in addressing the issues. If the teacher seems receptive, indicate in a nonthreatening, nonjudgmental way what might solve the problem.

GET TO KNOW THE TEACHER

A personal relationship with the teacher—even on a preliminary level—will help the conversation flow in an easy, relaxed, friendly way. Know the teacher's personality. Is she secure, insecure, flexible, or rigid? Having a sense of her will help you in forming an alliance and a bond of mutual respect. Remember, you are both trying to understand, explore, and educate yourselves about your child. This is the best emotional environment for helping your child to reach his greatest potential.

TRY TO RESOLVE CONFLICTS DIRECTLY

It's possible that the conference won't resolve a difference of opinion; you may end up disagreeing with the teacher about your child's situation. Despite your open-mindedness and patience, you may find that the teacher isn't particularly observant, insightful, or capable.

First of all, it's certainly possible that you're dealing with someone who's mistaken about your child, or who has limited insights or professional skills. If so, you may ultimately need to seek intervention at a higher level, such as from the principal. It would be a mistake, however, to request intervention from the principal too soon. Work things out with the teacher to the degree possible. You may need a consultation with a guidance counselor, too, at some point. Explore these avenues before going to the principal.

STRIVE FOR OPEN COMMUNICATION

Mutual respect and nonjudgmental communication work best. State your concerns openly; don't resort to hints, sarcasm, or whining. If you're upset or frustrated, say so without being dramatic or accusatory. If possible, acknowledge the teacher's feelings, which will prompt her to be more responsive to your own emotions. Ask for clarification without threatening or putting the teacher on the defensive.

ACCENTUATE THE POSITIVE

Let the teacher know what you like about your child's experience at school. If possible, emphasize the positive over the negative. When a problem does arise, the teacher will be more open to listening to you if you've already acted supportive.

CONTINUING THE COMMUNICATION PROCESS

Whether or not your conference is the first interaction with the teacher, make it part of a long-term relationship. Try not to interact with the school only when there's a problem.

- *Make yourself known.* Send an occasional note to say hello and see if the teacher needs anything. Try to be helpful.

- *Call if you have more detailed information to share.* Alert the teacher to your concerns about present or future issues. Here again, collaboration works better than confrontation. Your child's teacher will appreciate being treated as a colleague and ally.

- *Be visible at your child's school.* Attend parents' nights and PTA or PTO meetings. If you don't have time to serve on a committee, offer to help on short-term projects. This is important not just for the school, but for your child's perception of you. The more involved you are, the more your child sees how important you perceive his or her education to be; in addition, the teacher will see that you really care, too.

- *Volunteer to be a homeroom parent.* This commitment simultaneously lets you contribute to the classroom and presents you as an ally right off. Work on a committee, the school newspaper, a fund-raiser, or a special project. Volunteering also helps you to get to know the principal and the other teachers for subsequent years.

- *Keep your sense of humor.* Parents and teachers are all human. You're all trying to do your best to help your child succeed educationally, socially, and personally.

- *Have a win/win attitude*, not an us-against-them attitude!

THIRTY-NINE

SECURITY, SAFETY, AND STRANGERS

WHAT ARE THE real issues concerning children, safety, and strangers? On the one hand, we sometimes overprotect children by withholding the information and guidance they need to make good, safe choices when confronting uncomfortable or threatening situations. On the other hand, today's media hype and tell-it-all attitudes may prompt us to give kids too much information, which can cause unnecessary anxiety and fear. But how much information is too much? How much is too little? How do you help your kids feel insightful and powerful as they deal with some of the negative aspects of modern life? At the same time, how do you protect their innocence and avoid creating undue fears and anxieties?

THE REAL RISKS

What many parents imagine when they worry about these safety issues is a suspicious looking stranger luring their child into a car as she walks home from school. This scenario isn't beyond possibility; however, it's not a frequent occurrence. Neither is another much-publicized type of occurrence—sexual abuse at a child care center. In fact, contrary to the popular images, adults who abuse children are not usually strangers to their victims. Approximately 2 percent of molestations take place in a day care center, family child care setting, or school. About 13 percent occur with strangers. The rest—approximately 85 percent—happen in the company of someone the child knows well. This may mean a baby-sitter, a neighbor, an uncle or aunt, a grandparent, a sibling, or a parent. Unfortunately, such incidents may be repeated. If the perpetrator fails to connect with the child they will try again; if they do connect successfully, they may repeat their behavior with the same child. It's also worth noting that there are many different forms of sexual abuse and molestation. Violent attack isn't the norm. Abuse can be far more subtle, even outwardly affectionate. That being said, it is still abuse.

HOW TO EDUCATE YOUR CHILD ABOUT SAFETY ISSUES

Since you can't always identify potentially unsafe situations, and since you can't supervise your children every second of the day, how can you protect your child from danger? The key is to empower your child to be assertive. This task means creating an environment in which your child feels comfortable raising questions and disobeying certain authority figures. How? The answer to this question takes us back to a discussion in chapter 31, "Parenting Styles," regarding the difference between flexible and inflexible parents.

Inflexible parents tend to raise children who are obedient to all authority figures simply because such persons are in charge. Children of authoritarian parents are less likely to question authority figures even when a request or command is clearly inappropriate. By contrast, flexible parents allow their children the leeway to make age-appropriate decisions themselves and, when necessary, to question authority figures.

The consequences of these differences aren't hard to predict. Excessive deference to all authority figures may leave some children at risk for compliance to inappropriate or even dangerous requests. If someone touches them inappropriately, such children may feel obliged to tolerate the intrusion. By contrast, children who have been granted more permission to question authority figures will be less at risk than children who are more passive and dependent. The result: Independent, assertive kids will probably speak up when facing situations that make them feel uncomfortable either physically, emotionally, or both. Children who respect themselves and take their own needs seriously are usually better able to protect themselves.

WHAT YOU CAN DO TO HELP YOUR CHILD

In addition to empowering your child to make careful decisions, you can help her by providing good information at carefully selected times about possibly dangerous situations.

YOUNGER CHILDREN

Preschool and early school-age kids don't need detailed or graphic discussions of these issues. Your remarks and questions should be simple and clear.

One of the crucial steps you should take at this stage is to teach your child the standard terminology for body parts. Once children are old enough to refer to their elbows, knees, and neck, there's no reason for them not to refer as well to their breasts, nipples, penis or vagina, and so forth. In fact, using euphemisms or cute nicknames ("wee-wee," "down there," etc.) can disorient children or make them uncomfortable. First of all, this alternate vocabulary gives a message that it's wrong to talk openly about certain parts of the body. Second, this message may make it more likely that if someone touches your child inappropriately, she will be too ashamed or frightened to talk about what happened. An accepting, relaxed use of all the names for the body parts gives a contrasting and much more positive message: that her body is beautiful, good, and natural; that there's nothing dirty or embarrassing about any part of it; and that it's fine to discuss human sexuality. It also empowers and encourages a child to set limits and boundaries by giving her confidence about her body, which in turn enables her to speak more openly if someone touches her and makes her feel uncomfortable.

OLDER SCHOOL-AGE CHILDREN

As your child enters the middle grades, her intellectual and emotional development will allow you to address these issues in more detail. Many schools have health modules that raise issues of assertiveness and privacy; you can pick up where the teachers leave off, discussing issues of personal safety. You may want to raise these issues regardless of your school's curriculum.

Clear, Simple Discussions
When you speak with your child, be specific but use age-appropriate examples.

- Assure her that if someone—whether a stranger or a relative—touches her in an unwanted way, she has the right to set limits. This is true even regarding being hugged or kissed, and so forth, if it makes her feel uncomfortable.

- Give your child permission to set limits even for you, your spouse, and others. For instance, many children don't want to be kissed in public. This attitude is extremely common among preteens and teenagers.

- Reassure her about privacy. Teach her to knock before entering your bedroom or the bathroom, and allow her the equivalent privacy as well.

By means of these clear discussions, you're helping your child learn some important lessons.

- Her body belongs to her and her alone.

- She decides who touches her, when, and how.

- If someone touches her in a way that doesn't feel comfortable or right, she can tell that person to stop.

- If someone asks to touch her, it's okay to say no.

- If that person won't take no for an answer, she can leave and, if necessary, run to the nearest safe place. Discuss possible places in advance.

- If approached by a stranger, she should keep her distance, refuse to cooperate or go along, refuse to get into a car, and refuse any and all invitations—to earn a prize, answer a survey, see something special (puppies, kittens, toys, etc.), or get her picture taken.

- If any situation like these should occur, she should tell you, her teacher, her principal, her child care person, or some trusted relative or friend at once even if—*especially if*—warned "not to tell."

- If some such incident takes place, it is *not* the child's fault.

These discussions can take place gradually, without barraging your child with information at one time, but imparting pieces of information as appropriate. Try not to avoid the opportunities to educate your child about safety issues; at the same time, try not to overwhelm or scare her, either. Admittedly, this goal is easier said than done. To simplify discussion, put these issues in the context of overall safety issues, such as crossing the street, using seatbelts, wearing a bike helmet, and so forth. Address more difficult topics on a gradual basis. If your child feels scared by or uncomfortable with these discussions, respect her need to control the quantity or timing of information. Go at her pace.

Playing "What If?"

One of the best ways to help children deal with these issues is to act out scenarios. The goal isn't to provide scary situations, but rather to help kids practice assertive behavior. Here are some examples of the game I call "What If":

- What if a stranger came to you and said, "Would you like to come into my house and see some kittens?"

- What if a stranger asked you to carry some toys over to his car?

- What if a stranger drove up, rolled down his car window, and asked you for directions?

- What if a stranger came up to you in a mall and asked you to do a survey in another room?

- What if a stranger offered to pay you money to model for them or get your photo taken?

Try out these scenarios and see how your children react. Then, depending on their understanding of appropriate responses, teach them what they need to know. Allow them to be assertive. Throw a few "curveballs" to see what happens. Problem-solve together.

Saying No

Another game to practice with your kids is "Saying No." Take turns asking each other a favor. Then try saying no in various ways. This will help your child grow accustomed to the verbal act of saying no without feeling guilty or intimidated. Experiment with various levels of refusal—ranging, for instance, from polite to emphatic to angry.

TEENAGERS

You can provide your kids with much more information once they reach their teens. This is a mixed blessing. On the one hand, teenagers are better able to process detailed practical and ethical questions; on the other hand, even teenagers may not be emotionally or socially mature enough to grasp all the ambiguities. They need the information, but they may not be ready to handle it. They may need particularly thoughtful guidance when dealing with complex situations, such as those involving their peers. So it's up to you as the parent to use your good judgment and intuition.

During all these developmental stages—from toddlerhood to young adulthood—you know your child better than anybody else, so it's your choice regarding how much you believe your child can handle. Some parents feel that abundant information is the key to safety. Others worry that too much detail is alarming. My own feeling is that you should find the middle ground: enough age-appropriate information to allow your child to protect herself yet not so much data that it's overwhelming. It's not an easy decision. To complicate matters, you'll have to make the judgment call time after time as your child grows and changes. The key messages at any age should be:

- Your child has rights and choices.
- If she isn't comfortable with a situation, she should say no and seek a trusted adult.
- You are always available to talk about questions, concerns, and feelings.

THE ISSUE OF "COMFORT LEVEL"

Depending on your personal and religious views—and on the views expressed within your own family of origin—you may feel relatively more or relatively less comfortable discussing sexual issues. The range of people's comfort levels is understandable. In any case, try to resolve your own feelings about sexuality before talking with your children about it. If you have difficulty with frank talk about these issues, consider speaking with your spouse, a friend, or a counselor to clarify your feelings about sexuality. Doing so before any discussions with your children can aid in feeling more relaxed, open, and comfortable during these crucial conversations.

FORTY

SELF-ESTEEM

Accoring to Urie Bronfenbrenner, a prominent psychologist, it's crucial for a child to feel loved and cherished by a parent or other primary caregiver—someone who feels that the child is the sun, the moon, and the stars. Why is this so important? Positive self-esteem is essential to a child's growth and development; children thrive in a state of unconditional love. A primary caregiver's love—whether that caregiver is a parent, a stepparent, an aunt or uncle, a grandparent, or someone else—is the key to any child's self-esteem.

Children who have good self-esteem are much more likely to be happy as they develop and grow. They are less likely to act in antisocial ways than are less confident children. They're less at risk for succumbing to peer pressure or antisocial behavior from other kids. They're more likely to be resilient and strong when coping with negative pressures from society. They are more likely to attain good, stable mental health. As adults, they are much more likely to succeed in all areas of work, relationships, marriage, and general happiness.

WHY SELF-ESTEEM MATTERS

You can help your child feel good about herself from the start by letting her come into the world with a feeling that you value and cherish her. By making it clear that you regard parenthood as a privilege, not a burden. By communicating to her that caring for her is the best thing that you could have ever done with your life. These messages get translated into how a child experiences your commitment, love, and care. That experience of love and acceptance will affect every other aspect of your child's life—family, school, career, and other relationships.

A child with healthy self-esteem feels lovable, attractive, and confident. This isn't to say that such children don't have moments of fear or doubt or insecurity; these feelings are inevitable, appropriate, and normal. For the most part, however, secure children feel that they're good enough as they are. They don't have to be perfect; it's okay to make mistakes. If they make mistakes, they can shrug their shoulders, laugh, and say, "Oh, well—I flubbed," then get back on their feet and try again. Kids with good self-esteem know that they're important and that their ideas, feelings, and opinions matter. They know that they have a right to be visible and have a voice in decisions. By contrast, kids with lower self-esteem tend to be self-denigrating, and less confident; they may also tend to be perfectionistic and inclined to blame themselves for everything that goes wrong.

Parents who build their children's self-esteem have trusting, open, honest relationships with their kids. They are good listeners. They separate the child's behavior from her spirit or nature. They don't lash out at a child when she misbehaves by making general criticisms like, "You're such a slob," or "You're so lazy." They make specific, nonjudgmental requests and comments instead. Such parents are authoritative in a warm, flexible, open way. At times of misbehavior, they communicate by saying, "I love you, but what you're doing right now is unacceptable." They separate the child's nature or character from her behavior.

MODEL GOOD SELF-ESTEEM

If you're insecure, if you lack confidence, or if you're self-denigrating, your attitude will speak louder than all the words in the world. You can love your child intensely, but if you don't love yourself as well, your actions will contradict your words. It's true that each child is his or her own person; at the same time, your child will mirror your behavior and attitudes almost continuously. How you perceive yourself will invariably influence your child's perceptions not only of you, but of herself as well.

BE NONJUDGMENTAL

Similarly, it's important that you respond nonjudgmentally to what you see your child accomplish. Suppose that your five-year-old brings you a piece of artwork from school. You could say, "That's a really nice picture, but maybe next time you could try more colors. You could make the dog's head bigger, too." These comments, though partially complimentary, diminish your child's effort. The unstated message is, "This picture isn't good enough." Instead, you should simply comment on your child's effort. Ask open-ended questions about the painting. Talk about how hard she worked on the project, what beautiful colors or strokes she used, how creative or imaginative the painting looks. Ask her to tell you about her picture and how she feels about it. By this means, you're developing a child's self-esteem—a sense of self-worth based on internal perceptions, not on external rewards. She'll grow in confidence and skill. She's less likely to look for an outside payoff when she believes she's worthwhile for her own independent efforts.

THE PATH TO GOOD SELF-ESTEEM

Generally speaking, I don't believe in stickers, stamps, or other token rewards for good behavior. It's much more effective (in my opinion) for a child to feel proud of herself from the inside rather than to rely on external rewards. If you tell your child, "I'll give you five dollars for every A you get," your child's focus will be on the monetary payoff, not on the real task at hand, which isn't good grades but trying hard and learning well. External rewards may complicate your child's development as a confident person; they may actually undermine self-esteem. Kids know when they're being bought off. Real pride comes from genuine accomplishment and from the love you provide in positive, nonjudgmental messages. You're proud not only of what she does—that is, of the "products" of her efforts—you're also proud of the process. You're proud of her effort. You're proud of *her*.

So by all means encourage your child to be independent and to explore opportunities in the world. Provide a variety of experiences that interest her. Listen to your child actively and paraphrase your child's feelings to make sure that you understand each other. Spend time one-on-one. Solo time with your child helps her feel cared about, attended to, and worthwhile. When you spend time together one on one, and when you tell your child she's everything a parent could ever wish for, you're giving her the message that she really *is* the sun, the moon, and the stars.

FORTY-ONE

SEXUALITY

Melinda's six-year-old son, Robbie, impulsively kissed a little girl's hand. The kids' teacher took Robbie to the principal, who sent the boy home. Melinda was appalled. "These are first-graders!" she told me. "They treated my boy liked he'd practically raped the girl! They said the school district had a no-tolerance policy on sexual harassment!" Yet she admits the district is in a bind; similar incidents elsewhere have resulted in lawsuits. "But I just couldn't believe it," Melinda laments. "Is there no common sense left?"

Jack and Ellie had spent many hours explaining the facts of life to Sam, their nine-year-old son. These sessions had been relaxed and comfortable for everyone involved. After one recent conversation, however, during which the family had talked in detail about sexual intercourse, Ellie asked her son if he had any questions. "Yeah!" Sam half-shouted. "Are you telling me you guys do that for fun?"

"I made the mistake of letting my daughter pick out her own swimsuit," Lisa explains about her fourteen-year-old, Brianna. "You have to understand—she looks twenty-one and has a figure like a supermodel. So what does she pick out? A pure white filmy tank suit. You know that old warning moms give their daughters about how some bathing suits look transparent when wet? Forget about wet! Now, I want Brianna to feel proud about being beautiful, but she doesn't see there's a problem. No matter what she looks like, she's still too naive to grasp how prancing about in that wispy little thing is gonna affect every male in sight."

FOR PARENTS, HELPING children understand sexuality is most importantly a matter of communication. Your child will come to terms with different aspects of sexuality at different developmental stages; by helping her learn what she needs to know at each stage, you'll give her an incomparable gift.

I don't mean "communication" in a strictly verbal sense. What you tell your child—answering her questions, responding to her concerns—is certainly important. Much of what I call communication, though, is nonverbal. Your respect for yourself as a man or woman, your affection toward your spouse or partner, your sense of ease with your child's development from babyhood to womanhood—these and the other silent statements you make will inform her as fully as any words you speak about sexuality. Likewise, any disrespect you show yourself, any contempt you show your spouse or partner, and any discomfort you manifest about your child's development will deliver other messages.

SEXUALITY IN A MUDDLED CULTURE

What you communicate to your child about these issues is crucial because the culture surrounding us is profoundly muddled about sexuality. On the one hand, contemporary America is awash in sexual images. It's impossible to go shopping, watch TV, listen to the radio, or open a magazine without experiencing a bombardment of sex-charged propaganda. Sex sells, and the corporate world knows it. In addition, new media like the Internet are popular to some degree for providing easy access to sexy Web sites. The irony is that in the midst of this often feverish imagery, we Americans are often tense and conflicted in our attitudes toward sex. We aren't nearly as liberated as we imagine. Despite all the sex acts shown in movies, despite all the double entendres in TV sitcoms, despite all the exposed flesh in magazine ads, despite all the pornographic sites on the Web, the United States is in many ways a surprisingly desexualized country. The reason: We tend to forget that sexuality isn't just a question of body parts; it's a dimension of our deepest human nature. Sexuality isn't something a person *does*, but rather part of what a person *is*. And by forgetting this dimension of sexuality, we often confuse ourselves—and our children.

Compounding the problem are the additional risks involved in sexual relationships as the twenty-first century begins. Sexuality has always carried with it both the potential for ecstasy and the risk of despair. In recent decades, however, the riskiest aspects of sex have grown even more risky. The AIDS epidemic has made sexuality a life-or-death gamble, and other sexually transmitted diseases have also raised the stakes. Now even more than in the past, it's crucial that parents teach their children everything possible about responsible decisions concerning sexuality.

HOW TO HELP YOUR CHILD UNDERSTAND SEXUALITY

There's no question that helping children deal with sexual issues can create anxieties for many parents. First of all, it's a complex subject. Second, the issues can provoke a lot of personal anxiety. Third, the stakes are high for both parents and children. If you can confront the situation openly and honestly, however, you'll do a great service to your family.

EXPLORE YOUR OWN FEELINGS

One of the most important steps you can take is also one that many parents find difficult. I'm referring to the task of exploring your own feelings about sexuality. To do so, you don't necessarily need to share your beliefs, recollections, or emotions with anyone else, though doing so can be beneficial. (The ideal choice—assuming your relationship permits—would be sharing this process of exploration with your spouse or partner.) The goal is simply to understand what you feel about sexuality. Some questions to consider:

- What were your family's attitudes about sexuality?
- Did your family members consider sexuality to be normal, natural, and good, or did they think of it as abnormal, unnatural, or sinful?
- What are your earliest memories of yourself as a sexual person?
- Do you recall your early sexual experiences as pleasant or unpleasant, happy or unhappy, comfortable or uncomfortable?
- Were you ever reassured by others about your sexuality, or were you scolded, punished, or abused?
- Who explained sexual issues to you? (For instance: parents, grandparents, aunts or uncles, siblings, friends, schoolmates.)
- What sorts of attitudes did your teachers have about sexuality, and what impression did these attitudes have on you?
- How and when did you start becoming aware of other people as sexual persons?
- What were your feelings about yourself during puberty and your teens?
- Are you sexually at ease with yourself now? If not, what makes you feel uncomfortable?

Thinking over these questions will help you understand the process you experienced in coming to terms with your sexuality as a child, as an adolescent, and as an adult. As you consider the questions, keep in mind that there are no "right" or "wrong" answers—simply a process of clarifying your own experience as a human being and the place that sexuality has within that experience. To the degree that you can understand your own past, you will be relatively free to help your child understand her own sexuality unencumbered by any misgivings you feel.

If sorting through these issues leaves you feeling frustrated, angry, confused, or sad, don't be alarmed. Many of us (probably most) have struggled with the meaning of sexuality in one way or another. For some people, it's a question of coping with parental or societal "messages" during childhood or adolescence— messages, for instance, that sex is bad or dirty. For others, it's a question of sexual orientation—whether one is heterosexual, homosexual, or bisexual. For still others, it's a question of confronting societal stereotypes—such as the prejudice that beautiful people are sexy, while ordinary-looking people are less sexual. Few people go through life without working hard to define themselves as sexual beings. If you feel that you need help in coping with legacies from your past, consider asking for assistance from a well-trained psychotherapist. Facing your uncertainties will help both you and your family.

CREATE POSITIVE IMAGES OF SEXUALITY IN THE HOME

The best way to make sexuality a positive experience for your child is good role-modeling. If your marriage shows your child what a good, healthy, loving relationship is like, you'll teach her more by your example than through any words you speak. Show her that respect, kindness, friendship, and love are the fundamental components of a good bond. Model good communication, mutual respect, and an equitable sharing of power. If you look after one another, enjoy being together, and manifest genuine affection, your child will have the best possible start in her sexual development. If you are a single parent or in a same-sex relationship, the same guidelines can apply for role modeling: positive, healthy intimacy and nurturing attitudes. Whether your child observes you in a partnership, a close intimate relationship, or in a dating relationship, you will be the most powerful role model for positive images of sexuality.

BE AWARE OF THE STAGES OF SEXUAL DEVELOPMENT

As part of our societal confusion about sexuality, American culture tends to regard children as essentially asexual until puberty. The truth is, we are sexual beings from conception till death. How we feel sexually and how we express our sexual nature will change from one life stage to the next, but being male or female is simply part of being human.

One of the best contributions you can make to your child is to understand the stages of sexual development that she will undergo throughout the life cycle. (See the Resource Guide for some insightful books that provide an overview of human sexuality.) By learning about these issues, you'll be better prepared to help your child as issues arise.

LET YOUR CHILD OBSERVE NATURE

Another good way to help children understand sexuality is by letting them observe nature. Their observation doesn't have to be part of a health curriculum; kids are simply curious about the natural world. Helping children feel comfortable with nature is an important contribution to their understanding.

When I worked with preschoolers and kindergartners, I'd often take the kids to a place called Drumland Farm, near the day care center where I taught. I'd schedule our visits to coincide with the time of year when piglets were being born and chicks were hatching so that the children could watch the reproductive process in a very natural, nonthreatening way. Although the birth of baby animals is only one component in kids' understanding of sexuality, it's especially useful for very young children, since they relate so easily to young animals. Every child I've known reacted to this experience in a positive way.

DISCUSS ISSUES WITH YOUR CHILD

Open, relaxed, frequent discussions with your child are crucial. If you can help your child feel comfortable seeking you out for information and problem solving, you have won half the battle.

- *Don't resort to infrequent, dramatic "facts-of-life" discussions.* Avoid lecturing your child. Be careful about overwhelming her with too much information at once. Discussions should be interwoven with everyday conversations—ideally, in response to your child's own questions—and keep the discussions relatively short.

- *If possible, follow your child's lead.* Your child may well approach you with questions. Try to respond casually and immediately. If the circumstances are awkward (such as the proverbial supermarket checkout line), give a brief explanation, then pick up the subject at a more auspicious time.

- *If necessary, take the initiative.* Some children acquire our culture's ambivalence about sexuality so early that they hesitate to ask any questions. By assuming that sexual matters are "dirty," they stay silent even while their minds buzz with questions. If you sense that your child feels this kind of shyness, you may need to take the initiative and inquire about issues that may be troubling her.

- *Respond as comfortably as possible.* If your child asks a question that you find embarrassing, turn the question around. Responding to how babies are made, for instance, you can ask, "How do *you* think babies are made?" or

"Where do *you* think babies come from?" Then provide your child with age-appropriate information. Answer simply and directly. If your child wants a more detailed explanation, she'll continue the dialogue. (Her answer may also serve as a barometer of where she is developmentally.)

- *Use age-appropriate books and materials.* An abundance of printed and video materials now exist to help parents explain sexuality to children. A visit to any large bookstore should yield many resources. As always, your initial task will be to determine what's suitable for your child's age and personality, but you won't lack for possibilities. (One caveat: before sharing these materials with your child, do your homework, researching books and articles for content, accuracy, and appropriateness for your child's age group. Also, monitor your own response to these materials. The quality and content may vary, so take the time to feel confident about your choices.)

SCHOOL HEALTH CURRICULA

Most public schools start sex education around fifth grade. Usually presented as part of a health curriculum, these sex education modules can be an important contribution to your child's learning about sexuality. The usual emphases are the physiological changes typical during puberty—hormonal changes, menstruation, development of secondary sex characteristics (pubic hair, breasts, voice changes, and so forth). In general, I applaud schools for pursuing these important aspects of the curriculum. Two caveats, however:

One, many sex education modules are limited in scope. Because some members of our communities object to sex education in the schools (and sometimes express their objections through litigation) school districts often step carefully as they design their health modules. The level of detail in classes can be rather minimal. Discussions can be vague or squeamish. For instance, teachers may be allowed to mention masturbation but prohibited from stating that among teenagers, masturbation is common among girls, nearly universal among boys, and harmless for members of both sexes. Although there have been positive changes recently in the quality of school health curricula, too many programs neglect to provide information about positive, healing relationships. Many health modules say little or nothing about the deeper issue of communication as the foundation for developing respectful, loving intimacy, or about how a relationship of this sort can lead to more enjoyable sexual intimacy. In addition, many curricula make little or no mention of birth control—an omission that, in light of current statistics for teenage pregnancy, seems benighted. Don't expect sex education modules to provide your child with everything she needs to know.

Two, even a thoughtful sex education program in your local schools doesn't absolve you from responsibility in helping your child understand sexuality. As the parent, you're still the best, most reassuring source of information for your child, and you're a crucial player in your child's process of learning what she needs to know. Just as you might not understand everything about your child's other studies, you may not understand everything she learns in health class. But you're important as a resource and interpreter. Be available to answer questions. Help your child think through what she's learning.

FORTY-TWO

SIBLING RIVALRY

THERE ARE NO siblings without rivalry. Within every family, the children will compete for their parents' love and attention. This competition lingers even into—and throughout—adulthood; grown men and women often strive to gain the place of being the best-loved child in their parents' hearts. Why? It's possible that from an evolutionary perspective, individual children gain advantage through sibling competition. Throughout human history, the children who have survived have tended to be those who have successfully gained their parents' attention, concern, and sustenance. In short, children stand to benefit by being the best-loved.

THE NATURE OF SIBLING RIVALRY

To be the best-loved, a child must be unique. Uniqueness requires, first of all, a separate identity from the other siblings. To some degree, this state of separation is inevitable. Each human being has a built-in drive for self-definition. Children also have individual personalities and interests. The differences between one child and another occur in part because humans are born with innately different abilities, talents, and likes and dislikes; in addition, children almost invariably strive to distinguish themselves from one another. You've probably seen many families—perhaps including your own—in which kids stake out private "turf." One child has a strong interest in sports. Another likes science. Another is fascinated by art and music. Such differences of interest are often a consequence of genuine preferences, but they also reflect the children's drives to win the parental recognition and love. Sibling rivalry is basically a struggle for this position. The children are trying hard to form their own identities and, in so doing, to gain the parents' special favor.

A firstborn son or daughter often has a particularly difficult time with sibling rivalry. After all, this child has experienced the bliss of undivided parental love. Then, if another child arrives on the scene, the new baby may create a discontent for the firstborn. Even the most thoroughly well-adjusted child may feel a sense of confusion and hurt. Regardless of age, every firstborn child probably wonders why the newcomer is around at all. (Terri, a three-year-old, raised the matter of her newborn brother at once gently and bluntly: "Mommy, can that baby go home now?") The firstborn's unstated questions are, "Why have they replaced me?" and "Wasn't I lovable enough?" The result: great tension, pain, and anger. The firstborn may either express or suppress his feelings of hostility, hurt, and betrayal.

EARLY STAGES OF SIBLING RIVALRY

How can you help your firstborn when the new baby arrives? First, encourage an independent relationship between your older child and the baby to ease rivalrous feelings. If possible, include the firstborn in baby care activities, since this new role as the "big kid" may help the older child to feel appreciated and respected. Possibilities include helping to bottle-feed the baby, assisting the parents, and playing with the baby. It's crucial not to sideline the firstborn. In addition, it's important to allow the firstborn the opportunities to develop a relationship with the baby. By all means safeguard the baby from the hazards of attention from a well-intentioned but inexperienced sibling; at the same time, give them a chance to be together. The older child will eventually accept his younger sibling, but the process will take time.

ACCEPT YOUR FIRSTBORN'S FRUSTRATIONS

Avoid saying things like, "You shouldn't feel that way," or "How can you be jealous of this tiny little baby?" Try to identify and validate your older child's feelings. Saying, "Isn't the baby a pain sometimes?" or "Doesn't that crying bother you?" will ease the firstborn's worries or guilt about his own hostility.

DON'T PLACE THE OLDER CHILD IN AN INAPPROPRIATE ROLE

You can give him special tasks, since this will help him feel included and responsible—but there's a fine line between that and making the older child the caregiver or pseudo-parent.

LATER STAGES OF SIBLING RIVALRY

Sibling rivalry will probably intensify when the baby starts to walk, talk, and become a more active member of the family. These later stages are demanding for parents, since the second child's toddlerhood may complicate the task of finding time with the older child. Still, it's very important for parents to give each child his or her fair share of focused attention. It's very important to do things with your kids one-on-one, rather than always as a family unit. Rivalry will increase if one sibling gets more attention than another. The likeliest adversaries may be same-sex children who are close in age, since parents often perceive these children more as a unit than as separate individuals. They may be closer or more distant when they're older; in any case, same-sex children of similar age need to be treated as individuals. (This suggestion applies to twins, triplets, and other multiple births as well.)

Rivalry can increase when parents don't model cooperative problem solving. It's important for parents to model good communication for their kids, since children will often pick up on the anger or stress in the parents' relationship and may reflect those same tensions toward the siblings. Imitation of the parental relationship also affects issues of intimacy. Sometimes a parent's favoritism toward one child over another intensifies normal rivalry. This can be very detrimental. Likewise, if one child gets on your nerves because of person-ality or behavioral issues, it's important to ask the other parent to help out. You may also identify with one child over another because that child has the same position in the family as you did in yours. If you're a firstborn, for instance, you may identify more easily with your own firstborn child. On the other hand, you may identify with a child whose personality complements your own. (That is, a child who resembles you in the negative ways may really "push your buttons"; by contrast, a dissimilar child may aggravate you less.) In short, try to give each child a fair share of time and attention and try to do things preventively so that sibling rivalry doesn't escalate.

SIBLING RIVALRY AS REHEARSAL FOR LIFE

Another reason why sibling rivalry is important is that it's a dress rehearsal for relationships. Human relationships are complex. Children need consider-able practice to master the skills required for getting along with others. To complicate matters, no relationship is perfect, and we often feel ambivalent about even the people who matter most to us. Children must learn how to negotiate their different social roles and issues around emotional connective-ness and communication. Sibling relationships serve many functions, but one of the most important is that they provide children with a dress rehearsal for socialization in the wider world—how to accept others, how to compromise, how to deal with feelings, how to express emotions. During the early years, it's very important to help your children put words to their emotions so that they can learn to communicate rather than to lash out physically. Sibling relationships are a perfect way to practice communication about feelings and needs.

Another issue regarding sibling rivalry is that kids sometimes need a break from each other. They spend a lot of time together; they get on each other's nerves; they feel stressed. As with any intimate relationship, you sometimes need time alone, a chance to calm down, or an opportunity to get in touch with yourself. So those are times when kids need to do things separately from one another. If an older child must always take a younger child on outings, the result can be increased anger and resentment between the siblings. For this reason, it's important not to ask the older child always to have the younger child present or to include the younger child when a friend comes over to play.

PROBLEM SOLVING BETWEEN SIBLINGS

- *Find time to be alone with each child.* Don't try to do everything as a family. At least occasionally, take each child on a separate outing.

- *See your child as a separate individual.* Even if your children seem similar and compatible, acknowledge different interests and traits.

- *Be a good role model for your children.* This issue is especially important regarding how you and your spouse communicate. Let your kids see you sort things out, work together, and compromise.

- *Don't try to "solve" sibling rivalry.* Let your children find some of the solutions to their conflicts. Guide your children, but listen carefully to everyone and don't take sides. Be somewhat but not overly involved. Make suggestions; then let the kids generate their own options.

- *If fighting becomes physical and out of control, separate the kids until they calm down.* Then encourage them to talk and negotiate a solution.

- *Avoid pitting one child against the other or encouraging competition between siblings.* Don't say, "Your sister is better at sports (or science, art, etc.) than you are," or "Why can't you be more like your brother?" Such statements just increase the competition and the rivalry and makes your child feel rejected. This approach also ups the ante in terms of how they have to fight for the position of the best-loved child.

- *Avoid dismissing your child's emotions regarding sibling rivalry.* Statements such as, "You shouldn't feel like that," or "You're not being nice to your brother," or even "Be nice to the baby" can be counterproductive. Instead, validate their feelings: "This must be tough for you," or "I'm sure the baby is getting on your nerves," or (to an older child) "I felt that way, too, when my baby brother (or sister) was born." Empathize with your own child about what he or she is feeling.

- *Realize that the change is not going to come about without some stress.* Sibling arguments aren't just a challenge; they also provide an opportunity for kids to learn how to deal with the world. They are a catalyst for change and growth rather than just a crucible of family torture.

- *Have a positive attitude and a sense of humor.* Try to see sibling rivalry as a vehicle for children to learn about themselves and others, empower themselves, and reinforce their own autonomy. Praise their individuality, uniqueness, and intelligence. Encourage their ability to solve problems on their own. With just a little guidance and care from you, they can figure it out.

- *Remove yourself from the room, if necessary, and do something else if your kids seem to be "playing to an audience" during a conflict.* They may end up solving their problems more quickly alone. If so, back off and distract yourself.

FORTY-THREE

SINGLE PARENTHOOD

AN ACQUAINTANCE NAMED Sheila once explained to me what she finds both thrilling and difficult about running marathons. "It's not the physical exertion," she said. "I'm strong, I have good stamina, I love running, and I'm single-minded about getting to the finish line. What's hard is the loneliness. No matter how many people are running, no matter how many others are cheering from the sidelines, I'm still there all by myself. Ultimately it's *my* race. And I have to run it alone."

Hearing these words, I impulsively told her, "I know how you feel."

Sheila looked puzzled. "Really? I didn't think you were into marathons."

"I'm not," I answered. "But I'm a single parent."

THE LONELINESS OF THE LONG-DISTANCE PARENT

Single parenthood is now more common than ever. Once rare within American culture, families with just one parent are now a large minority: the Children's Defense Fund estimates that almost 50 percent of American children will spend part of their childhood living with only one parent. The percentage is likely to increase in the years ahead. Despite the growing presence of single parents within our society, however, some politicians, members of the clergy, and cultural critics deride one-parent families as an aberration. But single parents are here to stay, and the tasks and burdens they face deserve careful attention and strong support.

Why has the number of single parents increased so rapidly? Here are some of the major contributing factors:

- More than half of all marriages end in divorce.

- Single mothers, though often less affluent than married parents, now have greater economic opportunities for supporting children alone.

- A small but growing number of divorced fathers gain custody of their children.

- Unmarried women have greater social leeway now in choosing to adopt or bear children.

- Gay men have increased opportunities to adopt children.

- Lesbians, too, have opportunities to adopt or bear children.

- A growing number of grandparents are raising their grandchildren.

In short, people of many different backgrounds are either becoming single parents or, increasingly, are choosing single parenthood. The result is that single parenthood has "gone mainstream." Generally speaking, the stigma attached to raising a child alone has diminished. Many Americans who tackle the work of parenting their children alone do so eagerly, skillfully, and successfully.

Yet the fact remains: Parenthood is a hard race to run, and it's even harder if you're running it alone.

EASING THE STRESS OF SINGLE PARENTHOOD

If you're parenting a child on your own, what can make the tasks easier and less lonely? I know that there's no simple answer. There are, however, some approaches to the situation that can make your life simpler, less stressful, and more satisfying.

RELY ON THE OTHER PARENT, IF POSSIBLE

Most single parents are flying solo as a result of divorce. This outcome usually means that one parent (usually the mother) has custody. The circumstances can range from amicable co-parenting to total disengagement by one parent (usually the father). Obviously your situation as a single parent will depend on your custody arrangement and on the nature of the relationship you have with your ex-spouse. A contentious or hostile relationship may mean that you're raising your child not only alone, but practically under siege. What I often see, however, is that even relatively mild resentments can prompt the custodial parent to ignore or refuse help from the other parent, a situation that's understandable on an emotional level but often risky for the child.

In most cases, the noncustodial parent is a crucial contributor to your child's well-being. Your relationship with your ex may be unpleasant, but you need to support and sustain your child's relationship with her other parent if at all possible. The stakes are high on every level—financial, developmental, and social. In addition, your own circumstances may benefit from shared parental duties following divorce; you're more likely to maintain your stamina, health, and emotional well-being if you aren't carrying the whole burden all the time.

- *Focus intensely on your child's well-being.* Love your children more than you dislike your ex. Disengage from your hostility. Respond imaginatively to your child's need to love both her parents.

- *Don't undercut your ex's parenting skills.* Pushing him aside, sabotaging his efforts, belittling his gestures, or criticizing him needlessly will backfire, at least in the long run, affecting your child in negative ways. You may feel rightly pleased to have the custodial role, but relegating your ex to second-class parenting status will pointlessly increase his anger and humiliation, which in turn humilates and shames your child.

- *Never use your child as a pawn.* Maligning your ex puts your child in a no-win situation: If she sides with you, she violates her bond with her other parent; if she sides with him, she violates her bond with you. Avoid exhibiting behavior that reveals your own insecurity or possessiveness.

- *Do everything possible to nurture your child's relationship with her other parent.* Children need both parents! She will benefit from her closeness with each of you. The only exceptions to this rule: If your ex breaks major promises or is abusive, seek help from the court-appointed guardian to address your concerns.

FIND BACKUP SUPPORT

All parents need to be part of a community; the situation is even more crucial for single parents. By "community" I mean both an extended family—your parents, siblings, and other relatives—and members of the larger group of people around you. Get as much help and support as you can find. The benefits will serve you well, since you'll feel less isolated and stressed; in addition, your children will feel more secure, too, by knowing that there's a backup system around them.

Some members of this system are pretty obvious, such as close relatives or neighbors. Cast a wider net, though: There may be community resources you haven't considered. Many church and temple congregations are supportive of single parents. Your local PTA or PTO may also have a network of single parents who are especially eager to help each other out. Community centers sometimes have single-parent support groups, too. What's most important is not to "go it alone." You need someone available who can help you if your car breaks down, if your child gets sick at school, if you're stuck in traffic, and if Murphy's Law strikes in any other way.

A related suggestion: think through contingencies. In a two-parent household, each parent is the other's backup; as a single parent, you're the whole show. Consider in advance how you'll respond to crises and setbacks. What if you are hit by a bad virus? Who can you call for help? Who's around if you have an emergency in the middle of the night? Many single parents feel that they're burdening people, but people may be far more willing to help than you imagine.

Practical support isn't the whole issue here; you should consider your needs for emotional support as well. Again, friends and relatives are ideal. Sometimes, though, you need to widen your network. Church or synagogue support groups can offer emotional sustenance for single parents. In addition, parents education classes and support groups can be immensely helpful. The key is to find other people who understand the tasks and trials you face. In addition, one of the biggest stresses for single parents—particularly for those with young children—is that you don't have a "sounding board" to bounce ideas off. A source of reliable, nonjudgmental advice is crucial. Don't carry the burdens alone.

Nurture Yourself

As I stress repeatedly throughout this book, you need to replenish your energy throughout the parenting years. This recommendation holds true for all parents, but it's even more crucial if you're raising children alone. You can't run on empty. No matter how earnest you are about doing everything on your own, you'll deplete yourself eventually. The consequences will harm your child as well as you. For ideas on what you can do, see chapter 49, "Taking Care of Yourself."

Dealing with Single Parenthood by "Default"

Even if you're married, you may *feel* like a single parent. Some of the most stressed-out parents I know are women (and a small but increasing number of men) whose spouses work extremely long hours or travel a great deal. This can be a new spin on the old Ward and June Cleaver arrangement: one spouse stays home with the kids while the other brings home the bacon. Given current work schedules, though, it's rough on everyone. (Even Ward Cleaver came home each day by six.) What's outwardly a dual-parent household ends up single parenthood by default. The stay-at-home parent ends up carrying the whole domestic/child care burden.

How do you deal with this kind of situation? My earlier recommendations hold true here as well. Rely on your spouse. Find backup support. Nurture yourself. In addition, see chapter 32, "Parenting As Partners," for a more extensive discussion of collaborative parenting.

DON'T PARENTIFY YOUR CHILD

One good aspect of being a single parent is that you may have a lot of one-on-one time with your child. This situation can lead to a very close parent-child relationship, which is wonderful for both sides. My only caveat is this: don't get overly dependent on your child's support, praise, or emotional sustenance. As a single parent, you face stresses and demands so severe that there's a risk that you'll parentify your child—that is, you'll put your child in the role of taking care of *your* needs. This is an understandable but risky situation. Switching the roles in this manner is stressful and unfair to your child, since a child shouldn't have to carry this kind of adult responsibility for anyone, *especially* a parent.

My advice: Track your behavior and emotions closely. If you feel that you're putting unfair emotional burdens on your child, seek assistance from a friend or relative who can be a reliable confidant. If necessary, locate a therapist or counselor who can serve the same role. There's nothing wrong with needing help, comfort, insight, and consolation; the important thing is to find an appropriate source—a mature, nonjudgmental adult, *not* your child.

WATCH OUT FOR SIBLING RIVALRY

Single parenthood can lead to intense sibling relationships. Precisely because there's only a mother *or* a father at home, brothers and sisters may be aware of the intense pressures on that parent, which in turn may lead siblings to seek emotional comfort from each other. This situation isn't necessarily bad; close sibling ties are often wonderful and can even be closer and stronger than when the marriage was intact. In many families, siblings become each others' best support. But if you sense that tension and acrimony between your children are running high, deal with the circumstances before they deteriorate. Ideally, seek help from a trained counselor or family therapist.

WHEN DADS ARE SINGLE PARENTS

I'm delighted when dads assume a major parenting role. Tens of thousands of American fathers have started to take on greater child-rearing responsibilities each year, and this trend will change our culture in many ways. Still, the situation isn't without some drawbacks, including some that chiefly affect the dads.

One is that many fathers feel socially isolated. If a mother moves to a new neighborhood, she can easily find other moms with like-aged children within a few weeks; for dads, though, the task is more difficult. It's not necessarily that there aren't other men around with primary-parent responsibilities. The catch is that men don't always feel comfortable socializing with each other when parenting is the chief common ground. Exceptions exist. I've spoken with men throughout the country who have set up informal groups where their children can play while the dads hang out together. This sort of development is wonderful. But many other men tell me that even when they're aware of other primary-parent dads in the area, they're reluctant or uncertain about making contact. The same men often feel less than fully welcomed—or even feel ostracized—by some mothers' play groups, which often serve in part to meet women's social needs. Others may feel patronized by women who insist on offering unsolicited advice.

How should men respond to these situations? My chief recommendation is not to be shy about finding the resources you need. Ask around to see if other primary-parent dads live in your neighborhood. Local preschools may have bulletin boards advertising fathers' play groups. Churches and synagogues, too, may offer resources specifically for fathers. Your local library may have story hours and other activities that dads can attend with their children. If all else fails, visit the library or the local playgrounds on Saturday mornings, when many fathers who work regular jobs during the week may be present with their kids.

One last issue. I believe that primary-parent dads should be deeply proud of what they're doing. American culture gives very little praise to men who focus time and attention on their children, yet the tasks involved are among the most important that anyone can perform. If you're taking a major role in raising your kids, I congratulate and salute you. Celebrate yourselves, dads—not as Mr. Mom, as many fathers speak of themselves, but as Mr. Dad. Fathers, like mothers, are capable of being superb parents. You have every right to take pride in your role as a father.

THE PRIDE OF THE LONG-DISTANCE PARENT

Being a single parent can be one of the toughest challenges anyone can face. The work is hard; the tasks never seem to end; it's stressful to have sole responsibility for a child's well-being. Solo parenthood can be exhausting, overwhelming, frustrating, stressful, lonely, and scary. I know because I was a single parent myself for many years. I'll admit that I found single parenthood difficult in many ways.

At the same time, being a single parent somehow worked out anyway. I managed to set up a good support network, so that I was able to find help when I needed it. All kinds of wonderful people became part of my life—and part of my son's life, too. Despite the stresses of raising a child alone, I discovered that I had many opportunities to grow and change. So there's far more to me now—

more strength, more confidence, more empathy, more insight, more patience, more delight in life—than there was before I became a parent. I really know what I'm made of. Throughout the course of raising my son, I've had to look deep into my heart and soul, decide what I believe, determine what I want to do, and figure out how to accomplish what's necessary. Has this process been easy? Of course not. On the contrary, it's been incredibly hard. Still, it's been worth it.

What has been most valuable and most wonderful about this situation is simply the gift of being my son's mother. The situation would have been easier under other circumstances, but ultimately that doesn't matter. Being Jason's mom is simply how my life turned out. I can't imagine it any other way. I love my son and rejoice in his presence in my life.

Being a single parent can be hard at times, but it's often good. If you're in this situation, you probably feel as I do. You regret what has been difficult but, accepting your own emotions, you simply get back to work. You struggle with the tangled issues that crop up each day, then move on. You wish that life could be easier but ultimately accept your situation or else try creatively to change it. In any case, I urge you to trust yourself, praise yourself, honor yourself. Do right by your child—and delight in a hard job well done.

FORTY-FOUR

SLEEP

To PARAPHRASE THE legendary football coach Vince Lombardi, "Fatigue makes bozos of us all." There's probably nothing that makes parents feel crankier, crabbier, and crazier than the loss of sleep that accompanies many stages of raising children. Sleep deprivation can leave even a happy, easygoing person feeling miserable. Every chore becomes more difficult. It's harder to cope with everyday demands. It's impossible to find energy for enjoyable activities. It's easy to become irritable, anxious, and even depressed. As if the tasks of parenthood weren't already hard enough, you often have to go through the motions while feeling like a zombie.

None of this will be news to most parents. Even parents-to-be know that sleep loss comes with the turf. I wish I could reassure you that it's a short-lived phenomenon—something destined to ease after your newborn has been home for a few months. Unfortunately, the situation isn't quite so simple. Yes, newborns settle in and settle down. Your child will gradually develop a sleep routine. You, too, will catch some z's and regain your sanity. Yet I feel compelled to add that sleep issues crop up throughout the parenting years, and you're better off knowing that some rough water lies ahead than pretending it's all smooth sailing.

AGE-RELATED SLEEP ISSUES

Most of the difficulties that parents face in getting their children to sleep (and keeping them in bed till dawn) are age-related. Here's a quick breakdown of developmental stages and the sleep issues that children typically experience.

NEWBORNS

Newborn human babies are not inherently diurnal—that is, they aren't by nature inclined to sleep during the night and stay awake during the day. They sleep when they're tired and wake when they're rested. Most newborns sleep about sixteen to eighteen hours per day, but the periods of sleepiness and wakefulness follow the babies' physiological needs rather than the clock. Within a few months, however, most babies start to establish a sleep/wake pattern throughout the day. Parents who strive for consistency in bedtimes and wake-up times will reinforce the baby's process of settling into a normal daytime/nighttime schedule. Other variables include feeding patterns, the child's temperament, health issues (illness, prematurity, disabilities, etc.), and the surrounding environment (noise level, presence of other children, etc.).

INFANTS

Infants' sleep—or lack thereof—causes parents some of the greatest fatigue they'll experience throughout the parenting years. Here are some factors that affect how infants sleep (or fail to).

Feeding

A newborn baby's digestive system is not mature. Infants often experience discomfort in digesting food—even milk—which makes sleep difficult. Even breast-fed babies may experience discomfort, since certain foods that the mother eats (such as broccoli, cabbage, and orange juice) may cause gas in an infant. In addition, digestion and excretion may be uncomfortable for some infants.

Another cause for sleep difficulties is specific feeding issues. A feeding routine—consistent but not too rigid—is important. Most babies may start sleeping through the night at around three to five months of age. Bottle-fed babies often sleep through the night earlier than breast-fed babies, since breast milk is more easily and quickly digested, leaving the child hungrier sooner. Consult with a pediatrician if you have specific feeding concerns.

Neurological Issues

Babies are often neurologically immature in ways that complicate their falling asleep and staying asleep. Sometimes a calm rushing noise can soothe the child. To calm a jumpy infant, consider using one of the standard ploys, such as a musical teddy bear, running water, a music box, or a low-noise vacuum cleaner in the background. Some teddy bears and other stuffed toys now contain sound-generating microchips that mimic a pulsing sound similar to what babies hear in utero—a noise that infants often find especially lulling.

Teething

Although some medical authorities question whether teething can disrupt children's rest or change their moods, many parents believe that their babies simply don't sleep well or are fussier when cutting a new tooth. It's not hard to imagine why. Teething pain can be considerable by day; why should it diminish entirely at night? Many babies have trouble getting a restful night's sleep while teething. What's a helpful response? Ask your pediatrician or nurse practitioner for specific remedies.

TODDLERS

By toddlerhood, most children have outgrown most of the issues that disturb infants' sleep. However, the ups and downs aren't over yet.

Motor Development When a child reaches toddlerhood, she will experience a great surge in her motor skills. Walking, running, jumping, and moving in many other ways are new and complex skills that children acquire and perfect at this time. For many children, this developmental surge involves nighttime as well as daytime activity: the muscles move even during sleep. Toddlers may have a hard time "turning off" their urge to move, which may result in less-sound sleep and periodic wakefulness.

Developmental Adjustments Children change in other ways during toddlerhood. One developmental adjustment is separation anxiety. Even if your child has shown only minimal concern about your absence at bedtime, she may feel much more concerned about your whereabouts from about age one. One common manifestation of this concern is anxiety about where the parents are at night, whether they will come when called, and so forth. The need for closeness, comfort, and reassurance at this time can be intense, often continuing through the early preschool years as well. In addition, children who have only limited contact with her parents by day often manifest a greater need for parental contact at night. This craving can prompt your child to come to your bed, crawl in, demand a chance to snuggle, and so forth.

Nightmares, Night Terrors, and Sleepwalking Around late toddlerhood, two common sleep disturbances may occur: nightmares and night terrors. Both are fairly harmless, though often upsetting to both children and parents. Nightmares are what they seem—scary dreams that upset your child. Your main response should be simply to reassure your child, calm her, and convince her to go back to sleep. Letting her crawl into your bed may solve the short-term problem but may also lead to a reliance on this form of comfort in the longer run.

By contrast, night terrors aren't really nightmares; they are a state of severe agitation without an accompanying dream. Your child may not wake up from a night terror, but simply calm down and resume normal sleep. Again, simply reassure her and put her back to bed.

Finally, sleepwalking is worrisome to adults but fairly common; roughly 15 percent of all children sleepwalk at some point before age fifteen. Contrary to popular assumption, a sleepwalker isn't dreaming at the time. The main issue here is to make sure that your child isn't at risk from falling down a staircase or injuring herself in other ways. Railings, gates, and other forms of childproofing are crucial to ensure your child's safety.

Changes of Routine and Other Causes of Stress Almost any change in family routine can disrupt a child's sleep pattern. Typical situations include a parent's or sibling's illness, the arrival of a new baby, parents' marital difficulties or work problems, and disruption in the household (guests, noisy neighbors, etc.). Even stresses that primarily affect the parents can be transferred to your child, since children are highly sensitive to their primary caretaker's emotions.

Effects of TV and Other Media I'm amazed by how many parents let preschoolers, even toddlers, watch television before bed. "They know it's all fantasy," many parents insist. First of all, many young children *don't* know it's all fantasy; even bright, worldly children often have little conception of what's real and what's unreal. Second, many children who know that a program is fantasy may still be troubled by what they see. Violent dramas and cartoons, especially, can disturb the sleep of children who, during daylight hours, will watch TV seemingly unaffected. How should you respond? Go easy on the shows. Limit your child's exposure to violence, death, monsters, and even "harmless" action videos and programs. I believe it's appropriate to be generally conservative in this regard. Guide your child and monitor what she's watching. Decrease anything that may be troubling.

"Willful" Disruption? Confronted with a sleepless child, many parents tend to feel that such wakefulness is a form of misbehavior. In fact, this parental response is rarely appropriate. Don't take personally your child's inability to sleep. It's incredibly depleting to get up in the night and deal with a restless child, but there's usually a reason for what is happening. The issues are your child's development, your child's fears and anxieties, your child's physiological needs. Children at these early ages don't calculate to make their parents' lives miserable.

PRESCHOOLERS AND SCHOOL-AGE CHILDREN

Children ages three to ten generally have stable sleep patterns. Unless there are significant physical or psychological issues, your child probably sleeps a fairly regular nine to twelve hours per night. The main issue facing most parents of preschool and school-age children is the transition between evening and bedtime.

However, some anxieties and stresses can disrupt children's sleep at this stage. Young children react to stress and tension in various ways, including at night. Typical disruptive stresses include:

- Moving to a new house
- Any change in routine, such as a new day care provider, a new teacher, or a new school
- An upcoming holiday
- The death of a friend or family member
- Illness
- The death of a pet
- Violence on television
- Going on a vacation
- A shift to a higher level of functioning or achievement

PRETEENS AND TEENS

Just when you thought it was safe to go back to bed, your child will arrive at her preteen and teenage years. Parents often find this developmental stage reassuring in one way—teens and preteens sleep well—but exasperating in another— teens go to bed late and don't want to get up! Because the issues during adolescence are so different from what parents deal with during other stages of childhood, however, we'll address them later, in chapter 50, "The Teen Years."

STRATEGIES

How can you proceed so that your child learns to fall asleep alone, stay asleep, and sleep through the night? These are the most common tasks that parents face regarding their children's sleep patterns.

ESTABLISH A BEDTIME ROUTINE

The most crucial step you can take is to establish a bedtime routine for your child. Start from infancy and continue onward. Newborns sleep sporadically, of course, so that a predictable routine is elusive for several months. By the time your child reaches the age of three to five months, however, you should have some patterns established. Build on these patterns as your child grows. Think in advance about what's feasible, given your child's individual needs; check with your pediatrician if you need advice; be consistent. Consistency is, in fact, the key. Whatever you do to establish calm, and regular bedtime habits for your child will pay off dramatically over the years.

STAY CALM EVEN WHEN YOU'RE STRESSED AND TIRED

If you feel frustrated about your child's behavior at bedtime, she will pick up on your feelings, which will complicate the situation. You should remain calm, cool, and neutral about the ups and downs of preparation for bedtime. Start the routine with a positive attitude. Try to keep things simple: give a bath, nurse an infant or tell a story to an older child, put her to bed, but that's it. Keep it short. If your child wants something extra—more food, another book, or whatever—proceed with caution. It's common for children to construct elaborate bedtime rituals that complicate their efforts to fall asleep and soon drive parents crazy.

DON'T EXPECT YOUR CHILD TO FALL ASLEEP WHEN SHE'S NOT TIRED

Figure out when your child really is tired. Don't compare your child to her siblings or to other children, since every child has a different personality. Some children need more sleep than others. Some children need more activity during the day before they can calm down and relax. Try to build these bedtime routines into special moments between you and your child so that it's a bonding experience. With an infant, this means singing, rocking, and cuddling. For older children, it means reading or telling stories, chatting, or planning the next day. Make bedtime a calm, peaceful moment when you both can be together and connect.

PROVIDE A TRANSITIONAL "LOVE OBJECT"

If your child seems anxious about sleep, offer a doll, a plush toy, or a special pillow as a comfort object. Many children find this kind of comfort profoundly reassuring. The only risk is that your child will focus on a single toy or doll to the exclusion of all others, so that loss or damage to it will jeopardize her ability to fall asleep. One solution: "rotate" comfort objects from the start. If your child feels attached to each of several toys, there's less risk that only one of them is adequately comforting.

ENCOURAGE A WIND-DOWN PERIOD

If you want your child in bed by around 8:00, start a transition toward sleep by 7:15 or 7:30. Don't kid yourself that starting at 8:00 is sufficient, since 8:00

will inevitably lead to 8:10, 8:15, and 8:30. Plan ahead. Start the snacks and the bath early; shift to the stories or prebedtime activities with plenty of extra time; then proceed to lights-out on time. Again, consistency is everything. If you're too easygoing about what happens and when, your child will push bedtime back further and further.

TRY TO BE BORING

This sounds odd, but try to be boring. This is particularly important if you're reassuring your child in the middle of the night, nursing her, or comforting her. You're not there to entertain the troops. Make it quick and simple—not a lot of fun. Leave the amusing or entertaining activities for daytime. The prebedtime phase—reading, telling stories, singing lullabies, and so forth—should be soothing but quiet and comforting, not entertaining in a way that stimulates too much.

DON'T OFFER FOOD RIGHT BEFORE BED

A quick drink of water before bed is fine, but more abundant beverages or food is probably a mistake. Offer snacks much earlier in the evening. Food right before sleep may be stimulating rather than relaxing, and bedtime routines that include eating have a tendency to grow more elaborate over time.

DON'T GIVE CHOICES THAT DELAY THE WIND-DOWN

Too many parents follow the child's lead during bedtime routines. You want, of course, to allow your child some voice in what happens—which stories to read, which songs to sing. But again, keep it simple. You're in charge. Most children will happily stay up and play, but this can have negative consequences (mostly fatigue) the next morning. By all means specify the rules ahead of time, then follow them consistently.

TAKE TURNS WITH YOUR SPOUSE

If possible, you and your spouse should take turns putting your child to bed. This arrangement obviously isn't possible for single parents, and it may be difficult for some couples with a clear-cut division of labor. Still, do whatever allows you to divide the responsibility.

- *It's important for your child to learn flexibility.* If she grows accustomed to only one parent's routine at bedtime—the specific kinds of help provided, the games played, the stories told—she may insist on doing things just so and in no other way. This rigidity may be stressful for both parents and potentially disruptive (at least in the long run) for the child.

- *Taking turns fosters the child's intimate relationship with both parents.* It also provides each parent with an opportunity to develop an inside view of the child's feelings and thoughts.

- *Taking turns eases the burden on each parent.* It's exhausting to be the only parent allowed to perform the bedtime ritual; it locks that parent into a confining role. If the designated parent is then unable to be present— whether because of a work obligation, a social commitment, or illness— your child may be irate or inconsolable. This kind of situation isn't good for anyone in the family.

There's an additional dimension to this situation. When your daughter reaches age two or three, she may insist on being put to bed only by her father. A boy this age, too, often insists on being put to bed only by his mother. This situation can be awkward but is, in fact, developmentally age-appropriate. How should you respond? Sometimes it's easier simply to go along with this request, as it fits the child's need for a special relationship with the parent of the other sex. Sometimes, given practical aspects of your situation, you may need to be less accommodating. In any case, the "rejected" parent shouldn't take the child's attitude personally. It's simply part of your child's development as a person.

Don't Use the Bed or Bedtime As a Punishment

Punishing your child with an early bedtime or using her bed as a time-out place will probably backfire. It can be a big mistake to make the child's bed or bedroom into something negative. Use some other form of disincentive—time out in another location, taking away TV time, and so on. But avoid anything that causes your child to associate bedtime and sleep with punishment, deprivation, or even the temporary withdrawal of your affection. This is important because children (especially toddlers and preschoolers) struggle with issues of separation from the parents. Anxiety over separating from you at bedtime may already be intense; don't complicate the issue by further depriving your child at a time when her sense of security may be tenuous.

On the contrary, do everything you can to make your child's bed, bedroom, and bedtime seem inviting, embracing, and comfortable. The standard props are helpful: cozy decorations, a night-light, a cup (with a lid for younger children) with some water. Make sure she knows you're available if she needs you, and reassure her you'll be there when she wakes up in the morning. Allow her to take a stuffed animal, doll, safe toy, blanket, pillow, or other comfort object to bed. All of these props and reassurances help decrease separation anxiety.

FORTY-FIVE

SPIRITUALITY

I N SOME RESPECTS, nothing is more down-to-earth than raising children. Feeding, bathing, and dressing kids, taking care of them when they're sick, playing with them when they're healthy, and teaching them what they need to know are all tasks grounded in the minutiae of daily life. Some of these tasks are delightful, but others are repetitive, even tedious. A few tasks (such as changing diapers) are unpleasant. Many are exhausting. Almost all demand a degree—sometimes a large degree—of self-denial. The day-to-day care of children is hard work. At times even the most committed parents feel as if they're just going through the motions.

So what does parenthood have to do with spirituality? How does the down-to-earth, day-to-day routine of raising children connect with the quest for ultimate significance?

The answers to these questions vary in accordance with your definition of spirituality and your means of expressing it. But here are two ways of perceiving how parenthood and spirituality intersect. First, spirituality is at times an expression of parenthood, and vice versa. Second, spirituality is at times a relief from the stress of parenthood. Both perceptions are valid, and both are useful.

THE HOUSEHOLDER'S PATH

Many spiritual traditions teach directly or indirectly that the earthly nature of parenthood doesn't contradict a need for spiritual pursuits; on the contrary, the earthliness of raising children is part of what makes parenthood spiritual. This concept appears in Christian, Jewish, and Hindu practices, among others. Hinduism is especially explicit about how family life is essentially a spiritual practice.

In Hindu tradition, one of the paths one can choose to follow toward spiritual fulfillment is that of the householder. The householder rejects both the path of worldly pursuits (wealth, fame, and sensual delights as ends in themselves) and the path of otherworldly pursuits (asceticism, holy orders, and renunciation of material goods). Instead, the householder takes a middle way that accepts both the reality of the flesh (sex, childbearing, child-rearing, and the nature of ordinary earthly life) and the reality of the spirit (prayer, meditation, and other disciplines). The day-to-day tasks and rhythms of parenthood are central to the householder's path. This path is an end in itself—the task of giving children what they need to thrive; simultaneously, it is a means of undertaking a personal quest—the pursuit of selflessness. By focusing on your children's needs, you move beyond your own desires, which opens your heart and mind to higher states of understanding. It's precisely by serving others that you develop as a deeper, wiser human being.

Some people, including many American women, may object to this view of parenthood and spirituality. Isn't this just the same old patriarchal party line that has held women captive within a restrictive parenting role? "Look after the kids because self-denial is fulfilling" is certainly a mantra that mothers have heard for thousands of years, and the notion that a mother's duty resides in serving others has been used to constrain women in many cultures. So the objection can be valid. However, what I'm describing doesn't apply just to mothers. Fathers, too, can find the potential for growth and profound insight in devoting themselves to their children. And as is true for many kinds of spiritual pursuits, you can find both great fulfillment and great risk in what outwardly appear almost identical actions. Attending to your children's needs in ways that damage your own identity, or that results in bitterness or resentment, is far different from attending to your children's needs in ways that deepen your understanding of yourself and that result in appreciation, delight, and love. I wouldn't presume to know whether anyone else will benefit or suffer from perceiving parenthood as a spiritual path. This situation is one where each parent can find the answer only in the core of his or her own being.

Although this topic is personal and individual, following are some suggestions on how to combine child-rearing tasks and spirituality.

FORMAL RELIGIOUS PRACTICES

Many people find that participation in formal religious practices is at the core of family spirituality. Membership in a church, temple, or mosque becomes the hub that parenting turns around, or at least it is the compass that allows parents a clear sense of direction. If this situation suits your purposes, I urge you to pursue it in the ways that truly serve your children's needs. The only drawback I see in some situations is when parents take part in formal religious activities "for the kids' sake"—a decision that often backfires. If you're expecting your children to acquire a belief system that you yourself don't hold, there may well be negative consequences. Kids are equipped with built-in, shockproof hypocrisy detectors and will set you straight if they perceive that you're merely going through the motions.

INDIVIDUAL OR ALTERNATIVE PRACTICES

Exploring a spiritual path on your own can also be a salutary task during parenthood. Many religious traditions offer insights into the delights and difficulties of parenthood. For this reason, spiritual pursuits can help you understand the meaning of what you're facing as a parent, and certain spiritual practices can ease the fatigue and tension and loneliness that are common during the parenting years.

YOGA OR MEDITATION

Many people find the practice of yoga or meditation (or both) useful as ways of reducing stress, alleviating emotional burdens, and exploring the self. For thousands of years, practitioners of yoga have used this discipline as a method for easing physical and mental strain; in addition, the more advanced yogic techniques can allow access to the mind's inner reaches. Meditation of various sorts can offer similar benefits—not just relaxation but also insights into the nature of your personality. At many stages of parenthood—from the physical rigors of the baby and toddler years all the way to the great uncertainties of the teen years—yoga and meditation are wonderful ways to center yourself.

SPORTS

For some people, sports and other forms of exercise can have an almost spiritual effect by releasing pent-up stresses and allowing a process of self-centering. Some people, for instance, find that jogging, swimming, hiking, or bicycling can create a nearly meditative state of mind: by occupying the body with a rhythmic form of exertion, these activities release tension and free the mind from nagging concerns.

OTHER PATHS

Here are some other activities whose spiritual dimensions have helped many people overcome the stress of parenthood:

- Practicing t'ai chi, Sufi dance, or other forms of physical meditation
- Dancing, singing, playing a musical instrument, painting, or practicing some other art

- Hiking, swimming, running, or engaging in other sports
- Devoting time to volunteer activities

OTHER APPROACHES

In addition to the age-old disciplines I've touched on above, there are other, less formal ways to address spiritual concerns and release internal energy that fatigue and worry can block. (I'm using the word "spiritual" in a loose sense here—not so much to mean religious, but rather to mean fundamental or central to the great unanswerable questions of life.)

FIND AN ALLY

You don't have to go it alone. No matter how much you're convinced that you can tackle the process of parenthood unassisted, you'll almost certainly do better if you have an ally for the voyage. This ally is, ideally, your spouse. If a husband and wife are emotionally close, they will provide each other with invaluable sustenance as they attend to their children. Of course this alliance isn't always feasible. In addition, even spouses who are close friends and reliable partners may need other allies as they face the rigors of parenthood. Such an ally can be a friend, a relative, a counselor, a psychotherapist, or a member of the clergy. Whoever it is, though, it's important that this person be someone who will listen nonjudgmentally. Find someone you really trust.

KEEP A JOURNAL

You can also write down your feelings about parenthood and explore them in a journal. The only rule in this method is not to censor what you write. Your feelings aren't right or wrong, good or bad. They just *are*. It's important to have an uncensored way of getting those feelings out, and a journal is an excellent means to this end. See chapter 33, "The Past," for further discussion of journals.

EXPLORE YOUR DREAMS

Another powerful aid in exploring the spiritual aspects of parenthood is keeping a log or journal of your dreams. Dreams are, in fact, one of the best windows into this aspect of your personality. This journal should be separate from the cathartic free-association journal already discussed.

Here's how it works. Keep a notebook by your bed. Jot down your dreams when you wake. Later, when your schedule allows, compare and contrast what you read in your dream journal with what happens that day, or what happened the day before. What do your dreams indicate about your unconscious mind through your dreams? How do the dreams connect with events during the day? Your goal isn't simply to record and collect your dreams, but to understand them within the context of your whole life.

You have several options for how to proceed. Option one is to attempt to understand your dreams unassisted. This is a difficult path to pursue; although feasible, it's not one I recommend, since dreams are often confusing and sometimes upsetting. Option two is taking your dream journal to a psychotherapist to explore together, reaching insights into what your unconscious mind is working through. As is true when pursuing other kinds of psychological insight, having a guide will generally serve you well. Objective perceptions of your dreams may lead to insights you'd otherwise miss. Option three is exploring your dreams in the context of a dream workshop. I advise careful assessment of this option: although some people who organize dream workshops are insightful and sensitive, others are poorly trained and sensationalistic. Consider reading Jeremy Taylor's *Dream Work* or Montague Ullman and Nan Zimmerman's *Working with Dreams* or other thoughtful books about dream analysis. (See the Resource Guide for specific citations.)

FORTY-SIX

SPORTS

M OST KIDS LOVE sports. They love the excitement, the challenge, the playfulness, and the payoff. They enjoy the attention that playing well can provide. They like being a part of something that American culture regards as a transcendent experience. And they often revel in the physical pleasures of sports—the feelings of strength, energy, precision, even exaltation.

THE PROS

Sports have much to offer children:

- Sports lure kids away from TV, video games, and other sedentary pastimes.

- Sports involve vigorous activity, which heightens physical and emotional well-being.

- Sports help kids develop their physical abilities, especially large motor skills and coordination.

- Sports help kids develop social abilities—team playing, sportsmanship, strategic thinking, effective communication, ability to follow a game plan, ability to honor commitments, and leadership skills.

- Sports provide children with safe, positive outlets for aggression.

- Sports help kids discharge tension from the day, which in turn helps them sleep better at night.

- Sports can bolster kids' self-esteem by building a greater repertoire for self-confidence, self-esteem, and skill building.

- Sports help kids increase their attention span.

- Sports get kids off the streets.

- Sports gives kids the opportunity to interact with role models and other mentors, which can be crucial at several stages of development.

Kids' participation in sports can help parents, too. If your child is active in organized sports, for instance, you may gain some much-needed downtime from parenting duties and some additional support and social contacts.

THE CONS

But there are some notable drawbacks to sports as well:

- Sports can tempt parents to live inappropriately through a child's activities.

- Sports can pressure children into taking part in activities at odds with their personal interests or basic nature.

- Sports can foster unrealistic parental expectations.

- Sports can lead to serious injuries, including broken bones, torn ligaments, concussions, etc.

- Sports can lead to stress-related problems, such as obsession with the game, anxiety, etc.

- Sports can be expensive.

- Sports can encourage a winning-is-everything attitude that damages a more open attitude toward life.

- Sports can disrupt children's willingness to do varied activities, or to play independently of adults' plans and expectations.

- Sports can jeopardize self-confidence in children who are less skilled, less interested, or less practiced than others.

These disadvantages can spread to parents. Many moms and dads find their lives commandeered by children's sports activities—by taking part on committees, by attending athletic meets, and especially by chauffeuring kids endlessly to games and practice sessions.

ARE SPORTS TOO BIG A DEAL?

Kids today have more access to organized sports than children did in the past. To some degree the welter of activities reflects the growth of sports in the wider world; in addition, there are more sports programs available because many parents no longer feel comfortable letting their kids play unsupervised outside of the home. Fewer parents have abundant time at home; those who do may be preoccupied with other matters. Some parents also ease their guilt by scheduling intensive sports: they may be absent during the week, but they try to make up for their absence by scheduling organized activities each week or weekend. Sports give parents a way to participate in their child's life and to give something back in return.

I sometimes wonder whose needs all these sports are serving—the kids' or the parents'. Perhaps it's easier for parents to take their children to an organized activity where other adults will be present. It's less lonely and less boring for parents. This is understandable; still, the situation is unfortunate in some ways—less flexible, less spontaneous, more businesslike. Even "fun" can start to seem pressured. Time off becomes more and more like work, complete with schedules, goals, and rigorous activity.

THE IMPORTANCE OF BALANCE

Sports have a tremendous potential for positive effects in a child's life, and I suspect that there's more benefit than harm overall. But the situation is mixed. I know some families in which sports demand much of the parents' free time, and in some families sports are an obsession that excludes other areas of children's development. Some children end up feeling that unless they focus on sports and excel at them, they're failures. This attitude isn't healthy for either children or their parents.

Once again we come back to the question of balance. If sports are a welcome addition to your family life; if your child enjoys the sport in question; if she learns new skills and gains pleasure and confidence from playing it; if the sport is only one of several important activities in her life; and if your own parental duties aren't stretched excessively by your child's commitments—in short, if you and your child can keep your sense of balance—then the situation is probably fine. If, on the other hand, sports are a burden on your family; if your child isn't really interested or doesn't enjoy playing the sport; if she finds participation tedious, frustrating, or unpleasant; if the sport becomes an obsession that disrupts other activities; if sports always take precedence over other areas of development; or if your child's activities make your parental duties burdensome—in short, if the whole situation seems out of balance—then you need to evaluate what's happening.

In general, children have a pretty good sense of balance about where sports fit into their lives. Sports are certainly at the top of many children's lists of fun things to do. For the most part, kids have a pretty good internal guidance system about when to play and when to get out of the game. They learn the sport, play hard, then quit when they're tired. Unfortunately, it's *parents* who often lose their sense of balance. They often take sports too seriously, push their children too aggressively, and feel less committed to the process (playing the game) than to the product (winning). It's the parents' attitude that often transforms sports from a source of fun into a burden.

Last year I watched a wrestling match at the middle school in a friend's town. Most of the kids on the wrestling team probably wanted to be there, and they were clearly psyched to face their opponents and do their best. Even the coaches seemed sensible about the match—supportive of the kids and not too pushy. The parents, though, were appalling. They hollered at the children, screamed at the referee, and sometimes even looked ready to assault each other. The situation was unpleasant all the way around but especially so for the competitors. One little boy seemed especially hard hit. He couldn't have been older than six or seven. He had lost his match and, feeling frustrated, had started to cry. As if he wasn't miserable enough, the boy's father berated him in public. "Your friends will think you're a loser!" he yelled, letting everyone hear. "Pull yourself together and act like a man!" This scolding humiliated the boy still further.

Well, that's wrestling, you say—a primordial sport that brings out primordial passions. I wish the explanation were really so easy. The truth is, I've seen this same sort of behavior at soccer matches, baseball games, skating competitions, you name it: the parents scream, abuse the referee or umpire or judges, and model immature social behavior. This kind of behavior is bad enough in its own right; worse yet, it's contagious. Children see their parents modeling bad sportsmanship, so they imitate what their parents do. Vanquishing the opponent is the goal. Winning is all. Forget about civility or the pleasures of playing the game. The whole situation is out of balance.

GIVING SPORTS THEIR PROPER PLACE

Despite my misgivings about what I consider the inflated importance of sports in our society, I'm not *against* sports. I love sports. I play several sports and I encourage my son to do the same. What I find objectionable is the way that parents sometimes distort sports into more than they ought to be.

LET YOUR CHILD HAVE HER OWN DREAMS

Kids often dream of being great athletes. That's fine—it's a good dream, one that usually does no harm even when it doesn't come true. If nothing else, the dream of athletic prowess helps empower children and enables them to get good exercise, have fun, and imagine a kind of excellence that's concrete enough for them to grasp so early. However, many children get involved in sports not because of their own dream but because of their parents' dreams. One father I know always wanted to be a football star, but his own efforts during high school and college hadn't taken him high enough. So he pushed his son to join the local football team, play hard, and win the accolades that the father had never gained. What the son enjoyed was competitive rowing—a sport that his father didn't like or understand. Great tension developed between father and son. It was all very sad and pointless. If the father wanted to play football so badly, he should have gotten together with his own pals to throw the ol' pigskin around.

GRAB THE OPPORTUNITIES

On the other hand, sports can provide a good chance to support your child and encourage her to do what she enjoys. It's important to back her if she really wants to pursue a sport. You don't have to push her into doing more than she wants; just praise and support her for participating, doing her best, playing fairly, and seeing the sport in a wider context. In short, grab the opportunities to make sports enjoyable and worthwhile. Emphasize the process, not just the end result, of the sport. Subtly stress the importance of gaining confidence, learning new skills, and enjoying the camaraderie of teamwork. Taking part in these ways can boost your child greatly.

TAKE PART FAIRLY

If you're involved in a supervisory role—as a coach, for instance—make sure that your presence isn't unfair. I don't mean unfair just to the other kids; you could be putting your own child on the spot, too. It's difficult and confusing for a child to have her own parent be the coach *and* her parent. First of all, you may end up demoralizing her if you have to correct or criticize her in front of other children. Second, you may leave her open to accusations that you favor her, give her special privileges, assign her the best positions to play, and so forth. Make sure that all kids have the opportunity to play; rotate their positions; let everyone practice new skills. If possible, try to counteract the effects of overly competitive parents. Third, she may resent the enormous amount of time you spend with other kids, especially if you're not spending enough time with her one-on-one.

PICK THE RIGHT SPORT AT THE RIGHT AGE

It's also important to focus on sports in age-appropriate ways. Almost all young children enjoy kicking or throwing a ball around, but that doesn't mean you should sign them up for junior soccer or Little League baseball. Let your child have a say in the level of her participation. If she wants to pursue a sport seriously, she'll let you know; you don't have to push too hard. Research now suggests that pushing backfires anyway: children who start playing competitive sports early in elementary school often burn out by middle school. High expectations may prompt kids to rebel at some point, perhaps rejecting organized sports entirely.

Another consideration: Pick the right sport. I'm not totally against rough sports like football and hockey, but caution is appropriate. Football, especially, has a high injury rate, and orthopedic damage is disproportionately harmful to children, whose bones and joints are still developing. And lest I seem to be picking on macho sports—I have serious misgivings about some aspects of gymnastics, which, despite its esthetic delights, can sometimes take a high toll on young gymnasts' bodies.

DON'T NEGLECT ACADEMICS

I believe it's a mistake to emphasize sports of any kind over academic skills. Yes, sports are important. No, not everyone is an academic high-achiever. But mastering the highest level of academics appropriate for each child is ultimately better than athletic prowess. Even among gifted athletes, only a tiny fraction go on to professional careers. Most kids must pick a profession or trade among the standard choices. Encouraging a child to neglect her studies can seriously backfire. Never mind that sports stars make astronomical salaries; few people will ever attain those high earnings. It's just as well that your child recognize reality as soon as possible.

BE AWARE OF HIDDEN MESSAGES

For all that's good about sports, the *culture* of sports often carries hidden messages. An obvious example is the often arrogant behavior of sports stars at the high school level. Many high-achieving athletes, especially boys, garner so much adulation that their egos rapidly inflate. In its relatively harmless forms, this egotism shows up as swagger and puffery; in more harmful forms, it can manifest itself as gender bias, racism, and intolerable self-importance. An extreme instance of this phenomenon shows up in *Our Guys*, Bernard Lefkowitz's portrait of a group of high school athletes in Glen Ridge, New Jersey, who became so convinced of their personal supremacy and social invincibility that they sexually abused a retarded teenage girl. Many sports encourage boys to develop in limited, self-indulgent ways, splitting off from their feelings and staying emotionally distant from others.

FORTY-SEVEN

STEPPARENTS AND BLENDED FAMILIES

"AND THEY LIVED happily ever after. . . . "
If only real life worked out as neatly as a fairy tale! But it doesn't. Love can fade, marriages can fall apart, and families can split up and regroup.

People who remarry and create blended families invariably face unique opportunities and crises. On the one hand, they have new love relationships to savor, which can offer solace and delight; on the other hand, many partners in second marriages struggle with feelings of failure and anguish. There's often a tension between excitement about the future and sadness or frustration over the past. Couples may feel a profound desire to capture something they experienced earlier in family life, to avoid past mistakes, or to take advantage of a second chance at making the fairy tale come true. The emotional stakes are high.

I believe that divorce is not a failure; instead, it's the acceptance of having taken a relationship as far as possible, then acknowledging its limits. Divorce is unquestionably a difficult, stressful experience, however, and the task of building a second marriage and a second family is challenging as well. What stepparents face involves many of the rigors that are central to parenthood, and then some. It's a strenuous situation. (For a discussion of how divorce affects children, see chapter 10, "Divorce.")

If you're a parent or stepparent in a blended family, there are special approaches to take throughout the parenting years.

BE AWARE OF YOUR EXPECTATIONS

Parents in blended families may have certain expectations typical of their new situation—expectations that can complicate the tasks of raising children.

EXPECTATION #1—HEALING PAST WOUNDS

When entering a second marriage, many couples feel a need to soothe lingering pain and heal past wounds. This attitude is understandable in the aftermath of separation and divorce. However, these expectations are often unrealistic. The new couple, for instance, may assume that everyone in the blended family will feel an immediate sense of bonding, harmony, and love. The bad times are over; family life will be blissful the second time around.

Unfortunately, this attitude is a setup for disappointment. Family life is at least as complex the second time around. As a result, family members often feel shocked and disappointed when they face the inevitable adjustments, difficulties, challenges, misunderstandings, and differences of opinion. You can't heal old wounds quickly. You can't create a new family in a short time. Excessively high expectations can wreak havoc on the new family—or at least slow the real process of adjustment.

EXPECTATION #2—MAKING EVERYONE HAPPY

Another common expectation among parents in blended families is that they can make everyone happy. They'll satisfy every family member's needs. They'll maintain an identical relationship with their biological children while establishing close bonds with their stepchildren. And they'll somehow accomplish this great feat of parenthood while nurturing their new marriage at the same time.

It's a very tall order. First of all, you can't *make* other people happy. You can provide the material and emotional circumstances in which they may thrive and grow; you can offer support, insight, and affection; you can try to solve problems affecting others. But children in a blended family have their own tasks to tackle and their own relationships to explore. To some degree, what parents can realistically do is to be nurturing and patient. The rest of the process will take hard work and the passage of time.

EXPECTATION #3—FEELING LIKE THE ORIGINAL FAMILY

Many people expect a blended family to feel like their original family unit. There may, in fact, be similarities with what they experienced the first time around. But the new family is a different group of people with different backgrounds, different experiences, and different histories. How likely is it that the new family will seem the same as the first one? Not very. I'm not even convinced that it's a good sign if it *does* feel exactly like the first. But people's expectations for this outcome are high, and this state of mind puts additional pressure on the new blended family.

EXPECTATION #4—FEELING THAT THE FIRST FAMILY WAS THE "REAL" FAMILY

Another common expectation is more of a feeling or longing—namely, that the first family was the "real" family, and that the new family somehow doesn't stand up compared to the one that preceded it. This attitude is often the aftermath of the fairy-tale fantasy. If the romantic ideal is to fall in love, marry, and live happily ever after, what does that say about the blended family? Many people look back on their past family life with longing despite the difficulties—even misery—they experienced. Illusions die hard. As a result, the new, blended family may not seem as romantic as the first family, and members of the family may feel cynical or skeptical about their new situation.

In reality, all families are complicated. All families have their ups and downs. All families have assets and liabilities. All families face risks and opportunities. Every parent and child brings baggage from his or her past family experiences. It's true that blended families face more complicated tasks in some respects; there are often more players in the family drama, and their interactions frequently form a more complex web of relationships. But the nature of this situation doesn't mean that the first family unit was better, or that the blended family isn't blessed with great potential for love and mutual support. The spouses' motivations to succeed may be higher than before. The parents' skills, maturity, and wisdom may have increased over the years. The combination of personalities in the family may be especially promising. Everyone's coping skills may be greater than in the past.

In short, blended families often have great potential for satisfying their members' needs.

HELPING YOUR CHILD ADJUST TO A BLENDED FAMILY

It's important to accept from the start that adjusting to a blended family will challenge your child in many ways. Don't underestimate the magnitude of the task she faces in adjusting to a new family. She has been accustomed to living with certain people in certain ways; in addition, she will have her own legacy of feelings in response to the divorce. She will also have her own responses to changes in her parent-child relationship.

At the same time, don't underestimate her ability to adapt to the new situation. Children are amazingly flexible. Your child may, in fact, adjust more readily and easily to the blended family than you do.

TAKE TRANSITIONS SLOWLY

Children often react strongly to change. The reactions can be especially strong when change involves aspects of the parents' relationships such as dating, engagement, and remarriage. As an adult, you have a right to seek the affection you need; for your child's sake, though, take the transitions slowly. Introduce your children to potential new partners little by little. Avoid rushing into new domestic arrangements, such as having a partner move in. If you decide on a major change, such as remarriage, take your time tying the knot. Children experience a great sense of loss when their parents divorce; in the aftermath, they are highly sensitive to the side effects of a parent's love relationships *no matter how positive the emotional consequences for the parent.* Give your child as much time as possible to adjust to major changes in family structure. Try to make your decisions in a child-centered, not adult-centered, way.

DON'T EXPECT QUICK ACCEPTANCE

Similarly, don't assume that just because you've developed a relationship with a new partner, your child is going to accept this person with open arms. The same holds true if you are the stepparent entering your prospective spouse's family unit. From the child's point of view, the stepparent is invading her turf both physically and emotionally. She will be struggling with a tangle of different (often conflicting) emotions. The nature of the reaction will differ depending on the child's age, maturity, personality, and past experiences, but most kids will take their time accepting a stepparent. This is a normal situation. To the degree that you can accept it, understand it, and work around it, you'll give a great gift to the whole family.

MAKE GRADUAL CHANGES TO DOMESTIC ARRANGEMENTS

Even when your child reaches a state of feeling comfortable with the new family situation, avoid disruptive moves or even reallocations of space within your home. Let your child maintain her own living space to the degree possible. Of course many blended families end up in new settings: one spouse and one or more children move to the other spouse's home, or they all end up in a new house. Some degree of disruption is inevitable. Still, step carefully.

Even forcing your child to share a room with a stepsibling may be emotionally disruptive. Do whatever will prompt your child to feel the least intruded upon or displaced. If you can't arrange for each child to have his or her own bedroom, at least allow each child a separate area to store belongings—closet space, a set of drawers, or some other private space.

DON'T FORCE NEW RELATIONSHIPS OR AFFECTION

Kids will follow their own sense of timing in forging new relationships within the blended family. Don't force them to feel affection or a sense of connection before they're ready. Make sure they know there will be a period of adjustment for everyone, and reassure them that you don't expect everyone to feel instant love for each other. Above all, emphasize that you don't expect the stepparent to replace anyone's biological parent. It's acceptable to state that you want everyone in the blended family to treat everyone else with respect, but don't anticipate profound depth of affection right away.

An important corollary of this situation: avoid anything that intensifies alliances or rivalries along family lines. When a couple I'll call Jesse and Maria got married, for instance, each adult brought two children to the new family. Jesse's kids were understandably closer to Jesse than to Maria, and Maria's kids were closer to their own father than to Jesse. This is a predictable and acceptable situation. But Jesse tended to treat the children in markedly different ways—with open preference for his own—which created great tension for everyone. It's difficult but crucial to be fair and open-minded toward everyone in a blended family. Don't play favorites in ways that kids will find demoralizing. Don't let children play one parent off the other. Make sure that rules and guidelines are clear and fair.

REASSURE YOUR CHILD ABOUT YOUR LOVE

Be sure, too, that you reassure your child over and over that she isn't being "replaced" by your new spouse or by your stepchildren. Tell her that the love you feel for her is totally different from what you feel for your marital partner. Make sure she knows that no one can take her place. Say this in words but also demonstrate it in your actions, including special one-on-one time with your child.

DON'T BE SHOCKED BY YOUR CHILD'S EMOTIONAL REACTIONS

No matter how carefully and thoughtfully you deal with the situations I've described, your child will react intensely to these changes. Depending on your child's age, personality, and maturity, common reactions include sulking, verbal sniping, acting out, giving you the "silent treatment," and throwing tantrums. You and others within the blended family may then react in turn with anger, frustration, irritability, or depression. The situation can become difficult for everyone.

However, it's important not to overreact. Don't take your child's behavior personally. Of course it *is* personal in some ways, but you need to keep your cool. What you're witnessing isn't really a response to you—whether you're the stepparent or the biological parent—as much as it's a response to the losses that the child has suffered. The creation of a blended family is in some respects the most concrete evidence that the old family is gone forever. Your child is grieving over that loss. But children express grief in roundabout ways, including anger. (As the saying goes, sometimes it's easier to be mad than sad.) What appears to be anger or hostility may in fact be grief and sadness.

Your child may also struggle with divided loyalties. She may feel attached to you yet angry that you've created a new marital relationship. She may feel relieved to have a stepparent and stepsiblings yet competitive and jealous toward them. Try to accept these kinds of ambivalence. Just as adults feel many emotions as they establish a blended family, so do children. What complicates the situation for kids isn't just their less sophisticated understanding of the changes, but also—especially—their lack of choice in what has happened.

DON'T GET CAUGHT IN THE CROSSFIRE

One of the most common dilemmas that parents face in blended families is getting caught in various sorts of crossfire. By this I mean tension, arguments, and other conflicts between two or more members of the family.

Let's suppose, for instance, that there's a conflict between Leon and his son Michael. Michael's stepmother, Pauline—who has been married to Leon for only six months—feels tempted to intervene; she'd like to help her husband and her stepson sort through their differences. But her effort puts Pauline in the crossfire. After a longer period of adjustment, Pauline's intervention may be useful, but it's risky at a point when the new family members are settling in together. Other kinds of crossfire (such as between your new spouse and his or her ex-spouse) can be just as risky. Still other kinds, such as between stepchildren, may require both parents to intervene.

- *Don't malign the other parents.* If you criticize your spouse, your ex-spouse, or your spouse's ex, you may raise tensions and complicate everyone's tasks. Criticism can also make children defensive about their own biological parents. When possible—even if it requires biting your tongue—be supportive and nonjudgmental.

- *Try not to take obvious sides with your own children.* This is one of the hardest tasks for parents in blended families. Playing clear favorites, however, can create enormous stresses all the way around. Try to sort through issues in advance with your spouse; set rules as fairly as possible for everyone.

- *Stay clear of a disciplinary role toward your stepchildren.* Avoid assuming the role that rightly belongs to the child's biological parent, especially regarding discipline. In my opinion, only the biological parent should administer discipline. You can't successfully discipline a stepchild—or any child—

unless you have a significant emotional bond and history with that child, so stay out of that triangle if possible. If you disagree with the nature of the discipline, sort out your differences in private rather than undercutting your spouse on the spot.

- *Don't accept bad behavior.* Although you shouldn't take a full parental role toward your stepchildren, neither should you tolerate unacceptable behavior. Each biological parent should let the children know that although they don't have to love or even like their stepparent, they must treat him or her with respect, dignity, courtesy, and civility. The children shouldn't be allowed to abuse or insult the stepparents. Everyone must follow the same house rules.

- *Be prepared for developmental ups and downs.* Depending on the children's ages, personalities, and prior experiences, they may take out frustrations on the stepparents at various developmental stages. Toddlers and teenagers are notorious for being obstinate or obnoxious in their behavior toward stepparents, but the situation can be rough at other ages as well. (See chapter 50, "The Teen Years," for a further discussion of teen psychology.)

- *Don't expect the crossfire to ease overnight.* Most blended families take an extended period of living together to sort out the family members' differences and grow comfortable together. Emotional crossfire can be intense for months or even years. You may sometimes feel that the ordeal is more than you can tolerate, but many stepparents muddle through and eventually reach a point of equilibrium.

- *Remember that all families experience crossfire.* The situation you face in a blended family may be more complex than in nonblended families, but it's not unique. The drama of family life always includes alliances, triangles, and a process of emotional give-and-take.

HELP CHILDREN TO BOND WITHIN THE BLENDED FAMILY

As I mentioned earlier, you shouldn't expect the members of a blended family to feel the affection toward stepparents and stepsiblings that they feel toward biological parents or siblings. You can, however, take certain steps to help family members develop a deeper bond with each other. None of these steps will have an instant, transformative effect on the overall situation; they can, however, help out over time.

- *Find family activities that the children enjoy as a group.* Go on outings, get involved in sports, or pursue hobbies together. Group activities require planning and patience, but they can create a sense of common endeavor that brings family members together.

- *Find some projects that the children might enjoy doing one-on-one with a stepparent.* If you have an ability that appeals to your stepchild—skill in sports, for example, or cooking, fine arts, or a knowledge of computer technology—your skill may become the basis for sharing enjoyable times. Such activities can lead in turn to an increased sense of connection. Children can start to see that the assets of having a stepparent around far outweigh the deficits.

- *Avoid doting on your new spouse to the point of excluding the children.* Ignoring the kids during conversations, telling jokes they don't understand, flirting, or focusing on your spouse in other ways can make children—and especially stepchildren—feel left out. This situation can be especially problematic for adolescents, who already have a heightened sense of sexuality and may feel resentful about observing the adults' interactions.

- *Don't force your stepchild to be affectionate.* Kids often have clear-cut comfort levels regarding physical affection. Your stepchild may take a long time to return your gestures. In response to this situation, don't overreact. Don't pull back and decide never to try again; just back off, let some time pass, and express your affection at another time.

- *Be aware of hypersensitivities about favoritism.* Children are finely tuned regarding their right to a fair share of the family "goods." At times their perceptions are appropriate; at other times they cross the line into absurdity. One child told me, for instance, that she resented her mother because she gave the girl's stepfather more food than she herself received. Never mind that the stepdad was a grown man outweighing the child by a hundred pounds; she perceived food as a sign of affection, and her stepfather's servings violated her sense of justice. What's the solution? In this case, it wasn't a matter of serving the dad less or the child more; rather, the mother needed to reassure her child about the durability and abundance of her love.

- *Communicate openly.* It's important for the stepparent to acknowledge that the early stages of life as a blended family are difficult. Depending on the child's age and sophistication, be open to what's happening. Say things like, "It's complicated getting to know each other, isn't it?" or "If you need to talk about what you're feeling, just let me know." The child may or may not respond, but your openness to her feelings is reassuring in its own right.

- *Again, be careful about discipline.* Hasty or excessive participation in the disciplinary process can jeopardize long-term trust. Leave discipline up to the biological parent until the stepparent has a more established role. Your patience will pay off as the stepparent-stepchild bond develops.

THE SPECIAL ISSUES FOR WIDOWS AND WIDOWERS

In closing, here's a brief discussion regarding blended families in which one parent is a widow or widower. Many of the issues we've discussed already will apply here as well. There's a particular element, however, that bears mentioning.

A child who has suffered the loss of a parent through death has experienced one of the most traumatic forms of bereavement possible. Many children respond to such a loss by idealizing the deceased parent. This response is understandable; even so, it presents a stepparent with special challenges. It's hard to measure up as a parent when your predecessor is enshrined in the child's recollection. This situation also presents your stepchild with an even greater challenge regarding loyalty. If she chooses to love you, is she betraying her deceased parent? Of course not—but *she* may not feel that way. The result is a complex tangle of feelings within the child's mind.

- Emphasize that you are in no way attempting to "replace" your stepchild's deceased parent.

- Don't pressure the child to call you Mom or Dad; be flexible about what she chooses to call you, even if she wants to use your first name.

- If she "slips" and calls you Mom or Dad, don't bring attention to it; just let it go unacknowledged.

- Be open to discussions about the deceased parent, including—if the child suggests it—seeing photos.

- Emphasize that you're not jealous or competing with Mom or Dad; you're just trying to do your best.

- Accept the possibility that the child won't want to do certain activities with you, since certain pastimes may be central to the parent-child relationship. Find your own new activities to do together.

- In general, follow the child's lead in establishing an emotional connection between the two of you.

FORTY-EIGHT

STRESS

STRESS IS HERE to stay. It's simply part of the postindustrial world. We're all too familiar with the phenomenon of stress in our everyday lives. Whether the issue is scheduling, carpooling, job pressures, economic difficulties, or hassles with family and friends, the demands we face are intense—and so are the stresses that result from them.

Urie Bronfenbrenner, Professor of Human Development and Family Studies in Psychology at Cornell University in Ithaca, New York, has this to say about the pace of modern life:

> In a world in which both parents usually have to work . . . every family member through the waking hours from morning until night is "on the run." The need to coordinate conflicting demands of job and child care . . . can produce a situation in which everyone has to be transported several times a day in different directions, usually at the same time—a state of affairs that prompted a foreign colleague of mine to comment, "It seems to me that in your country most children are being brought up in moving vehicles."

WHY ARE WE ALL SO FRANTIC?

Ironically, research indicates that Americans actually have more leisure time today than in the past. A number of reasons have been offered as to why we feel stressful despite this fact.

- Leisure time isn't clear-cut—people often take work assignments home, or on vacation.

- Wages and salaries have been relatively stagnant for several decades. Money doesn't go as far as it did for past generations.

- Workers now put in more hours on the job, and more families include two wage-earners.

- Tight schedules tend to make people more self-centered, frazzled, and negative-minded; there's a downward spiral in many people's attitudes.

- Retirement and job security are uncertain.

- Family members often spend less time together, which can fragment activities and raise tensions.

- The media heighten expectations about material reward and focus people's concerns on themselves rather than on others.

- Electronic gadgets and intense entertainment media pervade life, leaving little room for introspection or relaxation.

THE CONSEQUENCES OF STRESS

The consequences may vary from person to person, but some typical complaints are:

- Loss of interest or joy in pleasurable activities

- Significant increase in weight or appetite

- Increase or decrease in energy level

- Difficulty sleeping or maintaining energy levels or stamina

- Feelings of pessimism, negativity, and low self-esteem or confidence

- Somatic (bodily) complaints—headaches, stomachaches, backaches, etc.—or vague, undiagnosable illnesses

- Irritability, increased frustration, pervasive distraction, anxiety, or inability to concentrate

- Habitual impatience

- Excessive competitiveness or feeling "driven"

- Difficulties at work or school—problems maintaining good grades, concentrating, or keeping up

- Problematic social relationships

- Feelings of helplessness, hopelessness, or depression

HOW SHOULD YOU RESPOND?

Unfortunately, there's no easy way out. Modern life isn't going to turn into a mellow funfest. Stress isn't going to go away anytime soon; we're going to have to cope with it—and stress can be a positive force. Fortunately, there are many ways to deal with it—not only for ourselves, but as good role models for our children.

- Observe what stresses you (or your child).

- Determine whether you can deal with stress directly by changing something—by simplifying your schedule, rearranging your plans, marshaling your resources, or changing your priorities.

- Consider the possibility that you can't change the source of your stress but must instead change your *attitude* about the stress.

- Don't expect everything to go as you wish. Instead, be open to all possibilities.

- Don't see changes as necessarily bad, but rather as challenges and opportunities.

- Be gentle with yourself—and with your child.

- Laugh at yourself and your quirks and your mistakes.

- Accept your own human imperfections. Don't take things too personally.

- Take time now and then to be alone. Sometimes that's all you need to get some perspective. Read a book. Take a long shower or a bubble bath. Watch your favorite TV show. Take a walk. Get out into nature. Take a hike. Go for a run. Ride your bike. Go for a swim.

- Eat well. A stressful schedule can tempt you to skimp on meals.

- Get enough rest. Adults need about eight hours of sleep per night, but most of us average only six or seven.

- Count your blessings—not just the stresses and negative aspects of life. Keep a journal noting what's going *well*. Or keep a list of the funniest things you and your kids have said.

- Separate work and parenting whenever possible. Attempting to work while entertaining a young child, especially, is often an exercise in futility. Compartmentalize your tasks. Carve out moments in which you give your child undivided attention so that it doesn't stress you out more. Filter out work-related demands by means of answering machines and e-mail. Celebrate and protect the time you have with your child.

- Find time with your spouse or partner. If you're a single parent, find time with someone you're close to. You need time with adults to recharge your batteries.

For more detailed suggestions about how to manage the stress of parenting, see chapter 49, "Taking Care of Yourself."

FORTY-NINE

TAKING CARE OF YOURSELF

WHEN I GIVE lectures and seminars about parenting, I ask how many members of the audience manage to take fifteen minutes of the day to look after themselves. Mind you, we're not talking about two hours, an hour, even half an hour—just fifteen minutes. Yet few people raise their hands. Among the mothers, especially, the response rate is almost zero.

Small wonder. Many women are not only working outside the home, looking after children, and taking primary responsibility for domestic duties; they're also caring for elderly parents, assisting at their children's schools, and helping friends and neighbors. Fathers, too, are intensely busy and stressed, whether with family activities, work obligations, or both. Everyone's load is heavy. This situation isn't altogether bad: Many people feel that although time is tight, life is meaningful. Still, there's always the risk that if day-to-day demands are excessive and unrelenting, something has to give. Some people find themselves at the breaking point. Under these circumstances, even a tiny problem—a child leaving a dirty sock in the middle of the living room floor—can be the last straw.

If you find yourself in this frayed state of mind, you need to take better care of yourself. This task is crucial. It isn't self-indulgent; on the contrary, it can make a positive contribution to everyone in your family. If you give and give until you feel empty inside, you'll have little to offer your spouse and children. You'll tend to be irritable and resentful, begrudging even other people's reasonable expectations. You'll be less able to enjoy what's good about family life and more stressed out when times are difficult. In short, failing to look after yourself is as dangerous to your family's well-being as failing to look after your children. It's important and imperative that you provide yourself with at least the minimal physical and emotional sustenance you need.

This recommendation means different things to different people, but what follows are some general suggestions and tips.

PAY ATTENTION TO YOUR MOOD

Parenthood is so demanding that almost everyone feels ambivalent about it at least some of the time. Even the most committed, talented, generous, energetic parents sometimes feel weary or depressed. This state of mind is understandable. It isn't a failing—it's just a response to the limitless demands of family life. Don't clobber yourself for feeling this way; just accept the mood and work around it.

At the same time, it's important not to make any major decisions when you're feeling low. Low moods will generally pass. If possible, stall on deciding about crucial matters until your spirits rise. Size up the situation later. It's also worthwhile to get someone else's input—your spouse's, partner's, or a trusted friend's—if you can't avoid making a particular decision when you're emotionally stressed. Avoid relying only on your own perspective if you feel that pressures or fatigue have altered your ability to judge situations accurately.

Parenthood can feel confining, even suffocating. As a parent, you lack certain kinds of freedom and flexibility that nonparents take for granted. Although you know this situation goes with the turf, it can still be frustrating. Don't criticize yourself for feeling this way now and then; all parents do whether they'll admit it or not. A sense of being confined or constrained doesn't mean that you made the wrong decision about having children—only that you need some time alone to replenish your emotional resources. Later sections of this chapter will offer specific suggestions.

CONSIDER THE PAST

Parenthood often brings up issues concerning your own childhood experiences. The dreams, expectations, wishes, fears, and anxieties left over from your own childhood make parenting a fertile ground for frustration, confusion, longing, resentment, or sadness. At times intense emotions surface when you least expect them. Something your child says may trigger a memory of your own family experiences. The words that you yourself speak may startle you, prompting you to exclaim, "My God, I sound just like my parents!" These experiences can be baffling, even alarming, but they're not really surprising. Parenting skills aren't innate; they are largely a learned experience, and your experience with your own parents will have an enormous effect on your own attitudes as a mother or father.

I can offer two suggestions for how to deal with the past.

One is to confront it directly. Find a well-trained, compassionate guide—

ideally, a therapist or counselor—who can help you explore the implications of your own upbringing. This path is often strenuous, and I wouldn't recommend it to everyone. It requires a significant commitment in time and money. However, it's invaluable as a way of discovering how your own experiences as a child affect your behavior and decisions as a parent. It can ease the stress and anguish you feel, and it can limit the unwanted side effects that your own past can exert on the present.

My other suggestion is to control the past's effects by learning new skills. You don't have to let your past experiences determine how you raise your own children; by acquiring new techniques or changing your understanding of child development, you can take better control of the situation. Does this option sound too simplistic or mechanistic? It doesn't have to be. A good parenting workshop or seminar can provide practical information yet allow subtle insight into family life. The truth is, people get more training for driving a car than for being a parent. Precisely because parenting skills are learned, everyone can benefit from more information. The result can ease the pressure on you and help you to become the best parent possible.

KNOW WHO YOU ARE

One of the less delightful aspects of parenthood is suffering through everyone else's opinions on how you should raise your kids. People are full of opinions about the right parental attitude, the best kind of child care, the most effective schooling, the most productive activities, the proper kinds of friends, the best way to balance work and life, and so forth. You'll end up barraged with suggestions from all sides. Family members—parents, siblings, aunts, uncles, cousins—will offer their advice. Friends will make their own recommendations. People who don't even have children will eagerly set you straight. This situation is inevitable; avoiding it is hopeless. The task of fending off everyone's opinions is further complicated by the fact that people are so well meaning. Still, it's a frustrating situation, and many times this cacophony of tips can complicate and cloud your perceptions of yourself and your role as a parent.

Where does this leave you? Obviously, you must pick and choose. Take whatever information is insightful and constructive and feels comfortable for you; ignore the rest. Doing so is easier, though, if you know who you are from the inside out. This isn't an easy task. It requires some earnest soul-searching. Even so, it's worthwhile. You're much better off if you have a clear sense of your hopes, wishes, expectations, and goals. Ultimately you have to do what seems best for your child. Trust your gut instincts. You know yourself and your child better than anyone else. The more secure you are with your own opinions, the less reactive and vulnerable you'll be when you hear outside opinions or criticism. You'll be confident from the inside out. You'll know that you're doing the very best job you can do for yourself, your child, and your family.

DISENGAGE FROM THE GUILT TRAP

All parents struggle with guilt. As many people have noted, guilt comes with the turf. One of the reasons is internal: precisely because parenthood is such a huge, complex array of responsibilities, we all worry if we're up to the job. Another reason is external: society hassles us with contradictory opinions and criticisms. People are quick to judge parents' abilities and performances. Mothers, especially, tend to be held accountable for their children's shortcomings. The result? Among other things, it's easy to get caught up in the guilt trap.

But the implications are often out of sync with reality. Yes, you do have some power over your child's life. You have responsibility and input. That being said, you aren't so powerful that you truly determine how your child will think, feel, and act, how your child is going to behave, or who your child becomes. Other forces have power and input, too: peers, schools, and the rest of society. In addition, your child's unique genetic makeup influences his personality, temperament, and physiology.

How should you respond? By all means take responsibility. Gain control over whatever circumstances you can. Do everything possible for your child. At the same time, grasp the difference between those things that are truly within your control and those that aren't. You are responsible for the effort but not for the outcome. Don't complicate your life by carrying a load of guilt that will only complicate your parental tasks and possibly confound your best efforts. Don't take all outcomes personally. It's good to reach insights and figure out what you can do better, but there's a big difference between pushing yourself harder and beating up on yourself. Be the best parent possible; be a good role model for your children; live your dreams; reach for your goals. But be flexible, too. Take it easy not only on your kids, but on yourself.

REJECT PERFECTIONISM

During the parenting years, perfectionism can be one of your worst enemies. Parenthood is by nature an imperfect process. Children have almost infinite needs; parents have finite energy, ideas, resources, and patience. Given this setup, how can your actions as a parent ever attain perfection? Even striving for perfection will drive you—and perhaps your child—crazy. A better strategy: accept both yourself and your child as imperfect. In doing so, you'll be gentler with yourself and more accepting of your child. That approach will ease a lot of the stress and pressure during the parenting years. Your child will make mistakes, and so will you. Your child will have victories, and so will you. Welcome to the human race.

The truth is, both you and your child will learn much more from your failures than from your successes. In addition, an easygoing, tolerant atmosphere is usually the one in which children thrive best. An atmosphere in which everything has to be done "right"—in accordance with some preconceived notion—isn't conducive to children achieving their greatest potential. It increases pressure and may thwart your child's efforts to perform well and enjoy life.

MAKE TIME FOR YOUR MARRIAGE

The foundation of family life is the parents' marriage. If the marriage is shaky or tense, its instability can jeopardize the children's well-being. This situation leads to a conundrum: on the one hand, the parents need to focus on their children, but focusing on kids *to the exclusion of the marriage* can undercut everyone's best efforts. The level of intimacy, cooperation, love, and respect that the partners share will greatly influence their satisfaction. The relative stability and warmth of your marriage will also influence how your children establish intimate relationships in the future. In short, nurturing yourselves as husband and wife is one of the best ways for you to nurture your children.

REACH OUT FOR HELP AND SUPPORT

In many families, one parent—often the mother—has a primary child care role. This arrangement may be a matter of choice or a matter of necessity. Either way, it's easy for mothers to end up overwhelmed by the magnitude of parenting responsibilities; there's simply no way that one parent can tackle all the tasks of raising children and not end up exhausted.

There are no easy answers, but I believe that two issues lie at the heart of the dilemma.

One is that fathers need to get more involved. I make this statement well aware that roles are changing, and that many American dads spend far more time with their children than fathers did in the past. In response I can only shout "Bravo." The willingness of some American men to tackle a larger, fuller parenting role is a wonderful development. Still, there's a long way to go. Many Americans, male and female alike, continue to see men in a strictly secondary role as parents. Even some men who claim to want more involvement don't follow through and actually do the work. The result is a continuing burden on women's shoulders.

In response to this situation, men should, first, take on still more child care duties. Perhaps this isn't feasible, you say, given current corporate policies. Maybe not. American corporations certainly have a long way to go in supporting their employees' family needs. But as Arlie Hochschild portrays the current issues in her recent book *The Time Bind*, many Americans—among them both blue- and white-collar workers—have access to flexible work situations that they often choose not to utilize. This situation holds true for many women as well as men. Regarding men, though: Only 19 percent of American fathers take advantage of paternity leave arrangements. Work conditions don't fully explain fathers' relatively low involvement in domestic duties. American men simply need to do more.

Second, American women need to be more flexible in accommodating their husbands' contributions to the cause. Many fathers have told me that although they want to be involved in their children's day-to-day care, they find their wives reluctant to cede control over this traditionally female role. And some of these wives are the same women who have rightfully asked that their husbands get more involved! In a sense, this contradiction is understandable: even mothers who want more spousal parity within the home struggle with issues of sex-role identity. Fair enough. But while sorting through these legitimate issues, it's crucial for women not to undercut their husbands' willingness to contribute their time and effort. (I discuss these issues in more detail in chapter 16, "Fathers," and chapter 32, "Parenting As Partners.") If parenthood is going to be a true partnership, mothers have to cede some of the territory.

CONSIDER JOINING A SUPPORT GROUP

Many support groups exist for parents. (See the Resource Guide for suggestions.) You can also look in your area's newspapers for listings of groups, seminars, and workshops. Likely sponsors are nonprofit parenting organizations, Jewish Children and Family Services, United Way, and Catholic Charities. If there's nothing available in your town, call some of these agencies. They may be able to direct you to appropriate resources. Your local community college or hospital may also suggest good support groups; some HMOs do as well.

Should you consider joining a support group? That's a question only you can answer. Many people shy away from this option; they feel uneasy about talking in a group. Obviously this issue is one that you need to examine thoughtfully. In general, however, most support groups are nonthreatening; you don't have to take part if you're uncomfortable. Participation isn't mandatory. The goal is simply to discuss parenting issues; to share personal stories that others may find relevant; and to consider options or acquire skills that may make parenting easier and less stressful.

Support groups offer the advantage of helping you feel less isolated. You see that others have problems similar to your own. Support groups help you feel that you're not totally alone with your problem, and that other people share at least some of your circumstances. Likewise, if you're "stuck" on a particular issue, a support group can help you to reach beyond yourself to support another person. It can also help you to feel certain emotions that you might have repressed, since understanding another person's feelings can help you understand your own.

Are there drawbacks to support groups? At times. One risk is that you'll spend some time listening to stories about others' situations that ultimately aren't so relevant to your own. Another is that you may feel an obligation to discuss your own circumstances when you'd prefer not to. Regardless, these risks are minimal—support groups tend to have a nonjudgmental, live-and-let-live attitude—and their advantages outweigh their drawbacks. Making new friends and expanding your social networks can be a wonderful experience; it's certainly very comforting and nurturing, too, to know that you don't have to parent your children in isolation.

FIND GOOD CHILD CARE

Whatever cooperation, support, and involvement you obtain from your spouse or partner, it's also crucial that you find good, dependable ancillary child care. This is true whether you're considering full-time, part-time, or occasional help. It's important that for your own sense of security and reassurance and self-esteem, you know that your child is well attended when out of your immediate care. Such arrangements will ease a lot of your guilt and, in turn, diminish the tension and stress that can complicate your life as a parent.

PERKS

Finally, here are some other, more specific suggestions for taking care of yourself—small things that can make a difference.

- Have lunch with a friend.
- Take a walk.
- Indulge yourself—get a massage or a manicure.
- Join a parenting support group.
- Take a warm bath.
- Read a book.
- Treat yourself to a take-out meal.
- Get some exercise you enjoy.
- Hire a mother's helper to take some pressure off your shoulders.
- Treat yourself to some household cleaning help.
- Trade child care with a parent in the neighborhood.

FIFTY

THE TEEN YEARS

"TURN DOWN THE stereo!" "Get off the phone!" "Clean up your messy room!"

Are these words you've heard yourself yelling over and over? If you've heard yourself shouting these typical directives at your teenager—much to your dismay, and to their discontent—you're not alone. It's stressful having a teenager in the house, and conflicts are all but inevitable.

But there are two sides to this story. Being a teenager isn't a picnic, either. By its very nature, adolescence is a time of dramatic, often stressful change. The magnitude of the physical, intellectual, and emotional transformation that human beings undergo during adolescence has always been difficult. To complicate matters, teens today face much more complex social and personal challenges than in times past.

Parents often wonder what is normal for a teenager. Why do teenagers act out? What are they really trying to say? What do they really want or need? How can parents cope with their teens' crises while the parents themselves deal with mid-life? These are among the issues that weigh most heavily on parents' minds during their children's teen years.

THE HEART OF ADOLESCENCE

Adolescence is a time when kids desperately want the privileges of adulthood yet hold on desperately to the advantages of childhood. It's a love-hate relationship. They don't want to take on the responsibilities, decision making, and hard work of adulthood, yet they desperately want to grow up. As a result, they are ambivalent about letting go and moving on. They vacillate between a craving for independence on the one hand and dependence on their families on the other; they regress into childhood for a while, then move forward into independence, individuation, and separation from their family. This process is often frustrating for parents.

No matter how frustrating, though, this process of vacillation is entirely normal. In fact, it's the very heart of adolescence. The great psychological theorist Erik Erikson calls this developmental stage Separation and Individuation, during which children separate from their families and develop an individual sense of self. To do so, they need to know that their families are present as a strong support system. It's similar to the behavior that children often display during toddlerhood: as they set off to explore the world, they make a big show of independence; at the same time, they desperately need to know you're there, and they'll come running back, hugging you and clinging to you, when the world depletes or frightens them. Just before they're ready to take a new developmental leap, they're often even clingier and moodier than usual. There are vast differences between toddlers and adolescents, of course, but this process of advancement and retreat is similar in both age groups. In this sense, adolescence is almost a recurrence of the "terrible two's"—a complex mixture of craving for independence and intensified fear of separation from what's known and safe. As a result, this is a crucial time for teenagers to feel secure.

An additional complication to the situation is that this process occurs at a time when most parents are going through mid-life and don't feel particularly stable, secure, or energetic. Many parents feel anxious about aging, medical problems, financial worries, college costs, marital or other relationship problems, and the tasks of caring for elderly parents. Teens, meanwhile, are going through a lot of emotional turmoil, growth spurts, and hormonal changes. They desperately need for us to be stable to give them the consistency they need.

COPING WITH THE TEEN YEARS

Given the situation I'm describing, it's unlikely that many families will have a smooth ride with teenagers in the house. Ups and downs are inevitable. Still, things don't have to be as rough as many parents assume. By keeping the dual nature of teens in mind—intellectual abilities racing ahead of emotional maturity—you have a context for understanding many adolescent behaviors. What follows in this chapter is a series of recommendations to help you (and your child) ride out the ups and downs as well as possible.

Although it's difficult to maintain your equilibrium, try to treat your adolescent sons or daughters as intellectual peers. At the same time, you might try perceiving them as much younger children than their intellectual sophistication would suggest. You'll be dealing with someone who is sophisticated but sometimes emotionally immature. In fact, teens often act like very large two-

or three-year-olds. There's no question that under these circumstances, being objective—caring for the adolescent without transferring your own conflicts and inner feelings onto him—is difficult.

It's particularly difficult because the relationship may evoke unfinished business from your own past, including emotions from your own teen years regarding self-esteem, sexuality, identity, relationships, and career goals. This can be another tough time as well for revisiting the relationships you had with your own parents. In short, what psychologists call transference—shifting emotions from one person to another—is a big issue during this stage of parenthood. It's crucial to step carefully when you get upset with your teen. Stop yourself before you get entangled in this situation. Ask yourself these questions:

- Is this conflict about my own child's behavior, or is it about what's going on in my life?

- If it's a conflict I'm part of, is the problem in the present, or is it an issue that's unresolved from my own past—something I'm transferring onto my child?

- If I'm transferring my emotions onto my teenager, how can I focus instead on what's really happening *now?*

INVOLVEMENT

The most important thing you can do as the parent of a teenager is to stay involved. Tune in to your teen, his interests, and his social life. Stay aware of the music he likes, the movies he watches, the sports he plays, the friends he enjoys. Try to maintain contact with the parents of your teenager's friends to stay aware of their activities. Pay attention to his self-esteem—his overall appearance, body language, demeanor, and clothes. Does he look happy or sad? Does he seem healthy? Is he over- or underweight? These issues are important in their own right, but they can also indicate underlying problems. Issues of weight, for instance, can be an important barometer at this time. If you notice your teen either not eating or overeating, you should probably talk to a counselor. In addition, you should pay attention to his mood swings. Emotional shifts are normal during the teens, but if they are protracted or extremely intense, consider the possibility that there's an emotional or biochemical problem at work. Discuss this possibility with your teen first, then consider the option of an outside evaluation.

Seeking outside help is especially crucial if you see signs of withdrawal, obsession with death, or any kind of bizarre, irrational, erratic behavior, including dramatic changes in sleeping or eating patterns, agitation, or sudden hyper-cheerfulness after a long period of sadness or depression. Take these signs or symptoms seriously. If you suspect that your teenager is either suicidal or having suicidal thoughts, call your family pediatrician to ask for a psychiatric referral. It's important to rule out anything that may be out of the norm. (Also, see the Resources Guide.)

Trust your instincts. It's important not to overreact, but you shouldn't underreact, either. You are your teenager's parent; you know him better than anyone else. If you feel that his behavior is really out of the ordinary and has been lasting more than two or three weeks, it's appropriate to get an outside professional opinion.

If you aren't really sure about what's going on, ask your teen directly. "Are you feeling depressed?" "Are you worried about something?" "How long have you felt this way?" "What have you been thinking about?" Tell your teenager that you won't judge him; you'll listen helpfully. Tell him you love him, and you really want to help and find a way to help resolve this situation together.

Again, listen to your teen empathically. Stay involved. Guide him with praise. Paraphrase what he's telling you. Don't overreact. Say things like, "Tell me more," "So what happened next?" "What are your options?" or "So you're feeling angry or upset." Sometimes you don't need to fix the situation; you simply need to empathize and be a good sounding board. Let your teen make as many decisions as possible. Again, be empathic, validate his feelings, but don't feel that you're necessarily the person who has to solve the problem.

COMMUNICATION

When you comment on your adolescent's behavior, remember that adolescents are tenderhearted and insecure. Take some deep breaths and regain your composure before you speak with your teen. When you're communicating with him, try to separate his behavior from his person or character. Don't blame him as if he's fundamentally flawed. Blanket accusations ("You never clean up your room," "You don't listen to me," "You're a real slob," etc.) simply translate (in the teen's mind) to mean "You're no good," "We don't love you," "You're a real pain in the butt." Instead of attacking his character, focus more objectively. What is the specific problem? How can you solve it? When will the task be done, and how does he plan to accomplish it? Speak of the emotions involved, but do so less accusingly. "I felt frustrated when I came in and saw your room was a mess, because I asked you yesterday but you didn't clean it. I'm really tired and stressed out. Can you help me out here? Tell me when you're going to get this done and how you're going to do it."

Specific Tips Regarding Communication
- Don't attack your teenager with a lot of criticism or blame.
- Don't tear down your teen's self-esteem.

- Give constructive feedback without lecturing.

- Don't be syrupy sweet or overly emphatic—just straightforward, candid, and level.

- Keep your emotions as neutral as possible.

RUDENESS AND PROFANITY

Rudeness is a behavior that aggravates many parents. Here, too, it isn't simply what it seems. It may be part of the growing abrasiveness of American culture; at the same time, it's also an expression of your teenager's ambivalence, frustration, anxiety, and stress about growing up. It's also the tension created within the teen because he's growing up so rapidly. Words can be a way to distance a parent so that the teen can separate and individuate. They'll never admit it, but teens are scared and ambivalent about growing up. One of the ways that this stress gets discharged is through rudeness. Scolding them is understandable but potentially unproductive. Limit-setting is a better strategy. I recommend that parents allow their kids to express their feelings as long as they don't call their parents, siblings, or friends obscenities. If they want to curse the situation, the activity, or an object, that's okay; directing it at a person is not. This approach may not be genteel, but rigid prohibitions don't really work well anyway. Prohibiting specific words endows them with greater power. The result: teens will know they can "get" you by uttering the magic words. A more relaxed attitude toward profanity will actually deprive curse words of their power, which makes them less likely to be used.

PEER PRESSURE

Preteens and teens are often vulnerable to peer pressure. To some degree, this situation is inevitable; by its very nature, adolescence is a time when children's allegiances shift from their parents to a peer group. But the degree of allegiance varies. There are teens whose limited sense of self-confidence leaves them vulnerable to their peers' every expectation. Other teens, however, have a stronger core identity, so that peer pressure is only one element they consider in making decisions and establishing a sense of self. Research shows that a strong family support system, highly involved parents, and a high degree of self-esteem are the core elements that enable teens to resist peer pressure. By contrast, teens who are more susceptible to peer pressure often have rigid, authoritarian parents; these children haven't had much practice making their own decisions while growing up, which leaves them less able to resist a strong leader. Other teens who are at risk are those whose parents are lackadaisical or permissive, or who aren't available emotionally; this scenario often prompts teenagers to look for a group to fill the role of their families.

A recent article in the *Journal of the American Medical Association* reports that teens and preteens who feel secure, who have close relationships with at least one parent or immediate family member, and who also feel supported at school, were less likely to engage in risky behaviors. This outcome was clear regardless of race, education, religion, and socioeconomic background. The more that families and school personnel are involved with teenagers, the lower the risk of teenagers experimenting with smoking, drinking, taking drugs, or having premature sexual involvements. Why? The likeliest explanation is that under these circumstances, teens feel that they have someone to talk to without being judged. They feel confident of being heard, listened to, validated, and respected. Having these insights helps your teen mature and reach his or her greatest potential. And it will certainly build closer, more intimate relationships between you and your teenager.

SETTING LIMITS

Setting limits is a crucial aspect of parenting teens. Remember, you have to set reasonable limits, just as you did when they were younger. Set the limits clearly in advance so that there's an understanding of what you expect. Ask your teen to negotiate with you; come up with possible solutions or options *together* for what can be done in a situation. For instance, if your daughter has a special activity that she wants to do when you plan to be out of town, try to compromise. Maybe you'll go out of town this time but next time you'll stay home. Or maybe this time you'll stay home and next time you'll go out of town. Be flexible but firm. Emphasize that everyone in the family needs to compromise.

It's important for you to know what your teenager's schedule is and to understand what your teenager has been through during the day. Sometimes teenagers seem obstinate, arrogant, and resistant to pitching in when, in fact, the core issue might be a reaction to some other experience. It might be that they had a horrendous experience at school. Or else they may be feeling a sudden lack of confidence. Or they may be having a hormonal mood swing. So keep in mind that an emotional outburst could be a delayed response to a specific event.

On the other hand, it's true that teenagers can sometimes simply act obnoxiously. If so, you should indicate that pointlessly abrasive behavior is unacceptable. You're a person, too; you have a right to be treated decently. Be firm with your adolescent. Make it clear that there's only so much that a parent can take. Never allow yourself to be verbally or physically abused. If that sort of problem is occurring, you need professional help.

After you've set some clear limits (including reasonable expectations) make the consequences clear regarding any violations of the rules. Indicate the consequences for misbehavior. Make sure that the punishment fits the crime. Don't over- or underreact by setting an inappropriate punishment. Being either too harsh or too lenient will jeopardize your parental authority. When it's appropriate, make exceptions to the rules. Try to be as human as possible with your teenager. Admit that you've made your own share of mistakes. Show that you understand the difficulties of adolescence and identify with the feelings and the confusion that adolescence brings on.

DIALOGUE

Ideally, dialogue starts well before your child becomes a teenager. It's crucial anyway, but especially when discussing loaded subjects like sex, drugs, smoking, and violence. At first you may find that discussing sex is difficult, especially if your parents had a hard time talking with you about this subject. But it's important to resolve some of your issues from your teen years and to try to be available and less self-conscious. Try to be a good resource for your teenager. This will help him to feel comfortable coming to you with any question without feeling that you're going to overreact or be judgmental. The best way to turn off a teen is to either ignore him or overreact. Ignoring him can create a feeling that you don't care; overreacting can prompt him to regard you as hysterical and not worth his time or energy. These responses can also make him feel guilty. Teens are often very self-critical; they pick on themselves physically, emotionally, sometimes much more brutally than we could ever imagine. Parents have a lot more power than they realize, so be careful how you exercise that power. It may not seem at times that your teenager wants to please you, but he needs your approval and love as much as you need his, if not more so.

TEENS' EXTERNAL AND INTERNAL IMAGES

Teenagers are tough but tender. They have very thin skin. The slightest feeling that you're displeased with them puts them over the edge. They are very insecure during this period of time; it doesn't take very much to hurt their feelings. Of course, from their standpoint, it's okay for them to hurt *our* feelings—they're not terribly empathic. As a result, it's very hard not to take to heart what they say. But the number one rule is, *Don't take it personally*. Put aside your own personal problems and moods. Stay in the moment. Respond in a calm, cool, and collected manner to deal with your teenager's mood swings.

SCHEDULES AND ACTIVITIES

If your teen doesn't want to go on a family outing, how do you respond? First of all, try to give him as much advance notice as possible. Teens often won't tell you that there's going to be a concert, a dance, or a movie that interests them. As a result, you should work out in advance who needs to be where. Find out what's on their agenda; let them know what's on yours. Then compromise to accommodate one another's plans. During the teen years, try to give your child independence whenever possible. Allow him to develop his own social activities and friendships. Don't burden him with expectations of having to join family outings and activities all the time. He'd rather be caught with his pants down than be caught at a movie, dinner, or the mall with his parents. This attitude is a typical attitude of most adolescents. Again, don't take it personally.

TEENS' STRESS LEVELS

When teenagers seem lazy and indifferent, they're often just physically and emotionally drained. Teenagers deal with many pressures that adults underestimate. Some of these pressures are external, such as school assignments and social situations. Some are internal, including the side effects of growth and other physical changes. As a result, you should be both firm and understanding. Set limits. At the same time, be loving, tender, and understanding. This is admittedly a difficult task, since teens are much more provocative than when they were two or three.

THE PSYCHOLOGICALLY ASTUTE PARENT

The preceding discussions are admittedly just an overview of parenting a teenager. Summarizing my advice briefly, though, I'll stress the importance of being a psychologically astute parent. Research indicates that kids with at least one parent who is sensitive to psychological issues will be at lower risk for acting out or indulging in high-risk behaviors or submitting to peer pressure. What does this mean? The psychologically astute parent does some of what I've already mentioned. You should:

- Listen actively without interrupting.

- Be empathic, paraphrasing what your teen tells you but not passing judgment.

- Validate his feelings.

- Show your teenager in loving ways that you care and that you're listening to what he says.

- Show your teen kindness; be positive, reinforcing his fragile ego.

- Don't let your teen be verbally abusive.

- Be a positive role model for the behavior you expect.

- Be available when your child wants to talk.

- Set appropriate limits when necessary, and be consistent.

Accept that at this stage of child development, you can never be truly "right" in his eyes. (As for being cool, forget it!) He needs something to rebel against to separate from you, to become his own person, and to form his own identity. If you go along with everything and don't show your discontent, your teen will up the ante. In short, allow him something to rebel against. In that way a little reaction isn't so bad. It's how we react—the amount, intensity, and duration— that matters. So go ahead, set limits, and be firm, but also be fair. Allow your teen his independence. Pick your battles carefully. Don't insist on winning every battle, since doing so may mean you lose the war. A lot of times you just have to let go and not react. And sometimes you have to set firm limits.

Celebrate your teenager's soul, his spirit, his heart. There's a good chance that he will drive you half-crazy, but this is also a time of tremendous growth and great change. Your teen will become much more sophisticated—developing more intimate, deeper relationships with himself, with his friends, with the world around him, and with you.

Keep your sense of humor. Learn to laugh. Try to remember what it was like to be a teenager. As my son, Jason, at age fourteen, said: "Hey, Mom, lighten up. I know my life is shallow, but I'm just a teenager. Your life is really neurotic. Why can't adults just have fun and laugh? Why are you guys always so *serious?*"

FIFTY-ONE

TWENTY-FIRST–CENTURY PARENTING

FAMILY RELATIONSHIPS ARE in tremendous flux today, and under tremendous strain.

- Nuclear families and extended family structures are changing.
- Divorce rates have reached all-time high levels throughout the United States.
- People spend a smaller fraction of their lives as part of anything that resembles a traditional family.
- American families today are showing more signs of stress and conflict than ever before.
- Families are fragmented and schedules are often complex and chaotic.
- Current social trends stress the primacy of the individual over others; in more psychological terms, we live in an increasingly narcissistic culture.
- Leisure and intimate relationships often end up on the back burner.

Sizing up these trends, it's easy to wonder what families have to offer people in an age of fragmentation and individualization. Whatever families do offer, what does this mean about parenting in the twenty-first century? In what ways will it differ from parenting today? What will be the challenges and opportunities for parents in the decades ahead? Who will be taking care of America's children?

THE MILLENNIUM AS A GOOD-NEWS/BAD-NEWS JOKE

My expectation is that parenting in the twenty-first century will be a tangle of positive and negative features. The bad news is that family life will be a continuation of the balancing and juggling acts that people face today. Blended families—those formed when spouses remarry—will present many challenges, since the rules of love, loyalty, commitment, and responsibility will remain complex. This family structure in turn sets up a very different kind of social system, including values, roles, and relationships. With these changes in the American family—compounded by changes in technology—our roles and relationships will tend to become more distant, mechanical, and formal. So much for the bad news.

The good news in the twenty-first century is that there will be a wider range of opportunities. There will be more flexibility in terms of the choices regarding family structure and acceptable behavior. This is the flip side of the uncertainty described above: family structures may be more nurturing because there will be less rigidity in terms of what constitutes a family. This flexibility will enable us as a society to become much more resilient and able to more easily adjust to change. It will present opportunities to celebrate the range of possibilities inherent in human experience.

On a practical level, parenting in the twenty-first century will require you to make much more effort in finding creative ways to be involved day-to-day in your child's life. Staying focused and connected to your child's needs—and balancing them with increasing economic and personal needs—will take a lot of time. This situation will also demand close attention so that you can stay connected with your child.

HOW PARENTS SHOULD RESPOND

In response to these pressures, here's a brief list of ways in which you'll have to address various parenting issues as we start the new millennium:

SET YOUR PRIORITIES

All individuals face societal pressures, some of them negative. Consumerism, reliance on vicarious entertainment, and a sense of disconnectedness from other people are just three aspects of the problem. Parents often wrestle with these issues as their children grow and change. The upcoming decades will only intensify this struggle. One of the big issues, then, will be deciding what's personally important rather than merely what society defines as significant. You should therefore clarify your own family values and prioritize what's important to you—what is optimal for your own and your child's growth and development. Prioritizing what you value will be essential if you intend to stay focused in a fast-paced, highly technological world.

HELP SCHOOLS CHANGE THEIR TRADITIONAL WAYS OF DOING THINGS

Schools must adapt to the changes ahead. Some of this adaptation will fall to academic professionals—teachers, administrators, and curriculum experts. Some of the responsibility, however, resides in parents. Three instances of possible changes are lengthening the school day, letting parent-teacher conferences occur at night, and encouraging working parents to be involved during after-school hours. Others include having schools remain open longer and on weekends for family activities. In addition, parents can use e-mail, voicemail, and fax to keep in touch with teachers.

RESIST TECHNOLOGICAL HYPE

There's a strong tendency for Americans to adapt almost any new technology that becomes available. Some new developments are, in fact, productive and empowering. Others backfire dramatically. High-tech communications hardware, for instance, was supposed to simplify worklife and lead to increased leisure time. Instead, the pervasiveness of communications gadgets means that there's no place where people can be inaccessible. The result: you're always "at work" even when you're not. The boss can find you at home, in your car, on a plane, or at the beach. In response to this invasiveness of technology, you'll need to slow down the pace of life so you can be "in the moment" with your child. Try to filter out external demands and expectations. Find ways to focus on the family and each person in it. Simplify, simplify. The more you chase after the pot of gold at the end of the consumerist rainbow, the more it will elude you. Just enjoy the little moments that are so precious in life. (For a further discussion of computer-related issues, see chapter 7, "Computers and Kids.")

MAKE TIME TO RELAX

Get regular exercise. Take simple outings rather than grand, expensive vacations. Carve out time that is solely family time. Do whatever you can to recharge your batteries. (For details on this issue, see chapter 15, "Family Life.")

GET IN TOUCH WITH SPIRITUAL VALUES

Meditate, do yoga, practice a spiritual discipline. Volunteer time to contribute something to others. Focus on commitments and connectedness rather than on acquiring power, status, and material goods. This is going to help balance some of the movement of our society and give us a better balance in our families. (See chapter 45, "Spirituality.")

REACH OUT TO YOUR COMMUNITY

It really does take a whole village to raise a child; in this day and age, you're going to have to use all your networking resourcefulness to keep life from becoming too chaotic. Find help from schools, religious establishments, recreational programs, town facilities, libraries, and other resources. Also, plan ahead for school schedules, vacation schedules, and sick time.

REJECT CONSUMERISM

People put too much stress on themselves to achieve more, buy more, and have more. So—starting from the inside out—make your interior life a higher priority than external gratification. This won't be easy: material seductions in the twenty-first century will be difficult to resist. You'll have to have a strong sense of yourself to be able to know what's important for you. Try not to let the fast pace of life control you. Take control; celebrate what the twenty-first century can offer you in terms of opportunities, information, and education without allowing it to control your life and your family life.

FIFTY-TWO

VACATIONS AND TRIPS

A RUSSIAN FRIEND and I were discussing work, family issues, and the meaning of life. I mentioned at some point that I would soon be taking a vacation.

"Where are you going?" asked Lilya.

"I'm taking my son to Florida," I told her.

She looked puzzled. "But you said this would be a vacation."

"Right."

Lilya now seemed downright perplexed. "You're taking your child."

I nodded.

"But how can it be a vacation," she asked, "if a child is with you?"

NO REST FOR THE WEARY?

There's some truth in my friend's words. Vacations are supposed to be relaxing; travel with kids is anything but. The rigors of getting from A to B are often stressful, and the demands that kids make "on the road" can drive parents to look back wistfully on the rough-and-tumble workplace. Still, Americans place a premium on togetherness and most often take vacations as a family.

Vacations can certainly be part of what draws family members together. How can you prevent the opposite from happening? How can you keep relaxation from becoming a new source of stress and fatigue? Where's the happy medium? How can vacations end up more than mere drudgery?

OPTIONS AND ALTERNATIVES

It's a peculiarly American assumption that a family should do everything together. For all that's good about the we're-all-here-together attitude, it has its limitations, too. I'm not suggesting that you must go off by yourself, either, but don't rule it out. If you're married, you and your spouse need time by yourselves at least now and then. Getting away together—even for just a day or two—can be marvelously rejuvenating both to your marriage and to your commitment to your kids. If you're a single parent, taking a break from family duties can be at least as crucial. Assuming you can arrange safe, reliable child care, everyone may benefit from your getting a brief respite from parenthood.

What are some other alternatives?

One possibility is to find a vacation spot that has varied activities—some involving kids, others without. Many family resorts provide on-site child care and kid-friendly activities. Sometimes resorts provide special instruction in swimming, tennis, or other sports that appeal to children's interests. These flexible arrangements can allow you the option of being alone or with one or more family members.

A more cost-effective possibility is to "divide and conquer." This is an option for two-parent families in which one adult takes one or more children on a trip while the other parent and one or more children stay home; later, the other parent takes another child or two on a different trip. This arrangement limits some of the togetherness that can make family travel satisfying, but it prevents some of the stress as well. It's also cheaper than having the whole family travel at once. In addition, it can be a useful tactic if your kids have widely diverging interests, since you can treat one child to specific activities that may not appeal to everyone. (An example: a teenage boy who hates hiking doesn't have to accompany his sister to walk parts of the Appalachian Trail, while his sister can avoid her brother's beloved skateboard jamboree.)

PLAN, PLAN, AND KEEP ON PLANNING

For family travel, logistics are everything. *Plan your vacation.* This is crucial under most circumstances, but never more so than when you have kids in tow. Take into account your children's ages, personalities, and needs. Spontaneity is great, but the risks you face with kids on board are far greater than when you're on your own. If nothing else, planning can ease the routine wear-and-tear that sometimes makes family vacations so exhausting.

AIM FOR THE RIGHT AGE LEVEL

Choose a vacation that's age-appropriate. Having fun doesn't have to be a big production or cost a lot of money. Complicated trips may actually increase the pressure that kids feel, which will quickly raise tension levels throughout the family, and parents often resent having to spend piles of cash on trips that family members seem not to enjoy. What's the answer? Aim for the right age level.

Younger Children

For younger children, day trips may be preferable to longer trips anyway; when they're comfortable and relaxed in secure, familiar surroundings, toddlers and preschoolers may feel far happier than in new places. Activities can be amazingly ordinary. Plant a garden together. Go out to lunch. Splash around in a wading pool. Do a baking project. Play games. Go to the park. Have a picnic. Go to the beach, a lake, or a local state park for the day. Toss a ball around. Blow bubbles. Draw with sidewalk chalk. Fly a kite. Sometimes kids even get excited about chores that adults wouldn't even consider entertaining, such as washing the car, painting a bookshelf, or weeding a garden. Exotic locales aren't necessary. In fact, some of the best, most relaxing vacations can happen when you stay home and tap into local activities.

School-Age Children

Kids aged five to ten often seem to need more complex distractions than younger ones, but this assumption may be deceptive. Yes, grade school children can demand elaborate entertainment—organized sports, summer camps, classes, workshops, and structured play. However, I'm convinced that much of the impetus toward complicated entertainment for this age group comes from the parents. As recently as three or four decades ago, children generally kept themselves amused and entertained. Parents' organizational abilities weren't required or even tolerated. Today, American parents often feel they have to play social secretaries for children most or all of the time. Some of this response comes out of concern for kids' safety. That's understandable. Even so, I think the pendulum has swung too far the other way. Children need freedom and leeway to play and explore. Vacations used to be—and ought to be—a time for kids to relax and follow their own noses for a while. Parents can set limits, serve as resources, and intervene when necessary, but I see no need for school-age children to demand that their parents serve as cruise directors.

If you feel a need to travel, choose a vacation where you can explore a new place or activity. Such vacations are often activity-oriented trips, but they provide far-reaching memories and can give children experiences outside of the classroom that expand their horizons.

Preteens and Teenagers

The situation grows more complex and contradictory as adolescence approaches and arrives. Preteens and teens are potentially more independent, and they are detaching themselves from parents' values, routines, and interests. They don't want parents to call the shots on how they entertain themselves.

They far prefer to go about their own business. However, kids this age have a growing capacity for getting into difficulties that range from the trivial (forgetting which bus to take home) to the significant (hanging out with trouble-making friends) to the calamitous (having an unsupervised party when you're out of town). Vacations are potentially times of great family closeness, but teens may not see the situation that way.

Ideally, you might provide your teen with some peer-oriented activities in addition to family-oriented trips. One time-tested possibility is summer camp. Most camps focus on the peer group, yet adults supervise all activities. In addition to traditional outdoorsy camps, some concentrate activities on a particular sport, art, or discipline: soccer, computers, music, and so forth. Many communities offer similar arrangements in miniature—day camps, often scheduled in units of two or three weeks—which are more affordable than sleep-away camps. Whether or not your teen chooses to take part in such activities, however, it's not unreasonable for you to insist on participation in some family trips. The key to success here is to bring your child into the decision-making process. Suggest the possibilities; allow time for everyone to sort through the options; try to make a group decision. Also, another option, mentioned earlier, is to let your teen bring along a friend.

KEEP YOUR EXPECTATIONS LOW

There's already enough pressure to have a great time on vacation; don't raise the stakes until it becomes a burden. Keep things simple. If possible, shoot low. Your vacation doesn't have to be a Disney World extravaganza. Figure out what your family needs rather than what some travel agent feels you ought to have.

Unfortunately, many parents try to compensate for lack of time with their kids by doing something extraordinary. Vacations become a form of compensation. The hidden message is, "I've been so busy that I feel guilty, but now I'll make it up to you." Yet when I ask children and adults what they remember most about their time together as a family, people often mention simple things. Riding on a train with their parents, having a pillow fight, or exploring nature—these are often the events that stick in their memories. It's not necessary to stay at a fancy resort. Sometimes kids remember those things, but most often it's simply spending time together that people recall and cherish. It's the feelings of closeness—not the activities—that count.

TRIPS AND TIPS

Here are some suggestions about family travel and vacations.

ADVENTURE TRAVEL

One of the big trends in tourism is adventure travel. This is travel with a focus on exotic lands, extreme sports, rugged forms of transportation, or a combination of all these. Adventure travel is great as long as it's safe and age-appropriate. Ask your travel agent about family-oriented places that would meet your budget and children's interests.

FOREIGN TRAVEL

If you can afford it, nothing opens children's eyes like foreign travel. The newness of another country can be challenging, even stressful, but it's a wonderful experience that starts to show kids the world's size and complexity. The main drawback is expense. Keep in mind, though, that for the cost of a week at Disneyland you could probably spend a week in parts of Europe, Canada, or Latin America instead.

SURVIVING ONE ANOTHER

Pace yourself. If you have younger children, don't plan to drive for hours and hours. Travel is hard. Travel for shorter periods of time whenever possible. If time is a concern and you have congenial relatives, stay overnight with family. The goal isn't to go around the world in eighty days; it's to have a good, interesting experience.

ON-THE-ROAD ACTIVITIES

- Have your kids keep a journal.
- Have them draw pictures of their experiences.
- Collect mementos from the trip—whatever will help them cherish their experiences and learn along the way.
- Play car versions of games—stickers, magnetic checkers, dominoes, Scrabble.
- Play other car games, like "I Spy," counting cars, license plates, and map reading.
- Listen to audiotapes.
- Make up a story with each person taking turns to add parts to the plot development.

AIRPLANE TRAVEL

Air travel these days is abundant, fast, and relatively cheap. Even so, it's getting more and more stressful, with packed airports and crowded flights. Surviving the flight is less a matter of air safety than somehow tolerating grouchy fellow-passengers, surly flight attendants, and sardine-can accommodations. Under these circumstances, how can you raise the odds of flying somewhere with your kids and arriving with your sanity intact?

- Make sure you have a change of clothes for each member of the family in your carry-on bag, in case the airline loses your luggage.

- For babies and toddlers, bring a full day's supply of bottles, diapers, and other supplies on board. Don't assume you won't get delayed, diverted to the wrong airport, or stuck in a landing stack-up.

- Let the kids chew gum if they experience clogged ears on takeoffs and landings. Dental hygiene can take a brief holiday under the circumstances.

- Pack snacks for everyone. If you've ever tried to survive a long flight on a single packet of peanuts, imagine how you'll fare with hungry kids around.

- Ask for any special kids' packets from the flight attendant. Many airlines offer little bags of souvenirs, games, crayons, and so forth.

- Plan a nonstop flight if possible, and choose kid-friendly airlines.

IS THERE LIFE AFTER VACATION?

Despite the gripes that many parents utter following family vacations—"Now I can go back to work and get some rest!"—most people enjoy the special trips and occasions they spend with their children. Partly it's the time spent together. Partly it's the fun of exploring new places together. Partly it's the delight of seeing the world through kids' eyes. The stresses of traveling as a family are genuine and abundant. It's crucial to pick activities and accommodations carefully. If you step carefully, though, it's worth the effort. You'll have good times together, and your children will remember their vacations as doors that opened on new and often remarkable views of the world.

FIFTY-THREE

VALUES

TEACHING YOUR CHILD values begins with the process of developing your child's conscience, which generally starts to develop around his fifth or sixth birthday, though this process can start somewhat earlier. (Development varies to some extent from one child to another.)

What is a conscience, and how does a child develop one? *Webster's New Collegiate Dictionary* defines conscience as "restraint or exercise over one's impulses, emotions, or desires." Teachers and parents often define conscience as including these features:

- Acceptance of responsibility to follow the rules at home and at school

- Socially acceptable behavior

- Learning to tame anger

- Developing kindness, empathy, and an ability to share

- Developing patience

- Developing an ability for autonomous thinking

- Tolerance for frustration

- Ability to delay gratification

Young children have many primitive drives. They generally have poor impulse control; they learn to control their temper and to learn right from wrong by being socialized. Initially, parents and teachers must provide external incentives to foster this process—that is, they express approval or disapproval. Later, the child will be less dependent on adults' outside "shaping" of behavior;

they will begin to develop ther own internal controls. When a sense of conscience does emerge at around the child's fifth or sixth year, it's a good start. However, the conscience may not become a stable part of his personality until the ninth or tenth year. And it won't be completely independent of parental guidance until the last phase of adolescence, as the child moves into young adulthood.

Psychologists have learned that the way in which parents set limits in the early years actually sets the stage for later self-control. Self-control is crucial, and children who lack it are at risk for a number of personal and social difficulties, including:

- Conflicts with parents and teachers

- Difficulty in developing friendships

- Lack of self-discipline, which makes life frustrating

- Difficulties with academic achievement, which could lead to low grades and falling short of academic goals, hence difficulty getting into high school programs, college, etc.

- Difficulties in building a successful career

- Possible troubles in developing intimate relationships

FOSTERING CONSCIENCE IN YOUNG CHILDREN

How do you help your child develop a conscience? How do you help him develop that inner self-discipline that's necessary to control his behavior from the inside without being dependent on external rewards or punishments?

OFFER UNCONDITIONAL LOVE

A parent's love is crucial. Best of all is unconditional love—loving your child regardless of his behavior. Separate your child's behavior from his being (soul, nature, etc.) at times of conflict. Tell him, "I love you, but I don't like your behavior just now." Young children want to please their parents. They definitely want love and approval. Your approval is a powerful tool.

SET UP SIMPLE RULES AND GUIDELINES

Let's say your two-year-old daughter is throwing sand. Instead of saying, "Why are you doing that?" say simply, "The sand stays in the sandbox." Or reinforce the rules in a positive way. "I know it's hard to wait your turn, but you have to. Can you sing a song while we wait? Or play a game? Then it'll be your turn." Make positive suggestions.

ARRANGE THE ENVIRONMENT TO OPTIMIZE EXPLORATION

Minimize the word *no*. Too often we quell the behavior without an explanation. With younger children it's hard to provide an explanation, but some younger children are very bright and verbal. With those children, you can explain to them why they can't do something or why they need to wait. Arranging the environment to help a younger child optimize the choices and exploration helps greatly.

REDIRECT OR SUBSTITUTE

If your son is hitting your daughter, simply saying no won't solve the problem. Children have aggressive impulses. Hitting other kids is unacceptable, but hitting a punching bag is acceptable. A child's destroying your phone isn't acceptable, so buy an old broken telephone and let the child play with that. Redirect or transfer aggression in positive ways. Let kids blow off steam by tearing old newspaper, knocking down bowling pins, or going outside to run around.

USE GUILT CAREFULLY

Appealing to a child's sense of guilt is necessary for the development of self-control and perceiving right and wrong. Don't overdo it, but don't hesitate to invoke guilt selectively. An example: your son has taken a neighbor's toy. "How would you feel," you ask, "if Johnny took *your* toy?" Or, "How do you think Johnny feels right now?" Those are appropriate questions. In the long run, a mild experience of guilt can lead to developing empathy. It can reinforce the behaviors and values that you want to instill in your child—kindness, sharing, patience, and self-control.

ALLOW DELAYED GRATIFICATION TO HELP DEVELOP PERSISTENCE

Spend time with your child and increase his attention span. That's possible through reading books, building with Legos, doing art projects, etc. Helping a child see a project through from beginning to end can help foster a stick-to-it mentality. Almost every aspect of American culture emphasizes instant gratification. Kids lose their attention span all too quickly as they adapt to the pace of TV, video games, and computer games.

FOSTERING CONSCIENCE IN OLDER CHILDREN

Here are some tips for developing a conscience in school-age children.

ASSIGN MEANINGFUL, AGE-APPROPRIATE RESPONSIBILITIES

Ask your child to take on specific tasks, chores, or responsibilities that fit his abilities. Don't do tasks that your child should accomplish on his own. Be consistent in your requests, and follow through on your expectations. Instill a sense of group responsibility—doing what needs to be done as part of being a family. Gently point out to your child when he's being self-absorbed and needs to be more attentive to other people's needs.

STICK TO A REALISTIC SCHEDULE

Help your children to make up a daily schedule for study time, homework, chores, and so on. Don't be overly rigid, especially with younger school-aged children. You don't want to make the schedule a punishment; emphasize that it's a normal part of daily family life. Try to make it fun.

LISTEN ATTENTIVELY

Validate your child's feelings. Try to figure out what's bothering him, and why. Praise and reinforce your child when he is patient, kind, or thoughtful, and when he perseveres at something.

USE ROLE-PLAYING TO HEIGHTEN EMPATHY

Ask your child to imagine how his acting out affects his classmates, his teacher, and family members. "How would you feel if you sat quietly and waited to be called on but another child called out first?" Help him develop a conscience and empathy. Assist his efforts to become more aware of other people's feelings, desires, and needs.

NEGOTIATE AND RESOLVE CONFLICTS

If your child takes part in thinking about and evaluating his behavior, he'll be much more likely to follow through when trying to cooperate. Ask your child, "If you were the parent, what would you do?" Many times if you say to your child, "Well, what do you think the punishment should be?" children will generally dish out far more rigid punishments than you could ever think of. So include the child in the process; give him a warning, then a chance to respond. Don't be too quick to punish, but don't be permissive, either. Stay somewhere in the middle. A balanced approach is important in developing your child's conscience.

TEACH PERSISTENCE AND RESPONSIBILITY

If your child agrees to go somewhere, insist that he follow through. Stress that you need to fulfill your commitments unless there's an unavoidable disruption, such as illness or a family event. Help your child understand commitment and responsibility. Sometimes you have to turn down an invitation because of a prior commitment—homework, for instance. Teach your child he must honor his obligations.

BE A GOOD ROLE MODEL

If you're impatient, inconsistent, unreliable, or disrespectful of others, your child will pick up on your behavior. If you urge him to be nonjudgmental yet you constantly pass judgment on others, he'll notice and model his behavior after yours. If you demand that he tell the truth while you speak dishonestly yourself, he'll quickly learn this behavior. The words are age-old but worth repeating: Practice what you preach.

FIFTY-FOUR

VIOLENCE

Julia, the thirty-six-year-old mother of three children in elementary school, worries constantly about their safety. "First there was that shooting in Tennessee. Then one in Oregon. Then the one in Kentucky—kids killed in their own schoolyard. I keep telling myself it can't happen here. You know what scares me? Whenever those things happen, the people there say, 'I never thought it could happen here.'"

....

"I've tried to monitor what my kids watch on TV and limit how much violent stuff they see," *says Rob, the father of two teenage boys.* "They know they won't watch a lot of graphic violence at home. But when they're with other families, there's not much I can do. Their pals log on to bizarre Web sites, play video games I can't even stand hearing about, and watch all kinds of movies I wouldn't tolerate. Should I prohibit them from hanging out with those guys? These are good kids, mind you. I just keep hoping they have their heads on straight and won't be affected."

....

Merrie learned from her daughter, Alexa, that a boy at school was hassling other kids. He'd taunt them, threaten to hit them, and boast about being the toughest dude around. The school authorities were aware of the problem and had disciplined the boy but seemed reluctant to expel him. "If this were back when I grew up," *Merrie explains,* "I'd figure this kid was just a bully. That would be bad enough but not cause for lying awake all night. Nowadays you can't be sure. Maybe this kid is just a pain in the butt—or maybe he's a psycho ready to go berserk."

I N AN ERA when twelve-year-olds are capable of gunning down their class-mates, where are your children safe? In a country where almost half of all households contain firearms, when can you feel confident that your kids aren't at risk of injury or death? In a culture in which the staples of TV and movie entertainment include murder, rape, torture, explosions, dismemberment, and decapitation, what can prompt you to feel comfortable with your children's impression of reality?

The United States is one of the most violent countries in the Western world, and to some degree everyone is at risk from a plague we've allowed to spread throughout the land. At the same time, the *level* of risk varies. Depending on where you live and what precautions you're willing to take, you can diminish the degree to which your children are at risk from violence.

THE CAUSES OF VIOLENCE

First of all, it's important to understand the causes of violence in America.

AVAILABILITY OF GUNS

Although many Americans express concern about violence at the hands of criminals, a greater danger lies within the home. More than 40 percent of American households with children contain firearms. The death toll from firearms in this country is staggering: 38,505 in 1994 and climbing. Americans are fifteen times more likely to be killed by gunfire than Europeans. Nearly 29 percent of those persons who died from firearm injuries in 1994 were between the ages of fifteen and twenty-four years old. The firearm industry and advocacy groups such as the National Rifle Association continue, of course, to absolve guns, gun manufacturers, and gun owners from any responsibility for this carnage. However, the easy availability of firearms throughout the United States at least sets the stage for, and may well contribute more directly to, a death toll unparalleled in any other industrialized nation. It's true that rage and other destructive impulses will always lead some people to lash out violently, but a rifle or pistol in the hands of an enraged or deranged person can do far more damage than most other weapons would if firearms were more difficult to obtain.

MODELING OF VIOLENT BEHAVIOR

In families where domestic violence exists, children will tend to model their own behavior after the aggression they perceive. Yelling, screaming, fighting, hitting, and other forms of abusive behavior become part of the context that children consider "normal"; they are more likely to emulate those behaviors as they mature. Similarly, children whose parents spank them are more likely to vent frustration aggressively than are children who have not been subject to corporal punishment. Witnessing any kind of severe domestic violence is especially traumatic to children and may lead to posttraumatic stress disorder in children, teens, and adults.

POVERTY

According to some researchers, a significant source of violence is poverty. Even a quick look at statistics for violence show that they tend to correlate positively with poverty: The poorer an area is within the United States, the higher its overall incidence of violent crime. One can draw a variety of conclusions from this situation. My own belief is that until this country addresses the root causes of poverty, we will suffer the consequences, including a high crime rate.

AVAILABILITY OF DRUGS AND ALCOHOL

High levels of poverty tend to correlate with increased consumption of drugs and alcohol; high rates of drugs and alcohol usage correlate in turn with increased crime rates. However, children in all sectors of society are at risk of violence in settings where high levels of drugs and alcohol use play a part.

VIOLENCE IN THE MEDIA

By age ten, most American kids will have watched tens of thousands of violent acts on television, including thousands of murders. Ironically, Saturday morning cartoons often have an even higher rate of violent acts (five to six per hour) than shows during the prime-time evening slot. Whether TV violence affects children directly remains unclear. (See chapter 29, "The Media.") Overall, however, I find it hard to believe that there isn't *some* sort of correlation. The cause-effect relationship may be indirect, but it's unlikely that a constant, long-term TV diet of violence, gore, and death doesn't have an effect on children. The situation now grows even more complex as violent video games and Web sites spread in popularity.

In response to this barrage of violent entertainment, some psychologists have offered several theories on whether children's viewing of violent shows perpetuates yet more violence.

One theory suggests that violence can be cathartic. That is, children, adolescents, and adults who watch violent programming can fantasize harmlessly about what they observe, thus releasing tensions, which may help alleviate rage and aggression. According to this theory, viewing violent shows may actually be beneficial; it prevents rather than promotes violence against others.

A second theory suggests that children who view violent shows run the risk of modeling their behavior after what they see. In this sense, violent programming teaches violence. Children observing repeated acts of aggression will tend to perceive violence (not insight, negotiation, and compromise) as the preferable means for solving problems. This theory suggests that violent entertainment doesn't cause violence but makes it more likely.

A third theory suggests that repetitive viewing of violence may desensitize children and may even prompt real-life violence. Although this theory isn't implausible, and though certain incidents in the news give it credence, psychologists and other researchers have performed minimal research to support or prove this theory. It's based on anecdotal evidence rather than on solid, hard statistics. Much more research needs to be done on this issue.

HUMAN NATURE

Many people I know say with resignation that human beings are, after all, inherently aggressive, so what can we do? This is an unfortunate attitude. Although biologists, anthropologists, psychologists, and other researchers are well aware that *Homo sapiens* have a history of violent behavior that spans and even predates our development as a species, I'm concerned that chalking up violence to human nature is taking the easy way out. The reality of the situation is far more complicated. I believe that for all that's wonderful about our country, much of the blame for the violence all around us lies squarely with cultural choices we've made. Even a quick comparison with Canada—a country with a history and a material culture similar to our own—is cause for great discomfort. While Canadians experience 4.31 gun-related deaths per 1,000 inhabitants of their country, citizens of the United States experience 14.24 deaths per 1,000 inhabitants. (The English suffer only 0.41 gun-related deaths per 1,000 inhabitants; the Japanese, only 0.05.) What does this show? You can draw your own conclusions. If nothing else, it verifies what many American parents feel: Gun violence is a significant risk to their children.

PROTECTING YOUR CHILD FROM VIOLENCE

Which brings us back to our basic dilemma. Given the widespread violence of contemporary life, how can you protect your child?

FOSTER GOOD SELF-ESTEEM

You can't personally transform the whole world from a violent place into one where peace and gentleness reign supreme; you can, however, make your own home a peaceful, gentle place. And the most crucial way to do so is to foster your child's self-esteem.

If your child believes that he is fundamentally good, lovable, and worthy of respect, his strong self-esteem will help to insulate him from violence. He'll be less susceptible to being bullied or pressured by peer groups. Children with low self-esteem and low confidence are much more likely to tolerate abusive behavior by bullies; as a consequence of their heightened need for social acceptance, they're more likely to imitate aggressive or hostile behavior. Confident, self-affirming children are more likely to follow an internal sense of right and wrong, and they're less likely to follow tyrannical leaders within their peer group.

A related issue is that children with high self-esteem and confidence are less likely to feel pent-up and angry, hence less prone to express frustrations through aggressive acts. They will more often trust people around them—parents, teachers, other adults, and peers—to hear their concerns and help them solve problems without resorting to violence.

ENCOURAGE GOOD PROBLEM SOLVING

From an early age, encourage your child to solve problems creatively. All children experience rivalries, misunderstandings, and other conflicts with others; however, their manner of solving these conflicts will differ depending on what they've learned from their parents and other adults. If your child learns that aggressive behavior isn't the proper way to solve conflicts, he'll be ahead of the game in dealing with the world. Emphasize the need to solve problems with brains, not brawn. Problem solving is a value that children must learn first and foremost from their parents. Help your child figure out ways to prevent fights by talking, compromising, and negotiating. Although teaching your own child good conflict resolution obviously won't solve the wider issues, it's an important contribution. Helping children to negotiate and settle differences without fighting is a primary way to decrease violence in peer groups.

ENCOURAGE YOUR SCHOOL TO IMPLEMENT CONFLICT-RESOLUTION PROGRAMS

Encourage your school or school district to implement seminars or workshops on communication, mediation, and conflict resolution. Education is paramount. Even if you're active in teaching your own child good conflict-resolution skills, the overall issues are community wide. Many children lack the proper role modeling to teach them good skills for social relationships; with parents often busy, indifferent, or entirely absent, these children don't adequately understand how to get along with others and celebrate each others' differences. Violence is a learned behavior. The more we can educate our children to relate to each other imaginatively, and the more we stress a zero-tolerance approach to prejudice, violence, and hate crimes, the less opportunity kids will have to imitate the aggressive, simplistic behavior they see around them.

LIMIT ACCESS TO VIOLENT GAMES AND PROGRAMMING

Parents should exert their authority to limit their children's viewing of violent TV, movies, and video games. There's no reason to let kids set their whole entertainment agenda. I don't advocate total prohibition of violent material; banning all contact with violent media can miss opportunities for crucial parent-child discussions. However, it's important to set age-appropriate limits consistent with your values. Especially if you have younger children, feel free to restrict access to violent shows and games regardless of what other parents are doing. The same may hold true if your child is experiencing a crisis (illness, disability, or the effects of parents divorcing) or if your child has trouble distinguishing between fantasy and reality.

PRACTICE GOOD GUN SAFETY

With more than 211 million firearms in U.S. homes, guns are unquestionably one of the greatest hazards to American children. My belief is that a home is safest if there are no guns present at all. People who keep guns in the home put themselves and their families at risk, particularly when the firearms are kept loaded and in an unsecured location. In 1995, for instance, there were 1,225 unintentional shooting fatalities in the United States, and many of the victims were children. I recommend that if you currently own guns, you consider disposing of them. If you are concerned about intruders, investigate home security systems. I am aware that guns are a sports-related fixture in many households, however, and that many responsible people feel that owning firearms contributes to their personal safety. That being said, I believe that good gun safety is a total obligation for responsible parents. If you must own guns, keep them properly stored—*unloaded, locked in a safe, with the ammunition locked in a separate place*—and make sure that there's no bullet left in the chamber.

INSIST THAT OTHER PARENTS PRACTICE GUN SAFETY, TOO

Even if you practice good gun safety, your child is at risk when other parents fail to do so. Not a week goes by without children dying as a result of gun-related accidents. Until recently, many American parents felt hesitant to inquire of other moms and dads regarding household gun safety, but now this situation is beginning to change. It's becoming more common and socially acceptable for parents to inquire among each other about this issue. I strongly urge you to make such inquiries part of your overview of your child's social scene. Some parents may take umbrage, but they shouldn't; they should feel reassured by your willingness to check. Just as you shouldn't be ashamed to make sure that your child will be visiting a household with a responsible parent at home, you shouldn't be ashamed to ask about this crucial element of safety.

Practice Good Risk Analysis

It's easy to lose track of the basic safety issues. In recent years, for instance, there's been widespread press about schoolyard shootings. The incidents have been horrific and inexcusable. However, focusing on these tragedies to the exclusion of other problems does everyone a disservice. In 1997, forty children died in schoolyard violence. During the same year, almost 1,225 children died in gun-related accidents. Another 9,000 died in auto accidents. No tragedy eliminates the horror and sadness of some other tragedy. My point, however, is legitimate: it's important to practice good risk analysis. If you lie awake worrying about your child's safety at school, for instance, but let him ride unrestrained in the family car, you focus on a small risk and ignore a far greater one.

Certain external risks, however, warrant close attention. If you feel that one of your child's fellow-students is behaving dangerously toward others, it's right and proper to flag the situation to the school authorities. Many schools (and some parents) neglect children's psychological health. There's a constant risk that parents will wait for someone else to intervene, thus delaying any effort to address the problem. Likewise, if you sense that your own child seems disturbed by violence—either as potential perpetrator or potential victim—you should take action. Typical warning signs:

- Your child indicates that he has either witnessed or heard about acts of violence at school or in the neighborhood.

- Your child acts excessively fearful, moody, withdrawn, aggressive, or edgy.

- Your child complains frequently of symptoms that seem psychosomatic.

- You believe that your child is involved with a high-risk peer group.

- Your child shows signs of abusing drugs or alcohol.

- You perceive other symptoms of depression, psychological trauma, or anxiety in your child.

- Your child has protracted or frequent outbursts of anger.

- You perceive that your child seems unable to stay in touch with reality.

If you feel that your child is at risk in any of these ways, consult a health care professional, counselor, or therapist. These signs may indicate other sorts of problems that warrant attention. This book's Resource Guide also lists sources of information including help lines, Web sites, and books. Don't try to deal with the issue alone. After discussing the situation with your physician or counselor, consider bringing the problem to the attention of your child's teacher, principal, or other school authorities.

KEEPING KIDS SAFE IN AN UNSAFE WORLD

Some years ago I asked a wise friend of mine—a writer who is the father of two grown sons—if he ever stopped worrying about his boys. "Hell, no," Sy told me. "I still lie awake wondering if they're okay." His answer shocked me. Sy was almost eighty at the time; his sons must have been in their forties. Yet his words made sense. "Once you're a parent," he went on, "you're always a parent. Period. I don't care if you reach a hundred and your kids are in their seventies. You never stop wondering and worrying. It just goes with the territory."

He's right. There's no way around it. The tasks of raising children may change and diminish, but the commitment to being concerned lasts forever. One of the greatest, hardest tasks that parents have always undertaken is to protect their children. The world has always had elements of danger. The issues may have shifted during our unpredictable times, but the core dilemma remains the same.

How should you keep your kids safe in a potentially unsafe world? I'd give anything if I could tell you—or myself—the answer to that question. Lacking the perfect response, though, I'd say this: Trust yourself. Follow your hunches. Listen to the wisest, most thoughtful people around you. And love your child unconditionally. If your child knows and trusts your love—and can respect the limits you set—he will gain a confidence, self-control, and resilience that will protect him throughout his journey through life better than anything else you could provide.

FIFTY-FIVE

WORK-TO-HOME TRANSITIONS

Many PARENTS TELL me that they feel as if they have two selves: a work self and a home self. They perform a certain set of duties and tasks in the workplace, then shift to another set of duties and tasks when they rejoin their family. The transition often creates a daily jolt. It's a common problem—one that many Americans find unnerving—and the problem has several separate solutions.

DEALING WITH HUNGER AND FATIGUE

It may sound simplistic, but dealing with late-day hunger and fatigue is a big issue, and not just for children but for adults as well. How do you get from the end of school and work to a calmer place? Many factors may help, but rule one is to avoid hypoglycemic burnout (low blood sugar). Many parent-child conflicts are caused—or at least aggravated—by plain old hunger. So by all means have some snacks in the car for both yourself and your children when you pick them up. Sandwiches and fruit are good options. Sugary snacks are less ideal, though some kinds of cookies and crackers may be perfectly acceptable. The main goal is to prevent your kids from running out of steam.

THE WORK/HOME TANGLE

Many people find it difficult to separate work and home life. Returning home to your family, it's easy to brood about everything you've left undone at work. Once you're back at work, it's just as easy to obsess about the endless tasks of family life. This state of mind is understandable in many ways; you can't help but ponder your many roles simultaneously. There are always deadlines, problems, and crises. There will always be some worries about what remains to be done. It's hard to slow down the wheels and disengage from the issues of the day. Even so, it's important not to obsess unnecessarily. Focus on the present. Prioritize. Keep a notepad or calendar to keep track of important tasks. Delegate whenever possible. However, try not to do everything at once; it's a sure route to stress and may not solve your problems anyway.

PERSONALITY ISSUES AT WORK

It's hard to detach from people problems. It's hard to keep work relationships in balance because they matter and they unquestionably affect you. But remember, work isn't a substitute for family. Your co-workers are precisely that: people you work with. They may also be friends—even close friends—and your commitment to them matters, but less profoundly than your bond to your family members. You can certainly take their assessment of you personally, but their opinions and needs shouldn't have the same level of meaning as those of the people you're closest and most committed to. Keep the situation in perspective. The job is a job. It's not your whole life. This is easier said than done, I know. But when you transfer work anxieties to your home, the result can wreak havoc with the rest of your life. Don't give the people at work too much psychological power over the rest of your life.

LOWER YOUR STANDARDS

Simplify whatever you can. Don't set impossibly high standards. It's fine to own a pretty house; it's enjoyable to have an attractive yard; it's fun to cook a fancy meal now and then. But forget about celebrity mavens of perfect home-keeping and gourmet cooking who may inspire dreams (nightmares?) of greater domestic glory.

KEEP FOOD SIMPLE

Cook in batches; freeze portions for later use. Don't fix complex meals if you don't have time. Don't feel guilty about using frozen or instant meals. Resort to fast food now and then—though it isn't ideal, you're better off salvaging your sanity than fretting about the occasional McBurger.

EASE UP ON REGIMENTED BATHTIMES

If your children are past toddlerhood, they'll be fine with a bath every couple of days except in hot weather or when they're playing sports. A nightly bath may not be necessary. (In winter, children's skin may suffer from excessive dryness anyway.)

PACE YOURSELF ON HOMEWORK

Your kids may be better off leaving homework until after dinner; they may be too hungry and wound up earlier. Although homework is important, many children can't do their assignments without at least intermittent parental involvement. Consider postponing homework until the kids are fed and more relaxed. Some kids can finish their work in the morning. If your child is too tired to do a particular assignment, write a note to the teacher requesting more time.

DON'T GO OVERBOARD ON TELEVISION

Allow kids to watch some TV. If you make it taboo, watching TV is precisely what they'll crave. The same holds for video games. (For a longer discussion of these issues, see chapter 29, "The Media," and chapter 7, "Computers and Kids.") At the same time, feel free to set limits when needed.

INTERACT WITH YOUR KIDS

Many parents avoid involvement with their children during the bumpy late-afternoon/early-evening hours. It's not hard to see why. Everyone is tired; the kids are cranky; people have differing, often conflicting, needs. It's tempting to shunt the kids aside to the TV or to ignore them altogether. This may be a big mistake, however, especially if the procedure becomes habitual. Your children may have school experiences they need to discuss with you. They may simply want to be held or comforted. How can you size up the situation and proceed creatively?

If family tensions run high, use a procedure I call HALT. HALT is an acronym that prompts you to ask, "Am I hungry, angry, lonely, or tired?" You can use this procedure to scan your own state of mind, and you can use it on your kids, too. Are they hungry? Are they angry? Are they lonely? Are they tired? In short, what's going on with them? Sometimes you know something's wrong, but you're not sure what. HALT can help you diagnose the situation. Did they have a difficult, stressful time at school? Are they not feeling well, or are they just fatigued because they're stressed out? If you can size up the situation objectively, you're ahead of the game. You won't take children's emotional outbursts or fussiness so personally, and you'll have a better chance to solve the problems facing you.

Your kids may need attention without even knowing it. Sometimes chaotic or obnoxious behavior is simply an ineffective way of asking for reassurance.

With younger children, simply offer a hug or a lap to sit on, offer them cookies and milk, or give them a warm bath. Anything that calms them down will help. Older children probably won't ask outright for parental comfort; you may have to say, "Come over here. What happened today at school?" or "Please get off the computer for a while so we can hang out together." Keep them company. Older kids often need attention as much as little kids. They may resist at first, but if you make it a routine to talk and process the day, they'll get used to it. They may not let you know it, but this ritual will help them feel cared for and loved. Kids need your undivided attention, so carve out blocks of privacy and solitude to be there for them.

USE TECHNOLOGY (CAREFULLY)

Although high technology is a mixed blessing—something that can complicate rather than simplify your life—judicious use of gadgetry can ease stress.

USE AN ANSWERING MACHINE

This is almost inevitable nowadays. Make it your electronic butler. Screen calls. Weed out the marketing reps. Ignore anyone else whose requests aren't crucial. Let your friends know in advance that you're rarely available at certain hours; they're almost sure to be sympathetic.

USE A CAR PHONE

Car phones, too, are becoming almost a given. However, phones can become a slippery slope because overuse of this technology means you're never "away"; people can always find you. In addition, phone use in cars apparently leads to a higher rate of accidents. Even so, having a car phone can ease anxiety and stress if you're concerned about your child's whereabouts, pickup times, road emergencies, and so forth. A crucial compromise: If at all possible, avoid driving and using the phone at the same time.

GET A BEEPER

This is an inexpensive solution to several problems. Your child or the school can reach you easily, which is reassuring, especially if your work keeps you in constant motion.

PLAN AHEAD

Family life is so hectic that often it's hard to do more than simply stumble from one obligation to another. There's a risk, too, in getting too obsessed with controlling the upheaval. Surely there's a happy medium. What I recommend, generally speaking, is pow-wows on weekends to plan ahead. Try to include the children in these discussions whenever possible.

The key issue here is distributing obligations. It's deadly for either parent to feel that he or she must do everything, or even all of any one thing. Obviously each family will have to find its own balance point. In a perfect world, the weight would fall evenly on two parents' shoulders; in reality, it's going to be far more unpredictable. It's important to talk things out.

- Figure out what needs to be done.

- Decide who's available.

- Parcel out tasks.

- Sort through the consequences of these "assignments."

- Trade off tasks, if possible.

- Be flexible, understanding, and nonaccusatory.

- Try to factor in some R&R—ideally, both time together and time apart.

- Make a schedule.

- Be ready to turn on a dime if things don't work out as planned.

- Keep talking about what needs to be done, how you feel about the situation, and so forth.

- Don't let resentments fester.

- Tinker with your plans and procedures as time passes.

GIVE KIDS RESPONSIBILITY

Children need responsibility; they love to be involved and needed. When your child is old enough, let him help you shop, plan a meal, set the table, take out the trash, or feed the dog. Don't be rigid about chores, but don't hesitate to assign them. Emphasize that you're all working together. Give them plenty of positive reinforcement for helping you. All too often, children don't get asked to help out in the home. This situation is all too permissive and ignores several opportunities—for children to learn domestic skills, to take on responsibility, to see family life as a common endeavor, and to take pride in work well done. Some children, however, are given too much responsibility and feel burdened by a parental role. Both extremes are unfortunate. Find the happy medium.

MAINTAIN A FLEXIBLE ATTITUDE

If you can't solve a problem, perhaps you can change your attitude about it.

- Be flexible about your plan—don't expect a particular outcome.
- Keep your sense of humor.
- Recognize that adulthood is a state of being able to adapt, cope, and adjust.
- Admit that life isn't perfect. Sometimes things won't be easy or fun; sometimes the best you can do is muddle through.

INDULGE YOURSELF

Last but not least, try to indulge yourself again. A little TLC after the kids are fed, bathed, and put to bed can do wonders for your body, mind, and soul. It doesn't have to be elaborate. Just soothe yourself a little. Have a bubble bath. Do some exercise. Call a friend. Walk the dog. Read a good book. Have something special to eat. Take a nap or meditate.

Your home should be an oasis—a place where you can wind down, relax, and decompress. Take care of yourself so you can take care of your kids as well as possible.

THE DAYS ARE LONG BUT THE YEARS ARE SHORT

PARENTS OFTEN ASK me if there's a key to successful parenting—an essence of insight and skill that makes parenthood easier and more effective. The short answer: no. The tasks of raising children are so various, so complex, so subtle, and so protracted that they can't be reduced to a single key or essence. Even a long book like *The Parenting Survival Kit*, with nearly five dozen chapters and hundreds of subtopics, can only begin to address the intricacy of its subject. Of course I can't help wishing that I *did* know the secret essence of parenthood—if nothing else, it would make my own life easier!—but so far that discovery has eluded me.

In concluding this book, however, I'd like to offer some final reflections that I've found useful both in my own efforts as a mother and in discussing parenthood with other parents. I'm not in any way providing these reflections as "Seven Easy Tips to Better Parenting." Rather, I intend them merely as lenses that you can look through and, I hope, use to perceive yourself and your children more clearly.

TRUST YOURSELF

These words echo the fundamental advice of this century's preeminent parenting expert, Dr. Benjamin Spock: "You know more than you think you do." Your judgment is basically good. You have a fundamental desire to be a good parent. You probably have a better grasp of parenting issues than you imagine. Although parenting skills are learned rather than innate, you have almost certainly acquired a substantial amount of parenting "lore" over the years. In addition, you know yourself and your child better than anyone else. This knowledge, combined with your capacity to learn and grow, will serve you well throughout the parenting years. Confidence in your abilities and goals will be one of the most valuable gifts you can give yourself and your child.

ACCEPT YOUR OWN IMPERFECTIONS

Don't expect to be a flawless parent. On the contrary, accept your own human imperfections. Being a parent means making one mistake after another. There's no way around it; the tasks of parenthood simply don't lend themselves to precision, and much of what takes place throughout day-to-day family life is inherently sloppy, messy, and ambiguous. Mistakes go with the turf. In fact, mistakes are a *necessary* part of the process. Sometimes you have to make a mistake before you can learn; it's precisely from your mistakes that you see what needs to be done. Fortunately, children are flexible creatures—durable, resilient, and forgiving. Do the best you can, keep learning, and accept your kids' own imperfections in turn.

ASK FOR HELP WHEN NECESSARY

Trusting yourself and accepting your imperfections doesn't mean you have to proceed alone. Precisely because parenthood is so demanding, difficult, and protracted, you can benefit from others' experience and wisdom. Your own parents, siblings, relatives, and friends may be useful resources of information and reassurance. In addition, many other resources exist to help you survive and thrive during the parenting years. Books, parenting support groups, and parent-educators can be supremely reassuring and helpful as you work through the stages of parenthood. Find the support you need.

ACCEPT YOUR CHILD AS UNIQUE

Precisely because every human being is one-of-a-kind, your child will have individual needs, interests, capabilities, tastes, and shortcomings that influence his development. To complicate matters, every parent is also unique, with specific talents, experiences, personal history, abilities, flaws, and virtues. The combination of the child's individuality with the parent's individuality results in a complex, unpredictable interaction. It's tempting to let your expectations or preferences guide the process of parenthood. To some extent, these expectations or preferences are appropriate; part of being a parent is following your sense of what's right and good. Keep your child's uniqueness in mind, however. He will ultimately develop into who he is, not who you (or anyone else) believes he ought to be.

PERCEIVE PARENTHOOD AS A DANCE

The process of parenthood isn't linear; neither is it a consistent progression. The cliché about taking one step forward, two steps back, is never truer than when dealing with parenthood. As children develop, there's almost always a regression before a progression; kids often hunker down and "retreat" to an earlier stage of behavior before moving forward to acquire new skills.

In many respects, the most useful metaphor in describing parenthood is to perceive it as a dance. Dancing isn't linear, yet every style of dance has its own order, its own rules and rhythms. Not only that: dancing is a partnership. Dance partners work together, yet each has a different role. In the dance of parenthood, sometimes the parent leads, sometimes the child. The dance can be smooth and graceful, with parent and child in harmony. The dance can also be awkward—the partners out of step, stumbling over each other's feet—and that's frustrating but normal. Even the most accomplished dancers can't always be graceful or harmonious. How should you respond? Just enjoy the process. You'll be in tune most of the time, and you'll learn the steps as you go.

EXPECT TO BE CHANGED

Few experiences can be as challenging and transforming as parenthood. My sense of things is that most people are significantly, even radically, changed by the parenting years. Generally the change is positive: Men and women become kinder, more generous, more thoughtful, more flexible, and more imaginative as a consequence of being parents. It's true that the consequences for some people are negative; parenthood can be burdensome, even destructive, under certain circumstances. Even so, I'd say that most parents end up better and more substantial human beings as a result of raising children. However, even when the outcome is happy, the process can be strenuous and frustrating. Change isn't easy for any of us. Parents, like children, can suffer growing pains. But the transformations that the parenting years can create may well end up among the most powerful experiences of your life. Brace yourself—then prepare to become more than you were before. By being a parent, you'll probably learn as much about yourself as you learn about your child. Parents and children inspire, guide, and teach one another.

SAVOR THE MOMENT

Above all, value what you have. Many parenting tasks are difficult, and some are tedious and frustrating, so it's understandable that certain days seem to grind on and on; still, the whole span of raising a child will pass with breathtaking speed. As an old saying puts it, "The days are long but the years are short." The child who so recently learned to walk will be off to college before you can imagine. Savor the moment. Experience every aspect of parenthood as fully as possible. Watch your child closely; listen carefully; open your heart to who he is and what he feels. To look after your child with love, laughter, and wonder as you watch yourself and your child grow—what could be more challenging, exhilarating, and fulfilling?

RESOURCE GUIDE

A COMMON SOURCE of frustration throughout the parenting years is a feeling that you have to solve a problem on your own. Even the most competent mom or dad can feel demoralized and exhausted by a sense of isolation. Fortunately, an increasing number of resources can help you with the problems you face. Sometimes what you need is a specific answer to a specific question; at other times, it's a general sense of solidarity with other parents. Finding resources takes some effort; but in some respects the task of finding information about parenthood is getting easier, not harder, as the years pass.

This section of *The Parenthood Survival Kit* therefore serves to bring possible resources to your attention. I've categorized the listings carefully; however, some organizations' services overlap, so please check the whole list to make sure you aren't missing a good source of help. Also, note that some resources are clearinghouse or umbrella organizations, not direct providers of services. They won't provide direct services to you, but they can inform you of specific agencies or groups that offer such services in your community.

The Resource Guide contains three sections:

- Organizations and Associations
- On-Line Information
- Further Reading

ORGANIZATIONS AND ASSOCIATIONS

A large number of organizations can provide useful information on specific issues and problems that may arise during the parenting years. These organizations usually focus on a problem or cluster of problems rather than more general tasks of parenthood. Here's a sampling, presented in alphabetical order by general category:

ALCOHOL AND DRUG ABUSE

American Council for Drug Education
164 West 74th Street
New York, NY 10023
212.758.8060 or 800.488.DRUG

Center for Substance Abuse Treatment
Information and Treatment Referral Hotline
11426-28 Rockville Pike, Suite 410
Rockville, MD 20852
800.662.HELP

CoAnon Family Groups
P.O. Box 64742-66
Los Angeles, CA 90064
310.859.2206

Cocaine Anonymous
3740 Overland Avenue, Suite G
Los Angeles, CA 90034
213.559.5833 or 800.347.8998

Hazelden Foundation
Pleasant Valley Road
P.O. Box 176
Center City, MN 55012
800.328.9000

Nar-Anon Family Groups
P.O. Box 2562
Palos Verdes Peninsula, CA 90274
310.547.5800

Narcotics Anonymous
P.O. Box 9999
Van Nuys, CA 91409
818.780.3951

National Clearinghouse for Alcohol and Drug Information
P.O. Box 2345
Rockville, MD 20847-2345
301.468.2600 or 800.729.6686

National Council on Alcoholism and Drug Dependence
12 West 21st Street, 7th Floor
New York, NY 10010
800.622.2255

National Council on Alcoholism, Inc.
12 West 21st Street
New York, NY 10010
212.206.6770

National Families in Action
2296 Henderson Mill Road, Suite 300
Atlanta, GA 30345
404.934.6364

CHILD ABUSE

American Professional Society on the Abuse of Children
407 South Dearborn Street, Suite 1300
Chicago, IL 60605-1111
312.554.0166

National Committee for the Prevention of Child Abuse
P.O. Box 2866
Chicago, IL 60690
312.663.3520

CHILD CARE

National Association of Child Care Resource and Referral Agencies
1319 F Street, N.W., Suite 810
Washington, DC 20004-1106
202.393.5501

National Child Care Association
1029 Railroad Street, N.W.
Conyers, GA 30207-5275
800.543.7161

CHILD SAFETY

National Child Passenger Safety Association
P.O. Box 841
Ardmore, PA 19003
215.525.4610

National SAFE KIDS Campaign
111 Michigan Avenue, N.W.
Washington, DC 20010-2970
202.939.4993

EDUCATIONAL ISSUES

Bank Street College
610 West 112th Street
New York, NY 10025
800.727.7243

Work and Family Life
6211 West Howard Street
Chicago, IL 60648

EXCEPTIONAL CHILDREN

Association for Children and Adults with Learning Disabilities
4156 Library Road
Pittsburgh, PA 15234
412.341.8077

Council for Exceptional Children
1920 Association Drive
Reston, VA 22091-1589
703.620.3660

Dyslexia Research Foundation
600 Northern Boulevard
Great Neck, NY 11021
516.482.2888

National Center for Learning Disabilities, Inc.
99 Park Avenue, 6th Floor
New York, NY 10016
212.687.7211

FOOD AND NUTRITION

Bulimia Anorexia Self-Help, Inc.
522 North New Ballas Road
St. Louis, MO 63141
314.567.4080

National Association for Anorexia Nervosa and Associated Disorders
P.O. Box 7
Highland Park, IL 60035
708.831.3438

HEALTH ISSUES

American Academy of Pediatrics
141 Northwest Point Boulevard
P.O. Box 927
Elkgrove Village, IL 60009-0927
847.228.5005 or 800.433.9016

American Cancer Society
1599 Clifton Road, N.E.
Atlanta, GA 30329
404.320.3333 or 800.ACS.2345

American Diabetes Association
National Center
P.O. Box 25757
1660 Duke Street
Alexandria, VA 22314
703.549.1500 or 800.ADA.DISC

American Foundation for the Blind
15 West 16th Street
New York, NY 10011
212.620.2000

American Heart Association
7272 Greenville Avenue
Dallas, TX 75231-4596
214.373.6300 or 800.242.1793

The Arthritis Foundation
67 Irving Place, 2nd Floor
New York, NY 10003
212.477.8700

Cancer Care, Inc.
1180 Avenue of the Americas
New York, NY 10036
212.221.3300

Cancer Information Service
Office of Cancer Communication
NCI, Building 31, 10A07
9000 Rockville Pike
Bethesda, MD 20890
800.4CANCER

Multiple Sclerosis National Society
733 Third Avenue
New York, NY 10017-3288
800.344.4867

National Head Injury Foundation
1776 Massachusetts Avenue, N.W., Suite 100
Washington, DC 20036
800.444.6443

National Kidney Foundation
30 East 33rd Street
New York, NY 10016
800.622.9010

LOSS AND BEREAVEMENT

Accord Aftercare Services
1930 Bishop Lane, Suite 947
Louisville, KY 40218
800.346.3087

Center for Death Education and Research
Department of Sociology
909 Social Science Building
267 Nineteenth Avenue South
University of Minnesota
Minneapolis, MN 55455-0412

The Compassionate Friends
P.O. Box 3696
Oak Brook, IL 60522-3696
708.990.0010

MARRIAGE AND RELATIONSHIPS

Academy of Family Mediators
4 Militia Drive
Lexington, MA 02173
617.674.2663

American Association for Marriage and Family Therapy
1133 Fifteenth Street, N.W., Suite 300
Washington, DC 20005
202.452.0109

Association for Marriage and Family Therapy
800.374.2638

MEDIA

Action for Children's Television (ACT)
10 University Road
Cambridge, MA 02138
617.876.6620

MENTAL HEALTH ISSUES

American Association of Psychiatric Services for Children
1200-C Scottsville Road
Rochester, NY 14624
716.236.6910

SANDWICH GENERATION/CARE OF THE AGING

American Senior Citizens Association
P.O. Box 41
Fayetteville, NC 28302
919.323.3641

Children of Aging Parents
Woodbourne Office Campus, Suite 302A
1609 Woodbourne Road
Levittown, PA 19057-1511

215.945.6900 or 800.CAPS.294

SELF-HELP

National Self-Help Clearinghouse
Graduate School and University Center
City University of New York
25 West 42nd Street, Suite 620
New York, NY 10036
212.354.8525

SINGLE PARENTHOOD

Parents Without Partners
401 North Michigan Avenue
Chicago, IL 60611-4267
312.644.6610 or 800.637.7974

Single Parents Association
602.758.5511 or 800.704.2102

STEP-PARENTHOOD

Step Family Association of America
650 J Street, Suite 205
Lincoln, NE 68508
800.735.0329

STRESS

Parental Stress Line
800.632.8188

VIOLENCE

Educational Fund to End Handgun Violence
110 Maryland Avenue, N.E., Box 72
Washington, DC 20002
202.544.7227

National Domestic Violence Hotline
800.799.SAFE

National Organization for Victim Assistance
1757 Park Road, N.W.
Washington, DC 20010
202.232.6682

ON-LINE INFORMATION

As in other aspects of contemporary life, computer on-line services have increased our options for obtaining information on any of the issues listed above. That's the good news. The bad news is that the sources of information change often and unpredictably. (Even the means of contacting sources—that is, the particular on-line services for accessing particular databases—are in constant flux.) Although what follows is a list of specific on-line resources for parents, keep in mind that any list of resources will change over time. In addition, the quality of what's available varies from genuinely useful to gimmicky and shallow.

Here's a general overview of on-line information and how it may help you in dealing with issues of parenthood.

ON-LINE SERVICES

Commercial on-line services often have resources you can access to obtain information or find support. Typical services are *databases, bulletin boards*, and *discussion groups*. Databases are compilations of data on one or more subjects accessible by computer. Bulletin boards are electronic listings of topics, subtopics, and responses. Discussion groups (sometimes called "chat rooms") are real-time interactions between on-line participants. At the time of this writing, for instance, CompuServe, America Online, and Prodigy all have services of these several sorts. An example: Within its "Moms Online" area, America Online has resources that focus on parenthood; CompuServe and Prodigy have similar bulletin boards. In addition, each of these services can provide access to health-related databases with information about specific illnesses, caregiving resources, and other data that you may find useful.

THE INTERNET

You can also find information on the Internet. Most commercial on-line services provide either limited or complete Internet access; check your users' manual or on-line users' information for details. Direct Internet access through Netscape or other access software will serve the same purpose. Either way, you can obtain information or join Internet discussion groups on a wide variety of topics. People coping with many illnesses, for instance, have their own bulletin boards to share information and offer mutual support.

E-MAIL

Finally, electronic mail can provide a sense of contact with friends and relatives that can help to relieve the stress and isolation that's common during the parenting years. E-mail can be especially convenient, too, if you need to contact a number of people with the same message: for instance, you can send identical, simultaneous messages to any of your relatives who are also on-line.

SPECIFIC WEB SITES REGARDING PARENTHOOD

Here's a selection of Web sites that focus on parenting issues. With the exception of the first, most general heading—general parenting issues—I've organized these sites alphabetically by category and within each category.

General Parenting Issues

www.abcparenting.com
   Essentially a search engine for Web sites on parenting issues: pregnancy, parenting, and family life.

www.familyeducation.com
   Established by the FamilyEducation Network, this site provides educational information, with specific focus on issues as diverse as toddler behavior, home schooling, and learning disabilities.

www.parenthoodweb.com
   A libarary of articles covering many issues, including preganancy, children's products, and expert advice.

www.parent.net
   Information for parents on a wide variety of topics.

www.parents.com
   Parenting information from the publishers of *Parents*, *Child*, *Family Circle*, and *McCall's* magazines.

www.parentsoup.com
   Information, features, and on-line discussion groups.

www.parentsplace.com
   A "parents-helping-parents" community that offers advice, interactive tools, and firsthand wisdom from real parents; topics include infertility, illness, and bereavement.

www.parentzone.com
   A compendium of information on health, pets, home improvement, developmental stages, and parental interaction.

www.wholefamily.com
   A clinical psychologist's insights into marriage, teens, and parenting issues.

Attachment and Bonding

www.attach-bond.com
   A Web site intended to "help parents and professionals learn more about attachment parenting, . . . attachment disorder, bonding problems, adoption difficulties, attachment therapy," and other related issues.

www.focis.com
   Sponsored by the Foster Care Information Service in London, Ontario, this Web site has a good reading list of books regarding attachment and bonding.

Attention Deficit and Hyperactivity Disorder (ADHD)

www.oneaddplace.com
    Information, calendar of events, products, and professional services relevant to ADHD.

Computers

www.getnetwise.org
    Information and resources for parents regarding the Internet, including information on Internet safety.

www.netparents.org
    A source of information similar to getnetwise above.

www.safesurf.com
    The Web site for a group that's working to create an Internet rating standard for browsers.

www.thelist.com
    A list of Internet service providers (ISPs)—on-line "gateways" to the Internet.

www.worldvillage.com
    "Family Safe Software"—a list of 300 game, educational, and multimedia software programs.

Divorce

www.divorceinfo.com
    A detailed, text-intensive Web site designed to "help you survive your divorce."

www.divorcenet.com
    An extensive Web site with state-by-state resource centers, interactive bulletin boards, a "reading room," and other resources regarding divorce issues.

Exceptional Children

www.familyvillage.wisc.edu/tindex.htm/
    This site is "a global community of disability-related resources."

FATHERS

www.acfc.org
   The Web site for the American Coalition for Fathers and Children, a national fathers' rights advocacy group.

www.fathers4kids.org
   Multinational resources provided by the National Fathers' Resource Center, a fathers' rights advocacy group.

www.fathersworld.com
   A virtual community for men interested in fathers' issues, including balancing work and family.

www.slowlane.com
   "The online resource for stay-at-home dads."

FINANCIAL PLANNING

http://lifenet.com/
   A site with interactive calculators and other information to help guide you through major financial life events.

http://update.wsj.com/
   Continually updated information on markets, business, and investing, from *The Wall Street Journal*.

www.cheapsk8.com
   An on-line newsletter on living well on little money.

www.financenter.com
   A site providing information on buying a house, leasing a car, or paying an installment loan.

www.hoovers.com
   A guide for consumers and business professionals; provides data on companies.

www.wife.org
   A financial-planning Web site for women, sponsored by the Women's Institute for Financial Education.

FOOD

www.nalusda.gov/fnic/
   Data on healthful nutrition for children age two and older.

GIRLS

www.girlgamesinc.com
A monthly on-line newsletter for girls, featuring current events, women and girls' issues, and "herstory."

www.planetgirl.com
Fashion, beauty, sports, health, around the planet, entertainment and arts.

HEALTH ISSUES

http://KidsHealth.org/
Tips on keeping children healthy or helping them when they're sick.

www.drs4kids.com/
A pediatrician's information on topics concerning infants, children, and adolescents.

www.health.org
Information for children and adults about alcohol, drugs, and tobacco use and other health issues.

www.healthtouch.com/
Information on health, wellness, and illness.

www.kidsource.com
Information on education, health care, and product information for parents and children.

www.menninger.edu
An educational Web site sponsored by the Menninger Child and Family Center intended to spread useful information about psychiatric issues regarding children.

www.nejm.org
A weekly on-line version of the *New England Journal of Medicine*, with reports on important medical topics.

www.pslgroup.com/Docguide.htm
Medical news, literature, and alerts drawn from the Web's medical resources.

LOSS AND BEREAVEMENT

www.growthhouse.org
This site includes detailed information on family bereavement, helping children with illness and grief, the aftermath of miscarriage and stillbirth, and resources for the bereaved.

OLDER PARENTS

www.midlifemommies.com
  Intended for women who have children relatively late, this site includes information on mid-life pregnancy, financial issues, and the tasks of the "sandwich generation."

SCHOOL AND RELATED ISSUES

www.inetcom.net/inet/resource/K12/
  A parent help line with information about preschool education and its benefits.

SINGLE PARENTS

www.parentswithoutpartners.org
  A site for single parents with varied information.

www.singleparents.org
  A similar Web site maintained by a smaller organization.

www.singlerose.com
  Resources for single mothers.

TEENAGERS

www.education.indiana.edu/cas/adol/adol.html
  On-line support for teenagers, parents, and counselors, with a guide to various resources for teens.

www.jayi.com/so
  A thoughtful, challenging e-zine for teens.

www.parentingteens.com
  Varied information for parents on topics relevant to adolescence.

www.react.com
  A teen news, sports, and entertainment e-zine.

TRIPS AND VACATIONS

www.travelsource.com/index.html
  Resources on destinations, modes of travel, prices, etc.

www.cdc.gov/travel/travel.html
   The Centers for Disease Control's information about health issues world-wide, with data on recommended precautions and vaccinations.

www.channel1.com/users/brosius
   Information about campgrounds nationwide.

www.cntraveler.com
   The *Conde Nast Traveler* magazine's data on travel sites.

www.mapquest.com/
   An interactive atlas and map Web site.

www.nps.gov
   Detailed information on all U.S. national parks.

Violence

www.fvpf.org/fund/
   Information on domestic violence, prevention, and public policy reform.

www.gunfree.org
   A gun-control advocacy group with information about gun-control legislation and safety issues.

www.handguncontrol.org
   A lobbying group concerned with legislation on handgun safety and legislation.

Women's Issues

www.aauw.org
   Web site for the American Association of University Women, which is an advocacy group for women's and girls' issues in education.

www.academic.org
   Information for parents interested in bolstering their daughters' education.

ww.best.com/sirlouwmhp.html
   Current medical information and recent publications focusing on women's health.

www.uvol.com/woman/
   A newsletter focusing on issues of interest to women, including relationships, finances, parenting, fitness, and self-improvement.

www.women.com/
   Miscellaneous information of interest to women.

FURTHER READING

Books about parenthood have been part of American culture for about a hundred years, and the number and variety have increased almost exponentially since the publication of Benjamin Spock's *Baby and Child Care* in the 1950s. Any big American bookstore now contains hundreds, if not thousands, of parenting books. The catch: finding the information you need. Here's a selection of classic and current books on parenthood that covers most of the topics discussed in this book.

ATTACHMENT AND BONDING

Ainsworth, M. D. S., et al. *Patterns of Attachment: A Psychological Study of the Strange Situation.* Hillsdale, N.J.: Erlbaum, 1978.

Bowlby, John. *Attachment and Loss.* Vol. 1: *Attachment.* New York: Basic Books, 1969.

———. *Attachment and Loss.* Vol. 2: *Separation.* New York: Basic Books, 1973.

Klaus, Marshall, and Phyllis Klaus. *Parent-Infant Bonding.* St. Louis: Mosby, 1982.

BEHAVIOR AND CHILD DEVELOPMENT

Ames, Louise Bates. *Your One-Year-Old.* New York: Delacorte Press, 1982.

———. *Your Two-Year-Old.* New York: Delacorte Press, 1982.

———. *Your Three-Year-Old.* New York: Delacorte Press, 1982.

———. *Your Four-Year-Old.* New York: Delacorte Press, 1982.

———. *Your Five-Year-Old.* New York: Delacorte Press, 1982.

———. *Your Six-Year-Old.* New York: Delacorte Press, 1982.

———. *Your Seven-Year-Old.* New York: Delacorte Press, 1982.

———. *Your Eight-Year-Old.* New York: Delacorte Press, 1982.

———. *Your Nine-Year-Old.* New York: Delacorte Press, 1982.

———. *Your Ten- to Fourteen-Year-Old.* New York: Delacorte Press, 1982.

Ames, Louise Bates, et al. *The Gesell Institute's Child from One to Six: Evaluating the Behavior of the Preschool Child.* New York: Harper & Row, 1979.

Brazelton, T. Berry. *Infants and Mothers: Differences in Development.* New York: Delacorte Press/Lawrence, 1994.

———. *Touchpoints: The Essential Reference.* New York: Addison Wesley, 1992.

Brazelton, T. Berry, and Bertrand G. Cramer. *The Earliest Relationship: Parents, Infants, and the Drama of Early Attachment.* Reading, Mass.: Addison Wesley, 1990.

The Editors of *Parents* Magazine. *The Parents Answer Book: From Birth through Age Five.* New York: Golden Books, 1998.

Gesell, Arnold, et al. *The Child from Five to Ten*. New York: Harper & Row, 1977.

Gesell, Arnold, et al. *Youth: The Years from Teen to Sixteen*. New York: Harper & Row, 1977.

Greenspan, Stanley, and Nancy Thorndike Greenspan. *First Feelings: Milestones in the Emotional Development of Your Baby and Child*. New York: Viking, 1985.

Kagan, Jerome. *The Growth of the Child: Reflections on Human Development*. New York: W. W. Norton, 1978.

———. *The Nature of the Child*. New York: Basic Books, 1984.

Klaus, Marshall, and Phyllis Klaus. *Your Amazing Newborn*. New York: Perseus Books, 1998.

Leach, Penelope. *Babyhood: Stage by Stage from Birth to Age Two*. New York: Alfred A. Knopf, 1976.

———. *Your Baby and Child: From Birth to Age Five*. New York: Alfred A. Knopf, 1997.

———. *Your Growing Child: From Babyhood through Adolescence*. New York: Alfred A. Knopf, 1986.

Spock, Benjamin, and Steven J. Parker. *Dr. Spock's Baby and Child Care*. New York: Pocket Books, 1998.

BOYS

Abbott, Franklin, ed. *Boyhood: Growing Up Male*. Freedom, Calif.: The Crossing Press, 1993.

Bassoff, Evelyn. *Between Mothers and Sons: The Making of Vital and Loving Men*. New York: Dutton, 1994.

Blankenhorn, David. *Fatherless America: Confronting Our Most Urgent Social Problem*. New York: Basic Books, 1995.

Gurian, Michael. *A Fine Young Man: What Parents, Mentors, and Educators Can Do to Shape Adolescent Boys into Exceptional Men*. New York: Tarcher/Putnam, 1997.

———. *The Wonder of Boys: What Parents, Mentors, and Educators Can Do to Shape Boys into Exceptional Men*. New York: Tarcher/Putnam, 1997.

Miedzian, Myriam. *Boys Will Be Boys: Breaking the Link between Masculinity and Violence*. New York: Anchor Books, 1991.

Moore, Sheila, and Roon Frost. *The Little Boy Book: A Guide to the First Eight Years*. New York: Ballantine Books, 1998.

Olsen, Paul. *Sons and Mothers: Why Men Behave As They Do*. New York: M. Evans, 1981.

Phillips, Angela. *The Trouble with Boys: A Wise and Sympathetic Guide to the Risky Business of Raising Sons*. New York: Basic Books, 1994.

Pollack, William S. *Real Boys: Rescuing Our Sons from the Myths of Boyhood*. New York: Random House, 1998.

CHILD DEVELOPMENT

Erickson, Erik. *Childhood and Society*. New York: W. W. Norton, 1950.
Erickson, Erik. *Identity and the Life Cycle*. New York: International Universities Press, 1959.
Piaget, Jean. *The Construction of Reality in the Child*. New York: Basic Books, 1954.
Piaget, Jean. *Play, Dream, and Imitation in the Child*. New York: W. W. Norton, 1962.
Piaget, Jean. *The Child's Construction of the World*. Totowa, N.J.: Littlefield, Adams, 1967.

COMMUNICATION BETWEEN PARENTS AND KIDS

Elkind, David. *Parenting Your Teenager*. New York: Ballantine Books, 1983.
Faber, Adele, and Elaine Mazlesch. *How to Listen So Kids Will Talk*. New York: Avon Books, 1982.
Frayberg, Selma. *The Magic Years: Understanding and Handling the Problems of Early Childhood*. New York: Fireside, 1996.
Ginott, Haim G. *Between Parent and Child: New Solutions to Old Problems*. New York: Avon Books, 1985.
———. *Between Parent and Teenager*. New York: Avon Books, 1985.

COMMUNICATION BETWEEN SPOUSES

Tannen, Deborah. *You Just Don't Understand: Women and Men in Conversation*. New York: Ballantine Books, 1990.
Wallerstein, Judith. *The Good Marriage: How and Why Love Lasts*. New York: Houghton Mifflin, 1995.

COMPUTERS

Brook, James, and Iain A. Boal. *Resisting the Virtual Life: The Culture and Politics of Information*. San Francisco: City Lights Books, 1995.
Levine, John R., and Carol Baroudi. *The Internet for Dummies* (6th edition). Foster City, Calif.: IDG Books, 1998.
Pogue, David. *Macs for Dummies* (6th edition). Foster City, Calif.: IDG Books, 1998.
Postman, Neil. *Technology: The Surrender of Culture to Technology*. New York: Vintage Books, 1993.
Rathbone, Andy. *Windows 98 for Dummies*. Foster City, Calif.: IDG Books, 1998.
Shenk, David. *Data Smog: Surviving the Information Glut*. San Francisco: Harper San Francisco, 1998.

Slouka, Mark. *War of the Worlds: Cyberspace and the High-Tech Assault on Reality*. New York: Basic Books, 1996.

Stoll, Clifford. *Silicon Snake Oil: Second Thoughts on the Information Highway*. New York: Anchor Books, 1996.

CONFLICTS AND DISCIPLINE

Brazelton, T. Berry. *Touchpoints: The Essential Reference*. New York: Addison Wesley, 1992.

Crary, Elizabeth. *Without Spanking or Spoiling: A Practical Approach to Toddler and Preschool Guidance*. Seattle: Parenting Press, 1979.

Coles, Robert. *The Moral Life of Children*. New York: Atlantic Monthly Press, 1986.

Dotson, Fitzhugh. *How to Discipline with Love: From Crib to College*. New York: New American Library, 1982.

Dreikurs, R. *Logical Consequences: A New Approach to Discipline*. New York: Dutton, 1990.

Faber, Adele, et al. *How to Talk So Kids Will Listen and Listen So Kids Will Talk*. New York: Avon Books, 1991.

Frayberg, Selma. *The Magic Years: Understanding and Handling the Problems of Early Childhood*. New York: Fireside, 1996.

Ginott, Haim G. *Between Parent and Teenager*. New York: Avon Books, 1969.

Schulman, Michael, and Eva Mekler. *Bringing Up a Moral Child*. New York: Doubleday, 1994.

Scull, Charles. *Fathers, Sons and Daughters: Exploring Fatherhood, Renewing the Bond*. Los Angeles: Jeremy Tarcher, 1992.

Winnicott, D. W. *Thinking about Children*. Reading, Mass.: Addison Wesley, 1996.

Wright, Robert. *The Moral Animal*. New York: Vintage, 1994.

DIVORCE

Blau, Melinda. *Families Apart: Ten Keys to Successful Co-Parenting*. New York: G. P. Putnam's Sons, 1993.

Blume, Judy. *It's Not the End of the World for Teens*. New York: Yearling Books, 1986.

Diamond, Susan. *Helping Children of Divorce*. New York: Schocken, 1985.

Fassel, Diane. *Growing Up Divorced: A Road to Healing for Adult Children of Divorce*. New York: Pocket Books, 1991.

Gardner, Richard. *Boys and Girls Book about Divorce*. New York: Bantam Young Readers, 1985.

Kaufman, Taube S. *The Combined Family: A Guide to Creating Successful Step Relationships*. New York: Plenum, 1993.

Marguilis, Sam. *Getting Divorced without Ruining Your Life*. New York: Fireside, 1992.

Neuman, M. Gary. *Helping Your Kids Cope with Divorce: The Sandcastles Way*. New York: Times Books, 1998.

Wallerstein, Judith S., and Sandra Blakeslee. *Second Chances: Men, Women and Children a Decade after Divorce*. New York: Ticknor and Fields, 1989.

Dreams

Taylor, Jeremy. *Dream Work: Techniques for Discovering the Creative Power in Dreams*. Mahway, N.J.: Paulist Press, 1984.

Ullman, Montague, and Nan Zimmerman. *The Variety of Dream Experience: Expanding Our Ways of Working with Dreams*. Binghamton, N.J.: The State University of New York Press, 1999.

Drugs, Alcohol, and Tobacco

Garner, Alan. *It's O.K. to Say No to Drugs: A Parent/Child Manual for the Protection of Children*. New York: Tom Doherty Associates, 1987.

Perkins, W. M., and N. McMurtrie-Perkins. *Raising Drug-Free Kids in a Drug-Filled World*. Center City, Minn.: Hazelden, 1986.

U.S. Department of Health and Human Services. *Questions and Answers: Teenage Alcohol Use and Abuse*. Washington, D.C.: National Institute on Alcohol Abuse and Alcoholism, 1983.

U.S. Department of Justice. *Drugs of Abuse*. Washington, D.C.: Drug Enforcement Administration, 1988.

Energetic Children and Hyperactivity

Feingold, Ben. *Why Your Child Is Hyperactive*. New York: Random House, 1974.

Feingold, Ben, and Helene Feingold. *The Feingold Cookbook for Hyperactive Children*. New York: Random House, 1979.

Taylor, Eric, ed. *The Overactive Child*. London: Lippincott Williams & Wilkins, 1991.

Taylor, John F. *Helping Your Hyperactive/ADD Child* (2nd edition). Rocklin, Calif.: Prima Publishing, 1997.

Exceptional Children

Doman, Glenn. *What to Do About Your Brain-Injured Child*. Garden City Park, N.Y.: Avery, 1994.

Featherstone, Helen. *A Difference in the Family: Life with a Disabled Child*. New York: Basic Books, 1980.

Greene, Lawrence. *Learning Disabilities and Your Child*. New York: Fawcett, 1987.

Kirk, Samuel A. *Educating Exceptional Children*. Boston: Houghton Mifflin College, 1997.

Osman, Betty. *Learning Disabilities: A Family Affair*. New York: Random House, 1979.

Pernecke, Raegene, and Sara Schreiner. *Schooling for the Learning Disabled*. Glenview, Ill.: SMS, 1983.

Takacs, Carol A. *Enjoy Your Gifted Child*. Syracuse, N.Y.: Syracuse University Press, 1986.

Turecki, Stanley. *The Difficult Child*. New York: Bantam Books, 1985.

Turnbull, R., et al. *Disability and Family: A Guide for Decisions for Adulthood*. Baltimore, Md.: Paul H. Brookes, 1989.

FAMILY LIFE

Jones, Charles, Lauren Temperman, and Suzanne Wilson. *The Futures of the Family*. Englewood Cliffs, N.J.: Prentice Hall/Simon & Schuster, 1995.

Satir, Virginia. *The New People Making*. Mountainview, Calif.: Science and Behavioral Books, 1988.

Spock, Benjamin. *Rebuilding American Family Values*. Chicago and New York: Contemporary Books, 1994.

FATHERS

Brott, Armin A. *The New Father: A Dad's Guide to the Toddler Years*. New York: Abbeville Press, 1998.

Lamb, Michael, ed. *The Role of the Father in Child Development*. New York: John Wiley & Sons, 1976.

Louv, Richard. *Father Love: What We Need, What We Seek, What We Must Create*. New York: Pocket Books, 1993.

Osherson, S. *Finding Our Fathers: The Unfinished Business of Manhood*. New York: Free Press, 1986.

Pruett, Kyle. *The Nurturing Father: Journey Toward the Complete Man*. New York: Warner Books, 1987.

Scull, Charles. *Fathers, Sons and Daughters*. Los Angeles: Jeremy Tarcher, 1992.

Secunda, Victoria. *Women and Their Fathers: The Sexual and Romantic Impact of the First Man in Your Life*. New York: Delta, 1992.

Sullivan, S. Adams. *The Father's Almanac*. New York: Doubleday, 1992.

Williams, Gene B. *The New Father's Panic Book: Everything a Dad Needs to Know to Welcome His Bundle of Joy*. New York: Avon Books, 1997.

FINANCIAL PLANNING

Dappen, Andy. *Shattering the Two-Income Myth: Daily Secrets for Living Well on One Income*. New York: Brier Books, 1997.

Gardiner, Robert M. *The Dean Witter Guide to Personal Investing*. New York: E. P. Dutton, 1997.

Garner, Robert et al. *Ernst & Young's Personal Financial Planning Guide* (3rd edition). New York: John Wiley & Sons, 1999.

Heady, Christy and Robert K. Heady. *Complete Idiot's Guide to Managing Your Money* (2nd edition). New York: MacMillan Publishing Company, 1998.

Quinn, Jane Bryant. *Making the Most of Your Money*. New York: Simon & Schuster, 1997.

Schwab, Charles. *Charles Schwab's Guide to Financial Independence*. New York: Crown Publishers, 1998.

Waschka, Larry and Bill Staton. *Complete Idiot's Guide to Getting Rich* (2nd edition). New York: MacMillan Publishing Company, 1998.

FOOD

Buist, Robert. *Food Chemical Sensitivity*. Garden City Park, N.Y.: Avery, 1988.

Chernin, Kim. *The Hungry Self: Women, Eating and Identity*. New York: Perennial Library, 1986.

Smith, Lendon. *Feed Your Kids Right*. New York: Dell, 1979.

Spock, Benjamin, and Steven J. Parker. *Dr. Spock's Baby and Child Care*. New York: Pocket Books, 1998.

GENDER BIAS

Katz, Montana. *The Gender Bias Prevention Book*. Northvale, N.J.: Jason Aronson, 1996.

GIRLS

American Association of University Women. *Shortchanging Girls, Shortchanging America: A Call to Action*. Washington, D.C.: American Association of University Women, 1991.

Apter, Terri. *Altered Loves: Mothers and Daughters during Adolescence*. New York: Fawcett Columbine, 1990.

Brown, L. M., and C. Gilligan, *Meeting at the Crossroads: Women's Psychology and Girls' Development*. New York: Ballantine Books, 1992.

Gilligan, Carol. *In a Different Voice: Sex Differences in the Expression of Moral Judgment*. Cambridge, Mass.: Harvard University Press, 1982.

Kaschak, E. *Engendered Lives: A New Psychology of Women's Experience*. New York: Basic Books, 1992.

Pipher, Mary. *Reviving Ophelia: Saving the Selves of Adolescent Girls*. New York: Grosset/Putnam, 1994.

Scull, Charles. *Fathers, Sons and Daughters*. Los Angeles: Jeremy Tarcher, 1992.

Wolf, Naomi. *The Beauty Myth: How Images of Beauty Are Used Against Women*. New York: William Morrow, 1991.

HEALTH

Kunz, J. R. M, and A. J. Finkel. *American Medical Association Family Medical Guide*. New York: Random House, 1987.

Leach, Penelope. *Babyhood: Stage by Stage from Birth to Age Two*. New York: Alfred A. Knopf, 1976.

———. *Your Baby and Child: From Birth to Age Five*. New York: Alfred A. Knopf, 1997.

———. *Your Growing Child: From Babyhood through Adolescence*. New York: Alfred A. Knopf, 1986.

Lovejoy, F. H., and D. Estridge, eds. *The New Child Health Encyclopedia: The Complete Guide for Parents*. New York: Delacorte Press/Lawrence, 1987.

Neifert, Marianne. *Dr. Mom: A Guide to Baby and Child Care*. New York: Signet Books, 1986.

Samuels, Mike, and Nancy Samuels. *The Well Baby Book*. New York: Summit Books, 1979.

Sears, William, and Martha Sears. *The Baby Book: Everything You Need to Know about Your Baby from Birth to Age Two*. Boston: Little, Brown, 1993

Spock, Benjamin, and Steven J. Parker. *Dr. Spock's Baby and Child Care*. New York: Pocket Books, 1998.

JUGGLING WORK AND FAMILY LIFE

Dappen, Andy. *Shattering the Two-Income Myth*. Brier, Wash.: Brier Books, 1997.

Hochschild, Arlie, with Anne Machung. *The Second Shift: Working Parents and the Revolution at Home*. New York: Viking, 1989.

Hochschild, Arlie. *The Time Bind: When Work Becomes Home and Home Becomes Work*. New York: Owl Books, 1998.

Houston, Victoria. *Making It Work: Finding the Time and Energy for Your Career, Marriage, Children, and Self*. Chicago and New York: Contemporary Books, 1990.

Middleman-Bowfin, Gene. *Mothers Who Work: Strategies for Coping*. New York: Ballantine Books, 1983.

Oldes, Sally. *The Working Parents' Survival Guide*. New York: Bantam Books, 1983.

Shreaves, Anita. *Remaking Motherhood*. New York: Ballantine Books, 1988.

LET YOUR KID BE A KID

Chopra, Deepak. *The Seven Spiritual Laws for Parents: Daily Lessons for Children to Live By*. New York: Crown, 1997.

Elkind, David. *The Hurried Child: Growing Up Too Fast Too Soon*. Reading, Mass: Addison Wesley, 1988.

Hendrix, Harville, and Helen Hunt. *Giving the Love That Heals*. New York: Pocket Books, 1997.

LOSS, BEREAVEMENT, AND GRIEF

Bowlby, John. *Attachment and Loss*. Vol. 3: *Loss*. New York: Basic Books, 1980.

Edelman, Hope. *Motherless Daughters: The Legacy of Loss*. Reading, Mass.: Addison Wesley, 1994.

Grollman, Earl. *Explaining Death to Children*. Boston: Beacon Press, 1964.

———. *Living When a Loved One Has Died*. Boston: Beacon Press, 1974.

Krementz, Jill. *How It Feels When a Parent Dies*. New York: Alfred A. Knopf, 1981.

Kübler-Ross, Elisabeth. *On Death and Dying*. New York: Macmillan, 1969.

LeShan, Eda. *Learning to Say Good-by*. New York: Avon Books, 1976.

Myers, Edward. *When Parents Die: A Guide for Adults*. New York: Penguin Books, 1997.

Raphael, Beverley. *The Anatomy of Bereavement*. New York: Basic Books, 1983.

THE MEDIA

Carlson, Page, and Diane Levin, *Who's Calling the Shots? How to Respond Effectively to Children's Fascination with War Play and War Toys*, Santa Cruz, Calif., New Society, 1990.

DeGaetono, Gloria. *Television and the Lives of Our Children*. Redmond, Wash.: Train of Thought, 1993.

Mander, Jerry. *Four Arguments for the Elimination of Television*. New York: Quill, 1978.

Marie Winn, *The Plug-In Drug: Television, Children, and the Family*. New York: Viking, 1985.

McKibben, Bill. *The Age of Missing Information*. New York: Plume, 1993.

MOTHERS

Bassoff, Evelyn. *Between Mothers and Sons: The Making of Vital and Loving Men*. New York: Dutton, 1994.

Bernard, Jessie. *The Future of Motherhood*. New York: Penguin, 1974.

Chodorow, Nancy. *The Reproduction of Mothering*. Berkeley, Calif.: University of California Press, 1978.

Faludi, Susan. *Backlash: The Undeclared War against American Women*. New York: Crown, 1991.

Kelly, Marguerite, et al. *The Mother's Almanac*. New York: Doubleday, 1975.

Lerner, Harriet. *The Mother Dance: How Children Change Your Life*. New York: HarperCollins, 1998.

———. *The Dance of Anger*. New York: Harper & Row, 1985.

———. *The Dance of Intimacy*. New York: Harper & Row, 1989.

Towle, Alexandra. *Mothers*. New York: Simon & Schuster, 1998.

Parenting Styles

Brazelton, T. Berry. *On Becoming a Family*. New York: Delacorte Press/Seymour Lawrence, 1981.

Galinsky, Ellen. *The Six Stages of Parenthood*. Reading, Mass.: Addison Wesley, 1987.

Satir, Virginia. *The New People Making*. Mountainview, Calif.: Science and Behavior Books, 1988.

Parenting As Partners

Galinsky, Ellen. *The Six Stages of Parenthood*. Reading, Mass.: Addison Wesley, 1987.

Samalin, Nancy. *Loving Your Child Is Not Enough*. New York: Penguin, 1989.

———. *Love and Anger: The Parental Dilemma*. New York: Penguin, 1992.

Satir, Virginia. *The New People Making*. Mountainview, Calif.; Science and Behavior Books, 1988.

Steinberg, Lawrence. *Crossing Paths: How Your Child's Adolescence Triggers Your Own Crises*. New York: Simon & Schuster, 1994.

Play and Learning

Axline, Virginia. *Play Therapy*. New York: Ballantine Books, 1974.

Bruner, Jerome, A. Jolly, and K. Sylva. *Play: Its Role in Development*. New York: Penguin, 1946.

Cherry, Clare. *Creative Art for the Developing Child*. Belmont, Calif.: Fearon Teacher Aids, 1990.

Erikson, Erik. *Childhood in Society*. New York: W. W. Norton, 1964.

Marzollo, Jean, and Janice Lloyd. *Learning through Play*. New York: Harper & Row, 1972.

RACISM AND PREJUDICE

Feagin, Joe R., and Melvin P. Sikes. *Living with Racism: The Black Middle-Class Experience*. Boston: Beacon Press, 1994.
———. *Race Matters*. New York: Random House, 1993.

SCHOOL ISSUES

Elkind, David. *Miseducation: Preschoolers at Risk*. New York: Alfred A. Knopf, 1988.

SELF-ESTEEM

Briggs, Dorothy. *Your Child's Self-Esteem*. New York: Doubleday, 1975.
Clarke, Jean Illsley. *Self-Esteem: A Family Affair*. San Francisco: Harper & Row, 1978.
Glenn, H. Steven, and Jane Nelsen. *Raising Self-Reliant Children*. Rocklin, Calif.: Prima, 1989.

SEXUALITY

Bourgeois, Paulette, et al. *Changes in You and Me: A Book about Puberty*. New York: Andrews and McMeel, 1994.
Coles, Robert, and Geoffrey Stokes. *Sex and the American Teenager*. New York: Harper & Row, 1985.
Elkind, David. *Parenting Your Teenager*. New York: Ballantine Books, 1993.
Gravelle, Karen. *The Period Book: Everything You Don't Want to Ask (But Need to Know)*. New York: Walker, 1996.
Harris, Robie H. *It's Perfectly Normal: Changing Bodies, Growing Up, Sex, and Sexual Health*. Cambridge, Mass.: Candlewick Press, 1994.
Madaras, Lynda. *What's Happening to My Body? A Book for Girls*. New York: Newmarket Press, 1987.
———. *What's Happening to My Body? A Book for Boys*. New York: Newmarket Press, 1987.
———. *My Body, My Self for Boys*. New York: Newmarket Press, 1995.

SIBLING RIVALRY

Bank, Stephen P. and Michael D. Kahn. *The Sibling Bond*. New York: Basic Books, 1982.
Cassill, Kay. *Twins: Nature's Amazing Mystery*. New York: Atheneum, 1982.
Dunn, Judy, and Robert Plomin. *Separate Lives: Why Siblings Are So Different*. New York: Basic Books, 1990.

Faber, Adele, and Elaine Mazlesch. *How to Talk So Kids Will Listen and Listen So Kids Will Talk*. New York: Avon Books, 1982.

Greer, Jane, with Edward Myers. *Adult Sibling Rivalry*. New York: Fawcett Crest, 1992.

Leman, Kevin. *The Birth Order Book*. New York: Dell, 1985.

———. *Growing Up First Born*. New York: Dell, 1989.

SINGLE PARENTHOOD

Wayman, Anne. *Successful Single Parenting*. Deephaven, Minn.: Meadowbrook, 1987.

SLEEP

Ames, Louise Bates. *Your One-Year-Old*. New York: Delacorte Press, 1982.

———. *Your Two-Year-Old*. New York: Delacorte Press, 1982.

———. *Your Three-Year-Old*. New York: Delacorte Press, 1982.

Brazleton, T. Berry. *Toddlers and Parents*. New York: Dell, 1974.

Cuthbertson, Joanne, and Susie Schevill. *Helping Your Child Sleep through the Night*. Garden City, N.Y.: Doubleday, 1985.

Ferber, Richard. *Solve Your Child's Sleep Problems*. New York: Simon & Schuster, 1985.

Mindell, Jodi A. *Sleeping through the Night: How Infants, Toddlers, and Their Parents Can Get a Good Night's Sleep*. New York: HarperCollins, 1997.

STEPPARENTS AND BLENDED FAMILIES

Burns, C. *Stepmotherhood*. New York: Times Books, 1985.

Diamond, Susan. *Helping Children of Divorce*. New York: Schocken, 1985.

Eckler, James. *Step-by-Stepparenting*. White Hall, Va.: Betterway, 1988.

Kaufman, Taube S. *The Combined Family: A Guide to Creating Successful Step-Relationships*. New York: Plenum, 1993.

Nelsen, Jane, Cheryl Erwin, and H. Stephen Glenn. *Positive Discipline for Blended Families*. Rocklin, Calif.: Prima, 1997.

Rosen, M. *Stepfathering*. New York: Ballantine Books, 1987.

STRESS

Arent, Ruth. *Stress and Your Child*. Englewood Cliffs, N.J.: Prentice-Hall, 1984.

Carlson, Richard. *Don't Sweat the Small Stuff*. New York: Hyperion Books, 1997.

Chopra, Deepak. *The Seven Spiritual Laws for Parents*. New York: Crown, 1997.

Covey, Stephen. *The Seven Habits of Highly Effective People*. New York: Fireside, 1989.

Ginsberg, Susan. *Family Wisdom*. New York: Columbia University Press, 1996.

Houston, Victoria. *Making It Work*. Chicago and New York: Contemporary Books, 1990.

Pillsbury, Linda. *Survival Tips for Working Moms*. Los Angeles: Perspective, 1994.

Saltzman, Amy. *Downshifting*. New York: HarperCollins, 1991.

THE TEEN YEARS

Elkind, David. *All Grown Up and No Place to Go: Teenagers in Crisis.* 2nd ed. Reading Mass.: Addison Wesley, 1997.

Ginott, Haim G. *Between Parent and Teenager*. New York: Avon Books, 1969.

Kaman, Ben. *Raising a Thoughtful Teenager*. New York: Penguin, 1996.

Pipher, Mary. *Reviving Ophelia: Saving the Selves of Adolescent Girls*. New York: Grosset/Putnam, 1994.

Powell, Douglas H. *Teenagers: When to Worry and What to Do—A Guide for Parents*. New York: Doubleday, 1987.

Wexler, David B. *The Adolescent Self*. New York: Norton, 1991.

TWENTY-FIRST–CENTURY PARENTING

Chopra, Deepak. *The Seven Spiritual Laws of Success*. New York: New World Library, 1994.

Horney, Karen. *The Neurotic Personality of Our Time*. New York: Norton, 1994.

Jones, Charles, Lorne Tepperman, and Suzanna Wilson. *The Futures of the Family*. New York: Prentice-Hall, 1995.

Pipher, Mary. *The Shelter of Each Other: Rebuilding Our Families*. New York: Grosset/Putnam Books, 1996.

Rank, Mark Robert, and Edward L. Kain. *Diversity and Change in Families: Patterns, Prospects and Policies*. New York: Prentice-Hall, 1995.

Wright-Edelman, Marion. *The Measure of Our Success: A Letter to My Children and Yours*. New York: HarperCollins, 1993.

VACATIONS AND TRIPS

Tristram, Claire. *Have Kid, Will Travel: 101 Survival Strategies for Vacationing with Babies and Young Children*. New York: Andrews and McMeel, 1997.

Wheeler, Maureen. *Lonely Planet Travel with Children*. Oakland, Calif.: Lonely Planet, 1995.

VIOLENCE

Curran, Daniel, et al. *Social Problems, Society in Crisis*. New York: Simon & Schuster, 1996.

Gilligan, J. *Violence: Our Deadly Epidemic and Its Causes*. New York: Putnam, 1996.

Miedzian, Myriam. *Boys Will Be Boys: Breaking the Link between Masculinity and Violence*. New York: Anchor Books, 1991.

WORK-TO-HOME TRANSITIONS

Brazleton, T. Berry. *Working and Caring*. Reading, Mass.: Addison Wesley, 1985.

Hewlitt, Sylvia Anne. *When the Bough Breaks: The Cost of Neglecting Our Children*. New York: Basic Books, 1991.

Hochschild, Arlie. *The Time Bind: When Work Becomes Home and Home Becomes Work*. New York: Owl Books, 1998.

Hochschild, Arlie, with Anne Machung. *The Second Shift: Working Parents and the Revolution at Home*. New York: Viking, 1989.

PERMISSIONS

INDEX

ABOUT THE AUTHORS

Aleta Koman, M.Ed., is a nationally celebrated psychotherapist who has hosted or appeared as an expert on national and local television and radio shows. She has taught on many levels, including undergraduate and graduate programs in psychology and professional studies. She is the former director of the Ohebei Shalom Temple Early Childhood Center in Brookline, MA. Aleta Koman currently maintains a private practice as a psychotherapist, with emphasis on individual, marital, and family counseling. In addition, she offers corporate programs on personal, marital, and parenting issues; lectures on psychological topics to groups of adults and children; and provides consultative services in the private and public sectors. She is the co-author of *How to Mend a Broken Heart: Letting Go and Moving On* (Contemporary Books, 1997) and has produced a series of nationally distributed video- and audiotapes on issues of relationships and parenting. She has a son, Jason, who is fifteen.

Edward Myers is a freelance writer who specializes in psychology books, mainstream novels, and children's fiction. He has published two nonfiction books under his own name: *When Parents Die: A Guide for Adults* (Viking Press, 1986; Penguin Books, 1987) and *The Chosen Few* (And Books, 1982). He has also co-written or ghostwritten eight other books, including *How to Mend a Broken Heart: Letting Go and Moving On*, with Aleta Koman, M.Ed. In addition, Ed Myers is the author of a trilogy of novels—*The Mountain Made of Light, Fire and Ice*, and *The Summit* (New American Library, respectively 1992, 1992, and 1994)—and many children's books.

Edward Myers is the father of two children—Robin, thirteen, and Cory, eight.